Hollow Promises

The LAW AND PUBLIC POLICY: PSYCHOLOGY AND THE SOCIAL SCIENCES series includes books in three domains:

Legal Studies—writings by legal scholars about issues of relevance to psychology and the other social sciences, or that employ social science information to advance the legal analysis;

Social Science Studies—writings by scientists from psychology and the other social sciences about issues of relevance to law and public policy; and

Forensic Studies—writings by psychologists and other mental health scientists and professionals about issues relevant to forensic mental health science and practice.

The series is guided by its editor, Bruce D. Sales, PhD, JD, ScD(*hc*), University of Arizona; and coeditors, Bruce J. Winick, JD, University of Miami; Norman J. Finkel, PhD, Georgetown University; and Stephen J. Ceci, PhD, Cornell University.

* * *

Hollow Promises

EMPLOYMENT DISCRIMINATION AGAINST
PEOPLE WITH MENTAL DISABILITIES

Susan Stefan

AMERICAN PSYCHOLOGICAL ASSOCIATION

WASHINGTON, DC

Published by
American Psychological Association
750 First Street, NE
Washington, DC 20002
www.apa.org

To order
APA Order Department
P.O. Box 92984
Washington, DC 20090-2984

Tel: (800) 374-2721, Direct: (202) 336-5510
Fax: (202) 336-5502, TDD/TTY: (202) 336-6123
On-line: www.apa.org/books/
E-mail: order@apa.org

In the U.K., Europe, Africa, and the Middle East, copies may be ordered from
American Psychological Association
3 Henrietta Street
Covent Garden, London
WC2E 8LU England

Typeset in Times Roman by EPS Group Inc., Easton, MD

Printer: Sheridan Books, Ann Arbor, MI
Cover Designer: Berg Design, Albany, NY
Technical/Production Editors: Amy J. Clarke and Jennifer L. Macomber

The opinions and statements published are the responsibility of the author, and such opinions and statements do not necessarily represent the policies of the American Psychological Association.

Library of Congress Cataloging-in-Publication Data
Stefan, Susan.
    Hollow promises : employment discrimination against people with mental disabilities / by Susan Stefan.—1st ed.
        p. cm.—(The law and public policy)
    Includes bibliographical references and index.
    ISBN 1-55798-792-0 (cloth : alk. paper)
        1. Mentally handicapped—Employment—law and legislation—United States.
    2. Discrimination in employment—Law and legislation—United States.
    3. United States. Americans with Disabilities Act of 1990. I. Title. II. Series.

KF3469 .S74 2001
344.7301′594—dc21

                                                                                    2001022122

British Library Cataloguing-in-Publication Data
A CIP record is available from the British Library.

Printed in the United States of America
First Edition

To my Mother, Wes, and Jamie—again and always.

CONTENTS

ACKNOWLEDGMENTS

Behind every book like this there is a phalanx of cheerful, competent, patient, and unheralded librarians. I would like to first thank the University of Miami School of Law's library staff, including tireless reference librarians Clare Membiela, Carlos Espinosa, Janet Reinke, Tica Stanton, and Virginia Templeton. No medal or award could sufficiently repay "Interlibrary Loan Heroines" Sue Ann Campbell and Barbara Cuadras.

The University of Miami School of Law gave me summer grants to conduct the research and perform the writing necessary to complete this book over a three-year period. Dean Rick Williamson was particularly supportive during moments of crisis, when his background in diplomacy was evident. I was assisted in researching the book by Alan Jockers, Katrina Barcelona, Beth Wolt, David Daniel, Alan Poppe, Ben England, Marc Rothenberg, Larry Brown, Annie Fox, Alex Asuncion, Beth Nagle, Christine Giovannelli, Marina Luybimova, and Oswaldo Rossi. I would particularly like to acknowledge Travis Godwin, a law student who volunteered his time to help me when I lost research assistance one month before the manuscript was due. Finally, I would like to thank James D. Elmer, Esquire for invaluable assistance in the last stages of this book.

This book is the product of the contributions and support of many people. I have been blessed by the generosity and mentorship of Professor Bruce Winick, whose kindness and encouragement to me have spanned almost 10 years and who is a model of what an academic colleague should be—I thank him.

I also thank all the people who took the time to complete the survey that is at the heart of this book. The survey itself could not have been distributed without the help of David Oaks of Support Coalition International; the New York Commission on Quality of Care for the Mentally Disabled; Joseph Buffington of Florida State Hospital; Karen Milstein of the GrassRoots Empowerment Project in Madison, Wisconsin; Judy Lavine of the National Association of Rights Protection and Advocacy; and Tim Ravitch, a law student at the University of Miami School of Law. Nancy Frost compiled the survey results and did the computer wizardry that makes no sense to me. Joanne Manees was absolutely crucial in the final push to the finish line.

My husband Wes Daniels was patient and gave much substantive editorial assistance. Professors Michael Perlin, Marc Fajer, Tom Baker, Michael Fischl, and Clark Freshman helped me throughout the years with difficult intellectual struggles; I appreciate very much having first-rate scholars as pals. I would like to particularly thank Professors Michael Kelly of the University of San Diego Law School and Professors Ken Casebeer and Michael Fischl of the University of Miami School of Law for patient instruction in economics and labor issues.

There are many people whom I have never met but who have inspired me with their humanity and understanding. I would like to thank and acknowledge the leaders of the disability community, who have consistently refused exclusionary pressures from those in power and stood by people with psychiatric disabilities, especially under strong pressure from Congress at crucial moments in the Americans with

Disabilities Act debate. I would also like to thank Oliver Sacks, Robert Coles, Bob Hayman, and Judge William Wayne Justice, for whom I had the honor to serve as a law clerk. All are models of service, humanity, and compassion.

I have also been fortunate to meet many people while doing work with and for people with psychiatric disabilities who have impressed me with their courage, compassion, and integrity, including Mary Auslander, Susan Mann, Ruta Mazelis, and Diana Rickard. There are so many people who have devoted amazing amounts of time and energy to fight the good fight, people from whom I have learned tremendously: Len Rubenstein, Andy Blanch, Ira Burnim, Tim Clune, Becky Cox, Joel Dvoskin, Bob Factor, Bob Fleischner, Mary Gallagher, Jim Green, Diane Greenley, Debbie Hiser, Steve Schwartz, Ellen Saideman, Al Smith, and Cliff Zucker.

I acknowledge and honor my clients, all of whom inspired me, in particular Jennifer W. I mourn always the clients who have died, especially Elizabeth. You are not forgotten.

Finally, there are people that Laura Ziegler describes as truly "down with us" —Nancy Bowker, David Oaks, and Steve Gold—people who beyond their time and energy have committed their lives and souls to fighting the injustices that damage and kill people who are perceived as "crazy." Some of these people I am fortunate enough to call my friends, my community, and my inspiration: Tom Behrendt, Laura Cain, Peter Cubra, Emmett Dwyer, Beth Mitchell, Laura Prescott, and Laura Ziegler. Thank you.

Lastly, I would like to salute the memory of my friend Rae Unzicker, whose pragmatic advice and uncompromising principles have served as an example to me for the past 15 years. We remember her eloquence, her love of the finer things in life, and the largeness of her laughter at the obstacles she encountered. Her laughter was her signal battle cry, and I miss it so much.

INTRODUCTION

As you read this, millions of Americans are suffering from devastating emotional pain. Suicide is the sixth highest cause of death in this country for children between the ages of 5 and 14 years old and the third highest cause of death for young people between the ages of 15 and 24.[1] White males commit suicide at a higher rate than any other group in the population: Between the ages of 5 and 14, suicide is the third highest cause of death, and between the ages of 15 and 24, it is the second highest cause of death, exceeded only by "all accidental deaths."

It is not only boys who injure themselves. Millions of people, mostly women and girls, cut or burn themselves or engage in other acts of self-injury.[2] No statistics are kept on the number of people who cannot get out of bed in the morning, who cannot sleep night after night, who are afraid to leave the house, who sweat and tremble in anxiety or flashbacks, and who resist ugly or menacing voices that no one else can hear.

Some people who suffer in these ways reside in mental institutions. Others have full-time jobs as journalists, accountants, financiers, lawyers, and bankers—all professions and employment categories. There are two worlds of people with psychiatric diagnoses or severe emotional difficulties. The first world, those who have jobs and professions, do not differ from people in psychiatric institutions in the ways that are commonly supposed. For example, reading their self-accounts and testimonies, a vast array of social science research, and case law reveals that the difference between the two worlds is not the severity of their symptoms. Rod Steiger, the Academy Award–winning actor, recounted, "after I got rid of the gun, I locked myself in the guest room downstairs at night, and I wound up with burning sensations; clawing my skin and pounding on the wall for three days."[3] Television news correspondent Mike Wallace wrote, "I used to look up walking along, and the sky would shake."[4] These accounts are not particularly different from the accounts of people who were institutionalized for years. The difference is a complex combination of social supports, social and self-labeling, and employment.

These two worlds of people who are in severe emotional pain experience discrimination very differently. The people who self-identify by their jobs or professions —the journalists, accountants, and the rest—pretend or are told nothing is wrong, struggle and suffer in silence, and deny their weaknesses. This is in large part because they and their loved ones cannot imagine being considered part of the second world: As Kitty Dukakis, wife of former Governor Michael Dukakis, said, "when I think of mental illness I think of people who are schizophrenic, who are psychotic, who can't function in society, people with whom you and I wouldn't want to spend much

---

[1] *National Vital Statistics Report* 48(11) (July 24, 2000): Table 8.

[2] A. R. Favazza and K. Conterio, "The Plight of Chronic Self-Mutilators," *Community Mental Health Journal*, 24(1) (1988):22 (conservatively estimating the rate of self-injury at 750 per 100,000).

[3] Kathy Cronkite (Ed.), *On the Edge of Darkness: Conversations About Conquering Depression* (New York: Doubleday, 1994) at 46.

[4] *Id.* at 17.

time."[5] Mike Wallace said, "for years, depression meant the crazy house."[6] Over and over again, hospitalization—"ending up in the crazy house"—is identified as a point of no return by people in the first world. Even those who ultimately were hospitalized and returned did not seem to bring with them any new acceptance or understanding of the people they left behind: people who live in hospitals rather than just receive a short spell of treatment, people whose struggle and suffering is permanently public. Once the label is affixed, especially through state proceedings, the individual is on the threshold of the second world: people who are seen as a collection of weaknesses and deficits, whose lives are considered to chronicle struggle and pain without victory.

So the journalists, accountants, financiers, lawyers, and bankers distance themselves from their brothers and sisters in the crazy house, and society's image of "the mentally ill" is distorted to the detriment of both worlds. People who are employed in the mainstream world struggle to keep their diagnoses and symptoms secret and receive little understanding from colleagues and friends who tell them to "just cheer up." People in the second world, whose sufferings are all too public, are considered incapable of employment and find it nearly impossible to obtain employment in the mainstream world. The detriment of these sharply separated worlds of Americans with psychiatric diagnoses has become all too apparent since the passage of the Americans With Disabilities Act (ADA): Judges cannot understand that an individual can be simultaneously employed and have a major psychiatric diagnosis because few employed people with major psychiatric diagnoses have ever felt feel safe letting the world know who they are.

The ADA was passed in 1990, prohibiting employers from discriminating on the basis of disability, including mental disability. Employers may no longer ask applicants about their mental health and hospitalization histories. The ADA also requires employers to provide qualified employees accommodations to enable more people with disabilities to work and lead productive lives. Americans with disabilities, including Americans with mental disabilities, greeted the passage of the ADA with joy, anticipating the possibility of a less stigmatizing world, one where discrimination would be punishable by law rather than taken for granted as a matter of practice.

Almost 12 years after the ADA took effect, little seems to have changed for Americans with mental disabilities. The best the ADA has been able to accomplish is to change the workplace from one where applicants had to affirmatively lie about their psychiatric histories and diagnoses to an environment of "don't ask, don't tell." Meanwhile, in the decade since the passage of the ADA, the average American work week has gone up steadily, requirements for overtime have increased, and job stress has skyrocketed. Depression, anxiety, and other emotional disorders have increased correspondingly among employees. Even though the ADA ostensibly requires employers to provide accommodations to disabled employees, employees with psychiatric disabilities have had little success in enforcing this requirement because courts generally manifest little understanding either of mental disability or of necessary accommodations. A few judges have expressed disbelief in some diagnoses; others have repeated stereotypes about mental illness and violence. Sometimes these difficulties arise because judges have a hard time believing that people who have been

---

[5]*Id.* at 80.
[6]*Id.* at 17.

successful employees and have held challenging and demanding jobs can simulta-neously be mentally disabled for purposes of the ADA. One of the reasons for these judges' inability to comprehend this reality is that people with mental disabilities in the first world have kept so silent about their experiences and their conditions that there are few social images of people with severe emotional problems and successful work careers to enable judges to understand the plaintiff's situation.

This book begins by describing the centrality of work to almost every American and the significance of employment in dividing the two worlds of Americans with psychiatric disabilities. The first chapter describes the discrimination faced by Amer-icans with severe emotional difficulties, psychiatric diagnoses, or histories of treat-ment. Individuals who are successfully employed often feel forced to keep their diagnoses secret and face discounting or disbelief if they try to describe their strug-gles. Individuals who are publicly labeled as mentally ill cannot get competitive jobs and are consigned to volunteer work, part-time work, or work that makes little use of their skills and strengths. Chapter 1 also summarizes and critiques the existing research on the relationship between work and psychiatric disabilities.

Chapter 2 provides an overview of the laws relating to discrimination against people with disabilities, including Section 504 of the Rehabilitation Act of 1973 and the ADA. With a focus principally on the ADA, the chapter explains the provisions of the ADA and explains how to bring a claim under the ADA. It discusses in layman's terms issues such as exhaustion of administrative remedies and statutes of limitations.

Following chapter 2, the remainder of the book tracks the language of the ADA in explaining how it has been applied to people with mental disabilities. The ADA defines a disability as "a physical or mental impairment that substantially limits one or more major life activities." [7] Chapters 3 and 4 look at how courts have interpreted the meanings of *mental impairment* and what kinds of impairments have been con-sidered that "substantially limit major life activities."

Of crucial importance to people with psychiatric disabilities, the ADA also pro-tects individuals who are not disabled but who have a history of disability or are simply regarded as being disabled. Chapter 5 examines legal interpretations of those provisions of the ADA.

If a person fits into the statutory definition of *disability* under the ADA, he or she is protected from discrimination by the ADA. *Discrimination* is broadly defined by the ADA to include a variety of practices, from an employer asking questions about a potential employee's disabilities in an interview to refusing accommodations to a qualified employee with a disability. Employers have continually sought guid-ance and clarity on the definition of discriminatory practices and appropriate accom-modations as they relate to people with psychiatric disabilities. Employees are equally uncertain of their rights under the ADA.

Chapters 6, 7, and 8 examine discrimination in a variety of different ways. Chapter 6 explores the employer practices that actually cause the most damaging and disadvantageous difficulties to employees with mental disabilities: the creation or tolerance of abusive and extremely stressful work environments. Chapter 6 looks at the case law in this area and explores the possibility of more successful legal arguments to protect workers with psychiatric disabilities. Chapter 7 looks at other

---

[7] 42 U.S.C. 12102(2)(A) (Lexis Law Publishing 2001).

employer actions that are commonly litigated, such as referring an employee to a psychiatrist or for discipline for misconduct, and actions that are less commonly litigated, such as associational discrimination and retaliation for engaging in protected activities under the ADA. Chapter 7 also examines characteristics of successful litigation on behalf of people with mental disabilities under the ADA. Chapter 8 discusses the concept and practice of reasonable accommodation.

Similar to its the companion volume, *Unequal Rights: Discrimination Against People With Mental Disabilities and the Americans With Disabilities Act*, this book strives to include the voices of the people who suffer discrimination, the findings of the social science researchers, the basic case law, and the legal and policy suggestions for improving protections against discrimination. As in *Unequal Rights*, my efforts to write a book that is understandable to the layperson, helpful to the lawyer unfamiliar with this field, and valuable to experienced and sophisticated lawyers and policymakers has probably made it less than perfect for readers in each category. All readers should understand that case law develops in this area over time, and the case law cited is intended to give the reader both a background and a basic understanding of the issues in each category. I hope very much that I have succeeded.

A Word About Terminology

Names and labels are always potent, and nothing illustrates this more than the ongoing battle over the appropriate terminology to use when describing the condition that serves as the basis for some of the most potent discrimination in American society.

I have used *crazy* in the past because, like Stephen Morse and Judi Chamberlin, I believe that "for legal purposes it is more descriptive and carries fewer connotations about disease processes that beg important questions about self-control."[8] Ironically, Morse's preference for the word *crazy* is not reflected in the title of his piece, which refers to *mental disorder*—another term with its own connotations. The common associations with the term *disorder* or lack of orderliness describe some, but by no means all, people who are involuntarily committed. Descriptively, I marginally prefer the language of disorder to the language of disease, but overall I believe that *disability* captures the truth better (although still not to my satisfaction) than *illness*, *disorder*, or *disturbance*. Many (although far from all) people who have or are perceived as having these conditions agree that the "disability" language is less offensive than the disease language. Others insist that the metaphors of illness capture their condition. I believe they do this because of their yearning to avoid the stigma and blame associated with mental conditions. Research shows, however, that using illness language does not result in destigmatization.

Even deciding to use *disability* does not get one out of the woods. How does one characterize this disability? The Equal Employment Opportunity Commission, the Department of Justice, and most major researchers in the field of discrimination law describe it as psychiatric disability. The American Psychological Association resists this terminology as having unwarranted biological connotations and suggest-

---

[8] Stephen J. Morse, "A Preference for Liberty: The Case Against Involuntary Commitment of the Mentally Disordered," *California Law Review* 70 (1982):54, 58.

ing that these disabilities are solely classified and treated by psychiatrists. The results from an informal survey suggest that the term *emotional disability* is resisted by those who are described by these terms. I have therefore agreed to use *mental disability* wherever possible, despite reservations as to its lack of specificity. From my point of view, *mental disability* embraces mental retardation, developmental disability, and organic conditions. I use *psychiatric disability* when distinctions are necessary but otherwise use *mental disability* as the least controversial of terms.

Hollow Promises

Chapter 1
THE WORK EXPERIENCE OF PEOPLE
WITH PSYCHIATRIC DISABILITIES

The underlying premise of this title is that persons with disabilities should not be excluded from job opportunities unless they are actually unable to do the job.[1]

This book is about people with psychiatric disabilities, their experiences in seeking and maintaining employment, and the effect of the Americans With Disabilities Act (ADA) on those experiences. There is a growing literature by people with psychiatric diagnoses about their experiences, including experiences in the workplace. This body of work includes books written by single authors[2] and edited collections of accounts.[3] In addition, there are hours of testimony before state legislatures and

---

[1] U.S. House of Representatives, Committee on the Judiciary, Report on the Americans with Disabilities Act, p. 31.

[2] The best known of these are Hannah Green's *I Never Promised You a Rose Garden* (New York: Holt, Rinehart & Winston, 1964) and—thinly disguised as fiction—Mary Jane Ward's *The Snake Pit* (New York: Random House, 1946) and Sylvia Plath's *The Bell Jar* (New York: Harper & Row, 1971). Many people are aware of Clifford Beers's *A Mind That Found Itself: An Autobiography* (2nd ed., New York: Longmans, Green & Co., 1910), the account of F. Scott Fitzgerald of his breakdown, *The Crack-Up* (originally published in 1936, reissued New York: Laughlin, 1945), William Styron's *Darkness Visible: A Memoir of Madness* (New York: Random House, 1990), and Janet Frame's *Faces in the Water* (New York: G. Braziller, 1961). Less familiar are Barbara Field Benziger's *The Prison of My Mind* (New York: Walker, 1969), Wilfrid Sheed's *In Love With Daylight: A Memoir of Recovery* (New York: Simon & Schuster, 1995), Mark Vonnegut's *The Eden Express* (New York: Prager, 1975), Joshua Logan's *My Up and Down, In and Out Life* (New York: Delacorte Press, 1976). Kenneth Donaldson, the plaintiff in the U.S. Supreme Court case of O'Connor v. Donaldson, wrote *Insanity Inside Out* (New York: Crown, 1976). Earlier works include Alonzo Graves's *The Eclipse of a Mind* (New York: Medical Journal Press, 1942) and John Custance's *Wisdom, Madness, and Folly: The Philosophy of a Lunatic* (New York: Pellegrini & Cudahy, 1952); two older books of great value are Judi Chamberlin's *On Our Own: Patient-Controlled Alternatives to the Mental Health System* (New York: Hawthorne Books, 1978) and Janet and Paul Gotkin's *Too Much Anger, Too Many Tears: A Personal Triumph Over Psychiatry* (New York: HarperPerennial, 1992). Others include Huey Freeman's *Judge, Jury and Executioner* (Urbana, IL: Talking Leaves, 1986) and Persimmon Blackbridge's and Sheila Gilhooly's *Still Sane* (Vancouver, British Columbia, Canada: Press Gang, 1985). More recently, books on this subject include Susanna Kaysen's *Girl Interrupted* (New York: Turtle Bay Books, 1993), Tracy Thompson's *The Beast: A Reckoning with Depression* (New York: Putnam, 1995), and Elizabeth Wurtzel's *Prozac Nation: Young and Depressed in America* (Boston: Houghton Mifflin 1994). Although people tend to associate first-person accounts of psychiatric disabilities with poets and authors, many mental health professionals have also written accounts of their mental health problems, usually with titles indicating their professional status, for example Norman Endler's *Holiday of Darkness: A Psychologist's Personal Journey out of His Depression*, (New York: Wiley, 1982), Martha Manning's *Undercurrents: A Therapist's Reckoning With Her Own Depression* (New York: HarperCollins, 1994), and Kay Redfield Jamison's *An Unquiet Mind: A Memoir of Moods and Madness* (New York: Knopf, 1995).

[3] Dale Peterson, ed., *A Mad People's History of Madness* (Pittsburgh, PA: University of Pittsburgh Press, 1982); Roy Porter, ed., *The Faber Book of Madness* (London: Faber & Faber, 1991); Michael A. Susko, ed., *Cry of the Invisible: Writings From the Homeless and Survivors of Psychiatric Hospitals* (Baltimore: Conservatory Press, 1991); Seth Farber, *Madness, Heresy, and the Rumor of Angels: The Revolt Against the Mental Health System* (Chicago: Open Court, 1993); Maxine Harris and Jeffrey Geller,

Congress, including testimony supporting the ADA as well as bulletins and news-letters produced by various groups of people with psychiatric diagnoses. Because they are rarely polled as a group, only a few surveys of Americans with psychiatric disabilities have been done.[4] In preparing for this book, I conducted a survey about people's experiences of discrimination.[5] Responses to the survey indicated that peo-ple with psychiatric disabilities continue to experience many different forms of em-ployment discrimination, including being denied jobs, being fired when they revealed their disability or that they were taking medications, and enduring condescending or demeaning attitudes on the part of supervisors and coworkers. They reported being denied the opportunity to prove themselves capable of performing the job, being harassed and bullied by coworkers and supervisors,[6] and being fired during periods when they were adjusting their medication.

The survey also asked in what context people had experienced the *worst* dis-crimination, giving a large choice of possible answers, including housing, higher education, insurance, medical treatment, institutionalization, and public accommo-dations such as stores and restaurants. Employment led the list as the area in which respondents had experienced the worst discrimination: Of those who experienced any discrimination based on psychiatric disability, 33% identified the workplace as the environment in which they experienced the worst discrimination.

In 1990, when the ADA was passed, one of its principal goals was prohibiting discrimination against people with disabilities in the workplace. Today, many em-ployers are confused and resentful about the requirements of the ADA, and partic-ularly about how the ADA applies to people with psychiatric disabilities. Who is

---

Women of the Asylum: Voices From Behind the Walls 1840–1945 (New York: Anchor Books, 1994); Janine Grobe, ed., *Beyond Bedlam: Contemporary Women Psychiatric Survivors Speak Out* (Chicago: Third Side Press, 1995).

[4]Marsha Langer Ellison and Zlatka Russinova, *A National Survey of Professionals and Managers With Psychiatric Conditions: A Portrait of Achievements and Challenges* (Boston: Center for Psychiatric Rehabilitation, 1999), *available at* http://www.bu.edu/SARPSYCH/research/rtc1999/si_3.html; Jean Campbell and Roy Schraiber, *The Well-Being Project: Mental Health Clients Speak for Themselves,* (Sacramento, CA: California Network of Mental Health Clients, 1989); E. S. Rogers et al., *Massachusetts Survey of Client Preferences for Community Support Services* (Boston: Center for Psychiatric Rehabil-itation, 1991) (71% of people with severe mental disorders have an active interest in working and finding jobs).

[5]I make no claims of statistical training or expertise. However, no one with statistical training or expertise has undertaken a survey on the subject of how people with psychiatric disabilities or who are perceived as having psychiatric disabilities experience discrimination (although Jean Campbell and Roy Schraiber included some questions about discrimination in their excellent survey, *see* Jean Campbell and Roy Schraiber, *id., e.g.,* Q31: "Have you ever been discriminated against because you were or are a mental health client?," to which 52% answered yes; 41% answered that people treated them differently "all of the time" or "most of the time" when they found out they had received mental health services or had been psychiatrically diagnosed. Their survey also discusses issues of discrimination at 90–92). I wanted to seek as much current information as possible from the people who are supposed to be protected by the ADA. I circulated my survey to many groups representing people with psychiatric disabilities. The survey was posted at various sites on the Internet, was sent to several state psychiatric institutions, and was distributed at conferences attended by people with psychiatric disabilities. I received a total of 423 responses from people from all walks of life—from law professors to people who had lived more than half their lives in psychiatric institutions. These responses reflect the enormous heterogenity and variety of people with psychiatric disabilities as well as the commonality of their experience of discrim-ination. The questions in the survey are reproduced as Appendix A at the end of this book.

[6]Survey No. 247.

covered? What constitutes discrimination? What are reasonable accommodations? This book is an attempt to answer those questions, clear some of the confusion, educate and empower people with psychiatric diagnoses, and defuse employer resentment arising from misunderstanding the ADA's requirements.

Some of the confusion employers describe, however, is inherent in the nature of the ADA. Congress was determined that the ADA would be applied on an individualized, case-by-case basis, which means (at least in principle) that certainty and predictability are to some extent sacrificed to justice. If each case is judged on its own particular facts, it is more difficult to draw generalizations or hard and fast rules to cover the next case—or the next hundred cases.

Both employers and judges are uncomfortable with such an individualized approach. For employers, uncertainty represents cost. For judges, the individualized decisions required by the ADA seem to require unprincipled decision making. Therefore, courts have devised a series of rules to guide resolution of ADA cases, which have increased predictability. Some of these rules reflect selective emphasis of Equal Employment Opportunity Commission (EEOC) regulations, others involve rejection of EEOC regulations, and still others are judicially created to fill the interstices of the language of the ADA.

Unfortunately, many of these judicially created rules hinder or eliminate the remedy the ADA was designed to provide to people with psychiatric disabilities for discrimination in the workplace. Paradoxically, as social science research and individual accounts teach us more about the nature of discrimination against people with psychiatric disabilities, the law is being developed and interpreted in a way that is contrary to those teachings—a way that ultimately provides little or no protection against discrimination.

This book presents the voices and experiences of people with psychiatric disabilities and the research and case law to date in an effort to describe discrimination in the workplace against people with psychiatric disabilities and to answer questions of both employees and employers about how the ADA affects the workplace environment of employees with psychiatric disabilities.

The Work Experience of People With Psychiatric Disabilities

The Impact of Psychiatric Disability on the Desire and Ability to Work

Overwhelmingly, people in the United States want and expect to work.[7] Work is crucial to people's social identity. Americans with psychiatric disabilities are no different—they, too, want to work.[8] When asked to define "disability," people with

---

[7] See Sue E. Estroff, Donald L. Patrick, Catherine R. Zimmer, and William S. Lachicotte, "Pathways to Disability Income Among Persons With Severe, Persistent Psychiatric Disorders." *Milbank Q.* 75 (1997): 495, 523.

[8] Richard Bonnie and John Monahan, Eds., *Mental Disorder, Work Disability, and the Law* (Chicago: University of Chicago Press, 1997); Jean Campbell and Roy Schraiber, *The Well-Being Project: Mental Health Clients Speak for Themselves* (Sacramento, CA: California Network of Mental Health Clients, 1989) (74% of survey respondents considered meaningful work or achievement to be essential to well-being); E. S. Rogers, D. Walsh, L. Masotta, and K. Danley, *Massachusetts Survey of Client Preferences for Community Support Service* (Boston: Center for Psychiatric Rehabilitation, 1991) (71% of people with severe mental disorders have an active interest in working and finding jobs).

psychiatric disabilities responding to my survey repeatedly defined "disability" in terms of being unable to work. Responses to the question "How do you define or describe 'having a disability'?" included "being unable to perform work for which I was educated, trained and experienced"; "not being allowed to continue one's work"; "that illness which prevents you from working"; "not being able to work"; "not having the ability to perform or work as most people"; "someone who can't hold a job"; and "a limitation affecting one's ability to work."[9] Another question in the survey asked "Do you feel part of the community where you live? Why or why not?" Many respondents alluded to their employment status in answering this question: for example, "not as much since I quit my job. Employment was my identity."[10] In the United States, a job provides identity, friends, and social contacts. It also gives meaning and purpose to life:

> Working offers structure to one's day, an opportunity to expand one's social circle, and the chance to contribute. It also produces income, which creates new opportunities for community participation and expands one's role as a consumer within the community.[11]

Perhaps more importantly, "having a job and a place to live are the two key variables that serve to separate those ex-patients who can permanently stay out of hospitals and live a decent life from those who face the revolving door or life in back alleys."[12]

Although the majority of people with psychiatric disabilities believe employment is necessary for fulfillment and meaning in their lives, some are troubled by the primacy that American society places on employment as a source of personal identity:

> I guess I just feel that the work world as it exists is not made for some of us; that it would be good if what we can do were more valued; and if basic food, shelter, services and mobility were available to all human beings whether we "qualified" in some way or not. . . . I hate it that I must name myself in terms of the job I'm able to hold down and if I have trouble doing that I lose my value as a human being, no matter how good a friend or neighbor or parent I might be.[13]

---

[9]Survey No. 152, 243, 251, 269, 271, 273, and 274. *See also* Survey No. 104, 106, 116, 117, 139, and 250.

[10]Survey No. 335.

[11]G. T. Bellamy et al., eds., *Supported Employment: A Community Implementation Guide 16* (Baltimore: Brookes, 1988).

[12]Michael Perlin, "The ADA and Persons with Mental Disabilities: Can Sanist Attitudes be Undone?" *J. of Law and Health* 8 (1993–1994): 15, 35.

[13]Survey No. 212. This uneasiness with the American emphasis on productivity as the primary indication of personal value is not unique to people with psychiatric disabilities. It is also an ongoing concern of people with physical disabilities and their loved ones, as well as the elderly. Briefs submitted to the U.S. Supreme Court in recent cases involving the right to die expressed concern that people who were viewed as nonproductive would be encouraged or even coerced to exercise their right to die, *Vacco v. Quill*, 521 U.S. 793 (1997).

It is true that some people become so discouraged and demoralized, in part because of the rejection and cruelty of others[14] or because they hear so often about the limitations of their illnesses,[15] that they give up hope of working and adopt an identity based on being a "mental patient." But the reality for most people is summarized in this description by a woman with a history of serious mental illness:

> Work was really crucial in making me feel like a valuable person. Now in this society, and maybe it's not right and maybe we shouldn't think in this way, but as we know, work defines you. I used to go to parties and people would say, "What do you do?" and I'd say, "Nothing." . . . It was hard, it was very hard . . . To me, work is one of the most valuable things you can do to recover.[16]

This woman's observations about her own life are supported by research linking working with recovery from psychiatric disabilities, including disabilities as severe as schizophrenia.[17]

Not only do people with psychiatric disabilities want to work, but many people with extraordinarily severe psychiatric disabilities can and do work. And they do not simply work in the area one survey respondent called "the three f's—food, flowers and fertilizer—(fast food, yard work, and janitorial)."[18] They work in demanding, challenging jobs. People with severe psychiatric difficulties have included senators,[19]

---

[14] John S. Strauss and Larry Davidson, "Mental Disorders, Work and Choice," in Richard J. Bonnie and John Monahan, eds., *Mental Disorder, Work Disability and the Law* (Chicago: University of Chicago Press, 1997) at 117 (quoting Clyde, "a funny-looking guy" with a psychiatric history as saying, "You know it's hard working on a job looking the way I do, so people sometimes start making fun of me or picking on me. Hell, they don't have much else to do.").

[15] *Id.* at 116. For a persuasive account of the adoption of such an identity, *see* Sue Estroff, *Making It Crazy: An Ethnography of Psychiatric Clients in an American Community* (Berkeley: University of California Press, 1981).

[16] Quoted in John S. Strauss and Larry Davidson, "Mental Disorders, Work, and Choice," in Richard J. Bonnie and John Monahan, Eds., *Mental Disorder, Work Disability, and the Law* (Chicago: University of Chicago Press, 1997) at 105. This chapter is a particularly powerful piece in a generally excellent book, which I recommend to the reader.

[17] *Id. See also* Christine Ahrens, Jana Frey, and Suzanne Burke, "An Individualized Job Engagement Approach for Persons With Severe Mental Illness," *J. of Rehabilitation* 65(4) (1999): 17; S. Trotter, K. Mitzkoff, K. Harrison, and J. Kepps, "Supported Work: An Innovative Approach to Vocational Rehabilitation of Persons Who Are Psychiatrically Disabled," *Rehabilitative Psychology* 33(91) (1988): 27–36; C. J. Van Dongen, "Quality of Life and Self-esteem in Working and Nonworking Persons with Mental Illness," *Community Mental Health J.* 32(6) (1996): 535–548; W. A. Anthony and Andrea Blanch, "Supported Employment for Persons Who Are Psychiatrically Disabled: A Historical and Conceptual Perspective," *Psychological Rehabilitative J.* 11(2) (1987): 5–23.

[18] Survey response of D. E. (Survey No. 201). Rehabilitation literature has referred to the "four f's —food, flowers, folding, and filth," which represent food service, gardening, laundry or clerical work, and janitorial services, respectively. Gregory G. Garske and Jay R. Stewart, "Stigmatic and Mythical Thinking: Barriers to Vocational Rehabilitation Services for Persons With Severe Mental Illness," *J. of Rehabilitation* 65 (1999): 4.

[19] Lawton Chiles took Prozac for depression, and Tom Eagleton received electric shock treatment for depression. Judy Keen, "Florida's Chiles Returns to Fray; Vows 'Major Change'," *USA Today* (Jan. 8, 1991):2A; Beverly Beckham, "Editorial; Op-Ed; Shame's Out; Only Celebrity Matters," *The Boston Herald* (Jan. 14, 2000):O25; William Goldschlag, "Candidates Under Great Pressure to Release Intimate Health Details," *Daily News* (Dec. 14, 1999).

television journalists,[20] print journalists,[21] clinical psychologists,[22] astronauts,[23] authors,[24] and psychiatrists.[25]

These are not simply people who get very depressed. A recent national survey of 500 professionals and managers with psychiatric conditions reflected that 43.5% reported a diagnosis of bipolar disorder, 29.0% reported major depression, 11.5% reported schizophrenia or schizoaffective disorder, and 10.0% reported posttraumatic stress disorder or dissociative identity disorder. Of this group, 73.0% were employed full time, 83.0% had a college degree or higher, and 79.0% earned more than $20,000 a year.[26] These professionals and managers had histories of hospitalization: 64.0% had been hospitalized three times or more, and 25.0% had been hospitalized in the last 3 years.

Behavior that is generally considered indicative of serious psychiatric difficulties can and does coexist with a high level of functioning. For example, self-injury, such as cutting and burning one's self, is engaged in by "corporate executives,"[27] "teachers and insurance salesmen,"[28] and others. Dr. Richard Kluft, who specializes in treating multiple personality disorders, sees professionals with multiple personalities from fields such as medicine, business, and law.[29]

Many people have read Dr. Kay Jamison's book recounting her successes as an academic scholar and as the coauthor of a standard text on bipolar disorder as well as her wildly manic episodes and suicide attempts.[30] One recent book on psychiatric problems in the workplace noted that "schizophrenia can often mean a reduction in social and occupational abilities, but not usually as much as people think . . . Given this opportunity for renewed self-confidence, and appropriate continuing treatment, employees with schizophrenia should again be able to perform job responsibilities at the level of their peers."[31] Dr. Daniel Fisher, a man with a diagnosis of schizo-

---

[20]*See* Kathy Cronkite, *On The Edge of Darkness: Conversations About Conquering Depression* (New York: Doubleday, 1994) (Mike Wallace's account of his battles with depression).

[21]Tracy Thompson, *The Beast: A Reckoning With Depression* (New York: Putnam, 1995).

[22]Martha Manning, *Undercurrents* (San Francisco: Harper, 1994).

[23]Buzz Aldrin has manic–depression. *See* Dana Parsons, "Bad Moods: Manic–Depressives Worry About Violence Giving Ailment Bad Name," *L. A. Times* (Feb. 16, 1989): pt. 9, p. 1.

[24]William Styron, *Darkness Visible: A Memoir of Madness* (New York: Random House, 1990); Elizabeth Wurtzel, *Prozac Nation: Young and Depressed in America* (Boston: Houghton-Mifflin, 1994); Wilfrid Sheed, *In Love With Daylight: A Memoir of Recovery* (New York: Simon & Schuster, 1995).

[25]"Psychiatrist/Former Mental Patient Calls for Health Care Reform Based on the 'Empowerment Model' of Recovery From Mental Illness," *Newswire* (June 15, 1994).

[26]Marsha Langer Ellison and Zlatka Russinova, *A National Survey of Professionals and Managers With Psychiatric Conditions: A Portrait of Achievements and Challenges* (Boston: Center for Psychiatric Rehabilitation, 1999), *available at* http://www.bu.edu/SARPSYCH/research/rtc1999/si_3.html.

[27]Sandra Bloom, *Creating Sanctuary: Toward the Evolution of Sane Societies* (New York: Routledge, 1997) at 131.

[28]Armando Favazza, "Why Patients Mutilate Themselves," *Hospital and Community Psychiatry* 40(2) (1989): 137.

[29]Richard P. Kluft, "High-Functioning Multiple Personality Patients," *J. Nerv. Mental Dis.* 174(12) (1986): 722–726.

[30]*Id.*

[31]Richard H. Gabel, "Psychosis: Peculiar Behaviors and Inflexible Bizarre Beliefs," in Jeffrey P. Kahn, ed., *Mental Health in the Workplace: A Practical Psychiatric Guide* (New York: Van Nostrand Reinhold, 1993) at 395, 398.

phrenia, is a board-certified psychiatrist and national speaker on techniques of recovery.[32]

This is not to say that anyone with a diagnosis of schizophrenia could be (or would want to be) a high-powered lawyer or psychiatrist any more than anyone without such a diagnosis. Because of their condition, some people with schizophrenia may be barred from work for a substantial portion of their lives, but research has shown that neither diagnoses nor symptomatology alone are reliable predictors of a person's ability to work.[33] Although the research is divided and in some respects contradictory, it appears that the best predictors of successful employment for people with psychiatric disabilities are the degree to which an individual has social skills and prior successful work experience.[34]

Psychiatric disabilities do affect some people's ability to work. Many survey respondents answered a question about how their disabilities affected them by noting that they could work only part time,[35] that they could not work long hours,[36] that they were "slow,"[37] or that they had difficulty concentrating or focusing at work.[38] Many said that they felt full-time employment was too stressful.[39] Relatively few reported that they could not work at all.[40]

Others emphasized that it was not their mental disability that interfered with their work but rather the medication that they were taking.[41] In fact, the U.S. Supreme

---

[32] "Psychiatrist/Former Mental Patient Calls for Health Care Reform Based on the 'Empowerment Model' of Recovery From Mental Illness," *Newswire* (June 15, 1994); Stephen Johnson, "Forced Psychiatric Treatment Opposed," *The Houston Chronicle* (May 7, 1994):A36; Jerry Crimmins, "Mentally Ill Brainstorm Toward Recovery," *Chicago Tribune* (Jan. 18, 1998):C1.

[33] Hector Tsang, Paul Lam, Bacon Ng, and Odelia Leung, "Predictors of Employment Outcome for People with Psychiatric Disabilities: A Review of the Literature since the Mid-80s," *J. of Rehabilitation* 66(2) (2000): 19; W. A. Anthony and M. A. Jansen, "Predicting the Vocational Capacity of the Chronically Mentally Ill," *American Psychologist* 39 (1984): 537; William A. Anthony, "Characteristics of People With Psychiatric Disabilities That Are Predictive of Entry Into the Rehabilitation Process and Successful Employment," *Psychosocial Rehab. J.* 17 (Jan. 1994): 3, 4–5.

[34] Hector Tsang, Paul Lam, Bacon Ng, and Odelia Leung, *id.*, at n. 33. This study reviewed a total of 92 articles researching predictors of employment outcome for persons with psychiatric disabilities. The authors concluded that "premorbid occupational performance, which refers to work skills, work attitudes, work adjustment, community living skills and other relevant life experiences before the onset of mental illness, received most support ($N = 7$) in the literature as a significant predictor of posthospital employment. However, three studies concluded it was a nonsignificant predictor. Social skills ($N = 11$) and premorbid functioning ($N = 6$) also received support as a significant predictor of employment outcome from the studies reviewed. Unlike premorbid occupational performance, there were no studies concluding that these latter two aspects were nonsignificant predictors." *See also* William A. Anthony, *id,* 3–5.

[35] Survey No. 89, 262, 272, 274, 323, and 324.

[36] Survey No. 293.

[37] Survey No. 269 and 271.

[38] Survey No. 238, 313, 334, and 331.

[39] Survey No. 89, 248, 254, and 334. *See also* chapter 6, this volume.

[40] Survey No. 107, 250, 267, and 269.

[41] Survey No. 25, Survey No. 111 (respondent can not "work or go to school" because "my medicine impairs my memory"), Survey No. 114 ("I was fired for being 'slow and lazy' when I tried to explain that my medications weren't working or that I was having trouble changing prescriptions"), Survey No. 254 ("medication makes me tired"), Survey No. 255 ("When I first began taking medications, my employers told me to 'snap out of it.' I became defensive and ultimately lost my position in

Court has recently reaffirmed that a person can be disabled under the ADA because of the effects of medication he or she takes to treat an impairment and referred specifically to antipsychotic medications as an example of this phenomenon.[42]

In summary, simply knowing that an individual has a psychiatric diagnosis tells an employer little, if anything, about that individual's talents, abilities, and difficulties in the work arena, and whether and to what extent the psychiatric condition affects work performance. For some people, work performance is distinctly enhanced by certain kinds of psychiatric conditions: the literature is replete with the accomplishments of people with bipolar disorder during certain parts of "manic" phases.[43] One research study found that "persons with schizophrenia were likely to experience worsening symptoms in the presence of stressful employment, while the symptoms of those with affective disorder improved."[44] Others struggle with depression and perform so capably that their coworkers and customers never suspect that they are experiencing tremendous difficulties.

The Two Worlds of People With Psychiatric Disabilities

Work serves as the main distinction between two worlds of people with psychiatric disabilities in American society.[45] In the "first" world, people's primary identities do not revolve around their psychiatric disabilities. Roseanne Barr, Mike Wallace, Buzz Aldrin, and Kay Jamison are in some sense shielded from the stigma associated with the psychiatric conditions they have revealed to the public because they are successful and well known in their fields. Being successful at work may be one of the few things in American culture that overrides stereotypes about psychiatric disability (assuming that success in work preceded the disclosure of psychiatric diagnosis). People in the first world work in the mainstream. They often keep their diagnoses private—even secret—and consider mental illness primarily a medical problem. Treatment providers are seen as allies. Hospitalizations are rare and tend to last a few weeks or months at most.

People in the second world are publicly identified as mentally disabled—they are clients of the public mental health system or they receive public disability payments. This public identity overwhelms all individual strengths and differences. People in the second world are unlikely to be offered attractive employment. They fight

---

management through intimidation."), Survey No. 269; Survey No. 332 ("meds and work are limited because they do not always work good together").

[42]Sutton v. United Airlines, 527 U.S. 471 (1999) (rejecting the evaluation of a disability in its unmitigated state because "courts and employers could not consider any negative side effects suffered by an individual from the use of mitigating measures, even when those side effects are very severe). See, e.g., Steven T. Johnson, "Antipsychotics: Pros and Cons of Antipsychotics," RN 60(8) (Aug. 1997) (noting that antipsychotic drugs can cause a variety of adverse effects, including neuroleptic malignant syndrome and painful seizures).

[43]Kay Redfield Jamison, Touched With Fire (New York: Free Press, 1994).

[44]Edward H. Yelin and Miriam G. Cisternas, "Employment Patterns Among Persons With and Without Mental Conditions," in Richard Bonnie and John Monahan, eds., Mental Disorder, Work Disability and the Law (Chicago: University of Chicago Press, 1997).

[45]This theory is developed in depth in my book, Unequal Rights: Discrimination Against People With Mental Disabilities and the Americans With Disabilities Act (Washington, DC: American Psychological Association, 2001).

to keep custody of their children—and usually lose. They are often at odds with their treatment providers. They dread involuntary institutionalization and forced medication. All people who *reside* in institutions as opposed to receiving brief treatment in institutional settings are members of the second world. All people whose residential status is linked to their psychiatric status—those living in halfway houses, board and care facilities, and group homes—are members of the second world.

It would be too easy—and misleading—to ascribe the distinction between the first and the second worlds to social class, to severity of symptomatology, or to ability to function. In fact, many people in the second world were born into the middle class (the formation of the National Alliance of the Mentally Ill stemmed in part from upper middle class parents' frustrations with the treatment of their children by the public mental health system), and many lower middle class and poor people with severe mental disabilities function in tiring, demanding mainstream employment every day.

As to symptomatology, personal accounts tell of lawyers, doctors, accountants, journalists, and professors who hear voices, have delusions, go on manic spending sprees, cut themselves, burn themselves, and are suicidal. No symptom associated with "severe and persistent mental illness" has not been described by a successful professional.

Some would insist that the division between the first and second worlds is one of functionality. People in mental hospitals must be there because they cannot function in the world. People who receive public disability benefits simply cannot work. This, too, is misleading. It is misleading because many people are institutionalized inappropriately and could live in the community and because many people on disability benefits can work, and some do work. Most importantly, this approach is mistaken because it conceptualizes functionality as a static trait. The failure to acknowledge that functionality fluctuates is one of the crucial errors of both law and public perception. Scientific researchers have reported for decades that people with psychiatric disabilities experience fluctuations in the levels of competency and functionality, but the law exists in either/or categories.

Thus, people in the first world describe weeks and months of being unable to function, yet they continue to be perceived as functional.[46] People in the second world are not perceived as functional even when they write books, edit newsletters, organize protests, provide testimony to federal and state legislatures, manage drop-in centers, sit on federal government task forces and committees, become Internet experts, and successfully parent children. For example, Ken Steele was vice chair of the Mental Health Association for the State of New York and chair of its Governmental Affairs Committee.[47] He published a newspaper, *New York City Voices,* about mental health issues, founded a support group called Awakenings, and consulted with the New York Attorney General's Office. He lived on a monthly Social Security disability check of $587 in a state-subsidized apartment.[48]

Understanding the distinction between the two worlds is particularly important

---

[46] *See, e.g.,* William Styron, *Darkness Visible: A Memoir of Madness* (New York: Random House, 1990) and Kathy Cronkite, *On the Edge of Darkness: Conversations About Conquering Depression* (New York: Doubleday, 1994).

[47] Erica Goode, "With Help, Climbing Back from Schizophrenia's Isolation," *New York Times* (Jan. 30, 1999): sec. A, p. 1. Mr. Steele died on Oct. 7, 2000. Erica Goode, "Kenneth M. Steele, 51, Advocate for the Mentally Ill," *New York Times* (Oct. 12, 2000): sec. A, p. 27.

[48] *Id.*

because research findings and statistics are often presented as though they encompass all people with psychiatric disabilities even though the research participants are limited to people from the second world.[49] For example, the unemployment rate among people with severe psychiatric disabilities is often estimated at 85% or more. This rate may be accurate for people in the second world—those whose severe psychiatric disabilities have been publicly diagnosed and who have found themselves clients of state mental health programs. Research shows that people with severe psychiatric disabilities whose disabilities remain undiagnosed may do better in terms of being employed and avoiding discrimination.

It does a tremendous disservice to the social understanding of psychiatric disability to present it only in terms of the experiences of the inhabitants of the second world. It does an equal disservice to people in the second world, whose disabilities are so public, to erase all the people with the same diagnosis and the same difficulties in functioning who are employed and pass silently as unimpaired and nondisabled.

Employment Rates of Persons With Psychiatric Disabilities

Like statistics about mental illness itself,[50] statistics about the employment rates of people with psychiatric disabilities vary widely. As previously suggested, this variation may occur because the people who form the pool from which the statistics are gathered largely populate the second world: people who are publicly known to have a psychiatric diagnosis and who may already be on disability. These people are more readily available as research subjects simply because they are identifiable and grouped together: in institutions, on the rolls of the public mental health system, or on a list of people receiving social security benefits. Therefore, they have been studied far more intensively than the people who are scattered and integrated in the mainstream, many of whom have kept their diagnoses private and would not willingly identify themselves as having a psychiatric disability. Some studies do encompass both worlds: so-called household surveys, which depend on truthful self-reporting by household members, and the massive population surveys done over 10 years by the Epidemiological Catchment Area researchers.[51]

Not surprisingly, the results of surveys focusing on the second world paint a dismal employment picture: They portray a world in which 75–95%[52] of people with mental illness are unemployed. A statement by the National Association of State Mental Health Program Directors estimated the unemployment rate among people with severe psychiatric disabilities to be 85% or more.[53] However, surveys based on the population at large reflect that people with serious mental disabilities, although still underemployed compared with the general population, are employed at far higher levels.

Employment studies are also hard to compare with each other because some

---

[49] *See* articles cited at notes 33 and 34, *supra*, and 52 and 53, *infra*.

[50] *See* chapter 3.

[51] *See* chapter 3 for further discussion of these surveys.

[52] L. J. Spaniol and A. M. Zipple, "Family and Professional Perception of Family Needs and Coping Strengths," *Rehabilitation Psychology* 33 (1988): 37.

[53] National Association of State Mental Health Program Directors Position Statement on the Employment of People with Severe Psychiatric Disabilities (adopted Dec. 7, 1990).

consider any kind of employment as constituting "employment" for the purposes of the survey, including volunteer or unpaid employment. Other studies include any paid employment, that is, part-time employment, temporary employment, sheltered workshops, supported employment, state-subsidized employment, and self-employment. Some studies include paid employment except for sheltered workshops. Others include "competitive" employment but define *competitive* to include part-time work. Thus, surveys that define employment as "full-time, competitive employment" find far lower employment rates[54] than do surveys that define employment more broadly. In addition, employment statistics do not make distinctions between the different kinds of "full-time, competitive" jobs at which people are employed, for example, minimum-wage jobs without benefits versus salaried positions of relative permanence and status, with accompanying health and pension benefits.

Employment statistics rarely examine wage differentials between employees with psychiatric disabilities and nondisabled employees. Researchers who set out to examine these differentials and to distinguish between differentials due to actual differences in productivity and differentials due to discrimination found the largest "unexplainable wage differential" in the case of people with "mental, nervous or emotional problems." That group was also found to be the most subject to discrimination after eliminating those who reported they were unable to work and eliminating wage differentials based on productivity differentials.[55]

Discrimination Based on Psychiatric Disability in the Workplace

People with severe psychiatric disabilities want to work, and most can work. But when a psychiatric diagnosis of an employee or applicant becomes known, especially a diagnosis associated with a "severe" mental illness, employers and colleagues alike often assume that the individual is incapable of sustained and challenging employment. Although many physical conditions also require intermittent and unpredictable hospitalizations or medication adjustments, few people question the ability of a person who has suffered from, for example, a heart attack to return to work. This understanding usually does not translate to a similar understanding of psychiatric disability. If an individual receives a diagnosis of a serious psychiatric illness, those who are aware of it interpret future functioning through the lens of disability.

Mental health professionals, who should be in the front lines of education about mistaken attitudes about mental illness, often behave as though they share those attitudes and perpetuate them in the public and, worse, to their patients. One woman with a psychiatric diagnosis wrote, speaking of her experience:

> You have a cyclical disorder. After the second year at the same job and the second episode, your MHP [mental health professional] tells you it would be better if you worked part-time. You know you can work more than full-time when you're well,

---

[54]*See* note 52 (5% of NAMI relatives with mental illness were competitively employed on a full-time basis); William A. Anthony and Mary A. Jansen, "Predicting the Vocational Capacity of the Chronically Mentally Ill: Research and Policy Implications," *American Psychologist* 39 (1984): 537; William Anthony, M. R. Cohen, and R. I. Vital, "The Measurement of Rehabilitation Outcome," *Schizophrenia Bul.* 4 (1978): 365.

[55]Marjorie L. Baldwin, "Can the ADA Achieve Its Employment Goals?," *Annals of the American Academy of Political and Social Science* 549 (Jan. 1997): 45–46.

which is three-fourths of the year, and you can't work at all when you're ill, which is one fourth of the year. But he's the MHP, so you go along.[56]

One witness in support of the ADA before Congress told of a hospitalized psychologist with a PhD in chemistry being asked to sort socks as vocational rehabilitation.[57]

The EEOC reports that it receives more complaints about discrimination based on psychiatric disability than any other disability.[58] The survey also adds insights not readily available from reading social sciences research or court decisions. Some of the ill-treatment complained about in the surveys (being shunned or mistreated by coworkers,[59] being yelled at,[60] being "banned from participating in employee trips,"[61] and having a supervisor make sarcastic comments[62]) would not suffice under current law to create a cause of action for discrimination, but probably created a miserable environment in which to work, added to the stress already experienced as a result of the psychiatric disability, and in some cases precipitated breakdowns.

Many respondents to the survey also reported discrimination in the process of trying to find a job[63] or being turned down for jobs,[64] a situation that is very rarely litigated,[65] especially by people with psychiatric disabilities.[66] In fact, recent research suggests that employers may be more hesitant about hiring people with disabilities since the advent of the ADA. In some surveys, respondents related being discriminated against in promotion,[67] being fired when their employers learned their diagnosis,[68] and being fired for *not* telling their employer of their diagnosis.[69] Others reported being fired because of problems with medication[70] or lying about being

---

[56]Betty Blaska, "What It Is Like To Be Treated Like a CMI," in Jeanine Grobe, ed., *Beyond Bedlam: Contemporary Women Psychiatric Survivors Speak Out* (Chicago: Third Side Press, 1995), 28. This article first appeared in *Schizophrenia Bull.* 17(1) (1991). Betty Blaska committed suicide in 1997.

[57]Testimony of Lelia Batten to the U.S. Congress in support of the ADA, Arnold and Porter, A&P Committee Print 1990 (28B) at *1191–1204.

[58]Many respondents complained about harassment or ill-treatment by supervisors or coworkers when their diagnosis was revealed. Case law reflects these issues and highlights the reluctance of employers to involve themselves in resolving these problems (*see* chapter 6, this volume).

[59]Survey No. 247 (on the job "they knew I was mentally ill and were suspicious of me and never fully accepted me"); Survey No. 270 ("people at my job avoided and shunned me"); Survey No. 290 ("co-workers assumed poor judgment causes slow performance").

[60]Survey No. 334.

[61]Survey No. 290.

[62]Survey No. 255 ("my boss prodded me using statements such as 'Are you worried that you won't please me? I'm not your mother'").

[63]Survey No. 271 and 270.

[64]Survey No. 4, 11, 102, 103, 179, 195, 196, 199, 235, 246, and 271. One survey respondent wrote that he worked at a company that had defended ADA cases, and he reported that the common view was that it was easier to discriminate in hiring, because it was easier to justify failure to hire, than to discriminate by firing someone (Survey No. 43).

[65]Kathryn Moss, Michael Ullman, Matthew C. Johnsen, Barbara E. Starrett, and Scott Burris, "Different Paths to Justice: The ADA, Employment and Administrative Enforcement by the EEOC and FEPAs," *Behavioral Sciences and the Law* 17(29) (1999): 35.

[66]*Id.*

[67]Survey No. 37 and 108. (anxiety disorder).

[68]Survey No. 104. *See* also Survey No. 283 ("Have been fired in the past due to mental illness [anxiety disorder]).

[69]Survey No. 135.

[70]Survey No. 114.

hospitalized because of fear of discrimination.[71] Other reports of discrimination indirectly related to employment included respondents' frustration at being forced to choose between Medicaid benefits to cover health care and higher wages, which would mean losing those benefits,[72] and pain caused by "people saying you're just lazy when severely depressed" or "people saying you would rather have a label and be on disability than work."[73]

Interestingly, people who identified themselves as being discriminated against on the basis of psychiatric disabilities often reported that they were discriminated against because of some other characteristic, such as gender,[74] race or national origin,[75] sexual orientation,[76] and physical disability.[77] These people reported that they were often unable to discern the basis for adverse action. One respondent wrote,

> Getting a job was bloody murder! In Texas in the 70's every street dyke could find work except me. I don't know if I was too crazy, too damn yankee, or too Jewish. Maybe all three. I was afraid I'd starve or be dependent forever.

This information supports the finding of a recent study that "the social and demographic conditions which place some people at severe disadvantage in the labor market [such as age and race] operate even more strongly among those with mental conditions, suggesting that the presence of a mental condition makes a bad employment situation much worse than would be indicated by either the mental condition or the social and demographic characteristics alone."[78]

Discrimination as the Cause of Psychiatric Disability

Both case law and survey respondents underscore the causal relationship between discrimination at work and emotional breakdowns. One of the most significant findings of the survey is that discrimination has an enormous and detrimental impact on people with psychiatric disabilities, often triggering or exacerbating acute episodes of disability. When asked what impact discrimination had on their lives, many respondents reported an enormous impact, such as hospitalization, suicide attempts, and an inability to seek other employment. Following are some of their comments:

> I had a breakdown after they wouldn't let me student teach. Thought I would never be anything—hopeless—lasted 1–2 years.[79]

* * *

> I was devastated. I ended up in the hospital psych isolation room on a suicide watch.[80]

---

[71] Survey No. 93.

[72] Survey No. 236 and 238.

[73] Survey No. 256.

[74] Survey No. 23 and 170.

[75] Survey No. 54, 58, 90, 221, 234, and 238.

[76] Survey No. 12, 15, and 272.

[77] Survey No. 266.

[78] Edward H. Yelin and Miriam G. Cisternas, "Employment Patterns Among Persons With and Without Mental Conditions," in Richard J. Bonnie and John Monahan, eds., *Mental Disorder, Work Disability and the Law* (Chicago: University of Chicago Press, 1997) at 27.

[79] Survey No. 115.

[80] Survey No. 114.

* * *

I felt terrible for years. It has been a slow, painful adjustment.[81]

* * *

I couldn't understand this. I did my job well. Because of this I haven't worked since and that happened in 1993.[82]

* * *

I lost my self-worth.[83]

Researchers have confirmed that "the impact of discrimination and stigma on a person's job performance, for example, may be more deleterious than the effects of the illness itself."[84] This conclusion is something that courts have yet to consider in employment discrimination cases.

The Cost of Discrimination

To eliminate or reduce discrimination on the basis of psychiatric disability in employment would be of tremendous benefit to people with psychiatric disabilities and to the country as a whole. Not only are rates of labor force participation of people with psychiatric disabilities under the age of 45 far lower than those of people without disabilities, but they "consistently fall far below rates of all persons with disabilities in the same age group."[85] About one quarter of the people collecting Social Security Disability Insurance (SSDI) are people with psychiatric disabilities,[86] and at least 30% of recipients of Supplemental Security Income (SSI) are people with psychiatric disabilities.[87]

The substantial proportion of people on SSI and SSDI who are psychiatrically disabled should not, by itself, be surprising: The number of people with psychiatric disabilities in our population is far greater than the number who are blind; deaf; use wheelchairs; and are diagnosed with multiple sclerosis, HIV-seropositivity, and lupus, combined.[88] Proportionately fewer people with psychiatric disabilities receive dis-

---

[81] Survey No. 99.

[82] Survey No. 135.

[83] Survey No. 136.

[84] See n. 13 at 126 and Jeffrey Kahn, ed., *Mental Health in the Workplace: A Practical Psychiatric Guide,* at 396. (New York: Van Nostrand Reinhold, 1993).

[85] L. Trupin, D. S. Sebesta, E. Yelin, and M. P. La Plante, "Trends in Labor Force Participation Among Persons With Disabilities, 1993–94," *Disability Statistics Report* 10 (1997): 1–39.

[86] Social Security Administration, Annual Statistical Supplement, *Social Security Bull.* (Nov. 1998), Table 5D6, p. 231 (25.6% of disabled workers collecting SSDI benefits have a "mental disorder other than mental retardation." Women constitute a higher percentage of those collecting SSDI benefits on the basis of mental disorder [27.5% versus 24.3% men]).

[87] *Id.* Table 7F1 (32.2% of people receiving SSI have a "mental disorder other than mental retardation").

[88] Compared with 10 million people with serious mental illness, 350,000 people have been diagnosed with multiple sclerosis (The Multiple Sclerosis Foundation, *http://www.msfacts.org/answers3.htm*), between 500,000 and 1.5 million people have been diagnosed with lupus (Lupus Foundation of America, *lupus.org/info/def.html*), and about 1 million Americans are HIV-positive (AIDS Org., Inc., *http://www. aids.org/Fact Sheets/101-what-is-aids.html.*).

ability benefits than would be expected from their numbers in the population.[89] However, the number of people with psychiatric disabilities applying for and receiving federal disability benefits has increased dramatically in the past 15 years.

Another reason that people with psychiatric disabilities constitute such a high proportion of those who receive federal disability benefits may be that relatively few people with psychiatric disabilities collect private long-term disability benefit insurance. This is because most private long-term disability benefit plans pay benefits for psychiatric disabilities for only two years or exclude these disabilities altogether.[90] Courts have ruled unanimously that this kind of differentiation between benefits for physical and emotional conditions is permissible under the ADA,[91] which essentially shifts the economic burden of paying these benefits to the government and serves as a windfall for private for-profit insurance companies.

Compared with people with physical disabilities receiving SSDI and SSI, people with psychiatric disabilities begin receiving benefits at a younger age.[92] Thus, they have potentially more productive work years ahead of them (or more years of collecting government benefits). The increase in people with psychiatric disabilities receiving SSI and SSDI is attributable primarily to an increase in the number of people with affective disorders receiving these benefits. It is probably easier for employers to prevent people with affective disorders from becoming too disabled to work than people with psychotic disorders (whose relative numbers in terms of benefits have not grown in the past 10 years),[93] and it is likely easier to accommodate those with affective disorders in the workplace. However, employers have relatively little economic incentive to make efforts to retain employees with psychiatric disabilities when they only pay short-term disability benefits and the state or federal government shoulders the bill for any subsequent care.[94] By contrast, employers pay for the long-term disability benefits of people with physical disabilities, creating a significant incentive to invest in rehabilitation and return-to-work programs.

Yet, people with psychiatric disabilities—even severe disabilities—clearly want to work. People with psychiatric disabilities constitute the second largest category of people taking advantage of the SSI Work Incentive program, which permits people to earn up to $500 per month without losing their benefits.[95] Under the current

---

[89]*See* chapter 3.

[90]For an extensive discussion of private insurance companies' discrimination against people with psychiatric disabilities, see Susan Stefan, *Unequal Rights: Discrimination Against People With Mental Disabilities and the Americans With Disabilities Act* (Washington, DC: American Psychological Association, 2001).

[91]EEOC v. Staten Island Savings Bank, 207 F.3d 144 (2nd Cir. 2000); Kimber v. Thiokol Corp., 196 F.3d 1092 (10th Cir. 1999); EEOC v. CNA Insurance Cos., 96 F.3d 1039 (7th Cir. 1996); Parker v. Metropolitan Life Insurance Co., 121 F.3d 1006 (6th Cir. 1997).

[92]Kalman Rupp and Charles G. Scott, "Trends in the Characteristics of DI and SSI Disability Awardees and Duration of Program Participation," *Social Security Bull.* 59 (Mar. 1, 1996): 3.

[93]Kalman Rupp and David Stapleton, eds., *Growth in Disability Benefits: Explanations and Policy Implications* (Kalamazoo, MI: Upjohn Institute for Employment Research, 1998); Kalman Rupp and Charles G. Scott, "Trends in the Characteristics of DI and SSI Disability Awardees and Duration of Program Participation," *Social Security Bull.* 59 (Mar. 22, 1996): 3.

[94]This has been explicitly cited as a reason that some states mandate the provision of mental health benefits by any insurer selling insurance in their states, *see* Metropolitan Life Insurance Company v. Commonwealth of Massachusetts, 471 U.S. 724, 731 (1985).

[95]Social Security Administration, Office of Research, Evaluation and Statistics, Division of SSI

minimum wage, a person could work 20 hours a week for the minimum wage without exceeding $500 a month in earnings. People with mental retardation constitute almost half of participants in the Work Incentive program, and people with psychiatric disabilities make up one quarter of the participants.[96]

The Failure of the ADA to Limit Workplace Discrimination

One of the primary goals of the ADA is to promote employment opportunities for disabled Americans[97] and reduce their dependency on government benefits by prohibiting discrimination on the basis of disability.[98] People with disabilities also hoped that the advent of the ADA would broaden understanding about the skills and capabilities of Americans with disabilities.

The ADA was intended to protect people who could work from unthinking and damaging stereotypes. For people with psychiatric diagnoses who seek employment, one of the first issues is whether to disclose the diagnosis. Few people do so if they have any choice,[99] even though it probably means forfeiting many of their rights under the ADA.[100] Therefore, very few cases under the ADA involve discrimination in hiring.[101] One study shows that the only psychiatric diagnosis associated with a significant number of failure-to-hire complaints to the EEOC is schizophrenia.[102]

More often, psychiatric disabilities develop or are perceived to develop during

---

Statistics and Analysis, "Quarterly Report on SSI Disabled Workers and Work Incentive Provisions," Chart E (Mar. 1998).

[96]*Id.*

[97]Pub. L. No. 101-336; H. R. 101-485 (II), 51.

[98]42 U.S.C. § 12101 (West 1999).

[99]Some people with psychiatric disabilities obtain their employment through the efforts of agencies engaged in providing employment opportunities for people with disabilities, so that their disability will obviously be known. However, these people will sometimes have advocacy and assistance from the agency as well. Otherwise, cases reflect very few instances of people voluntarily disclosing disabilities, and those who do tend either to have relatively nonstigmatized disabilities or to work in professions that might be expected to be understanding, or both. Davidson v. Midelfort Clinic, 133 F.3d 499 (7th Cir. 1998) (employee disclosed Attention Deficit Disorder in interview).

[100]Under the ADA, employers may be liable for discriminating against a person they regard as disabled even if they do not actually know whether the person is disabled. However, employers are not liable for refusing to provide reasonable accommodations unless they knew or had reason to know that the person was disabled. This is discussed further in chapter 8.

[101]In searching thousands of cases, I found only Glidden v. County of Monroe, 950 F. Supp. 73 (W.D. N.Y. 1997) and a few cases charging failure to hire based on the results of a pre-employment exam, including Greenberg v. New York State, 919 F. Supp. 673 (E.D. N.Y. 1996) (applicant for correction officer position denied employment based on results of personality test) and Barnes v. Cochran, 944 F. Supp. 897 (S.D. Fla. 1996). There were a few cases in which there was a failure to re-hire, including Grenier v. Cyanamid Plastics, 70 F.3d 667 (1st Cir. 1995) and Olson v. General Electric, 101 F.3d 947, 949 (3rd Cir. 1996).

[102]Kathryn Moss, *Psychiatric Disabilities, Employment Discrimination Charges, and the ADA*, Final Report for the Mary E. Switzer Distinguished Research Fellowship (Project #H133F50029) (Washington, DC: National Institute on Disability and Rehabilitation Research, 1996), 43 (Table 8: only 9.7% of charges of employment discrimination by people with psychiatric disabilities involved failure to hire, but 19.1% of complaints by people with schizophrenia involved that charge.) Very few complaints were filed with the EEOC by individuals with schizophrenia, so the data may be less reliable because of the low sample.

the course of employment, often as a result of escalating personality conflicts with a new supervisor.[103] Thus, although the ADA was conceptualized as a way of broadening the employment opportunities for people with disabilities, it appears to be used more frequently as a method of protecting workers who have been disabled by the conditions of their work environment than as a protection for people with psychiatric disabilities trying to break into the work force.

Although some people known to be clients of the mental health system are hired through the efforts of mental health and vocational rehabilitation agencies, this kind of supported employment is rarely competitive, with a chance to rise high in the company or business. Over and over, survey respondents reported that the best opportunities for people who were known to be clients of the mental health system came from self-employment and entrepreneurial activities.

This is not to say that supported employment does not have its place. As one survey respondent wrote

> I would like to say that I am grateful for the job I have, and I think they take it pretty easy on me. If it weren't for them giving me a part-time job and being nice enough to be friendly to me so that I want to stay there, I wouldn't have much of a chance to feel competent or useful. So many thanks should be sent out to people who help.[104]

Although individuals in supported employment would probably have little difficulty in convincing a court that they meet the definition of disability for purposes of the ADA,[105] they are basically not part of mainstream competitive employment in America and they rarely sue employers. When they do sue, they do not win.[106] This is in part because courts have a difficult time viewing supported employment as "real" employment, rather than as make-work for people with disabilities,[107] and in part because the very "supportedness" of the employment convinces the court that the employer has provided ample reasonable accommodation.[108]

People with mental disabilities such as mental retardation or organic brain damage who are employed in low-level, nonsheltered employment and suffer intentional discrimination do tend to win if their cases come before a jury.[109] However, when it

---

[103] See chapter 6 for further discussion.

[104] The respondent did not fill out the survey, but simply responded in letter form, so the survey was not numbered or included in the data. On file with author.

[105] But see Phillips v. Wal-Mart Stores, 78 F. Supp. 2d 1274 (S.D. Ala. 1999) (stating that plaintiff who was in a coma for four months after a car accident; was left with a traumatic brain injury that required him to relearn how to speak, walk, and read; and was on Social Security for 14 years and had a Supported Employment certificate from Vocational Rehabilitation was not disabled for purposes of the ADA).

[106] EEOC v. Hertz, 1998 U.S. Dist. LEXIS 58 (E.D. Mich. Jan. 6, 1998) (excoriating EEOC for suing Hertz after Hertz provided plaintiffs with sheltered employment); Phillips v. Wal-Mart Stores, 78 F. Supp. 2d 1274 (S.D. Ala. 1999).

[107] Id.

[108] Drawski v. Department of General Administration, 1998 Washington App. LEXIS 84 (Wash. App. Jan. 9, 1998). The EEOC has issued ambiguous regulations regarding supported employment, making it clear that supported employment is not generally the same as a reasonable accommodation, but cautioning that in some circumstances such features of supported employment such as a job coach might be considered a reasonable accommodation, 29 C.F.R. § 1630.9.

[109] See, e.g., Taylor v. Food World, 133 F.3d 1419 (11th Cir. 1998); EEOC v. CEC Entertainment d/b/a/ Chuck E. Cheese, 2000 U.S. Dist. LEXIS 13934 (W.D. Wisc. March 14, 2000). Research on employer hiring and accommodations for people with mental retardation also shows some positive de-

comes to psychiatric disabilities, it would be fair to conclude that the ADA has failed to provide a remedy against employment discrimination. Surveys of appellate court decisions in employment discrimination cases under the ADA in 1999 show that employees prevailed in only 4.3% of the cases where a final decision was rendered.[110] This represents a decline from 8.4% between 1992 and 1997 and 5.6% in 1998.[111] This reflects all Title I ADA cases, including those brought by people with more socially acceptable disabilities. Cases involving employees with psychiatric disabilities show even less success.

The overwhelming failure of litigated ADA employment discrimination cases is not due to the fact that meritorious complaints are being resolved successfully at the prelitigation administrative level. A study looking at complaints made to the EEOC shows that only 14.7% of charges of discrimination on the basis of psychiatric disability were resolved favorably to the complainant.[112] It is interesting to compare the disabilities with the highest percentages of successful resolution of cases (mental retardation, 28.2%; kidney impairment, 24.2%; "other blood,"[113] 22.9%; asthma, 20.9%; and visual impairment 20.0%) with the disabilities with the lowest percentage of successful resolution of cases (chemical sensitivity, 9.4%; schizophrenia, 10.9%; alcoholism, 12.8%; dwarfism, 13.3%; and "other psychiatric," 14.2%).[114]

Some have argued that the ADA has had a substantial impact simply by its existence. Employers may be taking steps to ensure compliance short of complaints or litigation. For example, the highest proportion of successful resolutions of discrimination claims have taken place after the employer was notified that the EEOC had received a charge but before the EEOC staff had begun to investigate.[115]

However, there is little evidence that employers have overwhelmingly changed their practices to comply with the ADA.[116] Many employers are not even aware

---

velopments, *see* Peter Blanck, "Transcending Title I of the Americans With Disabilities Act: A Case Report on Sears Roebuck and Co.," 20 *Mental and Physical Disability Law Reporter* 278 (1996).

[110]John W. Parry, "1999 Employment Decisions Under the ADA Title I: Survey Update," *Mental and Physical Disability Law Reporter* 20 (May/June 2000): 348.

[111]*Id.*

[112]Kathryn Moss, *Psychiatric Disabilities, Employment Discrimination Charges, and the ADA,* Final Report for the Mary E. Switzer Distinguished Research Fellowship (Project #H133F50029; Washington, DC: National Institute on Disability and Rehabilitation Research, 1997): 27, Table 2 (People complaining of discrimination on the basis of physical disabilities did only marginally better, receiving beneficial outcomes in 16.3% of cases. "Beneficial outcomes" were defined as "withdrawal of the charge with benefits, successful conciliation, or settlement.")

[113]*Id.* This category includes anemia, sickle cell anemia, and lupus.

[114]*Id.* at 33, Table 4. This excludes the least successful category, charges of discrimination based on a relationship with a disabled person, which had a successful resolution in only 7.9% of cases.

[115]*Id.* at 55. "The finding that 94% of beneficial outcomes were obtained after a charge was filed but before an investigation was initiated or completed strongly suggests that the mere presence of the law and the threat of EEOC enforcement have a highly motivational impact apart from formal enforcement activities."

[116]Teresa Scheid, "Employment of Individuals with Mental Disabilities: Business Response to ADA's Challenge," *Behavioral Sciences & the Law* 17 (1999): 73 (finding that one-third of 117 surveyed businesses in a southern metropolitan area had a Title I implementation plan, 15% had specific policies for hiring those with mental disabilities, and 37.6% had hired such an individual). There appears to be no appreciable change from the time immediately following enactment of the ADA, B. J. Jones, B. J. Gallagher, J. M. Kelley, and L. O. Massari, "A Survey of Fortune 500 Corporate Policies Concerning

of the ADA, and of those who are, few have altered their practices.[117] When the U.S. Civil Rights Commission assessed how the EEOC was enforcing Title I of the ADA, it concluded that the goals of the ADA "of ensuring equal employment opportunities . . . are far from being met."[118] This conclusion is reflected in the responses to my survey question "Do you think the Americans with Disabilities Act can prevent these things [instances of discrimination] from happening to people?" Almost half the respondents answered "No."

For years, the number of charges filed with the EEOC related to psychiatric disabilities has been second only to the number related to back problems, and in 1998, charges filed by people with psychiatric disabilities constituted the single largest group of complaints.[119] This figure is often cited with covert or even overt disapproval and without any acknowledgment that psychiatric disabilities are among the most common disabilities in the United States, and therefore one would expect more charges related to psychiatric disabilities.[120]

The EEOC also dismisses psychiatric disability charges as unfounded at a higher rate than charges for any other kind of disability. The EEOC's actions mirror those of courts—of the hundreds of employment discrimination cases filed in the courts by people claiming psychiatric disabilities,[121] only a handful have achieved even limited success. Even when plaintiffs with psychiatric disabilities prevail before a jury, their cases are often reversed on appeal.[122] Some of the remarks of district court and appellate judges in these cases make it clear that the judges share the very attitudes that the ADA was passed to combat. For example, one well-known circuit court judge opined in a concurrence that a person with paranoid schizophrenia probably would not be otherwise qualified for employment, because "paranoid schizo-

---

the Psychiatrically Handicapped," *Rehabilitation J.* 57 (1991): 31 (fewer than 25% of surveyed companies had policies regarding the hiring of people with psychiatric disabilities).

[117] *Id.*

[118] U.S. Civil Rights Commission, "Helping Employers Comply with the ADA: An Assessment of How the United States Equal Employment Opportunity Commission Is Enforcing Title I of the Americans with Disabilities Act" (Sept. 1998): 2.

[119] This is due in part to the fact that, until very recently, the EEOC kept all complaints involving psychiatric disabilities under one category, "emotional/psychiatric impairments," with only two subcategories: "schizophrenia" and "other emotional/psychiatric impairments," whereas it divided physical disabilities into several subsets, including diabetes, hearing impairments, heart impairments, gastrointestinal impairments, back impairments, vision impairments, cancer, HIV, asthma, and neurological impairments. As of 1997, the EEOC separated psychiatric disability complaints into anxiety disorder, depression, manic-depressive disorder, schizophrenia, and "other." EEOC Basic Codes, on file with author.

[120] Interestingly, people with psychiatric disabilities are vastly underrepresented in charges filed with the Department of Justice, accounting for only 6.1% of charges. U.S. Civil Rights Commission, "Helping State and Local Governments Comply with the ADA: An Assessment of How the Department of Justice Is Enforcing Title II, Subpart A, of the Americans with Disabilities Act," Table 2.2 at p. 32 (Sept. 1998). This could be due to a variety of factors. First, the database is admittedly incomplete—the Department of Justice had figures relating to disability for only 2,315 complaints out of 10,065 received, *id.* at 32 and 33. Second, the relative underrepresentation of complaints by people with psychiatric disabilities might be due to the combination in the statistics of complaints under Titles II and III. Title III is primarily concerned with physical accessibility; thus it would not be the source of many charges from people with psychiatric disabilities.

[121] *See* Appendix B for a categorization of these cases according to disability.

[122] Van Stan v. Fancy Colors, 125 F.3d 563 (7th Cir. 1997).

phrenia often entails the sort of violent outbursts (or threats of violence) that an employer need not accommodate."[123] There was no indication in the case before the court that the plaintiff had acted violently or made any threats.

The reasons for these failures as well as a thorough analysis of the law to date, defining the obligations and responsibilities of employers, employees, and the government under the ADA, are explored in the upcoming chapters.

---

[123]Wilson v. Chrysler, 172 F.3d 500, 512 (7th Cir. 1999) (Easterbrook, J., concurring).

Chapter 2
DISABILITY DISCRIMINATION LAW AND DISCRIMINATION AGAINST PEOPLE WITH PSYCHIATRIC DISABILITIES

Discrimination on the basis of physical or mental disability is prohibited by federal law. This chapter reviews the federal laws relating to disability discrimination and explains how to bring a disability discrimination claim. It summarizes the most recent interpretations by the U.S. Supreme Court of the scope of the Americans With Disabilities Act (ADA). Finally, it examines other federal laws that impact individuals with disabilities, such as the Family and Medical Leave Act (FMLA) and the Fair Labor Standards Act.

A Basic Primer in Disability Discrimination Law

Federal, State, and Local Statutes

There are two principal federal statutes that forbid employment discrimination against people with disabilities. Section 504 of the Rehabilitation Act applies to any entity receiving federal funds and forbids discrimination based "solely" on disability.[1] Title I of the ADA prohibits any employer with 15 employees or more, as well as unions, referral agencies, organizations providing training or apprenticeship programs, and organizations providing fringe benefits, from discriminating on the basis of disability.[2] Title I of the ADA was intended by Congress to expand the coverage of Section 504 of the Rehabilitation Act by including employers who do not receive federal funds and eliminating the requirement that discrimination be based "solely" on disability.[3]

All states have statutes forbidding discrimination in employment on the basis of disability. A few states, such as Alabama and Mississippi, forbid discrimination only

---

[1] 29 U.S.C. § 794 (West 2000). The definition of "receiving federal funds" has generally been applied quite liberally and includes firms that receive assistance through the Federal Emergency Management Administration, Rivera-Flores v. Bristol-Myers Squibb Caribbean, 112 F.3d 9 (1st Cir. 1997), or training from a federal agent.

[2] 42 U.S.C. § 12111 (West 2000). The circuit courts are divided on whether Title II of the ADA, which prohibits discrimination by state and local governments, applies to employment discrimination by these entities. *Compare* Bledsoe v. Palm Beach County Soil and Water Conservation District, 140 F.3d 1044 (11th Cir. 1998) with Zimmerman v. Oregon Department of Justice, 183 F.3d 1161 (9th Cir. 1999). This question may lose significance in light of the holding and implications in University of Alabama v. Garrett, 531 U.S. 356 (2001), see discussion *infra* at pp. 34–35.

[3] For a comprehensive history of the passage of Section 504, *see* Susan Stefan, *Unequal Rights: Discrimination Against People With Mental Disabilities and the Americans With Disabilities Act* (Washington, DC: American Psychological Association, 2000); Richard Scotch, *From Good Will to Civil Rights: Transforming Federal Disability Policy* (Philadelphia: Temple University Press, 1984); and Joe Shapiro, *No Pity* (New York: Random House, 1993).

against people with physical disabilities[4]; Georgia forbids discrimination against people with mental disabilities but excludes people with mental illness or learning disabilities from its definition of "mental disabilities."[5] Connecticut, although it has considerable specific legislation protecting people with mental disabilities from discrimination, prohibits the use of numerical goals or quotas in employment—but only for people with mental disorders or histories of mental disorders.[6] In some states, such as Massachusetts, New York, New Jersey, Washington, and Connecticut, courts have construed the state antidiscrimination statutes to grant more protection or broader coverage than the federal antidiscrimination statutes. In addition, some municipalities, such as New York City, San Francisco, and Los Angeles, have codes prohibiting discrimination on the basis of handicap or disability.

To qualify for protection under the ADA, an employee must have a disability. "Disability" is defined in three ways:

> (A) a physical or mental impairment that substantially limits one or more of the major life activities of such individual;
> (B) a record of such an impairment; or
> (C) being regarded as having such an impairment.[7]

The ADA forbids any discrimination in the "terms and conditions" of employment, a broad definition that includes recruitment, hiring, promotion, transfer, employee benefits, training, fringe benefits, layoff, and termination. The statute specifically prohibits a number of different forms of discrimination, including using qualification standards, employment tests, or other selection criteria that screen out or tend to screen out individuals with disabilities; and failing to make reasonable accommodations for individuals with disabilities unless the accommodation creates undue hardship on the operation of the business.

One form of discrimination defined by the ADA of particular importance to people with psychiatric disabilities is asking an applicant whether he or she has a disability. This question cannot be asked, either in writing on an employment application or in person in an interview. An employer cannot ask an applicant about his or her history of injuries, hospitalization, commitment, or worker's compensation. Nor can an employer require an applicant to take a psychological or other medical

---

[4]See Ala. Code § 21-7-1 through § 21-7-5 (2000): This section of the code is entitled "Rights of Blind and Otherwise Physically Disabled Persons." The first provision of the section declares, "It is the policy of this State to encourage and enable the blind, the visually handicapped and the otherwise physically disabled to participate fully in the social and economic life of the State and to engage in remunerative employment." (Ala. Code § 21-7-1). Although Mississippi protects employees with any disability in state employment, having deleted "physical" from prohibition of discrimination on the basis of disability in 1998 (Miss. Code § 25-9-103(e), see also Miss. Code § 25-9-149) (prohibiting discrimination based on "any handicap" in state employment), Mississippi's general prohibition on employment discrimination provides, "No person shall be refused employment by reason of his being blind, visually handicapped, deaf or otherwise physically handicapped" and is limited to employees "supported in whole or in part by public funds." (Miss. Code § 43-6-15).

[5]O.C.G.A. § 34-6A-2 (7) (2000); see Bowers v. Estrop, 420 S.E.2d 336 (Ga. Ct. App. 1992) (confirming the intent of the legislature to exclude people with psychiatric diagnoses from statutory protection against employment discrimination).

[6]Conn. Gen. Stat. §§ 46a-61 (1999).

[7]42 U.S.C. § 12102(2) (LEXIS 2000).

test before offering him or her a job. An employer can, however, administer "personality tests" under some circumstances.[8]

To sue under the ADA, a worker must have experienced an "adverse employment action." Termination is obviously adverse, as is demotion; however, courts have concluded that requiring an employee to undergo a psychiatric examination or take leave because of emotional problems does not constitute an adverse employment action under the ADA.[9] Many district courts have also recognized a cause of action for a "hostile work environment," but the employment environment must be egregiously hostile for an employee to prevail under this cause of action.[10]

The ADA also requires employers to provide "reasonable accommodations" to their employees with disabilities. Like other definitions in the ADA or its regulations, a list of examples of reasonable accommodations is given rather than an actual definition.[11] A "reasonable accommodation" under the statute may include

> (A) making existing facilities used by employees readily accessible to and usable by individuals with disabilities and
> (B) job-restructuring, part-time or modified work schedules, reassignment to a vacant position, acquisition or modification equipment or devices, appropriate adjustment or modification of examinations, training materials or policies, the provision of qualified readers or interpreters, and other similar accommodations for individuals with disabilities.[12]

Other forms of discrimination include "utilizing standards, criteria or methods of administration (A) that have the effect of discrimination on the basis of disability; or (B) that perpetuate the discrimination of others who are subject to common administrative control."[13] For example, a police officer stated a claim under the ADA when he charged that the police department's requirement that a police officer could not return to work unless he or she could pass the firearms test from a standing position discriminated on the basis of disability.[14]

EEOC Regulations Under the ADA

The EEOC is the agency charged by Congress with interpreting the employment discrimination provisions of the ADA.[15] The EEOC has issued detailed regulations interpreting Title I of the ADA.

The EEOC has also issued documents to assist employers and employees in determining the requirements and protections of the ADA. These include commentary on its regulations; a technical assistance manual (also called a compliance manual); and enforcement guidances on subjects, including the ADA and worker's compensation, the ADA and applications for disability benefits, and the meaning of reason-

---

[8]*See* chapter 7, this volume.

[9]*See* chapter 7, this volume.

[10]*Id.*

[11]*See* the EEOC's definition of "major life activities," which similarly lists a noncomprehensive sample of major life activities as a definition, 29 C.F.R. § 1630.2(i).

[12]42 U.S.C. § 1211 (West 2000).

[13]42 U.S.C. § 12112(b)(3) (West 2000).

[14]Clark v. City of Chicago, 1998 U.S. Dist. LEXIS 464 (N.D. Ill. Jan. 12, 1998).

[15]42 U.S.C. § 12116 (West, Westlaw current through 1999).

able accommodations and undue hardship under the ADA.[16] The EEOC has also twice issued an enforcement guidance on what constitutes permissible pre-employment inquiries about disability.[17] The most recent guidance replaced, and considerably revised, a prior guidance that was the subject of considerable disgruntlement and protest from employers. No enforcement guidance, however, has received as much resistance and complaint as the one aimed at clarifying the obligations of employers to employees and applicants with psychiatric disabilities. This enforcement guidance, which the EEOC had been repeatedly urged to issue, was greeted with howls of outrage that far exceeded any previous response to an EEOC enforcement guidance.

The EEOC's regulations and guidances have received uneven deference from the courts. The circuits are split on several issues on which the EEOC has taken a firm position, from the question of whether a former employee has standing to sue under Title I to the issue of whether an individual must prove he or she is disabled in order to challenge an illegal preemployment inquiry about disability.

Although in *Bragdon v. Abbott,* decided during the 1998 term, the U.S. Supreme Court gave notable deference to implementing regulations by the Department of Justice construing the ADA, in 1999 the court questioned the validity of the ADA's implementing regulations at virtually every opportunity. In four of its five ADA decisions, the court explicitly and repeatedly left open the question of the validity of the regulations, stating six times that "we assume, without deciding, that such regulations are valid, and we have no occasion to decide what level of deference, if any, they are due."[18]

Bringing a Complaint Under the ADA

One of the questions in my survey asked what specific areas should be addressed in this volume. Many survey respondents asked how to persuade a lawyer to take their cases or for a simple explanation of the legal process involved in trying to bring their own lawsuits.

It is in fact extraordinarily difficult for people who have experienced discrimination on the basis of mental disability to gain access to the legal system. Many lawyers share the prejudices of the population at large. In 1998, a judge wrote to warn lawyers against their common mistake of "confusing the issue of mental illness with intelligence."[19] Public interest lawyers who do not share these misconceptions

---

[16]EEOC regulations and enforcement guidelines are available on the EEOC's Web site (http://www.eeoc.gov/) or from a number of treatises and manuals, including the *Federal Employment Practices Manual (FEP)*, published by the Bureau of National Affairs (BNA: Washington, DC: 1999).

[17]The most recent version is "Pre-Employment Disability Related Questions and Medical Examinations," in *EEOC Enforcement Guidance* 8 FEP Manual 405: 7191 (Washington, DC: Bureau of National Affairs, Oct. 10, 1995).

[18]Albertson's v. Kirkingburg, 527 U.S. 555, 563, n. 10 (1999); Olmstead v. L.C., 527 U.S. 581, 592 (1999), Sutton v. United Airlines, Inc., 527 U.S. 471, 480 (1999).

[19]Judge Robert W. Lee, "Mental Illness and the Right to Contract," *The Florida Bar Journal* 48, 49 (December 1998).

have many more cases than they can handle and are increasingly restricted by federal law in the work that they can do.[20]

Even when people with psychiatric diagnoses do obtain counsel, they may find themselves worse off than when they began. Stories of lawyers who take cases and do nothing—often after collecting retainer fees—abound. Sometimes clients' frustration with lawyers is misdirected and arises from a misunderstanding about procedural barriers to bringing suit or about necessary delays in the legal system. But often it appears that lawyers treat psychiatrically disabled clients worse than other clients. One woman who spoke to a lawyer about being charged for services that were never performed at a psychiatric hospital, such as a physical exam including palpations of the abdomen, was told by the lawyer that

> I may have been "unaware" (I have a psychiatric diagnosis, right? Therefore, obviously not credible)—unaware of whether I was at any time in a prone position or not? I know as well as the next person whether I'm seated or lying down, and I certainly know if someone palpates my abdomen, for crying out loud.[21]

Even when the lawyers do file litigation and pursue cases, they often lose, not because the claim lacked merit but because the defendants successfully used procedural arguments and defenses that prevented a court (which may not have been particularly sympathetic in the first place) from ever reaching the substance of the claim. It is thus crucial for both attorneys and clients to master the procedural requirements of litigation. This section is written for those who wish to increase their knowledge—and perhaps their frustration—about the workings of a legal system that permits at least three-quarters of ADA claims to be dismissed without a trial, often for procedural defects that seem mysterious and unrelated to the principal issues of the case.

Before You File a Lawsuit

Informal Attempts to Resolve the Problem

Sometimes a problem can be resolved through the intervention by an advocate or ombudsperson without legal action. Many employers have an employee or office designated to handle questions about discrimination. Some employment contracts require mediation or arbitration of grievances.[22] However, you should be aware that efforts to informally resolve the dispute do not stop the statute of limitations from running (see the discussion below). Be sure to obtain a complaint form and file with either the EEOC or state employment discrimination agency within 180 days of the discriminatory act. If the matter is resolved informally, you can always withdraw or dismiss your complaint.

There are a number of difficulties in trying to go to court over discriminatory injuries. First, lawsuits necessarily take time—at the very least, 6 months before a

---

[20]Legal services lawyers, for example, can no longer bring class actions. Protection and Advocacy lawyers are not permitted to take part in civil commitment hearings, *see* 42 U.S.C. § 10821(a)(1) (West 2000).

[21]Survey No. 164.

[22]*See infra* pp. 42–43 for further discussion of this issue.

complaint can even be filed in court[23] and then often 1–2 years before the trial commences. Second, some courts have held that bringing a claim on employment discrimination based on mental disability may mean that the defendant has the right to see the plaintiff's mental health records[24] or require that the plaintiff undergo a psychological examination by an expert of the defendant's choosing.[25]

There are two basic premises supporting these decisions. First, if a plaintiff contends that he or she has a mental disability under the ADA, that contention is crucial to the controversy in the case.[26] Thus, courts are more likely to refuse requests for access to the plaintiff's mental health records if the plaintiff does not allege that he or she is actually disabled under the ADA but rather claims protection because he or she was perceived by the defendant as disabled.[27]

The second is when a plaintiff asks for damages based on mental or emotional distress. Some courts have limited defendants' right of access to records to situations when plaintiffs claim extreme emotional distress (e.g., that the defendant caused a mental illness vs. "garden variety" mental distress claims).

When courts do permit psychological examinations, they generally refuse requests that the plaintiff's attorney be allowed to be present[28] or that the examination be taped. However, the raw data from any psychological testing must be turned over to the plaintiff's attorney,[29] and motions to reduce demands for excessively lengthy examination have succeeded.

Does Your Problem State a Legal Claim?

The next step is the point at which people usually go to a lawyer, namely, to find out whether their problem states a legal claim. People can get treated very badly without having any recourse at law. To discover whether you may be entitled to a legal remedy, you can either try to find a lawyer[30] or try to find the answer for yourself through legal research. Sometimes librarians can be helpful. If there is a

---

[23] See discussion about exhaustion of administrative remedies below.

[24] Although federal courts and most state courts recognize therapist-patient privilege with regard to confidentiality of mental health records (Jaffee v. Redmond, 518 U.S. 1 (1996)), a plaintiff who puts his or her mental condition at issue in a case is considered to have waived the privilege. Thus, the legal inquiry is whether plaintiff's claims put his or her mental condition at issue in the case, Butler v. Burroughs Wellcome, 920 F. Supp. 90, 92 (E.D. N.C. 1992); Patterson v. Association for Retarded Children, 1997 WL 323575 (N.D. Ill. June 6, 1997).

[25] Rule 35 of the Federal Rules of Civil Procedure, and many analogous state rules, permit a defendant to seek a court order for a mental or physical examination of a plaintiff (or defendant, or any person in the custody or control of a party to the lawsuit) if the mental or physical condition of the person is in controversy, or if there is good cause for the examination. See Douris v. County of Bucks, 2000 U.S. Dist. LEXIS 13473 (E.D. Pa. Sept. 21, 2000).

[26] Sarko v. Penn-Del Directory, 170 F.R.D. 127, 130 (E.D. Pa. 1997).

[27] Fritsch v. City of Chula Vista, 196 F.R.D. 562 (S.D. Ca. 1999); Ruhlmann v. Ulster County Dept. of Social Services, 194 F.R.D. 445 (N.D. N.Y. 2000).

[28] Hirschheimer v. ASOMA, 1995 U.S. Dist. LEXIS 18375 (S.D. N.Y. Dec. 12, 1995).

[29] Id.

[30] It is very difficult to find a lawyer who has experience in physical or mental disability law. A few suggestions: Pennsylvania has a toll-free disabilities lawyer referral service: (888) 712-0128; the National Bar Association's Commission on Mental and Physical Disability has a list of 4,000 lawyers who practice disability law; the Community Health Law Project in New Jersey sometimes represents people with psychiatric disabilities, although its primary work involves accessible housing, (973): 275-1175.

law school in your area, some law professors are willing to talk a problem through with you, or there may be a pro bono clinic at a nearby law school.

Before you seek legal assistance, you should first gather together every single document that relates to your problem: all letters, evaluations, and warnings you have received from your employer plus any letters your treatment professional may have sent your employer. Categorize or index these documents in a file or binder. Begin the binder with a concise, written factual summary of your problem, concentrating on dates and events and identifying the decision makers. If a document in your file or binder supports an assertion in your summary, cite the document. Doing these things does not necessarily mean a lawyer will take your case, but it helps people who want to help you. Always keep one copy of all relevant documents with you; do not give away originals if you can help it.

To succeed in court, a claim must be both legally meritorious and not barred by any procedural defenses. Courts have uniformly resisted suggestions to appoint counsel for plaintiffs in civil suits on the basis of disability. Suggestions that this is required under the ADA as a reasonable accommodation have been rebuffed, although in rejecting these claims federal courts have not seen fit to mention that they are not subject to the ADA. If you are going to try to do legal research yourself, there are a number of basic points that you need to research.

Statutes of Limitation

Under the ADA and the Rehabilitation Act

One of the first questions most lawyers focus on is when a particular discriminatory injury occurred. Sometimes the answer leads to the conclusion that there is no legal remedy whatsoever, no matter how egregious the action, because the statute of limitations has run out. This is very frustrating to people with psychiatric disabilities, who often have to spend a considerable amount of time trying to recover emotionally from the devastation caused by the injury, only to be told when they are ready to proceed that it is too late.

There are special complications related to the statute of limitations in disability discrimination suits. A substantial number of cases brought under the Rehabilitation Act and the ADA are dismissed as barred by statutes of limitations.[31] This is in part because neither the Rehabilitation Act nor the ADA contains its own statutes of limitations. Under these circumstances, the U.S. Supreme Court has ruled that courts must find the most appropriate analogue to the federal law in the law of the state in which the court is sitting and then apply that law's statute of limitations.[32] This leads to different states having different statutes of limitations for the ADA and Rehabil-

---

[31]Graehling v. Village of Lombard, 58 F.3d 295 (7th Cir. 1995); Wolsky v. Medical College of Hampton Roads, 1 F.3d 222 (4th Cir. 1993), *cert. denied*, 510 U.S. 1073 (1994) (claim of medical student with panic disorder under Rehabilitation Act barred by one-year statue of limitations); Baker v. University of Kansas Medical School, 991 F.2d 628 (10th Cir. 1993) (Rehabilitation Act claim barred by 2-year statute of limitations); Repp v. Oregon Health Sciences University, 972 F. Supp. 546 (D. Ore. 1997); Place v. Abbott Labs, 938 F. Supp. 1379 (1996); Toney v. U.S. Health Care, 840 F. Supp. 357 (E.D. Pa.), *aff'd*, 37 F.3d 1489 (3d Cir. 1994).

[32]Wilson v. Garcia, 461 U.S. 261, 266–67 (1985).

itation Act. Statutes of limitations for claims under these acts range from 180 days[33] to 1 year[34] to 2 years[35] to 6 years.[36] Often courts in the same state, and even the same district, determine different statutes of limitations for Rehabilitation Act[37] and ADA claims, although in some states, like Arizona, the statute of limitations is the same.[38]

The statute of limitations for ADA and Section 504 claims are not in any statute book; it is in case law. A law review article discussing disability discrimination claims in the jurisdiction (state) in which you live may also have this information.

Administrative Exhaustion Requirements and Statutes of Limitations

In addition to general statutes of limitations requirements, certain kinds of discrimination complaints require that before a person goes to court, he or she must first lodge a complaint with a specified administrative agency. If an employee of a private business[39] with 15 or more employees believes that he or she has been subject to discrimination on the basis of disability, he or she has 180 days to make a formal complaint to the Equal Employment Opportunity Commission (EEOC), which has field offices in every state.[40] If the state in which the individual lives has an equivalent organization (called a "FEPA," or "Fair Employment Practices Agency") with a "work-sharing" agreement with the EEOC, the individual has 300 days to file the complaint, either with the state agency or the EEOC.[41]

---

[33]McCullough v. Branch Banking & Trust Co., 35 F.3d 127 (4th Cir. 1994).

[34]Wolsky v. Medical College of Hampton Roads, 1 F.3d 222 (4th Cir. 1993); Solomon v. New York City Board of Education (E.D. N.Y. 1996).

[35]Madden-Tyler v. Maricopa County, 943 P.2d 822 (Ariz. App. 1997); Saylor v. Ridge, 989 F. Supp. 680 (E.D. Pa. 1998), Everett v. Cobb County School District, 138 F.3d 1407 (11th Cir. 1998) (2-year limitation for Section 504 in Georgia); Soignier v. American Board of Plastic Surgery, 92 F.3d 547 (7th Cir. 1996) (2-year limitation in Illinois).

[36]Doe v. County of Milwaukee, 871 F. Supp. 1072 at 1076–78 (E.D. Wisc. 1995).

[37]Cf. Noel v. Cornell University Medical College, 853 F. Supp. 93 (S.D. N.Y. 1994) (statute of limitations of three years for Rehabilitation Act employment discrimination action involving plaintiff with physical disability) with Solomon v. New York City Board of Education, 1996 U.S. Dist. LEXIS 20251 (E.D. N.Y. Mar. 25, 1996) (statute of limitations of one year for Rehabilitation Act employment discrimination claims involving plaintiff with psychiatric disability).

[38]Madden-Tyler v. Maricopa County, 943 P.2d 822 (Ariz. App. 1997).

[39]Employees of the federal government are covered under Section 501 of the Rehabilitation Act and are subject to different requirements, see 29 C.F.R. 1613. Most courts have held that employees of state and local governments can sue under Title II of the ADA without having to meet the procedural requirements imposed by Title I of the ADA, see Bledsoe v. Palm Beach County Soil and Water Conservation District, 133 F.3d 816 (11th Cir. 1998); Castellano v. City of New York, 142 F.3d 58 (2d Cir. 1998); Holmes v. Texas A & M, 145 F.3d 681 (5th Cir. 1998); Doe v. Univ. of Md. Medical Systems Corp., 50 F.3d 1261 (4th Cir. 1995); see also Zimmerman v. Oregon Department of Justice, 183 F.3d 1161 (9th Cir. 1999) (no right to bring employment discrimination case under Title II). The U.S. Supreme Court's decision in University of Alabama v. Garrett, which precludes state employees from suing for damages under the ADA, probably moots this issue as to state but not local governments.

[40]The ADA incorporates the procedural requirements of Title VII, see 42 U.S.C. § 12117(a), which requires individuals to follow the filing requirements laid out in 42 U.S.C. § 2000e-5. The locations of EEOC field offices are found in Appendix C (this volume).

[41]Technically, the law envisions that an individual would file the complaint with the state agency, which would then have 60 days of exclusive jurisdiction over the complaint. However, if an individual files with the EEOC within 300 days, the "worksharing" agreements usually involve the EEOC trans-

The content of this complaint or "charge" is important. Generally, an individual cannot later sue in federal court for discrimination that was not at least alluded to in the charge, and the individual's answer to the question about the latest date that discrimination occurred will often be relevant for purposes of determining the statute of limitations.

The EEOC has 180 days to investigate the complaint and find either "reasonable cause" to believe that discrimination has occurred or "no reasonable cause" to believe that discrimination has occurred. The EEOC may attempt to bring about a voluntary settlement of the dispute or try to mediate between the parties. If this is unsuccessful, the EEOC has the option of taking the case to court itself.

If the EEOC decides not to take the case, it issues a "right to sue" letter, which permits an individual to file in federal court within 90 days of receiving the letter. The EEOC issues a right to sue letter whether it finds reasonable cause to believe that discrimination has occurred, finds no reasonable cause, or makes no finding. If the EEOC does not respond within 180 days, an individual can also request a right to sue letter. Because the EEOC staff receives far more complaints than it can adequately investigate, let alone litigate, most cases proceed to court through the right to sue letter. It is crucial to note that unless the employer is a state or local government entity, a person cannot go to court without first filing a complaint, either with the EEOC or with a FEPA, and receiving a right to sue letter. Once the right to sue letter is received, the complaint must be filed within 90 days. The 90-day limit is not jurisdictional—that is, it does not relate to whether the court has the legal power to hear the case—thus, failure to meet the requirement can be excused for a variety of reasons.[42]

There are three ways in which a claim not made within the applicable period of time can be saved: The plaintiff may argue that the statute of limitations was tolled because of mental disability; the doctrine of equitable estoppel can be used if defendants persuaded a plaintiff not to make a complaint with the promise that they would not invoke the statute of limitations; or the plaintiff may claim that the injury is ongoing, constituting a "continuing violation."

Psychiatric Disability as Tolling Statutes of Limitations

Almost all states permit tolling of statutes of limitations because of a mental condition, variously described as being of "unsound mind,"[43] "insane," or "mentally disabled." The exact state of mind necessary to toll the running of statutes of limitations has always been the subject of litigation. Generally, the findings of courts in this area parallel the findings of criminal courts with regard to competence to enter pleas or stand trial: People who are psychotic, whose psychiatric problems clearly center on cognition, are generally considered incompetent to stand trial and to have conditions that justify tolling the statute of limitations.

---

mitting a copy of the complaint to the state agency, thus satisfying the requirement that the state agency receive a copy of the charge within 300 days. For a more detailed discussion of these requirements, *see* Melincoff v. East Norriton Physician Services, 1998 U.S. Dist. LEXIS 5416 (E.D. Pa. Apr. 20, 1998).

[42]Zipes v. TWA, 455 U.S. 385, 398 (1982); Truitt v. County of Wayne, 148 F.3d 644, 646 (6th Cir. 1998) (waiver, estoppel, and equitable tolling are excuses for failure to meet 90-day rule).

[43]Ariz. Rev. Stat. § 12-502 (Lexis Law Publishing 2001).

However, courts' holdings in the area of the kinds of mental conditions sufficient to toll the statute of limitations are equally if not more vulnerable to the critique directed at criminal court findings: The impact of disorders of mood and affect are disregarded by courts in criminal cases. Some clinicians have argued that people who are severely depressed might make decisions—such as to plead guilty or to fire their lawyers—that are distorted by their mood disorder. Whether depression affects people's ability to make decisions is much more open to debate than whether depression affects people's ability to act. Courts often appear to believe that filing a legal action is simply the product of a decision to bring litigation. The difficulty people with psychiatric disorders have—not dissimilar to people without psychiatric disabilities—in knowing how to go about contacting a lawyer and trying to persuade him or her to take the case, often involving repeated contacts, rejections, and discouragement, could be overwhelming to someone who is struggling with depression. When courts decide whether the statute of limitation should be tolled, they look solely to the individual's diagnosis and its effect on his or her daily ability to function as opposed to its effects on his or her ability to decide to bring suit and to pursue and retain legal counsel.

One category of plaintiff that has been more successful in tolling statutes of limitations are people whose mental disability was caused by the defendant they are seeking to sue. This may be one reason that some—but far from all—plaintiffs seeking to toll the statute of limitations because of disability produced by childhood sexual abuse have been successful.[44] If an individual had treatment in a hospital setting, it may be useful to excerpt the hospital's own charts and descriptions of the person while hospitalized to prove the mental state necessary to toll the statute of limitations.[45]

Equitable Estoppel

A defendant who persuades a potential plaintiff to try to resolve their differences informally can later invoke the statute of limitations to preclude a legal claim, as long as the defendant did not explicitly or specifically promise to waive a statute of limitations defense. A defendant who deliberately hides a plaintiff's cause of action from him or her cannot later claim protection from the statute of limitations—but this rarely is an issue in employment discrimination litigation. Any promises made by a potential defendant should be secured in a signed, dated document.

Continuing Violation

"Continuing violation" or "ongoing injury" is another difficult argument to make in employment discrimination cases. If a plaintiff is complaining about a discriminatory policy that continues to be in existence and continues to deprive the plaintiff of rights under the ADA, there may be a continuing violation.

[44] Jones v. Jones, 576 A.2d 316 (N.J. App. 1990); Nicolette v. Carey, 751 F. Supp. 695 (W.D. Mich. 1990); Petersen v. Bruen, 792 P.2d 18 (Nev. 1990).
[45] Shanley v. Brown, 1997 U.S. Dist. LEXIS 20024 (N.D. Ill. Dec. 4, 1997).

Remedies

Remedies provided by courts typically come in three forms: money (called "damages"), ordering someone to do something or stop doing something ("injunctive relief"), and simply finding that one's rights have been violated ("declaratory relief"). It is very hard to get declaratory relief if one is not also entitled to injunctive relief, damages, or both.

The question of whether discrimination law permits claims for damages is somewhat complex. One cannot seek money damages against the federal government for a violation of Section 504 of the Rehabilitation Act,[46] nor are damages available against a state employer for a violation of Title I of the ADA.[47] However, if one has been discriminated against by a state employer, the federal government can seek money damages on that person's behalf if the EEOC decides to pursue a claim for discrimination against the state employer. One may be entitled to seek damages against a state employer under state law, depending on whether the state has waived its sovereign immunity. Often when states waive immunity, they put a cap on the amount of damages a plaintiff can be awarded. Damages against private employers under Title I of the ADA are also capped since Congress enacted the Civil Rights Act of 1991.

Title I of the ADA, which prohibits discrimination in employment on the basis of disability, is one of the statutes covered by the Civil Rights Act of 1991. This statute makes explicit that compensatory damages are available under Title I of the ADA but limits them depending on the size of the employer's operation. It also eliminates the possibility of punitive damages under the ADA.

Title II of the ADA covers employment by "public entities"—state and local governments and their branches. It is highly likely that claims against states as employers under Title II of the ADA for damages are unconstitutional.[48] As for local governments, Title II was explicitly intended by Congress to have all the remedies available under Section 504 of the Rehabilitation Act. Therefore, the question of what damages are available under Title II is the same question as what damages are available under Section 504 of the Rehabilitation Act. It is clear that compensatory damages are permitted under Title II.[49] Since the U.S. Supreme Court decided that punitive damages were available under Title IX, dozens of district courts have held that punitive damages are similarly available under Section 504,[50] and a number of circuit courts have concurred that Section 504 permits the "full spectrum" or "full range" of damages.[51]

---

[46]Lane v. Pena, 518 U.S. 187 (1996).

[47]University of Alabama v. Garrett, 531 U.S. 356, 121 S.Ct. 955, 148 L.Ed.2d 866 (Feb. 21, 2001), see discussion *infra* at pp. 34–35.

[48]*See* discussion of University of Alabama v. Garrett, 531 U.S. 356 (2001), *infra* at pp. 34–35.

[49]Some courts have held or suggested that they are only permissible in cases of intentional discrimination, Ferguson v. City of Phoenix, 157 F.3d 668, 674 (9th Cir. 1998); Tyler v. City of Manhattan, 118 F.3d 1400 (10th Cir. 1997), but, as the dissent points out, this is not based on any conceivable reading of either the ADA or the Rehabilitation Act, neither of which makes any such distinctions.

[50]*See* cases collected at Burns-Vidlak v. Chandler, 980 F. Supp. 1144 (D. Haw. 1997).

[51]Pandazides v. Va. Board of Education, 13 F.3d 823 (4th Cir. 1994); Rodgers v. Magnet Cove Public Schools, 34 F.3d 642 (8th Cir. 1994); Waldrop v. Southern Co. Services, 24 F.3d 152 (11th Cir. 1994); W.B. v. Matula, 67 F.3d 484 (3d Cir. 1995).

Recent and Upcoming Supreme Court Decisions and Their Impact on the ADA

Upcoming Cases

In April 2001, the Supreme Court agreed to hear two cases presenting issues under Title I of the Americans With Disabilities Act, *Williams v. Toyota Manufacturing Co.,*[52] and *Barnett v. United Airways.*[53]

The *Williams* case involved a worker with carpal tunnel syndrome who had asked her employer for a job in quality control as a reasonable accommodation for her inability to perform her previous work. Although the Sixth Circuit had concentrated on whether the ability to perform manual tasks was a major life activity, the Supreme Court granted *certiorari* on a question that was hardly argued or briefed in the Sixth Circuit: "Whether the Sixth Circuit correctly held—in conflict with the established rule in other circuits—that an impairment precluding an individual from performing only a limited number of tasks associated with a specific job qualifies as a disability under the ADA."[54]

The *Barnett* case raises the question of whether an employer must provide a reasonable accommodation if to do so would conflict with a seniority system when the seniority system is not the result of a collective bargaining agreement. All courts to date that have considered the matter have concluded that an accommodation is not reasonable if it requires an employer to violate a collective bargaining agreement. The *Barnett* case involves a seniority system that is not required by an agreement with employee's union.

University of Alabama v. Garrett

On February 26, 2001, the U.S. Supreme Court decided, by a vote of 5 to 4, that Congress had overstepped constitutional limits by authorizing suits for money damages by private individuals against state employers for discrimination under the ADA. In *Board of Trustees of the University of Alabama v. Garrett,*[55] the court precluded actions for damages against the University of Alabama by Patricia Garrett, a nurse who charged she had been discriminated against because of her breast cancer, and by Milton Ash, who claimed that he was denied reasonable accommodations for his asthma.

The precise holding of the U.S. Supreme Court is that states cannot be sued for damages by private individuals under Title I of the ADA in federal court. The holding strongly implies that private individuals cannot sue states for damages because of employment discrimination under Title II of the ADA. U.S. Supreme Court case law also suggests that states cannot be sued in state court for damages arising out of employment discrimination under either Title I or Title II of the ADA.[56]

---

[52] 224 F.3d 840 (6th Cir. 2000).

[53] 228 F.3d 1105 (9th Cir. 2000).

[54] 20 Disability Compliance Bulletin Issue 4, p. 4 (May 3, 2001).

[55] 531 U.S. 356, 121 S.Ct. 955, 148 L.Ed.2d 866 (Feb. 21, 2001).

[56] Alden v. Maine, 527 U.S. 706 (1999) (recognizing that Congress cannot abrogate States' sovereign immunity from suit by individuals).

However, individuals can still sue local governments, such as county and city governments, for employment discrimination for money damages under Title I or Title II of the ADA. Individuals can also still sue state government employers for injunctive relief, such as the reinstatement or requirement of provided accommodations, under Title I of the ADA.[57] Using other federal statutory remedies, individuals can still sue state employers for damages for employment discrimination under Section 504 of the Rehabilitation Act if the employing agencies receive federal funds. The Federal Government, through the EEOC, may sue states for damages on behalf of individuals who have been discriminated against in employment.[58]

Individuals may also sue state governments for employment discrimination under state antidiscrimination laws if the state has waived sovereign immunity. Some states permit such actions to be brought[59]; others do not.[60] Of course, individuals can still sue private employers for damages for discrimination under Title I of the ADA.

There is some concern that the U.S. Supreme Court may turn its attention to the constitutionality of Section 504, in which congressional prohibition of discrimination by the states is justified as a condition for receiving federal funds. This so-called "spending clause" justification was last construed by the U.S. Supreme Court in 1987, when the court upheld Congress's right to require states to raise the drinking age to 21 years old in exchange for federal highway funds.

The Sutton Trilogy

On June 22, 1999, the U.S. Supreme Court issued its first interpretation of Title I of the ADA in a trilogy of cases raising a variety of issues under the ADA. In *Sutton v. United Airlines,*[61] *Murphy v. United Parcel Service,*[62] and *Albertson's v. Kirkingburg,*[63] the Supreme Court interpreted two major provisions of the ADA.

The principal decision in the trilogy is *Sutton v. United Airlines,* which involved two pilots rejected by United Airlines because they did not have uncorrected vision of 20/100 or better. The issue in *Sutton* was not whether United's policy was valid or discriminatory or whether safety concerns justified its exclusion of people with certain visual impairments. Rather, the court considered whether the pilots, whose corrected vision was 20/20 or better, should be able to invoke the protection of the ADA at all.

The EEOC, which issued the regulations for Title I, had interpreted the term *disability* to mean an individual's condition without regard to mitigating devices or medications. In doing this, the EEOC had ample support in the ADA's legislative history. Various Committee reports, in fact, had directed the EEOC to adopt this

---

[57]Board of Trustees of the University of Alabama v. Garrett, 531 U.S. 356, 121 S.Ct. 955, 968 n. 9 (Feb. 21, 2001).

[58]*Id.*

[59]*See, e.g.,* Marsh v. Department of Civil Service, 370 N.W.2d 613 (Mich. App. 1985), *appeal denied,* (interpreting Michigan's Persons with Disabilities Civil Rights Act, Ch. 37.1101 *et seq,* as subjecting state entities to suit).

[60]Arkansas, for example, has a constitutional amendment prohibiting its citizens from suing the state for damages, Ark. Constitution, Article 5, Section 20 (1999).

[61]527 U.S. 471 (1999).

[62]527 U.S. 516 (1999).

[63]527 U.S. 555 (1999).

interpretation. Under the EEOC's interpretation, the pilots, whose uncorrected vision was so poor that they could not conduct their daily affairs without corrective lenses, would be considered disabled. As previously noted, this interpretation would not ensure their victory against United Airlines. It simply gave them the right to litigate the validity of the airline's prohibition on pilots with uncorrected vision of 20/100 or worse.

The U.S. Supreme Court, however, foreclosed this possibility. It rejected the EEOC's position and its regulation as contradicting the facial language of the ADA. The court, in an opinion by Justice O'Connor, gave several reasons for this conclusion. First, the court said that determining the impact a condition in its unmitigated state would have on a person required "speculation." As Justice Breyer pointed out in dissent, however, the plaintiffs in *Sutton* had only to remove their glasses to demonstrate the impact of their visual impairment on their lives.

Second, the court said this rule would preclude courts from taking into consideration the negative impact that some devices or medications had on people's lives in determining whether they were disabled. In illustrating the possibility that medications could render someone disabled, the court's first example was psychotropic medications.[64] The court cited an article that pointed out that "antipsychotic drugs can cause a variety of adverse effects, including neuroleptic malignant syndrome and painful seizures."[65]

Third, the court placed great emphasis on the congressional finding that 43 million Americans were disabled. This number was too small to include people with visual impairments such as the plaintiffs. Rather, the court looked to a definition of disability that required ongoing functional impairment. It concluded that the congressional figure was derived from a survey that found that 37.3 million noninstitutionalized people older than age 15 had physical disabilities, and it inferred that the missing 5.7 million people could be explained by adding in the 943,000 noninstitutionalized people with activity limitation due to mental illness, the 947,000 noninstitutionalized people with activity limitations due to mental retardation, the 1,900,000 noninstitutionalized people younger than age 18 with an activity limitation, and the 1,553,000 people in nursing and related care facilities.

This kind of disability counting is extremely troubling. Although it suggests—correctly—that people who are institutionalized or live in nursing homes are automatically covered by the ADA because they are substantially limited in almost every major life activity, the conclusion that in the mid- to late 1980s only 943,000 noninstitutionalized people with psychiatric disabilities would have met the ADA's definition of disability cannot be sustained. By even the most stringent and narrow definition of severe mental illness, the number of noninstitutionalized people with psychiatric disabilities covered by the ADA would have been in the millions.[66]

The court's conclusion that disabilities must be considered in their mitigated state is devastating to the millions of Americans who control their conditions of bipolar disorder or depression with medication but are nevertheless afraid that if their employers discovered this fact they would face discrimination in the workplace.[67]

---

[64] 527 U.S. at 484 (1999).

[65] *Id.* (citing Johnson, "Antipsychotics: Pros and Cons of Antipsychotics," *RN* (Aug. 1997)).

[66] *See* chapter 3, this volume.

[67] *See, e.g.,* Kay Redfield Jamison, *An Unquiet Mind: A Memoir of Moods and Madness* (New York: Knopf, 1995).

The U.S. Supreme Court's decisions effectively insulate such discrimination entirely. If bipolar disorder under control with medication is not a disability, then employers can discriminate freely against people whose bipolar disorder is under control without being liable for discrimination on the basis of disability.[68] An employer could, under current interpretations of the ADA, fire someone because he or she has a diagnosis of bipolar disorder or takes lithium, and the employee would have no recourse under the ADA if the employee was not substantially limited in any major life activity.

Since *Sutton,* courts in a number of cases involving plaintiffs with psychiatric disabilities have raised the fact that the plaintiff is taking medication to mitigate the effect of the disability.[69] Of course, this raises the issue of whether a plaintiff who did not take medication would qualify as disabled; case law suggests that in many of those cases, plaintiffs fail to meet the "otherwise qualified" prong of the ADA.[70]

In finding that disabilities have to be considered in their unmitigated state, the U.S. Supreme Court explicitly refused to defer to the EEOC's contrary construction because the majority concluded that Congress had not empowered the EEOC to write regulations defining disability. The court reached this conclusion because the statutory language defining disability appears before Title I, and the EEOC is only authorized to write regulations interpreting Title I of the ADA.

In reaching this conclusion, the U.S. Supreme Court ignored Congress's endorsement of "the regulations issued by Federal agencies pursuant to" Section 504 of the Rehabilitation Act.[71] These regulations contained language specifically rejected by the court in the *Sutton* trilogy. In addition, each agency that has the authority to interpret the ADA, and every agency that has the authority to interpret Section 504 of the Rehabilitation Act, has defined disability (or handicap) in identical terms. This was not the only instance in *Sutton* where the court ignored both legislative history and case precedent. The U.S. Supreme Court majority also suggested in *dicta* that "work" might not qualify as a major life activity, in stark contrast to congressional intent as expressed in the ADA's legislative history and decades of judicial interpretation of Section 504 of the Rehabilitation Act and the ADA.

Although the ADA also prohibits discrimination on the basis of perceived disability, the U.S. Supreme Court endorsed a narrow reading of this provision. After rejecting the EEOC's regulations on ameliorative devices because the EEOC was not empowered to regulate the definition of disability, the court relied on other EEOC regulations defining disability to hold that to regard an employee as disabled, the employer must regard an employee as substantially limited in a major life activity. In the context of work, the employer must regard the employee as unable to perform

---

[68] *See* chapters 4 and 5, this volume, and Kevin S. Wiley, Jr., "Scaling Back the ADA: How the Sutton v. United Airlines Decision Affects Employees with Bipolar Disorder," 2 *Scholar* 355 (2000).

[69] Spade v. City of Walnut Ridge, 186 F.3d 897, 899 (8th Cir. 1999); Robb v. Horizon Credit Union, 66 F. Supp. 2d 913, 918 (C.D. Ill. 1999); Alderdice v. American Health, 118 F. Supp. 2d 856, 864 (S.D. Ohio 2000); Lusk v. Christ Hospital and Medical Center, 2000 U.S. Dist. LEXIS 2691 at *14 (N.D. Ill. Feb. 29, 2000); *but see* Taylor v. Phoenixville School District 184 F.3d 296 (3d Cir. 1999) and *Schumacher v. Souderton Area School District*, 2000 U.S. Dist. LEXIS 563 at *26 (E.D. Pa. Jan. 21, 2000) (requiring a more sensitive, fact-specific approach to cases involving plaintiffs taking psychotropic medications).

[70] This issue is discussed further in chapter 8.

[71] 42 U.S.C. § 12101(a) (Westlaw 2000).

a class of jobs or broad range of jobs.[72] An employer who only regards the employee as unable to perform his or her specific job because of disability would not be held to be discriminating on the basis of disability, even if the employer's perception was the result of discriminatory stereotypes.

These decisions are a misinterpretation of congressional directive. Although it is clear that, based on its legislative history, Congress expected disabilities to be considered in their unmitigated state, the court rejected this history because it concluded that the language of the ADA clearly dictated differently on its face. Yet the language of the ADA on its face also instructs the court that "nothing in this chapter shall be construed to apply a lesser standard than the standards applied under Title V of the Rehabilitation Act of 1973 [Section 504] or the regulations issued by federal agencies pursuant to such title."[73] Other language in the ADA instructed the EEOC to issue regulations to prevent "imposition of inconsistent or conflicting standards for the same requirements under this subchapter and the Rehabilitation Act."[74] The consistent reading of Section 504, and the regulations under Section 504, required consideration of handicap without regard to mitigating devices.

The Supreme Court also departed from its own Section 504 precedent in interpreting the "regarded as disabled" provision. In *School Board of Nassau County v. Arline,* the court concluded that if an employee was precluded from a job because of the employer's perception that he or she was handicapped, then the employee was regarded as handicapped for the purposes of the statute.[75]

Because of the ADA's requirement that its provisions must not be interpreted to provide less protection than the Rehabilitation Act, it would seem that *Arline's,* interpretation of when an individual is regarded as disabled would be sustained under the ADA. However, ironically enough, subsequent congressional legislation revised Section 504 to conform it to Title I standards,[76] therefore potentially weakening Section 504 rather than strengthening and harmonizing protection against disability discrimination under federal statutes.

Other Federal Laws Regulating Employment

The Family and Medical Leave Act

The Family and Medical Leave Act (FMLA) was a priority in President Clinton's campaign for the presidency, and it was the first piece of legislation he signed after he took office. The law applies to all employers who employ more than 12 workers (in contrast to the ADA, which applies to employers who employ more than 15 workers). Workers are covered under the FMLA after being employed for 1 year (in contrast to the ADA, which covers applicants for work and any employee). Title I of the ADA is enforced by the EEOC, whereas the FMLA is enforced by the Department of Labor.

---

[72] 29 C.F.R. 1630(j) (Westlaw 2000).

[73] 42 U.S.C. § 12201 (West 2000). The court cited this provision of the ADA to support its holding in *Bragdon v. Abbott,* 526 U.S. 1131 (1999).

[74] 42 U.S.C. § 12117 (West 2000).

[75] School Board of Nassau County v. Arline, 480 U.S. 273 (1987).

[76] *See* 29 U.S.C. § 794(d) (West 2000).

The FMLA requires employers to permit employees to take up to 12 weeks of unpaid leave per calendar year without losing their job under four conditions: the birth or adoption of a child; the placement of a child with the employee for foster care; the care of a spouse, parent, or child with a serious health condition; or a serious health condition that makes the employee unable to perform the functions of the position.[77] An employee is entitled to return to his or her position or an equivalent position with the same terms and benefits the employee had at the beginning of leave.[78] Like the ADA, the FMLA permits an employer to seek certification of a "serious health condition" from the employee's health care provider,[79] although unlike the ADA (at least statutorily), the FMLA gives an employer who has "a reason to doubt the validity" of an employee's serious health condition a right to seek a second opinion about the employee's health condition.[80]

Like the ADA, the FMLA gives an employer affirmative defenses that permit it to deny an employee restoration to his or her job. Under the FMLA, if an employee is a highly paid,[81] "key" employee, without whom the employer would suffer "substantial and grievous economic injury," the employer must notify the employee that he or she will not be restored to the job and give the employee a chance to return. If the employee does not return after receiving the notice, the employer may fill the job and deny the employee restoration to his or her prior position. The FMLA's "substantial and grievous economic injury" test is more stringent than the ADA's "undue hardship" test, which permits an employer to discriminate on the basis of disability if equal treatment or reasonable accommodation of disabled employees would create "undue hardship."[82]

A "serious health condition" under the FMLA includes "mental conditions that involve either inpatient care or continuing treatment by a health care provider."[83] The regulations provide that any condition that results in "inability to work more than three consecutive calendar days and involves treatment two or more times by a health care provider" constitutes a serious health condition.[84] As is apparent, the FMLA definition of "serious health condition" is considerably broader than the ADA's definition of disability.

Employees frequently bring litigation under both the ADA and the FMLA. In cases involving both acts, employees sometimes prevail on the FMLA count and lose on the ADA count.[85] In cases involving psychiatric disabilities, most notably, workers may be entitled to leave and reinstatement under the FMLA when their psychiatric conditions are brought about by stressful interactions with supervisors and the stresses of the general work environment, but not under the ADA.[86] In

---

[77] 29 U.S.C. § 2612(a)(1) (2000).

[78] 29 U.S.C. § 2614(a)(1) (2000).

[79] 29 U.S.C. § 2613(a) (2000).

[80] 29 U.S.C. § 2613(c)(1) (2000).

[81] The employee must be among the highest paid 10% of the employees within 75 miles of the facility at which the employee is employed, 29 U.S.C. § 2614(b).

[82] 29 C.F.R. § 825.218(d) (regulations of the Department of Labor).

[83] 29 U.S.C. § 2611(11) (West 2000).

[84] 29 C.F.R. § 825.114(a)(2)(i)(A).

[85] Kephart v. Cherokee County, 2000 U.S. App. LEXIS 18924 (4th Cir. Aug. 4, 2000) (employee loses appeal on ADA count because he failed to object to magistrate's report).

[86] Cf. Stekloff v. St. John's Mercy Health Systems, 218 F.3d 858 (8th Cir. 2000) ("The doctor emphasized that Ms. Stekloff needed a break from her work at St. John's because the environment in

addition, the fact that employees obtain work elsewhere is not held against them under the FMLA as it is under the ADA.[87] Unlike the ADA, courts have determined that individuals can be sued under the FMLA.[88]

Like the ADA, the FMLA has been subject to challenge in its application to state entities. As of this writing, the U.S. Court of Appeals for the 8th, 5th, 6th, and 3rd Circuits have held that state employers may not be sued under the FMLA.[89] The Supreme Court is likely to take up the issue soon.

Employment Retirement Income Security Act

The Employment Retirement Income Security Act (ERISA) is legislation designed to provide federal protection and regulation of employees' benefits. It was prompted by massive union and employer misappropriation of employee benefit funds in the 1970s, and it provides a uniform remedy for employees who believe they have been unjustly denied retirement or health insurance benefits.

The significance of ERISA to people with psychiatric disabilities arises when they wish to dispute denials of care by their employer-provided health insurance plan. Denial of care may involve failure to admit people to inpatient care,[90] failure to retain a person on an inpatient unit, failure to provide short-term disability benefits,[91] or, most often, failure to provide disability benefits after 2 years have elapsed. Most disability benefits plans distinguish between physical conditions and "mental, nervous or emotional conditions" and provide far less generous benefits for the latter.

In providing a uniform federal remedy, however, ERISA preempts all state remedies. This means that individuals cannot sue their employee health plans under tort law, contract law, or any other state law claims.[92] Congress is currently considering legislation that would permit individuals to sue HMOs.

---

her unit (and presumably in close proximity to the supervisor with whom she had her disagreement) was 'reinjuring a traumatized area of her life'.") *with* Weigel v. Target Stores, 122 F.3d 461, 469 (7th Cir. 1997) (denying request for additional leave).

[87] *Cf. Stekloff* ("we think that the key issue in this case is whether Ms. Stekloff's inability to work at St. John's is enough to show that she was unable to work for FMLA purposes and therefore was incapacitated within the meaning of the FMLA") *with* Weiler v. Household Finance Corporation, 101 F.3d 519, 524 (7th Cir. 1996) ("Weiler's claim amounts to a charge that she is only unable to work if Skonupka is her boss . . . whatever Weiler's problem was with Skonupka, it is not recognized as a disability under the ADA. The major life activity of working is not 'substantially limited' if a plaintiff merely cannot work with a certain supervisor.") *and with* Schniken v. Fortis Insurance Co., 200 F.3d 1055 (7th Cir. 2000) ("Standing alone, a personality conflict between an employee and a supervisor— even one that triggers an employee's depression—is not enough to establish that the employee is disabled so long as the employee could still perform the job under a different supervisor.")

[88] Meara v. Bennett, 27 F. Supp. 2d 288 (D. Mass. 1998).

[89] Townsel v. State, 2000 U.S. App. LEXIS 30716 (8th Cir. Dec. 5, 2000); Thomson v. Ohio State Univ. Hospital, 2000 U.S. App. LEXIS 29206 (6th Cir. Nov. 8, 2000); Chittister v. Dept. of Community and Economic Development, 226 F.3d 223 (3d Cir. 2000); Kazmier v. Widman, 219 F.3d 559 (5th Cir. 2000).

[90] Lazorko v. Pennsylvania Hospital, 237 F.3d 242 (3d Cir. 2000).

[91] Parelli v. Bell Atlantic—Pennsylvania, 2000 U.S. Dist. LEXIS 8074 (E.D. Pa. June 13, 2000).

[92] Pilot Life Insurance Co. v. Dedeaux, 481 U.S. 41, 43 (1987).

Fair Labor Standards Act

The Fair Labor Standards Act (FLSA) protects employees who receive hourly wages from being required to work more than a set number of hours per week without being paid overtime. It also sets the minimum wage that employers can pay employees. The FLSA may or may not apply to employees of sheltered workshops[93] or transitional employment programs[94] or to "workfare" for recent welfare recipients.[95] It does not apply to training programs when the company or organization providing the training receives no immediate benefit from the training and when completing the training does not ensure employment with the company or organization.[96] It does apply under some circumstances to employment in institutions by patients.[97]

Unions, Collective Bargaining, and the ADA

The ADA establishes certain federal statutory rights for employees. Some of these employees are also members of unions and bound by collective bargaining contracts. Tensions between the ADA and collective bargaining agreements come in two basic forms. First, most collective bargaining contracts are structured so that aggrieved employees must adhere to a prescribed set of steps in protesting employer action against them, including, in some cases, submission to binding arbitration. What is the impact of these clauses on an individual's rights under the ADA? Second, the ADA grants employees certain rights, such as the right to reasonable accommodations. What happens when a requested accommodation collides with provisions of the collective bargaining agreement, usually provisions involving rights accorded on the basis of seniority?

Congress considered these questions in some detail when it passed the ADA, and the EEOC has addressed both issues in its regulations. In addition, the Supreme Court has provided some guidance, at least with regard to the first question.

---

[93] Sheltered workshops employ approximately 250,000 individuals; Theo Liebmann and Ann Peters, "Employment Programs for Individuals with Disabilities: Reducing Poverty in America?" *Geo. J. on Fighting Poverty* 1 (1999): 132, 133.

[94] *Cf.* Tony and Susan Alamo Foundation v. Secretary of Labor, 471 U.S. 290, 200–01 (1985) (holding that recovering drug addicts who were "paid" with food, shelter, and clothing constituted employees under the Fair Labor Standards Act) *and* Archie v. Grand Central Partnership, 86 F. Supp.2d 262 (S.D. N.Y. 2000) (homeless participants of transitional employment program covered under the FLSA); Cincinnati Association for the Blind v. N.L.R.B., 672 F.2d 567 (6th Cir. 1982) *with* Arkansas Lighthouse for the Blind v. N.L.R.B., 851 F.2d 180 (8th Cir. 1980) (finding sheltered workshop employee outside of N.L.R.B. jurisdiction) *and* Goodwill Industries of Southern California, 231 N.L.R.B. 536 (Aug. 23, 1977) (finding that although Goodwill workers are "employees in the generic sense of the term," they cannot unionize).

[95] Johns v. Stewart, 57 F.3d 1544, 1555–56 (10th Cir. 1995).

[96] Walling v. Portland Terminal Co., 330 U.S. 148 (1947).

[97] If the labor benefits the institution or involves the operation and maintenance of the institution, then patients are employees protected by the FLSA, Souder v. Brennan, 367 F. Supp. 808 (D. D.C. 1973), Wyatt v. Stickney, 344 F. Supp. 387, 402 (M.D. Ala. 1972). Such employment, if unpaid, may also violate the Thirteenth Amendment to the Constitution, which forbids involuntary servitude, Johnson v. Hennse, 355 F.2d 129, 132, n. 3 (2d Cir. 1966).

The ADA and Binding Arbitration Clauses in Employment Contracts and Collective Bargaining Agreements

There is ample case law addressing the question of when an employee loses the right to bring a federal discrimination claim because of his or her agreement to an arbitration clause in an employment contract. This question involves the collision of two important principles: support for arbitration rather than litigation and the protection from infringement of people's statutory rights to be free from discrimination. Congress passed the Federal Arbitration Act in support of the first principle—it precludes federal judges from hearing or disposing of cases that are subject to arbitration agreements. The second principle, the right of a citizen to retain his or her statutory entitlements in the face of employer coercion to relinquish them, is considered essential to ensure that those statutory entitlements achieve their purpose.[98] The U.S. Supreme Court has addressed this question in three cases, one of which involved the ADA. Taken together, the cases stand for the proposition that an individual can bargain away the right to statutory protection by agreeing to binding arbitration in an individual employment contract.[99] However, if a union purports to waive individual rights to statutory protection, it must do so clearly and unmistakably—simply agreeing to binding arbitration does not suffice to accomplish this.[100] Courts have decided that a waiver is clear and unmistakable under two circumstances. If the agreement specifically refers to federal causes of action when it submits all grievances to binding arbitration or if a collective bargaining agreement explicitly incorporates the federal statutory guarantees as part of the collective bargaining agreement, identifying the antidiscrimination statutes by name,[101] then the waiver has been sufficiently clear and unmistakable. Even if the union did explicitly waive an employee's rights to bring an action in federal court, it is not clear that this waiver would be effective.[102]

Reasonable Accommodation in the Context of Collective Bargaining Agreements

One of the controversies under the ADA is whether an employer is required to make a certain accommodation when to do so would directly conflict with the seniority

---

[98]Brooklyn Savings Bank v. O'Neil, 324 U.S. 697, 704 (1945) ("a right conferred on a private party, but affecting the public interest, may not be waived or released if such waiver or release contravenes the statutory policy").

[99]Gilmer v. Interstate/Johnson Lane Corp., 500 U.S. 20, 33–35 (1991).

[100]Wright v. Universal Maritime Service Corporation, 525 U.S. 70, 80–81 (1998).

[101]Bratten v. SSI Services, 185 F.3d 625, 631 (6th Cir. 1999); Prince v. Coca Cola Bottling Company, 37 F. Supp. 2d 289, 293 (S.D. N.Y. 1999); Carson v. Giant Food, 175 F.3d 325, 332 (4th Cir. 1999).

[102]Alexander v. Gardner-Denver, 415 U.S. 36, 49–51 (1974); Barrentine v. Arkansas Best Freight, 450 U.S. 728, 745–46 (1981). Most courts have taken *Gilmer* to apply only to individual employment contracts, rather than union negotiated contracts, Tran v. Tran, 54 F.3d 115, 117–18 (2d Cir. 1995); Bratten v. SSI Services, 185 F.3d 625, 630–32 (6th Cir. 1999); Albertson's v. United Food and Commercial Workers Union, 157 F.3d 758, 760–62 (9th Cir. 1998); Air Line Pilots' Association International v. Northwest Airlines, 199 F.3d 477, 481–86 (D.C. Cir. 1999), judgment reinstated, 211 F.3d 1312 (D.C. Cir. 2000). However, the 4th Circuit has held that unions may waive individuals' rights to litigate their employment discrimination cases, Austin v. Owens-Brockway Glass Container, 78 F.3d 875, 880–86 (4th Cir. 1996).

provisions of a collective bargaining agreement. However, there seems to be little actual controversy: Virtually all courts have decided that such an accommodation is unreasonable as a matter of law.[103] This outcome is a little odd, because the legislative history of the ADA counsels a different approach altogether.

Reports by both the House and the Senate emphasize that the ADA obliged an employer to comply with its provisions, regardless of any inconsistent term of a collective bargaining agreement to which it was subject.[104] These reports also strongly imply that an employer has a duty to negotiate collective bargaining agreements in ways that allow it to comply with the ADA, rather than in ways that give it an excuse to not grant accommodations required by disabled workers.[105] In fact, the reports are detailed about the effect of collective bargaining agreements on an employer's obligations under the ADA. There are clear statements that the ADA does not require an employer to "bump" another employee to provide a reasonable accommodation. In addition, it is clear that the terms of collective bargaining agreements may be factors—but only factors—in assessing whether a job requirement is an "essential function" or whether complying with a proposed reasonable accommodation would constitute an undue hardship.[106] In both cases, "the agreement would not be determinative on the issue."[107] Thus, "an employer cannot use a collective bargaining agreement to accomplish what it otherwise would be prohibited from doing under this Act," and "the terms of a collective bargaining agreement that violate the Act can be challenged under the ADA."[108]

Commentators and scholars have pointed to these provisions in arguing that courts should take a balanced approach to ADA requests for reasonable accommodations that involve conflicts with collective bargaining agreements.[109] But courts

---

[103] Willis v. Pacific Maritime Association, 162 F.3d 561 (9th Cir. 1998); Aldrich v. Boeing Co., 146 F.3d 1265, 1272, n. 5 (10th Cir. 1998), cert. denied, 526 U.S. 1144 (1999); Kralik v. Durbin, 130 F.3d 76, 81, 83 (3d Cir. 1997); Eckles v. Consolidated Rail Corporation, 94 F.3d 1041, 1051 (7th Cir. 1996), cert. denied, 520 U.S. 1146, 117 S. Ct. 1318 (1997); Milton v. Scrivner, Inc., 53 F.3d 1118, 1125 (10th Cir. 1995); Foreman v. Babcock and Wilcox Co., 117 F.3d 800 (5th Cir. 1997). The 6th, 4th, and 1st Circuit Courts have not ruled on this question under the ADA, although all have given strong indications that they would join the majority of circuits, either through language in unpublished cases, such as Boback v. General Motors, 107 F.3d 870 (6th Cir. 1997) or through decisions in cases involving the Rehabilitation Act, such as Carter v. Tisch, 822 F.2d 465, 469 (4th Cir. 1987) and Shea v. Tisch, 870 F.2d 786 (1st Cir. 1989). The D.C. Circuit Court has explicitly declined to decide the question, see Aka v. Washington Hospital Center, 156 F.3d 1284, 1302, 1305 (D.C. Cir. 1998) (en banc).

[104] Report of the House Committee on Labor and Education, H.R. Rep. No. 101-485, pt. 2, at 63 (1989) ("Section 504's regulations provide that a recipient's obligation to comply with this subpart is not affected by any inconsistent term of any collective bargaining agreement to which it is a party. 45 C.F.R. § 84.11(c). This policy also applies to the ADA."); Report of the Senate Committee on Labor and Education, S. Rep. No. 101-485, at 31 (1989) (same as language in House Report).

[105] Id. ("Conflicts between provisions of a collective bargaining agreement and an employer's duty to provide reasonable accommodations may be avoided by ensuring that agreements negotiated after the effective date of this title contain a provision permitting the employer to take all actions necessary to comply with this legislation.")

[106] Id. ("If certain jobs are reserved for people with seniority, this may be considered in determining whether it is reasonable to assign a disabled employee without seniority to the job").

[107] Id.

[108] Id.

[109] See, e.g., William McDevitt, "Seniority Systems and the ADA: The Fate of Reasonable Accommodation after Eckles," St. Thomas L. Rev. 9(1997): 359; Eric H. J. Stahlhurt, "Playing the Trump Card: May an Employee Refuse to Reasonably Accommodate Under the ADA by Claiming a Collective

have been unwilling to adopt this approach, principally on public policy grounds. Several circuit courts have stated flatly that because several Rehabilitation Act cases had found that an accommodation was unreasonable if it conflicted with a seniority provision in a collective bargaining agreement,[110] Congress would have to specifically repudiate this position in the language of the ADA. Note that this position applies only to "direct" conflicts with bona fide seniority provisions of collective bargaining agreements that implicate the employment rights of other employees: "We most certainly do not here decide that all provisions of a collective bargaining agreement will preempt the employer's duty to reasonably accommodate."[111]

In addition, if a collective bargaining agreement has provisions allowing seniority to be bypassed in "exceptional circumstances"[112] or if it permits the union to waive a certain bargained-for concession,[113] there may be a requirement to ask the union to waive the concession in the individual case or to use that provision to reasonably accommodate a disabled employee. The 3rd Circuit Court concluded that an employer could not be held responsible if the union refused to grant the waiver, although it did not consider whether unions—which are also subject to the ADA[114] —have obligations to do so under these circumstances.

In one case, a collective bargaining agreement had a "handicapped transfer" provision that appeared to conflict with other provisions of the collective bargaining agreement. The D.C. Circuit Court remanded to the district court to see whether the provisions could be construed to harmonize with the ADA—a fact-specific question based on the understanding of the parties who negotiated the collective bargaining agreement and the practice of the union and the employer.[115]

Conclusion

In this chapter, I have tried to present an overview of the many issues and possibilities raised by legal action challenging discrimination in employment on the basis of mental disability. Although there are federal statutes that may be implicated, such as Section 504 of the Rehabilitation Act, and most state statutes prohibit employment discrimination, these statutes are often interpreted by reference to Title I of the ADA. The remainder of this volume is devoted to a close examination of the scope of protection provided by the ADA in actions charging discrimination in employment.

Bargaining Obligation?" *Labor L. J.* 9 (1993): 71; Robert A. DuBault, "The ADA and the NLRA: Balancing Individual and Collective Rights," *Indiana L. J.* 70 (1995): 1271.

[110] Shea v. Tisch, 870 F.2d 786 (1st Cir. 1989).

[111] Eckles v. ConRail, 94 F.3d 1041, 1046 (7th Cir. 1996).

[112] Buckingham v. United States, 998 F.2d 735, 741 (9th Cir. 1993).

[113] Kralik v. Durbin, 130 F.3d 76 (3d Cir. 1997).

[114] 42 U.S.C. § 12111(2).

[115] Aka v. Washington Hospital Center, 156 F.3d 1284 (D.C. Cir. 1998) (en banc).

Chapter 3
THE AMERICANS WITH DISABILITIES ACT
AND THE DEFINITION OF MENTAL IMPAIRMENTS

An individual's mental state is crucial in almost every category of law, from criminal law to contract law to family law. The law has developed many different terms to describe abnormal mental conditions that affect an individual's legal rights and responsibilities: *incompetent, insane, mentally ill,* and *mentally infirm* represent only a few of them.

Because the Americans With Disabilities Act (ADA) draws its terminology from Section 504 of the Rehabilitation Act, which was a nondiscrimination provision inserted into a vocational rehabilitation statute, the ADA uses vocational rehabilitation terminology to refer to mental conditions protected under the ADA. *Impairment* and *disability* are well-known terms in vocational rehabilitation that have been modified to serve the function of disability discrimination law.

Although the medical and rehabilitation communities generally use the terms *impairment, handicap,* and *disability,* confusion arises because different entities define each word differently. For example, the World Health Organization (WHO) defines *impairment* as "any loss or abnormality of psychological, physiological or anatomical structure or function."[1] Examples include a broken or missing finger or glaucoma. A *disability* is "a restriction of ability or lack of ability to perform an activity considered normal for the person."[2] A person with the impairment of a broken finger might have a disability of being unable to lift certain objects or catch a basketball; a person with glaucoma might be disabled in his or her depth perception or vision. A *handicap* is a "disadvantage for a given individual, resulting from a disability or impairment, that limits or prevents fulfillment of a role that is normal for that person."[3] If the broken or missing finger or glaucoma prevents an individual from playing sports, that would be a handicap. With psychiatric conditions, the impairment of depression might lead to the disability of being unable to sleep properly, resulting in the handicap of job loss.

In the United States, under the American Medical Association's *Guides to the Evaluation of Permanent Impairment,*[4] the definition of *impairment* is similar to that of the WHO: "a deviation from normal in a bodily part or organ system and its functioning."[5] However, unlike the WHO, the American Medical Association does

---

[1] *International Classification of Impairments, Disabilities and Handicaps* (New York: World Health Organization, 1980) at 47.

[2] *Id.* at 143.

[3] *Id.* at 183.

[4] *Guides to the Evaluation of Permanent Impairment,* (5th ed., Chicago: American Medical Association, 2000). This all-important book is used to determine Worker's Compensation and disability awards in most states. For a fascinating review of an earlier edition of the *Guides, see* Ellen Smith Pryor, "Book Review: Flawed Promises: A Critical Evaluation of the AMA's Guides to the Evaluation of Permanent Impairment," *Harv. L. Rev.* 103 (1990): 964.

[5] This definition is found in the *Guides'* glossary and defines impairment.

not refer to psychological function in its definition. In addition, Americans often blur the WHO's concepts of impairment and disability.[6] Americans generally use *disability* to mean what the WHO means by *handicap*; Americans no longer use *handicap* because disabled people find it offensive.[7] A *disability* is "an alteration of an individual's capacity to meet personal, social, or occupational demands or statutory or regulatory requirements, because of an impairment."[8] *Impairment* is seen as a purely medical judgment, whereas the disability created by the impairment is context specific, "subjective and value laden."[9] Ellen Smith Pryor has argued persuasively that *impairment* is also subjective and value laden,[10] because impairments are judged according to a standard of what constitutes "normal" abilities to accomplish an individual's "ordinary daily activities." Pryor points out that the American Medical Association's *Guides to the Evaluation of Permanent Impairment* refers to sports as "normal activities" for men and housework as a "normal activity" for women.

But beyond this, the impairment–handicap–disability model does not adapt well to emotional and psychological difficulties. The fundamental sorrows, despair, grayness, and broken hearts do not fit well into models that divide the body into component parts and measure impairments or deficits one part at a time, assuming that the findings represent some truth that will last beyond the next day or week. This chapter explores the meaning of mental disability as understood in legislation and through statistics and then closely examines some of the case law surrounding the ADA.

The Meaning of *Mental Disability* Under the ADA

The ADA states that the term *disability* means, with respect to an individual:

> (A) a physical or mental impairment that substantially limits one or more of the major life activities of such individual; (B) a record of such an impairment; or (C) being regarded as having such an impairment.[11]

A *mental impairment,* according to the regulations implementing Title I of the ADA

---

[6]For example, the *Guides* also define *impairment* as "an alteration of an individual's health status that is assessed by medical means," *id.* at 2.

[7]Report of the House Committee on Education and Labor, H.R. Rep. 101-485, pt. 2, at 50 and 51 (May 15, 1990) ("As with racial and ethnic epithets, the choice of terms to apply to a person with disabilities is overlaid with stereotypes, patronizing attitudes, and other emotional connotations. Many individuals with disabilities, and organizations representing such individuals, object to the use of such terms as "'handicapped person'" or "'the handicapped.'"). *See also* Report of the House Judiciary Committee, H.R. Rep. 101-485, pt. 3, at 26 and 27 (1990).

[8]*Id.*

[9]Deborah Stone, *The Disabled State* (Philadelphia: Temple University Press, 1984) at 110.

[10]Ellen Smith Pryor, "Flawed Promises: A Critical Evaluation of the American Medical Association's *Guides to the Evaluation of Permanent Impairment*," *Harv. L. Rev.* 103 (1990): 964, 967–973.

[11]42 U.S.C. § 12102(2) (West 2000).

includes "any mental or psychological disorder, such as mental retardation, organic brain syndrome, emotional or mental illness, and specific learning disabilities."[12]

Courts have generally found that all the best known diagnoses of mental illness constitute impairments under the ADA: schizophrenia,[13] depression,[14] and bipolar disorder.[15] Few defendants have contested that anxiety or panic disorders constitute impairments.[16] Some courts have questioned whether posttraumatic stress disorder (PTSD) is an impairment—or even exists—but they are in the minority.

Statistics About Mental Illness

How many people in the United States have any mental or psychological disorder? The answer depends on how broadly or narrowly "any mental or psychological disorder" is defined. The briefest search confirms that statistics regarding mental illness are extraordinarily confusing. For example, the ADA finds that "some 43,000,000 Americans have one or more physical or mental disabilities,"[17] but the most reliable epidemiological sources state that in 1990, the same year the ADA became law, 44.2 million American adults had a mental disorder found in the third edition revised of the *Diagnostic and Statistical Manual of Mental Disorders* (*DSM-III-R*).[18]

This is not necessarily contradictory. Not only does a *disability* as defined by the ADA require that a person have a physical or mental impairment, but it also requires that the impairment "substantially limit[s] one or more major life activities." A diagnosis therefore is not equivalent to a disability, although when it comes to psychiatric disabilities, society sometimes seems inclined to treat them as the same.

Because of the vast range of conditions that are called *mental illness* or that are found in the *DSM*,[19] an effort has always been made to distinguish between a mental

---

[12]29 C.F.R. § 1630.2(h). The validity of these regulations has recently been called into question by the Supreme Court, which noted that the EEOC had not been given authority by Congress to interpret the meaning of the term *disability.* Sutton v. United Airlines 527 U.S. 471, 479 (1999) ("No agency, however, has been given authority to issue regulations implementing the generally applicable provisions of the ADA, *see* 12101-12102, which fall outside Titles I–V. Most notably, no agency has been delegated authority to interpret the term.").

[13]Eusanio v. C.F., 1997 WL 374209 (W.D. N.Y. June 17, 1997); Bultemeyer v. Fort Wayne Community Schools, 100 F.3d 1281 (7th Cir. 1996).

[14]Smoke v. Walmart Stores, 2000 U.S. App. LEXIS 2478 (10th Cir. Feb. 17, 2000) at *7.

[15]Fitts v. Fed. Nat'l Mortgage Ass'n, 77 F. Supp.2d 9, 23 (D. D.C. 1999); Den Hartog v. Wasatch Academy, 129 F.3d 1076 (10th Cir. 1997).

[16]Reeves v. Johnson Controls World Services, 140 F.3d 144 (2d Cir. 1998); Zirpel v. Toshiba America, Info Systems, Inc., 111 F.3d 80, 81 (8th Cir. 1997).

[17]42 U.S.C. § 12101(a)(1) (West 2000).

[18]Ronald C. Kessler, Patricia A. Berglund, Shanyang Zhao, Phillip J. Leaf, Anthony C. Kouzis, Martha L. Bruce, Robert M. Friedman, Rene C. Grosser, Cille Kennedy, William E. Narrow, Timothy J. Kuehnel, Eugene M. Laska, Ronald W. Manderscheid, Robert A. Rosenheck, Timothy W. Santoni, and Max Schneier, "The 12-Month Prevalence and Correlates of Serious Mental Illness," in Ronald W. Manderscheid and Mary Anne Sonnenschein, eds., *Mental Health United States, 1996* (Washington, DC: Center for Mental Health Services, Substance Abuse and Mental Health Services Administration, DHHS Pub. No. [SMA] 96-3098, 1996) at 64. This article will henceforth be referred to as the National Comorbidity Survey, which is the survey that provided the data on which the study was based.

[19]*See* further discussion below about the diagnoses in *Diagnostic and Statistical Manual of Mental Disorders*, 4th ed. (DSM-IV) (Washington, DC: American Psychiatric Association, 1994).

illness and more disabling mental conditions. The term *chronic mental illness* was used for a while. After that term became disfavored because of its connotations of hopelessness, "severe and persistent mental illness" (which, frankly, does not seem much better) or "serious mental illness" or "severe mental illness" were adopted and are used to this day.

For many years, the number of people with serious mental illness was considered coextensive with the population of people in state mental hospitals. After deinstitutionalization, the term became harder to define, and ultimately a definition of serious mental illness was arrived at using a combination of certain diagnoses, duration of the condition, and level of functional impairment. For example, federal law defines *serious mental illness* for purposes of state block grants for mental health treatment as one 12-month *DSM* disorder other than substance abuse disorders and serious impairment.[20]

On the basis of the fairly stringent definition of serious mental illness described above, in 1990, the year that the ADA was passed, 10 million American adults—almost a quarter of the number of people found by Congress to be disabled—were "seriously mentally ill."[21] *Severe and persistent mental illness* is defined as a diagnosis of schizophrenia, schizoaffective disorder, manic–depressive disorder, autism, severe forms of major depression, panic disorder, and obsessive–compulsive disorder in a 12-month period.[22] The Center for Mental Health Services estimates that about 4.8 million people in the United States have severe and persistent mental illness. In contrast, 750,000 Americans are blind,[23] 2.5 million have some form of epilepsy,[24] and 15.7 million have diabetes.[25]

In one recent study, the civilian, noninstitutionalized population of the United States with schizophrenia, schizoaffective disorder or other psychoses, or "bipolar depression" or at risk for bipolar depression—the group of people referred to by the authors of the study as "severely mentally ill"—was estimated to be 3.3 million or 1.7% of the adult population in July 1996.[26]

The prevalence of schizophrenia and schizophreniform disorder is about 1.5% of the adult population.[27] This figure represents more than 2 million people. To put this figure in context, schizophrenia is 5 times more common than multiple sclerosis,

---

[20]ADAMHA Reorganization Act, Pub. L. No. 102-321, 106 Stat. 323, 380, 388 (1992).

[21]*Id. Serious mental illness* was defined as having one 12-month disorder from the following disorders—mood disorder, anxiety disorder, substance use disorder, antisocial personality disorder, schizophrenia, schizophreniform disorder, other nonaffective psychoses, somatization disorder, or organic brain syndrome—and being seriously impaired, with impairment defined as meeting any one of the following four criteria: (a) having severe mental illness, (b) planned or attempted suicide; (c) substantially interfered with vocational capacity; and (d) serious interpersonal impairment.

[22]Ronald C. Kessler et al., *id* at 60 and 63.

[23]National Federation of the Blind Web Site, http://www.nfb.org/aboutnfb.htm.

[24]*Epilepsy Facts & Figures, available at* http://www.epilepsy-ohio.org/Facts_and_Figures/facts_and_figures.htm.

[25]American Diabetes Association, http://www.diabetes.org/ada/c20f.html.

[26]Donna D. McAlpine and David Mechanic, "Utilization of Specialty Mental Health Care Among Persons with Severe Mental Illness: The Roles of Demographics, Need, Insurance, and Risk," *Health Services Research* 35 (Apr. 1, 2000): 277.

[27]Samuel J. Keith, Darrel A. Regier, and Donald S. Rae, "Schizophrenic Disorders," in Lee N. Robins and Darrel A. Regier, eds., *Psychiatric Disorders in America: The Epidemiological Catchment Area Survey* (New York: Free Press, 1991) at 38.

6 times more common than insulin-dependent diabetes, and 60 times more common than muscular dystrophy.[28]

Depression is far more prevalent than schizophrenia and schizophreniform disorder. Interestingly, although the National Depressive and Manic Depressive Association estimates that 17.4 million adults will experience an affective or mood disorder each year,[29] 28 million Americans are taking antidepressants.[30] Bipolar disorder —what used to be called manic–depression—has a life-time prevalence of only 0.8% of the U.S. population.[31] Posttraumatic stress disorder, however, has a lifetime prevalence of 7.8% of the population, with higher rates among women.[32]

The fact that the definitions of "serious" and "severe and persistent" mental illness are used as a way of allocating federal funds to the states for mental health treatment is significant. One of the principal reasons for distinguishing between "severe and persistent" mental illness and "serious" mental illness and other kinds of mental illness is because states are not permitted to spend federal funds for mental health services on anyone except people who meet this definition. Thus, people with certain diagnoses qualify for social benefits, such as insurance parity and federal and state funding of treatment,[33] whereas people with other diagnoses—such as PTSD —do not.

An overt effort has been made to equate "serious" mental illness with "biologically based" mental illness, in ways that strive to legitimize these psychiatric diagnoses by associating them with physical illness. A favorite synonym for serious mental illness is *brain disease,* and a favorite analogy for someone with mental illness is the diabetic who needs insulin to function. By implication, this approach minimizes all forms of nonbiological mental illness as not being serious.

This is fundamentally unfair. It is unfair because debilitation and anguish with nonbiological roots—such as PTSD from witnessing the carnage of Vietnam and dissociative identity disorder arising from years of severe childhood sexual abuse— cause as much pain and dislocation in the lives of people who have had these experiences as does depression or bipolar disorder. People who have emotional difficulties because of these experiences are equally in need of services, financial assistance, and help. In addition, some people who have had experiences of early childhood sexual abuse, traumatic accidents, or service in Vietnam receive diagnoses of schizophrenia or major depression. These people—but not those with the same experiences but different diagnoses—are eligible for parity of insurance coverage or state-funded services. In some cases, caring mental health professionals are driven to diagnose favored, although inaccurate, reimbursable diagnoses over other diagnoses that would leave the individual with a label and no treatment.

---

[28]An estimated 350,000 people in the United States have multiple sclerosis, according to the Multiple Sclerosis Foundation of America (Fort Lauderdale, FL).

[29]National Depressive and Manic Depressive Association, Overview of Depressive Illness and Its Symptoms, *available at* http://www.ndmda.org/depover.htm.

[30]Maya Szalavitz, "Mood Swings," *New York,* 26 Oct. 1998, 24.

[31]Lee N. Robins and Darrel A. Regier, eds., *Psychiatric Disorders in America: The Epidemiological Catchment Area Survey* (New York: Free Press, 1991) at 65–66.

[32]R. C. Kessler, A. Sonnega, E. Bromet, and C. B. Nelson, "Posttraumatic Stress Disorder in the National Comorbidity Survey," *Archives of Gen. Psych.* 52 (1995): 1048.

[33]The ADAMHA Reorganization Act, *supra* n. 18, established a system of block grants for states to fund community mental health services for adults with "serious mental illness."

The Principal Epidemiological Studies

The two principal epidemiological surveys of mental illness in the United States are the Epidemiological Catchment Area Survey (ECA)[34] and the National Comorbidity Survey (NCS).[35] The ECA was conducted at five sites and involved interviews of about 15,000 people. It concluded that about 32% of Americans had experienced a psychiatric disorder[36] in their lifetimes, and about 20% had experienced such a disorder in the past year.[37] In terms of the 1994 adult population, that translates into at least 38 million Americans having experienced a diagnosable psychiatric disorder in one year and at least 61 million Americans having experienced a diagnosable psychiatric disorder during their lifetime.[38]

The NCS, conducted later, put the results at an even higher level. The most recent edition of *Mental Health United States, 1996,* published by the Center for Mental Health Services, pooled ECA results from Baltimore[39] and NCS results to conclude that 44.2 million adult Americans experience a *DSM-III-R* disorder in any 12-month period.

One of the reasons that the figures in the study are so high is that the studies attempted to capture the total number of people with psychiatric disorders, not only people who had received a diagnosis of a psychiatric disorder.[40] In fact, the ECA

---

[34] Lee N. Robins and Darrel A. Regier, eds., *Psychiatric Disorders in America: The Epidemiological Catchment Area Survey* (New York: Free Press, 1991).

[35] R. C. Kessler, K. A. McGonagle, S. Zhao, C. B. Nelson, et al., "Lifetime and 12-Month Prevalence of DSM-III-R Psychiatric Disorders in the United States: Results From the National Comorbidity Survey," *Archives of General Psychiatry* 51 (1994): 8.

[36] The psychiatric disorders tested for included affective disorders such as depression and bipolar disorder, schizophrenia and related disorders, phobias and panic disorders, generalized anxiety disorders, obsessive–compulsive disorders, antisocial personality, substance abuse disorders, and somatization disorder, which is "the presentation of multiple physical complaints in multiple organ systems for which no organic cause can be found," Marvin Swartz, Richard Landerman, Linda K. George, et al., "Somatization Disorder," in Robins and Regier, n. 80, at 220. Anorexia and bulimia were tested for, but only 11 cases were found among 20,000 people, and so the category was not included in the final findings. Of these conditions, substance abuse disorders, including both alcohol and drug abuse, were the most common disorders, followed by phobias and generalized anxieties, at 343.

[37] Robins and Regier, n. 90, at 329. This included substance abuse disorders. The survey was conducted between 1980 and 1985.

[38] The adult, civilian, noninstitutionalized population of the United States in 1994 was 190.3 million, *Statistical Abstract of the United States* (Washington, DC: U.S. Dept. of Commerce, Oct. 1996), at 286, Table No. 456, Voting Age Population. The fact that these figures do not include the institutionalized population means that using them to determine the number of Americans with a diagnosable mental illness necessarily underestimates that number.

[39] The Epidemiological Catchment Area Study surveyed five metropolitan areas, including Baltimore. The Center for Mental Health Services used the Baltimore survey because it was the only site that included questions about impairment necessary for conclusions about the rate of serious mental illness, see below.

[40] To determine how many people in the population have various mental illnesses and whether they are diagnosed with those conditions or not, epidemiologists had to devise questions whose answers correspond to the diagnosis. These questions ranged from 19 questions for schizophrenia ("Have you ever believed people were watching you or spying on you?" "Have you ever believed that others were controlling how you moved or what you thought against your will?") and panic disorder to 33 questions for depressive episode and dysthmia. Answers to these questions serve as proxies for the conclusion that the person has the diagnosed condition.

showed that relatively few people seek treatment for psychiatric conditions,[41] and of those that do, most of them seek treatment from their doctors rather than from mental health professionals.[42] In addition, the study showed that

> a more than trivial proportion of those without an active disorder had been in treatment, 10% of those with a past disorder but no symptoms of that disorder in the past year, and 4% of those who had never had one of the covered disorders.[43]

Interestingly, 27% of people interviewed in psychiatric institutions were found *not* to have had a psychiatric disorder in the past year.[44] The authors explained this by hypothesizing that those people either had a psychiatric diagnosis not covered by the survey,[45] had "poor insight into their symptoms [that] made their report of symptoms incomplete,"[46] or were "in need of hospitalization despite not meeting criteria for a diagnosis, perhaps because they had very serious symptoms such as a suicide attempt."[47]

Epidemiologists are trying to uncover the "true" rates of these conditions in the population, not simply the rate of diagnoses of these conditions. As reflected previously, many people who are considered to have the condition have not received the diagnosis, and some who have received the diagnosis are not considered to have the condition.

These kinds of studies are particularly important in the area of discrimination on the basis of psychiatric disability, because they help to illuminate the extent to which discrimination is based on the disability and its manifestations, as opposed to only having a diagnosis. For example, pioneering work by Bruce Link showed that people with "treated (labeled) cases of psychiatric disorder have less income and are more likely to be underemployed than similarly impaired untreated (unlabeled) cases with comparable background characteristics."[48]

The Epidemiological Gap and Various Explanations

Although 10 million people are considered to be seriously mentally ill (i.e., diagnosed with a mental disorder that causes serious functional impairments), in 1997 only 2,279,498 received either Supplemental Security Income (SSI) or Social Se-

---

[41] "Only 19% of household residents with an active disorder in the current year reported either inpatient treatment in the last year or outpatient treatment in the last six months." Robins and Regier at 341.

[42] *Id.* at 100.

[43] Robins and Regier at 341.

[44] Robins and Regier at 339 and 340.

[45] The survey covered all major psychiatric diagnoses, including substance abuse disorders, organic brain syndrome, personality disorders, and so forth. The authors did not check to see whether the people they identified as having no psychiatric disorder were diagnosed with one of these disorders by the institution in which they resided.

[46] This was not considered a problem for those people in the community who had such poor insight that they had never sought treatment at all.

[47] Robins and Regier at 339 and 340.

[48] Bruce G. Link, "Understanding Labeling Effects in the Area of Mental Disorders: An Assessment of the Effects of Expectations of Rejection," *American Sociological Review* 52 (1987): 96, citing to Bruce G. Link, "Mental Patient Status, Work, and Income: An Examination of the Effects of a Psychiatric Label," *American Sociological Review* 47 (1982): 202.

curity Disability Insurance (SSDI) benefits for psychiatric disability.[49] At the end of 1990, 226,953 people were inpatients in psychiatric facilities.[50] Thus, only one-quarter of the people in the general population who would clearly meet the ADA's definition of disability are either receiving disability benefits or residing in institutions. What about the other three-quarters of these people? Where are they? What determines which quarter of this group gets disability benefits and which three-quarters do not? What determines who is institutionalized and who is not? What determines who works and who does not? One thing is clear: People with equally severe conditions live inside and outside institutions and receive benefits or do not. How people fit into each category is related to economic or social conditions more than it is to medical factors.

Although the standard response of the American public might be that the other 8 million people are homeless, in prison, or in jail, the real answer is more complex. The latest figures released by the Bureau of Justice Statistics put the total of seriously mentally ill people in prison or jail at 283,800,[51] whereas the number of homeless mentally ill people is estimated at about 200,000.[52] Although these figures are staggering, the half million people they represent do not account for the 7.5 million people estimated to be seriously mentally ill who are not receiving disability benefits, not institutionalized, not in prison or jail, and not homeless.

Disability scholars and economists have noted that the population of people considered disabled for the purposes of receiving disability benefits tracks economic conditions, with more people receiving disability benefits in hard times and fewer in times of prosperity.[53] There are various explanations for this. One is that losing one's employment, or fear of its loss, contributes to stress leading to disability,[54] so that hard times create an increase in psychiatric disability. A more common explanation is that disability is an elastic category describing marginal workers—workers who

---

[49]*Annual Statistical Supplement to the Social Security Bull.* (Washington, DC: Government Printing Office, Nov. 1998), at 219 and 304, Tables 5, D6, and 7 F.1.

[50]Richard W. Redick, Michael J. Witkin, Joanne E. Atay, and Ronald W. Manderscheid, "Highlights of Organized Mental Health Services in 1992 and Major State and National Trends," in *Mental Health United States, 1996* (1996), at 90 and 94, Table 7.4.

[51]Bureau of Justice Statistics, Special Report, "Mental Health and Treatment of Inmates and Probationers," NCJ 174463 (Washington, DC: Government Printing Office, July 1999).

[52]These figures are obviously tricky because they involve an estimate of the number of people who are homeless, a difficult proposition, and the proportion of those people who are seriously or severely mentally ill, an even more difficult task. The Federal Task Force on Homelessness and Severe Mental Illness estimates that there are 600,000 homeless people on any given night and defines homelessness to match the McKinney Act definition of homelessness, that is, a person "who lacks a fixed, regular and adequate nighttime residence" and someone whose primary nighttime residence is a supervised public or private shelter designed to provide temporary living accommodations; an institution that provides a temporary residence for individuals intended to be institutionalized; or a public or private place not designed for, or ordinarily used as, a regular sleeping accommodation for human beings." The Federal Task Force on Homelessness and Severe Mental Illness estimates that a third of these people are severely mentally ill, Department of Health and Human Services, *Outcasts on Main Street* (Washington, DC: Interagency Council on the Homeless, 1992). This represents only 5% of the 4 million people estimated to have a serious mental illness; *see* National Coalition for the Homeless Fact Sheet 5 (Apr. 1999).

[53]Deborah Stone, *The Disabled State* (Philadelphia: Temple University Press, 1984); Matthew Diller, "Entitlement and Exclusion: The Role of Disability in the Social Welfare System," *UCLA Law Rev.* 44 (1996): 361.

[54]*See* studies cited in Richard Warner, *Recovery From Schizophrenia: Psychiatry and Political Economy*, 2d ed. (Routledge, 1994) at 47–49.

are not considered too disabled to work when the labor pool experiences shortages but who appear clearly disabled when the labor pool is glutted.[55]

The first attempt to specifically examine the role of the economy in rates of mental illness was by Harvey Brenner, who tracked admissions to New York mental hospitals from the mid-1800s through the 1960s and found that admissions increased in times of economic decline and decreased in times of prosperity.[56] Later studies confirmed that the state of the economy was closely tied to admissions for working-age adults, but hospital capacity (the number of beds that needed to be filled) was the best predictor of admission for the elderly and for children.[57]

Economists look at numbers in the aggregate. The sociologist Sue Estroff and her colleagues investigated what moves individuals to apply for disability benefits. They conducted detailed interviews with people who had been hospitalized or had received treatment from outpatient mental health programs and who were "early and eligible" (i.e., soon after they were diagnosed with major psychiatric disorders and eligible for SSI and SSDI). By interviewing people and their self-identified most significant other, reviewing hospital charts and medical records, and examining several explanatory variables, Estroff and her colleagues were able to draw a complex and rich portrait of the forces that drive people to apply for disability benefits. They discovered that

> the perceived need for SSI/SSDI demonstrated by applicants is not bounded by demographic or diagnostic factors, but rather by what might be summarized as dysfunction, dependence and despair . . . Those who viewed themselves as comparatively in need financially, who were experiencing clinical and functional difficulties, who felt helpless and in despair about themselves, and who experienced themselves as submissively dependent on their families applied for disability income.[58]

Thus, regardless of the number of people who actually have conditions identified as mental illness, the economy and social and cultural conditions have a great deal to do with (a), who is identified as psychiatrically disabled; (b), whether the person self-identifies as mentally ill or is unwillingly labeled; and (c), the legal and social consequences of being identified as psychiatrically disabled. In other words, neither the individual's diagnosis nor his or her symptoms primarily determine if he or she is employed, receives disability benefits, is homeless, or is self-supporting.

ADA Case Law and Mental Impairment

Although disability is defined identically in the three major titles of the ADA, case law makes it clear that for the courts at least, disability means different things in

---

[55] Deborah Stone at n. 53.

[56] M. Harvey Brenner, *Mental Illness and the Economy* (Cambridge, MA: Harvard University Press, 1973).

[57] James Marshall and Donna Funch, "Mental Illness and the Economy: A Critique and Partial Replication," *J. of Health and Social Behavior* 20 (1979): 282; P. R. Ahr, M. J. Gorodezky, and D. W. Cho, "Measuring the Relationship of Public Psychiatric Admissions to Rising Unemployment," *Hospital and Community Psychiatry* 32 (1981): 398.

[58] Sue Estroff, " 'No Other Way to Go': Pathways to Disability Income Application Among People with Severe Persistent Mental Illness," in Richard Bonnie and John Monahan, eds., *Mental Disorder, Work Disability and the Law* (University of Chicago Press, 1997) at 87 and 88.

different contexts. When an employment discrimination case arises under Title I, courts focus sharply on the question of whether the plaintiff is disabled, and the vast majority of courts are finding that the plaintiff is not disabled. In cases charging discrimination by public entities or discrimination in public accommodations, defendants raise the question of whether the plaintiff is disabled far less frequently and with far less success. In most cases involving Title II (discrimination by state or local government entities), the plaintiff's disability is not questioned.[59] Nor is the question of whether a plaintiff is disabled an issue in many Title III cases (public accommodations such as restaurants and movie theaters).[60] When defendants do raise the issue in Title II and III cases, they are rarely successful in persuading the court of their position.[61]

This is not because Title II and III plaintiffs are more seriously disabled than Title I plaintiffs. Title I plaintiffs have diagnoses of serious mental illness such as schizophrenia[62] and bipolar disorder, are repeatedly psychiatrically hospitalized,[63] get electroconvulsive treatment (ECT),[64] attempt suicide or threaten to kill themselves,[65] and in general reflect a range of impairment that is similar to, or more severe than, the Title II and III plaintiffs.

Are There "Per Se" Psychiatric Disabilities?

The Supreme Court has addressed the issue of whether the ADA contemplates "per se" disabilities on more than one occasion. In *Bragdon v. Abbott,* the Court declined to rule that HIV-seropositivity was a per se disability,[66] while finding that it always substantially limited reproduction and sexual relations, which it found to be major life activities. Justice Souter cited *Bragdon* as supporting the proposition that "some impairments may invariably cause a substantial limitation on major life activities," whereas Justice O'Connor used *Bragdon* to support the proposition that "whether a person has a disability under the ADA is an individualized inquiry."

Again, in *Albertson's v. Kirkingburg,* the U.S. Supreme Court held that monocularity was not a per se disability but stated that

> this is not to suggest that monocular individuals have an onerous burden in trying to show that they are disabled. On the contrary, our brief examination of some of the medical literature leaves us sharing the Government's judgment that people with monocular vision "ordinarily" will meet the Act's definition of disability.[67]

---

[59]Roe v. County Commission of Monongalia County, 926 F. Supp. 74 (N.D. W.Va. 1996).

[60]*See,* however, Price v. National Board of Medical Examiners, 966 F. Supp. 419 (S.D. W.Va. 1997).

[61]*Cf.* almost any employment case with Musko v. McClandless, 1995 WL 262520 (E.D. Pa. 1995); Ellen S. v. Florida Board of Bar Examiners, 859 F. Supp. 1489 (S.D. Fla. 1994); and Pat Doe v. Judicial Nominating Commission, 906 F. Supp. 1534 (S.D. Fla. 1995); *but see* Price v. National Medical Examiners, 966 F. Supp. 419 (S.D. W.Va. 1997).

[62]Fuentes v. U.S.P.S., 989 F. Supp. 67 (D. P.R. 1997).

[63]Franklin v. U.S.P.S., 687 F. Supp. 1214 (S.D. Ohio 1988); Walton v. Mental Health Association of Southeastern Pennsylvania, 1997 U.S. Dist. LEXIS 18224 (E.D. Pa. Nov. 17, 1997) *aff'd,* 168 F.3d 661 (3d Cir. 1999); Pesterfield v. TVA, 941 F.2d 437 (6th Cir. 1991) (Rehabilitation Act case).

[64]Rasmussen v. Quaker Chemical Corp., 993 F. Supp. 677 (N.D. Iowa 1998).

[65]Pesterfield v. TVA, 941 F.2d 437 (6th Cir. 1991) (Rehabilitation Act case); Witter v. Delta Airlines, 138 F.3d 1366 (11th Cir. 1998); Doe v. Region 13 Mental Health-Mental Retardation Commission, 704 F.2d 1402 (5th Cir. 1983) (Rehabilitation Act case).

[66]Bragdon v. Abbott, 524 U.S. 624, 642 (1998).

[67]Albertson's v. Kirkingburg, 527 U.S. 555, 567 (1999).

Although many of the best known psychiatric diagnoses are clearly "impairments" under the ADA,[68] it is highly unlikely that any psychiatric condition will be considered a per se disability by the courts. It is clear that any mental condition considered to be a per se disability will have to be clearly and unmistakably identifiable. This means that the chances of psychiatric conditions being considered per se disabilities are diminished because they are so much more fluid than other medical conditions. Respected mental health professionals still debate whether "schizophrenia" covers a variety of discrete and distinctive conditions,[69] or whether "borderline personality disorder" describes a condition at all.[70]

Indeed, no psychiatric diagnosis has been acknowledged by all courts as reflecting a disability under the ADA. Courts have ruled that people with active hallucinations caused by schizophrenia are not disabled under the ADA.[71] However, schizophrenia and bipolar disorder are the diagnoses most likely to be considered disabilities under the ADA. In a 1998 decision, the 7th Circuit Court described bipolar disorder as one of the "recognized disabilities under the ADA."[72] However, this decision is in question since the U.S. Supreme Court's recent decisions in *Sutton v. United Airlines*[73] and *Murphy v. United Parcel Service*,[74] which implied that if an individual's bipolar disorder was controlled by the use of medication, it might not be considered a disability under the ADA. Nevertheless, the kind of crises that precede diagnosis and prescription of medications may give rise to a history of disability.

Neither schizophrenia nor bipolar disorder is the most frequent basis of ADA claims by people with psychiatric disabilities. By far, the greatest number of ADA claims are brought by people with depression. In addition, a surprisingly high number of claims are brought by people with PTSD. Courts have been unusually sympathetic to claims of PTSD by men, possibly because in many cases the origins of the stress are looked upon sympathetically by judges: the Vietnam or Gulf Wars as well as rescue work by firefighters and police officers.[75] Courts have been less sympathetic to claims of PTSD by women, even women who have been raped or assaulted.

---

[68] Eusanio v. C.F., 1997 WL 374309 (W.D. N.Y. June 17, 1997) (schizophrenia); Bultemeyer v. Fort Wayne Community Schools, 100 F.3d 1281 (7th Cir. 1996) (schizophrenia); Smoke v. Walmart Stores, 2000 U.S. App. LEXIS 2478 (10th Cir. Feb. 17, 2000) (depression); Fitts v. Fed. Nat'l Mortgage Ass'n, 77 F. Supp. 2d 9 (D. D.C. 1999) (bipolar disorder); Den Hartog v. Wasatch Academy, 129 F.3d 1076 (10th Cir. 1997) (bipolar disorder).

[69] M. T. Tsuang, W. S. Stone, and S. V. Faraone, "Toward Reformulating the Diagnosis of Schizophrenia," *Am. J. Psychiatry* 147 (2000): 1041; M. T. Tsuang, M. J. Lyons, and S. V. Faraone, "Heterogeneity of Schizophrenia: Conceptual Models and Analytic Strategies," *British J. of Psychiatry* 156 (Jan. 1990): 17.

[70] Aaron T. Beck and Arthur Freeman, *Cognitive Theory of Personality Disorders* (New York: Guilford Press, 1990) at 177 and 178. ("In some circles, 'borderline' is still used as a 'garbage can' diagnosis for individuals who are hard to diagnose or is interpreted as meaning 'nearly psychotic,' despite a lack of empirical support for this conceptualization of the disorder . . . Finally, . . . borderline personality disorder is often used as a generic label for difficult clients or as an excuse for therapy going badly.")

[71] Patterson v. Chicago Association for Retarded Citizens, 150 F.3d 719 (7th Cir. 1998).

[72] Duda v. Board of Education of Franklin Park, 133 F.3d 1054 (7th Cir. 1998) (collecting cases). *See also* Glowacki v. Buffalo General Hospital, 2 F. Supp. 2d 346, 351 (W.D. N.Y. 1998) ("bipolar affective disorder has been recognized as a disability under the ADA").

[73] 527 U.S. 471 (1999).

[74] 527 U.S. 516 (1999).

[75] Sherback v. Wright Auto Group, 987 F. Supp. 433 (W.D. Pa. 1997) and Berry v. City of Savannah, 1999 U.S. App. LEXIS 6728 (6th Cir. Apr. 1, 1999). *But see* Marschand v. Norfolk and Western Railway

The DSM *and the ADA*

The *DSM* is a manual of mental health disorders published by the American Psychiatric Association. Now in its fourth edition, it is known as *DSM-IV.* The *DSM-IV* contains a total of 374 disorders, a considerable increase over earlier editions.

Technically, a formal psychiatric diagnosis requires assessment on five axes. An Axis I diagnosis is a diagnosis of mental disorders, such as schizophrenia, mood disorders (e.g., depression), or anxiety disorders. Axis II is reserved for assessments of personality disorders. Axis III contains a listing of medical problems that may be of concern, Axis IV measures the severity of psychosocial stressors, and Axis V requires an assessment of global life functioning. Court cases usually refer only to an Axis I or Axis II diagnosis. Very few assessments involve all five axes.

For the most part, the fact that a plaintiff has a diagnosis found in the *DSM-IV*[76] is sufficient to persuade the court that the plaintiff has, at the very least, a mental impairment: "a court may give weight to a diagnosis of mental impairment which is described in the *Diagnostic and Statistical Manual of Mental Disorders* of the American Psychiatric Association."[77]

However, the Equal Employment Opportunity Commission (EEOC) warns that "not all conditions listed in the *DSM-IV* are disabilities, or even impairments, for purposes of the ADA."[78] Some conditions in the *DSM-IV* were expressly excluded by Congress from coverage under the ADA: "compulsive gambling, kleptomania, pyromania, various sexual behavior disorders, and substance abuse disorders resulting from current illegal use of drugs."[79] In fact, relatively few of the disorders cataloged in the *DSM-IV* are presented as disabilities in ADA litigation: A fairly comprehensive sampling of Title I cases revealed about 30 diagnoses cited by plaintiffs, with the great majority of cases represented by depression, anxiety disorder, and bipolar disorder (*see* Appendix B of this book).

One of the major questions as yet unresolved is whether the *DSM-IV* represents the outer limits of the definition of mental impairment. At least one court has held that "Congress only intended the mental disorders as defined by the American Psychiatric Association's *Diagnostic and Statistical Manual* may qualify as mental impairments potentially covered by the ADA."[80] Occasionally a court will find that a plaintiff has presented a material issue of fact sufficient to survive summary judgment even without a formal diagnosis of mental disability.[81]

Co., 876 F. Supp. 1528 (N.D. Ind. 1995) and Hamilton v. Southwestern Bell Telephone Co., 136 F.3d 1047 (5th Cir. 1998).

[76]The American Psychiatric Association's *DSM-IV* is the most widely used system of diagnosis in the United States by mental health professionals.

[77]Boldini v. Postmaster General, 928 F. Supp. 125, 130 (D. N.H. 1995) (Rehabilitation Act); Schmidt v. Bell, 1983 WL 631 at *10 (E.D. Pa. Sept. 9, 1983); Rezza v. U.S. Dept. of Justice, 1988 WL 48541 at *2–*3 (E.D. Pa. May 16, 1988), *recons. denied*, 698 F. Supp. 586 (E.D. Pa. 1988).

[78]"Enforcement Guidance on the Americans With Disabilities Act and Psychiatric Disabilities" (Washington, DC: EEOC, July 1997). All enforcement guidances are available on the EEOC's Web site (http://www.eeoc.gov) or through certain treatises available at most law libraries, such as the Federal Employment Practice Manual published by the Bureau of National Affairs.

[79]42 U.S.C. § 1221(b) (West 2000).

[80]Dertz v. City of Chicago, 1997 U.S. Dist. LEXIS 1956 (N.D. Ill. Feb. 19, 1997).

[81]Leisen v. City of Shelbyville, 968 F. Supp. 409, 416 (S.D. Ind. 1997).

However, a few courts have indicated skepticism about certain diagnoses found in the *DSM-IV*. This is not skepticism as to whether the diagnoses are severe enough to constitute an impairment or disability, but a skepticism that such conditions even exist. The conditions about which the courts have expressed this skepticism are not exotic or esoteric diagnoses, but relatively common ones, including PTSD and dissociative identity disorder. One court on its own dismissed two cases involving PTSD, concluding that PTSD was not a disability under the ADA as a matter of law. These decisions were quickly reversed on appeal, with the appellate court emphasizing the individualized nature of the inquiry required by the ADA.[82]

The Biological Model and Its Limitations

In most cases involving psychiatric disabilities, the court is willing to concede that the plaintiff's condition represents a mental impairment. The more difficult question is whether the impairment rises to the level of a disability. A faithful reading of the statute indicates that this is a strictly factual inquiry, involving the extent to which the impairment substantially limits major life activities. It is clear, however, that for many courts, the dividing line between disabling and nondisabling psychiatric conditions is discerned not by factual inquiries as to the extent of functional limitations created by the impairment but by the question of whether the impairment is "medical," "biological," or "chemically based." Virtually every case in which a mental impairment is ruled a disability makes reference to these words or phrases[83] (although being biological or chemically based is not always enough).[84]

Psychiatric conditions that are found *not* to be disabilities are those that are manifested through stress and interpersonal difficulties, even if these are serious enough to lead to complete breakdowns, medication, and hospitalization. A few courts have found that certain conditions, including job-related stress,[85] are not disabilities as a matter of law under the ADA.

The major problem with the courts' version of the biological model[86] is that it precludes them from properly understanding the nature of psychiatric disability. This legal model of mental disability, added to inherent problems in the nature of legal categorization, makes it inevitable that most mentally disabled plaintiffs will lose ADA claims.

Two characteristics of psychiatric disabilities, whose recognition is crucial to the achievement of fair results in ADA cases, have been ignored by almost all courts.

---

[82]Freeman v. City of Inglewood, 1997 U.S. App. LEXIS 11789 at *2 (9th Cir. May 16, 1997) (table case 113 F.3d 1241) (9th Cir. 1997); Hoffman v. City of Inglewood, 1997 U.S. App. LEXIS 11790 at *2 (9th Cir. May 16, 1997) (table case 113 F.3d 1241) (9th Cir. 1997).

[83]Duda v. Board of Education, 133 F.3d 1059 (7th Cir. 1998) (bipolar disorder is a "medically diagnosed mental condition").

[84]Davidson v. Midelfort Clinic, 133 F.3d 499 (7th Cir. 1998) (attention deficit disorder described as "chronic psychological disability resulting from chemical imbalance" but ruled not sufficiently limiting on major life activities to constitute a disability under the ADA).

[85]Mundo v. Sanus Health Plan of Greater New York, 966 F. Supp. 171 (E.D. N.Y. 1997).

[86]I am not making any arguments as to whether psychiatric disabilities are or are not actually biologically based, because that doesn't need to be resolved to present the problem here, which is how courts understand and apply their own distorted ideas of what it means for a condition to be biologically based.

Psychiatric Disabilities Are Contextual and Affected by Interactions

First, while disability in general is "not just a characteristic of individuals [but] results from the interaction between individuals who have . . . impairments with a resulting loss of function and the broader environment,"[87] this is particularly true of psychiatric disability. Psychiatric disability can be greatly exacerbated or greatly ameliorated by the quality of interpersonal contact and the nature of the environment. This is underscored with the greatest of urgency by people who have been diagnosed with psychiatric disabilities, both in their writings and in their litigation, and by experts, both in their research and in the evidence they present in court. It underlies almost every ADA case brought on behalf of people with psychiatric disabilities under any title of the ADA. The complex, interactive dynamic between psychiatric disability and an individual's environment means that courts must focus more on context and interaction to understand psychiatric disability. It is the gravest of misconceptions about psychiatric disability to assume that it will be an unchanging constant wherever the individual goes and however he or she is treated. However, courts have explicitly articulated precisely these assumptions: "a disability is part of someone and goes with her to her next job."[88] Courts use blindness and mobility impairments as baselines to determine disability: "After all, a visually impaired person will be visually impaired no matter what job he holds; a quadriplegic will be unable to walk whether or not he is employed."[89]

The biological model of mental illness contributes to courts' unwillingness to examine the effects of the environment on creating or profoundly exacerbating psychiatric disability. Although, of course, biological illnesses are also environmental and contextual—pollen and dust cause asthma, stress and overwork may cause heart attacks, and so on—courts are so imbued with the blindness/deafness/mobility impairment model that they sometimes refuse to hold that physical conditions are disabilities when they result from environmental triggers. Thus, although courts' refusal to credit impairments that become disabilities only in certain environmental contexts falls most heavily and consistently on people with psychiatric disabilities, it has also proven problematic for people with a variety of physical disabilities. For example, people with chemical sensitivities, who have severe reactions to cigarette smoke, or who have asthma are also people whose impairments only become disabilities in certain contexts, and many courts have refused to recognize their disabilities precisely because of the environmental context of the disability.[90] However, other courts have adopted the view that such people are handicapped or disabled.[91] A very few courts have even recognized that someone may have a psychiatric disability only in a certain work environment as long as the causes are physical (e.g.,

---

[87]Jerry Mashaw and Virginia Reno, eds., *Balancing Security and Opportunity: The Challenge of Disability Income Policy* (Washington, DC: National Academy of Social Insurance, 1996), 10.

[88]Weiler v. Household Finance Corp., 1995 WL 452977 at *5 (N.D. Ill. July 27, 1995).

[89]Dewitt v. Carsten, 941 F. Supp. 1232, 1237 (N.D. Ga. 1996), *aff'd mem.*, 122 F.3d 1079 (11th Cir. 1997).

[90]Heilwell v. Mount Sinai Hospital, 32 F.3d 718 (2d Cir. 1994).

[91]Byrne v. Board of Education, 979 F.2d 560, 566 (7th Cir. 1992) (teacher who could not work at two schools because of sensitivity to fungus at those schools raised a jury issue of disability); Vickers v. V.A., 549 F. Supp. 85, 86 (W.D. Wash. 1982) (individual who could only work in a smoke-free environment was handicapped).

claustrophobia[92] or agoraphobia[93]) rather than personal (e.g., a bullying or abusive supervisor). What courts cannot accept is the relationship between psychiatric disabilities and stress, overwork, or personal interactions. This is discussed in detail in chapter 6 in this volume.

The association between "legitimate" mental illness and biological etiology almost always includes a corollary assumption that the mental illness can be treated primarily by medication. Judge Posner recently stated the following without support or citation:

> Most mental illnesses today are treatable by drugs that restore the patient to at least a reasonable approximation of normal mentation and behavior. When his illness is controlled he can work and attend to his affairs, including the pursuit of any legal remedies he may have.[94]

There are two major problems with this assumption. The first is that the Supreme Court has recently decided—contrary to congressional intention as evidenced in ample legislative history—that disabilities must be considered in their ameliorated rather than unameliorated condition.[95] Thus, if Judge Posner is correct, employers will be free to discriminate on the basis of mental illness: If an employee takes medication, he or she will not be disabled under the Supreme Court's recent decisions. If an employee does not take medication, the employee will be seen as responsible for his or her own disability, and several courts have held that under these circumstances, an employee is not "qualified." Thus, under this biological perspective, only employees taking medication that does not work well—which actually encompasses a substantial number of people—will be eligible for protection under the ADA.

The second problem with the assumption that mental illness can be treated primarily by medication is that it essentially operates to preclude the kinds of workplace accommodations that employees with psychiatric disabilities most need. Depression, stress, or breakdown might best be accommodated by transfer to a different position, more structure, or not being screamed at by a supervisor. The assumption about treatability with medication means that at best the employee is granted a leave of absence to get therapy or adjust medication to better deal with being screamed at on the job.

Not only do these assumptions run counter to research and understanding of psychiatric disorders, they run counter to the understanding of impairment, disability, and accommodation by Congress and the EEOC. Implicit in Congress's recognition that the same impairment could have different effects on different people is the understanding that context is often determinative of whether a person is disabled or

---

[92]Neveau v. Boise Cascade, 902 F. Supp. 207 (D. Ore. 1995); Commission on Human Rights v. General Dynamics, 1991 Conn. Super. LEXIS 2704 (Nov. 22, 1991). The EEOC has implicitly assumed that claustrophobia is a disability by using it in one of its Enforcement Guidances as an example, see EEOC Enforcement Guidance, "Pre-Employment Disability Related Questions and Medical Examinations," *EEOC Compliance Manual* IV(B)(5)(b) (Oct. 10, 1995) at 5371, paragraph 6093 (if applicant voluntarily informs employer that he or she has claustrophobia, employer may ask how applicant will do job that involves fitting into tight spaces).

[93]Przybylak v. New York State Thruway Authority, 1997 WL 662346 (W.D. N.Y. Oct. 16, 1997).

[94]Miller v. Runyon, 77 F.3d 189 (7th Cir. 1996).

[95]Sutton v. United Airlines, 527 U.S. 471 (1999).

not. Both Congress and earlier Supreme Court decisions have recognized that the reactions of others are often a major disabling factor. The EEOC's regulations and guidance have underscored this fact, emphasizing that "the issue is whether an impairment substantially limits any of the major life activities of the person in question, not whether the impairment is substantially limiting in general."[96] The 3rd Circuit Court recently held that whether a given impairment substantially limits one or more life activities depends on a person's skills and abilities, which may themselves also limit job opportunities.[97]

Psychiatric Disabilities Are Episodically and Intermittently Manifested

A related issue, which has presented even greater problems for the courts, is the fact that most psychiatric disabilities (even the most serious ones) are manifested episodically or intermittently. Yet courts have distorted congressional intent to create a doctrine that "temporary" disabilities are not disabilities at all and have used this doctrine to exclude plaintiffs whose psychiatric problems fell well within the *DSM-IV* diagnoses and substantially limited them in major life activities.

The text of the ADA makes no reference whatsoever to the duration of the impairment or disability. Congress in its legislative history made clear that the ADA was not expected to apply to "trivial" impairments but did not refer explicitly to length of time as a necessary qualification to be deemed disabled.

The EEOC in its regulations listed "duration or expected duration of the impairment" as one of a number of factors to be considered in determining whether a person's impairment substantially limits his or her major life activity.[98] The comments to the regulations remark with regard to "duration" that "a broken leg that takes eight weeks to heal is an impairment of fairly short duration." The problem with this example is that very few employers would fire an employee because he or she had a broken leg—it is not a stigmatized impairment in the way that mental illness is stigmatized.[99] If accommodations were sought and denied, the leg would have healed well before the date a complaint could be filed in court.[100] But individuals who are severely depressed for 3–6 months,[101] unlike the employee with the broken leg, *are* fired. Even when an employee is fired for depression related to experiences with cancer or other illnesses, courts have artificially distinguished the two conditions and ruled the depression too "temporary" to be a disability.[102] Indeed, courts use terminology that describes many psychiatric disabilities when concluding that im-

---

[96] EEOC Memorandum, *Compliance Manual*, "Definition of the Term 'Disability'," 902.4(a).

[97] Mondzelewski v. Pathmark Stores, 162 F.3d 778 (3d Cir. 1998) (the court may properly take into consideration the plaintiff's lack of education and skills in finding that lifting restriction disables him from work).

[98] 29 C.F.R. § 1630.2(j)(2)(ii).

[99] *See* Sam Bagenstos, "Subordination, Stigma and 'Disability'," 86 *Va. L. Rev.* 397 (2000), for the suggestion that an analysis of whether a given condition was historically stigmatized is appropriate in determining whether it constitutes a disability under the ADA.

[100] *See* chapter 2, Exhaustion of Administrative Requirements.

[101] Brown v. Northern Trust Bank, 1997 U.S. Dist. LEXIS 13184 (N.D. Ill. Sept. 2, 1997).

[102] Sanders v. Arneson Products, 91 F.3d 1351 (9th Cir. 1996) (4-month depression considered separately from cancer and too temporary to constitute a disability).

pairments that are "episodic and intermittent"[103] or that "vary in intensity and are sporadic in nature"[104] do not qualify as disabilities.

Some courts, following the lead of Judge Posner in the 7th Circuit Court, have reflected an understanding that one can have a chronic disability that is manifested by intermittent impairments, which are characteristic of the disability, and still qualify for the protections of the ADA.

In part because Judge Posner stated explicitly and emphatically early on in ADA jurisprudence that the episodic manifestations of an underlying disability are entitled to accommodation,[105] some courts have followed this lead,[106] and the 7th Circuit Court has continued to re-emphasize the point.[107] As one of the only courts to even acknowledge this reality pointed out, deciding cases involving depression is particularly fact-specific because the "nature of the plaintiff's impairment is not consistent from day-to-day."[108]

The Disability–Personality Dichotomy

This boils down to nothing more than personalities.[109]

One of the key issues in disability discrimination law as it pertains to people with mental disabilities is how to draw the line between psychiatric disability and personality. This implicates a broad range of questions under the ADA and other disability-related statutes such as the Individuals with Disabilities in Education Act,[110] as well as sensitive criminal law and constitutional law issues.[111]

The ADA drafters and its implementing federal agencies clearly believe that a distinction exists between mental disability and personality. In accordance with the legislative history of the ADA, the EEOC's implementing regulations distinguish between "mental and psychological disorders," and "common personality traits such as poor judgment or a quick temper *where these are not symptoms of a mental disorder.*"[112] This regulation is frequently incompletely quoted by courts, which often stop the quotation marks at "temper." The truncated version of the quotation is cited by the courts as supporting the distinction between people with common personality

---

[103]Hamm v. Runyon, 51 F.3d 721, 725 (7th Cir. 1995).

[104]Glowacki v. Buffalo General Hospital, 2 F. Supp. 2d 346 (W.D. N.Y. 1998).

[105]Vande Zande v. State of Wisc. Dept. of Admin., 44 F.3d 538 (7th Cir. 1995).

[106]Dutton v. Johnson County, 859 F. Supp. 498, 506 (D. Kan. 1994) (episodic, intermittent, unpredictable migraines were a disability).

[107]Haschman v. Time Warner, 151 F.3d 591 (7th Cir. 1998).

[108]Mendez v. Gearan, 956 F. Supp. 1520, 1524 (N.D. Cal. 1997).

[109]Stewart v. County of Brown, 86 F.3d 107, 111 (7th Cir. 1996).

[110]Under the Individuals with Disabilities in Education Act, for example, students can be expelled for misconduct if it did not arise out of a disability, but cannot be expelled for disability-related misconduct. *Cf.* Commonwealth of Virg. Dept. of Educ. v. Riley, 106 F.3d 559 (4th Cir. 1997) and Doe v. Board of Educ. Oak Park, 115 F.3d 1273 (7th Cir. 1997) (OK to expel if *not* related to disability) *with* Kaelin v. Grubbs, 482 F.2d 595 (6th Cir. 1982) *and* Clyde K. v. Puyallup School Dist., 35 F.3d 1396 (9th Cir. 1996) (cannot expel because misconduct is sufficiently linked to disability).

[111]*See, e.g.,* Kansas v. Hendricks, 521 U.S. 346 (1997), raising the question of whether a man with pedophilia can be committed. The American Psychiatric Association took a position in its amicus brief that pedophilia was not a mental illness for commitment purposes, whereas the Menninger Clinic took an opposing point of view.

[112]29 C.F.R. pt 1630, app. § 1630.2(1) (2000) (emphasis added).

traits and people with mental disabilities and the conclusion that the ADA protects the latter and not the former.

The real question raised by the full quotation is how to distinguish when a quick temper or poor judgment is the result of a personality trait and when it is the result of a mental disability. When does a personal characteristic or a trait become a symptom? It sometimes seems that the transformation occurs with a mental health professional's wave of a magic diagnosis; this is not far from the case. In practice, courts usually require a diagnosis to conclude that a person has an impairment, and some courts insist on a physician's or psychiatrist's diagnosis. As one court stated explicitly,

> generally the plaintiff who asserts that they [sic] suffer from a medical condition must prove this through a medical diagnosis from a medical professional. This is necessary to distinguish between a claim of depression that is in actuality a personal conflict or mere temperament and irritability and a true medical condition of depression.[113]

This perception that the line between personality and disability is hard to draw has caused a great deal of disgruntlement and hostility against claims related to mental disability. Yet we freely extend tolerance to behavioral difficulties when we discover that they are related to a physical disability. Hypoglycemia, thyroid imbalance, brain tumors, AIDS, diabetes, and numerous other conditions may result in inappropriate behavior, which is understood and excused as a symptom of the physical condition.[114]

Another way of expressing the disability–personality distinction is to refer to temperament. Thus, the 7th Circuit Court found that a sheriff's conclusion that one of his deputies was "temperamentally unfit" for his position did not mean that the sheriff perceived the deputy to be disabled (even though the sheriff also ordered the deputy to undergo a series of psychological tests over a considerable length of time).[115] In another case, the 7th Circuit Court distinguished between "temperament or irritability" and true psychiatric disorders.[116]

Courts frequently construct the distinction between personality and mental disability as one involving frequency of occurrence in the population. If a given trait is common, it cannot reflect disability.[117] Many courts are indignant at plaintiffs for even suggesting the contrary[118] and warn explicitly that such claims will lead to the demise of protection against discrimination for people with "true" disabilities.[119]

---

[113]Alderdice v. American Health, 118 F. Supp. 2d 856, 864 (S.D. Ohio 2000).

[114]Gilday v. Mecosta County, 124 F.3d 760, 761 (6th Cir. 1997) (the diabetic employee's unpleasant behavior was due to his difficulty in regulating his insulin); Boelman v. Manson State Bank, 522 N.W.2d 73, 76 (Iowa 1994) (multiple sclerosis was the cause of the employee's behavioral difficulties); Bussey v. West, 86 F.3d 1149 (4th Cir. 1996) (multiple sclerosis made the employee irritable and lose her temper); Siciliano v. Chicago Local 458 3-M, 1997 U.S. Dist. LEXIS 20519 at *17 (N.D. Ill. Dec. 18, 1997) (diabetes).

[115]Stewart v. County of Brown, 86 F.3d 107 (7th Cir. 1996).

[116]Duda v. Board of Education of Franklin Park, 133 F.3d 1054 (7th Cir. 1998).

[117]Dewitt v. Carsten, 941 F. Supp. 1232 (N.D. Ga. 1996) ("[To accept claims of stress as constituting disability] would expand the scope of the ADA well beyond the scope of illnesses that Congress has indicated it was intended to cover. That is, many employees feel stress from their jobs.")

[118]Forrisi v. Bowen, 794 F.2d 931, 934–35 (4th Cir. 1986) (Rehabilitation Act claim); Mundo v. Sanus Health Plan of Greater New York, 966 F. Supp. 171 (E.D. N.Y. 1997).

[119]Pouncy v. Vulcan Materials Co., 920 F. Supp. 1566 (N.D. Ala. 1996); Daley v. Koch, 892 F.2d 212 (2d Cir. 1989); Forrisi v. Bowen, 794 F.2d 931 (4th Cir. 1986).

Despite the fact that the ADA cites the number of Americans with disabilities as 43 million[120] and that the most recent authoritative survey of mental illness suggests that more than one in four Americans will have a mental illness during their lifetime, courts with neither citation nor reflection appear to be saying that if something is common it cannot be a disability. But neither Congress nor disability researchers have ever suggested that disability is rare. Women are protected against gender-based discrimination even though they constitute a majority of the population. People over 40 years old are protected from age discrimination in employment, although they constitute a substantial proportion of the population.

Unfortunately, many of the most crucial and salient symptoms or characteristics of mental disability in the workplace can easily be considered "common personality traits." These include the inability to tolerate stress, difficulties with interpersonal and social relationships, and periodic difficulties in focusing and concentration. As the literature confirms, mental disability is not something separate and apart from personality, it simply represents extremes along a variety of cognitive and affective continua.

Another problem relates to where so-called personality disorders fit into the ADA. Although personality disorders are cataloged in the *DSM-IV*, which militates in favor of their being considered disabilities under the ADA, mental health professionals draw sharp distinctions between personality disorders and other "mental illnesses."[121] Some mental health professionals do not believe that personality disorders are mental illnesses, or at least do not believe that they are treatable. Personality disorders are also cataloged separately in the traditional diagnostic system: They are noted on Axis II, whereas other mental illnesses are listed on Axis I.

Yet people who are diagnosed with personality disorders are subject to all the negative implications of mental illness diagnoses, including involuntary commitment, forcible medication, loss of child custody, loss of employment, expulsion from the military without benefits, and more.[122] However, people diagnosed with personality disorders rarely receive any of the benefits associated with disability status, such as disability benefits, priority for receipt of mental health services, or exemption from criminal responsibility.[123] In addition, people with personality disorders are subjected to stereotypes that are just as harmful, or more harmful, than those associated with Axis I diagnoses, as reflected in the U.S. Civil Rights Commission's 1998 report on the EEOC's enforcement of Title I:

> Two commentators have wondered whether EEOC is requiring an employer to accommodate behaviors such as the paranoid employee's penchant for spreading false and destructive rumors, the borderline employee's manipulation of supervisors and

---

[120]42 U.S.C. § 12101(a)(1) (West 2000).

[121]Karin Mika and Denise Wimbiscus, "Responsibilities of Employers Toward Mentally Disabled Persons Under the Americans With Disabilities Act," 11 *Journal of Law & Health* 173 (1996/1997): 175 ("mental health professionals themselves disagree as to whether personality disorders . . . are properly characterized as mental illness") (gathering citations).

[122]*See* Susan Stefan, "The Impact of the Law on Women with Diagnoses of Borderline Personality Disorder Related to Childhood Sexual Abuse," in Bruce Levin, Andrea Blanch, and Ann Jennings, eds., *Women's Mental Health Services* (Thousand Oaks, CA: Sage, 1998). People with a history of a "basic personality disorder" are disqualified from employment with the U.S. Marshal's Service, Lassiter v. Reno, 885 F. Supp. 869, 874 (E.D. Va. 1995).

[123]*Id.*

co-workers, the histrionic employee's sexually provocative dress and innuendo, or the narcissistic manager's insensitivity and denigration of subordinates.[124]

In fact, the Civil Rights Commission was so concerned about the impact of including people with personality disorders among those protected by the ADA that it devoted several pages of its report to the subject and concluded by expressing doubt about the wisdom of "the [EEOC] guidance's assertion that personality disorders are potential disabilities under the ADA."[125] It hardly needs to be noted that no employee in the 17 years since the Rehabilitation Act and the ADA were passed has ever asked for the kinds of accommodations suggested by the U.S. Civil Rights Commission.

The personality disorders, especially borderline personality disorder, can be reflective of little more than the diagnoser's intense dislike of the person diagnosed. Some clinicians have even suggested doing away with the diagnosis of borderline personality disorder because its connotations are so pejorative. It is apparent from reading the Civil Rights Commission's report that its major concern is that conduct such as violence, or traits such as rudeness, obnoxiousness, or "being a jerk," which the Commission associates with personality disorders, should not be protected under the ADA.

To center this concern on personality disorders is itself a manifestation of discrimination against a particular set of diagnoses. As noted earlier, obnoxious or troubling behavior is associated with several diagnoses, including diabetes when insulin control is a problem,[126] organic brain damage,[127] and multiple sclerosis.[128] Yet only people with personality disorders are singled out for a discussion that certainly raises important issues regarding accommodation, workplace culture, and the rights of fellow employees.

As Joel Dvoskin wrote,

> there are some diagnoses that hurt people very much. All too often, the result of a psychiatric diagnosis is to stigmatize certain people as dishonest, unlikeable, and worst of all hopeless . . . no diagnosis hurts more than that of a personality disorder.[129]

---

[124] *Helping Employers Comply with the ADA: An Assessment of How the United States Equal Employment Opportunity Commission Is Enforcing Title I of the Americans With Disabilities Act* (Washington, DC: U.S. Civil Rights Commission 1998) at 122. Although the source of this "wondering" is cited, the U.S. Civil Rights Commission neither puts these remarks in quotations nor dissociates itself from them in the text or notes.

[125] *Id.* at 122.

[126] Gilday v. Mecosta County, 124 F.3d 760 (6th Cir. 1997); Siciliano v. Chicago Local 458 3-M, 1997 U.S. Dist. LEXIS 20519 (N.D. Ill. Dec. 18, 1997).

[127] Gasper v. Perry, 155 F.3d 558 (table case), 1998 U.S. App. LEXIS 14933 (4th Cir. July 2, 1998) (Organic brain damage led man to be "impulsive, disinhibited, excessively loquacious and have trouble reading social cues." One example of this behavior was that he took a fellow employee's umbrella with a duck head and, holding the head close to her face, made quacking noises at her. This kind of behavior raises questions about the extent to which work environments must expand the notion of what is socially acceptable in order to accommodate people with disabilities, and the extent to which accommodations must be made by fellow employees rather than the employer.)

[128] Boelman v. Manson State Bank, 552 N.W.2d 73 (Iowa 1994) (termination of employee whose multiple sclerosis made it difficult for him to get along with others was action taken on the basis of disability but was justified); Bussey v. West, 86 F.3d 1149 (table case), 1996 U.S. App. LEXIS 13290 (4th Cir. June 4, 1996) (employee whose multiple sclerosis made her "irritable" and "lose her temper" was not terminated because of discrimination on the basis of her disability).

[129] Joel Dvoskin, "Sticks and Stones: The Abuse of Psychiatric Diagnosis in Prison," *J. of the*

Another way in which a distinction is drawn between personality and disability is that the EEOC permits employers to conduct personality tests and screen for undesirable personality traits, but it does not permit psychological exams intended to screen for mental impairments or disabilities. Sometimes the line between these two kinds of tests is hard to discern. For example, in one case, a court ruled that a test that screened for "emotional instability" did not run afoul of the ADA because "emotional instability" was not itself a diagnosis of a mental impairment or disability.[130]

The Disability–Conduct Distinction

A concern about the ADA, unique to the mental disability area, is how to draw the line, if any can be sensibly drawn, between a psychiatric disability and the conduct of an individual. The manifestation of many physical disabilities (even the invisible disabilities) is not primarily through conduct. A blind person's inability to see or a person with quadriplegia's use of a wheelchair is not conceptualized as conduct or behavior. The distinction between disability and conduct is far more problematic with mental disability.

The view that people with psychiatric disabilities have no control over their behavior, which equates the behavior with the disability, may perpetuate the very stereotypes that the ADA was intended to eliminate. There is clearly a continuum of control over behavior, from the flailing of someone having an epileptic seizure or the screaming and aggressive behavior associated with some forms of Alzheimer's disease[131] to the criminal assaults committed by juvenile delinquents with mental health problems[132] and the ability that some people have to slow or speed their pulse and other bodily functions. But where do the actions of people with schizophrenia responding to commands by internal voices, the actions of people with multiple personalities, the impulsive and reckless purchases of someone with mania, the immobility of someone with severe depression, or the cutting of some women with histories of childhood sexual abuse fit on this continuum?

To assume (as many courts do) that there is a dichotomy between disability and conduct, and that the former cannot be the basis for discrimination but the latter can, causes other problems. If this is the case, then the only protection offered by the ADA is against adverse action based solely on diagnosis and nothing more. This reduces the ADA's protection for people with mental disabilities to one based on intentional discrimination alone, which is far less than individuals with other disabilities receive, and renders the requirement of reasonable accommodation meaningless in the context of mental disabilities. Some courts have held that if an individual could mitigate the effects of a disability by taking medication or seeking

---

California Alliance for the Mentally Ill 8(1) (1997): 20. *See also* George Vaillant, "The Beginning of Wisdom Is Never Calling a Patient Borderline," *J. of Psychotherapy Practice and Research* 1(2) (1992): 117–134.

[130]Thompson v. Borg-Warner, 1996 WL 162990 (N.D. Cal. Mar. 11, 1996).

[131]*See* Wagner v. Fair Acres Geriatric Center, 49 F.3d 1002 (3d Cir. 1995).

[132]*See* David B. v McDonald, 116 F.3d 1146, 1147 (7th Cir. 1997), *cert. denied*, 522 U.S. 1048 (1998) *judgment vacated by* 156 F.3d 780 (7th Cir. 1998), *cert. denied*, 525 U.S. 1145 (1999).

treatment, and did not do so, that individual could not prevail in a discrimination claim,[133] either because the person was not disabled or was not otherwise qualified or because the employer's actions could not be construed as discriminatory under the circumstances, since the employee in effect chose to engage in the conduct that led to termination.[134]

The truth of the matter is that to reduce the question to whether the individual could control the behavior, although an extremely common one in law, is simply the wrong way to address the disability/conduct conundrum. One of the ways in which a law ostensibly dedicated to prohibiting discrimination against people with disabilities in fact preserves and protects discrimination is by reducing the complexity of disability and behavior to a binary choice. The dichotomy between control–lack of control is false. As Joel Dvoskin has written, perhaps the problem is with making such a clear and non-overlapping distinction between disability and free will: "Our dichotomous scientific minds lead us to see things as either willful or the result of disability. I suspect a middle ground, where people with precious few alternatives for feeling better choose one that we find offensive."[135] The reality is one that the law has difficulties in accommodating: Having a psychiatric disability is a struggle, and behavior—or its absence—sometimes manifests that struggle. Perhaps a person has control over the choices he or she makes but cannot comprehend the entire range of choices available. Perhaps a person has control over the conduct but has impaired recognition of the consequences of the conduct. Perhaps a person has control over the conduct, but the negative consequences of the conduct should be mitigated out of recognition of the heightened obstacles the individual faces, just as tardiness rules might not be enforced strictly in the case of a person in a wheelchair who has to deal with a commuting environment constructed with the needs of able-bodied people in mind.

Many of the cases involving the disability/conduct distinction are sharply gendered. The cases involving women revolve around suicide attempts and self-injury; the cases involving men often revolve around threats, assaults, fights, and violence.[136] These cases raise very different issues. First, the suicide attempts and self-injury rarely involve the direct threat to the health and safety of others that Congress contemplates as a defense to the ADA.[137] Second, suicidal behavior and self-injury are more traditionally associated with mental disability, whereas fighting and assaults are not necessarily signs of mental disability. Thus, the EEOC *Compliance Manual*'s declaration that misconduct that results from a disability need not be excused if the employer would not tolerate such conduct from a nondisabled employee[138] may be

---

[133] Siefken v. Village of Arlington Heights, 65 F.3d 664, 667 (7th Cir. 1995); Overturf v. Penn Ventilator, 929 F. Supp. 895 (E.D. Pa. 1996).

[134] Franklin v. U.S.P.S., 687 F. Supp. 1214 (S.D. Ohio 1988) ("It is [the] plaintiff's election not to take her medication that has caused the incidents of arrest and violence and violations of the law. The choice being hers, it seems difficult if not impossible to understand why the actions of [the] defendant should be discriminatory.")

[135] Joel Dvoskin, n. 129 at p. 21.

[136] A residual category, which is not within the scope of this book, involves conduct related to alcohol and substance abuse, *see* DeSpears v. Milwaukee County, 63 F.3d 635 (7th Cir. 1995); Miners v. Cargill Communications, Inc., 113 F.3d 820 (8th Cir. 1997).

[137] *See* further discussion at pp. 153–158.

[138] EEOC Compliance Manual, 902.2(c)(4) (1995).

applicable to violence and fights in the workplace; it is harder to classify attempted suicide off the job as "misconduct" the employer need not tolerate. (For further discussion of misconduct and disability, see chapter 7.)

The EEOC policy also begs the key question of what kind of conduct an employer can rule out at work. The case of *Gasper v. Perry* highlights this question. This case involved a man who worked for a mapping agency and was apparently adequate at the skills of his job. However, he had suffered an accident that left him with brain damage, making him unable to readily respond to social cues. He asked embarrassing questions, such as how sports training bras differed from regular bras; he refused to let a fellow employee pass through a door unless she gave him a lick of her ice cream cone; and, upon encountering the same colleague with a duck-head umbrella in an elevator, he grasped it and pointed it at her face, quacking loudly. He got on his knees in front of another employee and begged her never to cut her hair. Although there had been no apparent problems with his first supervisor, after another supervisor was appointed, he began to be written up for misconduct. His fellow employees were uncomfortable with his conduct—some were even afraid—and demanded that he be fired.

The Court of Appeals categorized this as a case involving workplace misconduct and cited other misconduct cases, all of which involved violence or assault.[139] This is not a case of violence and assault that would be forbidden if engaged in by a nondisabled person; it is a case in which the behavior is different and disturbing *and* a direct result of the disability.

At first, this case may seem to raise the question of how much tolerance or accommodation for "difference" as a result of disability does the ADA require? Congress made clear in its legislative history that it considered discomfort with difference to play a major role in discrimination against people with disabilities: the famous comment of the zookeeper who excluded the boy with Down's syndrome because he would scare the chimpanzees[140]; the auction house that tried to remove two women in wheelchairs because they were "disgusting to look at"[141]; the boy with cerebral palsy who was excluded from the classroom because his appearance would have a "nauseating effect" on his classmates[142]; and the woman with arthritis denied a job at a college because "normal students shouldn't see her."[143]

Although most people understand that the ADA prohibits discrimination based on discomfort with differences that manifest themselves visually, differences that manifest themselves behaviorally are a different story. With few exceptions (such as mental retardation), society retains a lingering suspicion that inappropriate behavior is willful and could be controlled. Even when there is no question of an individual's ability to control such behavior (e.g., as a result of brain damage), the social discomfort generated by differences in behavior rather than differences in appearance is distinctly greater. In addition, society tolerates a greater range of difference in

---

[139]Gasper v. Perry, 1998 U.S. App. LEXIS 14933 (4th Cir. July 2, 1998) at *9. Even the Circuit Court recognized that the cases it cited involved "more egregious" misconduct; nevertheless, it characterized "inappropriate behavior when interacting with others" as misconduct.

[140]135 CONG. REC. S10718 (daily ed. Sept. 7, 1989).

[141]*Id.* (One woman, Judith Heumann, went on to become an assistant secretary in the Department of Education under the Clinton Administration.)

[142]*Id.* (Although rarely mentioned, this is a reference to a case at the turn of the century.)

[143]*Id.*

appearance than in conduct. Even behavior such as asking grocery store customers how their children are doing is cited by a district court as rendering a grocery bag boy unqualified for the job, because he was "talking too loudly."[144]

If "different" behavior that does not conform to the social norms of a particular workplace and community can be categorized as "misconduct" or as rendering the plaintiff unqualified for a job without further analysis, one of the principal purposes of the ADA—to prohibit loss of employment opportunities solely because people recoil from difference—will be defeated. This idea was rejected by courts when employers attempted to justify race and gender discrimination on the basis of the reactions of customers, and Congress explicitly prohibited employers from using the reactions of customers as an excuse for discrimination under Section 504 of the Rehabilitation Act and the ADA.[145]

Courts must look more carefully at the "different" behavior. First, if behavior is characterized as misconduct, is this behavior in which other employees have engaged and for which they have received differential discipline? In particular, is this behavior in which supervisors or those higher up in organizational status have engaged without discipline? Although no one can dispute that employers should not have to tolerate physical violence, some employers do tolerate it (in fact, some supervisors engage in it, see chapter 6). Disability-based conduct should not be punished if similar conduct not arising from disability is punished differentially or not at all.

Second, is the problem described as the reaction of customers or coworkers rather than an inability to do the job? If so, how long has the individual been employed? Has a new supervisor been assigned recently? In virtually all of these cases, it can be inferred that the catalyst for adverse employment action is the appointment of the new supervisor, who is not as comfortable with difference as a previous supervisor.[146] Supervisors can set the tone for how coworkers and even customers react to employees with disabilities.

This leads to an even more important insight, which is that "difference" is not an immutable concept. Employment environments and cultures are partially responsible for the definition and toleration of "difference." Workplace cultures vary dramatically. Behavior that could be interpreted as evidence of mental illness at IBM might be considered a sign of creativity and leadership in Silicon Valley.[147] Behavior

---

[144]Taylor v. Food World, 946 F. Supp. 937 (1996), rev'd, 133 F.3d 1419 (11th Cir. 1998). Many customers lauded Food World and the plaintiff for his efforts to work; others claimed to be made uncomfortable.

[145]29 C.F.R. pt. 1630 App. § 1630.15(a), 1630.2(l) (West 2000); Talanda v. KFC National Manpower Co., 140 F.3d 1090 (7th Cir. 1998).

[146]See Kent v. Derwinski, 790 F. Supp. 1032 (E.D. Wash. 1991); Taylor v. Food World, 946 F. Supp. 937 (N.D. Ala. 1996), rev'd, 133 F.3d 1419 (11th Cir. 1998); Gasper v. Perry, 1998 U.S. App. LEXIS 14933 (4th Cir. July 2, 1998). See also Warren Bates, "Unlucky Bagger Filed Lawsuit Against Supermarket Over Firing," Las Vegas Rev. J., May 1, 1998, at 7B (the bagger with Down's syndrome was fired for not paying 26¢ for lunch after working at Lucky's successfully for a number of years before a new supervisor was appointed).

[147]High-tech workers and chief executives are known to put octopuses in air conditioning vents: Jon Swartz, "Spotlight Turns on Comedic Costello, CEO of Cadence," Austin American Statesman (Oct. 20, 1997); wear Java decoder rings, multicolored balloon hats, and wear Hawaiian shirts and grass skirts while leading their production crews in the Macarena: Michelle Cole, "Micron Electronics Vows to Loosen Up," The Idaho Statesman (Sept. 8, 1998): 6B; see generally, Po Bronson, The Nudist on the Night Shift (New York: Random House, 1999).

that would merit discharge in some environments is described approvingly as "pranks" or as "temperament" when engaged in by members of major league sports teams.[148] Even more importantly, behavior that is tolerated or ignored in supervisors or directors is considered completely unacceptable in subordinates.

Conclusion

The question of whether an individual has a mental impairment under the ADA raises fascinating issues about the relationship between personality and psychiatric disability. Other questions concern the ways in which conduct manifesting mental impairment can be parsed from the impairment itself. The definition of "mental impairment" as "any mental or psychological disorder, such as . . . mental illness"[149] does not provide much in the way of enlightenment on these questions.

In practice, if a psychiatrist, doctor, or psychologist is willing to certify that an individual has a mental impairment, courts rarely question the conclusion. The interesting questions raised by attempting to define "mental impairment" are largely ducked, and the real interpretive action in the ADA comes in the second part of the definition of disability: whether the impairment substantially limits one or more major life activities. This issue is considered in the next chapter.

---

[148] Jim Prime with Bill Nowlin, *Tales From the Red Sox Dugout* (Champaign, IL: Sports, 2000) at 74–76 (baseball players tying up each other and taping a player's mouth shut).

[149] 29 C.F.R. § 1630.2(h) (Westlaw 2000).

Chapter 4
THE SUBSTANTIAL LIMITATIONS OF THE SUBSTANTIAL LIMITATIONS REQUIREMENT OF THE AMERICANS WITH DISABILITIES ACT

The discrimination hides inside the law, which is interpreted so narrowly.[1]

Employers are winning the vast majority of Title I cases by arguing successfully that Americans With Disabilities Act (ADA) plaintiffs do not meet the definition of disability under the ADA.[2] In most cases, the employee's mental condition is conceded to constitute an impairment under the ADA. However, the plaintiff's impairments are usually not seen as substantially limiting one or more of the plaintiff's major life activities. Courts have found that plaintiffs with cancer, emphysema, and schizophrenia are not substantially limited in their major life activities. In one case, a court found that a plaintiff who died of cancer during the course of the litigation from his condition was not substantially limited in major life activities under the ADA.[3]

By doing this, courts have followed a path that both the U.S. Congress and the Supreme Court considered and rejected[4]: the privileging of more visible and socially acceptable disabilities, such as blindness, deafness, and paraplegia,[5] which are always

---

[1] Survey No. 189.

[2] A comprehensive survey of 1,200 ADA cases decided by federal appellate courts since 1992 found that employers won over 90% of litigated cases, American Bar Association Commission on Mental and Physical Disability Law, "Study Finds Employers Win Most ADA Title I Judicial and Administrative Complaints," *Mental and Physical Disability Law Reporter* 22 (1998): 403. Another recent survey of 261 federal appellate ADA employment discrimination decisions showed courts siding with defendants in 209 cases. "Dismal Results for Plaintiffs," *Disability Compliance Bull.* 10 (Nov. 20, 1997): 10. The 10th Circuit sided with defendants in 94% of cases, the 4th Circuit in just under 93% of cases. *See also* "Courts Continuing Narrow Interpretation of 'Disability,' Case Study Shows," *Disability Compliance Bull.* 9(5) (March 27, 1997): 1 (only 6 findings of disability among 110 decisions).

[3] Hirsch v. National Mall and Services, 989 F. Supp. 977 (N.D. Ill. 1997).

[4] From the beginning, Congress has consistently made it clear that its definitions of *handicap* in the Rehabilitation Act and *disability* in the ADA were intended to be broad in scope; *see, e.g.*, Senate Committee on Labor and Public Welfare, S. Rep. No. 93-1297 (1974), *reprinted in* 1974 U.S.C.C.A.N. 6373, 6388.

[5] Courts in the course of ruling against plaintiffs claiming other disabilities repeatedly compare those conditions unfavorably with blindness, deafness, and paraplegia: "[High cholesterol] is wholly unlike blindness or paraplegia or the other conventional disabilities that trigger the protection of the ADA," Christian v. St. Anthony Medical Center, 117 F.3d 1051 (7th Cir. 1997); "determinations of disability must be made on a case by case basis . . . blindness and deafness will always substantially limit the major life activities of blind and deaf individuals," Runnebaum v. Nationsbank of Maryland, N.A., 123 F.3d 156, 166 (4th Cir. 1997) (en banc). Commentators have been even more explicit, calling blindness, deafness, and paraplegia "prototypical statutory disabilities" or "classic impairments," *see* James M. Zappa, "The Americans With Disabilities Act of 1990: Improving Judicial Determinations of Whether an Individual Is 'Substantially Limited'," 75 *Minnesota Law Rev.* 74 (1991): 1303, 1304, n. 14. Blindness has always been the most privileged of the disabilities; when Congress passed Title IX of the Civil Rights Act in 1972, it prohibited discrimination on the basis of gender or blindness in federally funded

found to substantially limit major life activities, and the exclusion of less acceptable disabilities, such as HIV infection, substance abuse, and psychiatric disabilities. By ruling in favor of an HIV-positive plaintiff, the Supreme Court reminded lower courts in *Bragdon v. Abbott* that the ADA was meant to have a broader scope and cover a range of disabilities.[6] It remains to be seen whether the holding in *Bragdon* will affect plaintiffs who have disabilities other than HIV seropositivity.

The "substantial limitation on major life activities" requirement of the disability definition in the ADA comes directly from the ADA's predecessor, Section 504 of the Rehabilitation Act. This statute was designed to provide vocational rehabilitation benefits to people with disabilities. The earliest definition of a *handicapped individual* was "any individual who (A) has a physical or mental disability which for such individual constitutes or results in a substantial handicap to employment and (B) can reasonably be expected to benefit in terms of employability from vocational rehabilitation services."[7] This definition sprang from the purpose of the statute as a whole, which was to define the group of handicapped individuals who qualified for rehabilitation and services. Within a year, Congress recognized the difficulties this definition presented to the antidiscrimination provisions of the Rehabilitation Act, and the definition was revised. The new definition, which parallels the current definition in the ADA, changed "substantial handicap to employment" to "substantial limitation in major life activities."

This language is useful when an employee is requesting an accommodation. Employers should not be required to provide accommodations to an employee unless the employee is substantially limited in one or more major life activities. However, the "substantial limitation" definition of disability defeats the purpose of the ADA when an employee is not requesting an accommodation, but is simply asking to be treated like every other employee. Employees are terminated, demoted, or transferred explicitly because of a physical or mental impairment and then lose discrimination claims because courts conclude that they are neither substantially limited in their major life activity nor regarded as such by their employer.

For example, in *Bridges v. City of Bossier*,[8] the defendant conceded that the only reason it refused to hire Bridges as a firefighter was because he had a mild form of hemophilia. Although Bridges presented considerable evidence that he could safely perform the duties of a firefighter, and the city conceded that it failed to hire him because of his condition, he lost. The court found that he was not disabled by his condition, and because the city only perceived him to be disabled for a narrow range

---

educational programs, 20 U.S.C. § 1681-1684. Blindness is also separated out in disability benefits law and is the only condition that entitles an individual to per se disability benefits without further proof of disability. Thus, under current law, Judge David Tatel of the D.C. Circuit who is blind, is entitled to receive disability benefits. In addition, many government programs that grant disability benefits grant more generous benefits to blind people, *see, e.g.*, Vaughn v. Sullivan, 83 F.3d 907 (7th Cir. 1996) (upholding Indiana Medicaid plan, which allows blind people but not other disabled people to disregard the Plan for Achieving Self-Support income when calculating their eligibility for Medicaid benefits).

[6]Bragdon v. Abbott, 524 U.S. 624 (1998). *See also* Anderson v. Gus Mayer Boston Stone, 924 F. Supp. 763, 774–75 (E.D. Tx. 1996) (finding blindness, deafness, and HIV-seropositivity to be per se disabilities).

[7]Vocational Rehabilitation Act of 1973, Pub. L. No. 93-112, 1973 U.S.C.C.A.N. (87 Stat.) 409, 414.

[8]92 F.3d 329 (5th Cir. 1996).

of jobs (including, of course, the job of firefighter), it did not regard Bridges as disabled under the ADA. The court never reached the question of whether the city's perception that Bridges' mild hemophilia prevented him from being a firefighter was accurate or based on myths and stereotypes.

To require a qualified employee who has clearly been subjected to discrimination on the basis of a condition or impairment, or perceived condition or impairment, to prove that he or she is either substantially limited in a major life activity or perceived as being substantially limited in a major life activity misses the point of how disability discrimination happens. This is particularly true when it concerns people with psychiatric disabilities.

People with psychiatric disabilities are not primarily discriminated against because of mistaken assessments of their abilities to conduct major life activities. The public is afraid of people with psychiatric disabilities; families are ashamed of them; friends are uneasy or vanish when they hear of a diagnosis; children taunt them; they are assaulted and killed by strangers. The depth of discomfort caused by the revelation that an individual has a mental illness is not associated with the perception that the individual is substantially limited in major life activities. Like people who are HIV positive or have AIDS, the degree to which people with mental illness can conduct their major life activities is essentially irrelevant to the uneasiness and fear the conditions engender in others. A finding that a plaintiff is not disabled means that the court does not have to determine whether an employer discriminated against the plaintiff.[9] If employer discrimination were the focus of Title I cases, a significant number of plaintiffs who lost at summary judgment because they were deemed to not fit the definition of disability would have at least gone to trial over the employer's actions against them.[10] Discrimination is considered to be a question of fact, best left to a jury to decide when it involves determinations of credibility. But the decision of whether a plaintiff is disabled or not is often viewed as a question of law for a judge to determine,[11] and a judge's determination that a plaintiff does not meet the definition of disability means that a jury never hears the plaintiff's allegations of discrimination.

Plaintiffs are losing these cases because disability discrimination law, unlike race or gender discrimination law, requires a showing that the plaintiff is a member of the protected class of disabled people before he or she can be granted any relief. The plaintiff must prove that he or she has a physical or mental impairment, has a

---

[9]Ellison v. Software Spectrum, 85 F.3d 187 (5th Cir. 1996) ("For the ADA claim, the court held that Ellison's breast cancer was not a requisite 'disability' within the meaning of the ADA. Therefore, it did not rule on the other elements of that claim: Likewise, because we conclude that summary judgment as to disability is proper, we need not reach those other elements.")

[10]Courts are accustomed to regarding allegations and denials of discrimination as raising material issues of disputed fact; however, most courts resolve the issue of whether the plaintiff is disabled on motions for summary judgment, see Paul Frisman, "Study Suggests Employees Treated Unfairly Under Americans With Disabilities Act," Conn. Law Tribune 25(16) (April 19, 1999): 1.

[11]Cf. Poindexter v. Atchison, Topeka and Santa Fe Railroad, 168 F.3d 1228, 1230 (10th Cir. 1999) (holding that whether a condition is an impairment and whether an activity is a major life activity are questions of law under the ADA), with Hall v. Claussen, 2001 U.S. App. LEXIS 3404 (10th Cir. Mar. 6, 2001) (appearing to retreat from Poindexter). See also Bridges v. City of Bossier, 92 F.3d 329, 333 (5th Cir. 1996) (whether an individual is substantially limited in a major life activity is a mixed question of law and fact).

record of an impairment, or is regarded as having an impairment,[12] and that the impairment must constitute or be regarded as constituting a "substantial limitation on major life activities."[13]

Substantial Limitation in Major Life Activities

The EEOC has defined "substantially limited in major life activities" as

> unable to perform a major life activity that the average person in the general population can perform or restricted as to the condition, manner, or duration under which an individual can perform a particular major life activity as compared to the condition, manner, or duration under which the average person in the general population can perform that same major life activity.[14]

Obviously, a significant concern in the definition of disability will be the delineation of those life activities considered to be "major" for the purpose of the ADA.

What Are "Major Life Activities"?

The text of the ADA does not define "major life activities," and the EEOC, the Supreme Court, and lower courts have spent substantial effort to flesh out the meaning of the phrase. In the process, they have laid bare a fascinating social anthropology of American culture and values. For example, the 9th Circuit Court concluded that even if an individual had difficulty staying awake and alert because of cancer treatment, if he could perform his job duties, he was not substantially limited in the major life activity of sleeping.[15] The 9th Circuit thus implicitly valued sleep only insofar as it enables an individual to work by concluding that a limitation on sleep is not substantial unless it precludes an individual from working. Another example is the court's struggle with whether housework is a major life activity,[16] their rejection of driving as a major life activity,[17] and the surprisingly limited discussion to date as to whether sex is a major life activity. Although the U.S. Supreme Court decided

---

[12]42 U.S.C.A. § 12102(2) (West 2000).

[13]*Id.* at § 12102(2)(A).

[14]29 C.F.R. § 1630.2(j)(1) (West 2000).

[15]Innes v. Mechatronics, 1997 U.S. App. LEXIS 18000 at *6–7 (9th Cir. July 14, 1997). This is certainly a mistaken interpretation of the ADA, and would lead to bizarre conclusions in the case of people like Stephen Hawking and Judge David Tatel, who have disabilities that substantially limit major life activities but work very well in their chosen professions.

[16]*Cf.* Marinelli v. City of Erie, 216 F.3d 354 (3d Cir. 2000) (holding that picking up trash and washing dishes are major life activities but that the "basic chores" are not because housework only amounts to a major life activity when it is necessary to maintain a healthy or sanitary environment), *with* Weber v. Steippit, 186 F.3d 907 (8th Cir. 1999) (basic chores of housework are major life activities).

[17]Chenoweth v. Hillsborough County, 250 F.3d 1328 (11th Cir. 2001) (noting in the case of an individual with epilepsy that "it would be at least an oddity that a major life activity required a license from the state" and asserting that driving could not be compared to seeing or learning); Sinkler v. Midwest Property Management Limited Partnership, 209 F.3d 678 (6th Cir. 2000) (driving phobia); Flemmings v. Howard University, 198 F.3d 857 (D.C. Cir. 1999) (questioning but not determining whether driving is a major life activity in a case involving an individual with vertigo and Meniere's Disease); Colwell v. Suffolk County Police Department, 158 F.3d 635, 643 (2d Cir. 1998).

that reproduction is a major life activity and strongly suggested that sexual activity in the absence of reproduction was also a major life activity,[18] the circuits have not uniformly accepted this approach.[19]

The EEOC has several levels of regulatory advice about what constitutes major life activities. The regulations list as examples caring for one's self, performing manual tasks, walking, hearing, seeing, speaking, breathing, learning, and working.[20] The *Interpretive Guidance* to the EEOC's regulations adds sitting, standing, lifting, and reaching, with citations to the legislative history of the ADA.[21] Interestingly, the *Technical Assistance Manual* lists all of these as examples of major life activities but substitutes "reading" for "reaching."[22]

These examples of major life activities are very much oriented to physical disabilities. Partially in response to the concerns of the mental disability community, the EEOC added examples of major life activities in its *Enforcement Guidance on the Definition of Disability* that reflected limitations associated with some mental disabilities, for example, thinking, concentrating, and interacting with others.[23] In its *Enforcement Guidance on the ADA and Psychiatric Disabilities,* the EEOC added "sleeping" as a major life activity.[24]

The circuit courts generally concur with the major life activities associated with physical limitations—walking, lifting, and performing manual tasks—although they have interesting ideas about what constitutes substantial limitations of those activities.[25] Not surprisingly, courts have been more reluctant to regard activities limited by psychiatric disabilities as major life activities. Thus, although most circuit courts consider personal interactions, sleep, and concentration to be major life activities, some have held that each of these activities is not a major life activity.[26]

---

[18]Bragdon v. Abbott, 524 U.S. 624, 638 (1998) (noting that "the sexual dynamics surrounding reproduction are central to the life process itself").

[19]*Cf.* McAlinden v. San Diego, 192 F.3d 1226, 1234 (9th Cir. 1999) (holding that sexual activity constitutes a major life activity) *with* Contreras v. Suncast, 237 F.3d 756, 764 (7th Cir. 2000) (refusing to decide the question of whether sexual activity independent of reproduction is a major life activity).

[20]29 C.F.R. § 1630.2(i) (2000).

[21]*Id.,* at app. (2000).

[22]*EEOC Technical Assistance Manual,* I-2.2(a)(ii) (Jan. 1992).

[23]*EEOC Interim Enforcement Guidance,* Section 902, "Definition of the Term 'Disability'."

[24] *EEOC Enforcement Guidance on the Americans With Disabilities Act and Psychiatric Disabilities,* EEOC Notice No. 915.002, Mar. 25, 1997.

[25]*See, e.g.,* Maynard v. Pneumatic Products Co., 233 F.3d 1344 (11th Cir. 2000) (upholding summary judgment against the plaintiff who could not sit in a chair for more than 15–20 minutes, bend at the waist, or walk more than 40–50 yards at a time because the plaintiff had not shown how far the average person can walk). Sometimes appellate courts reverse lower courts on these issues, *see, e.g.,* Lutz v. Glendale Union High School, 2001 U.S. App. LEXIS 7766 (9th Cir. Apr. 10, 2001) (reversing the district court, which granted summary of judgment to the defendant on the sole ground that the plaintiff with uncontrolled diabetes and who could not walk for even a minimal distance more than once every 2 months was not substantially limited in a major life activity).

[26]The First, Second, Ninth, Tenth, and Eleventh Circuits have recognized sleep as a major life activity. Criado v. IBM Corp., 145 F.3d 437, 442 (1st Cir. 1998); Colwell v. Suffolk County Police Dep't, 158 F.3d 635, 643 (2d Cir. 1998); McAlindin v. County of San Diego, 192 F.3d 1226, 1234 (9th Cir. 1999); Pack v. K-Mart Corp., 166 F.3d 1300, 1305 (10th Cir. 1999); Pritchard v. Southern Co. Servs., 92 F.3d 1130, 1134 (11th Cir. 1996). The Second Circuit recognizes reading as a major life activity. Bartlett v. New York Sate Bd. of Law Exam'rs, No. 97-9162, 2000 U.S. App. LEXIS 22212, at *23 (2d Cir. Aug. 30, 2000). The Third and Ninth Circuits have recognized interacting with others as a major life activity. Taylor v. Phoenixville Sch. Dist., 184 F.3d 296 (3d Cir. 1999); *McAlindin,* 192 F.3d

The problem with the requirement that an individual be substantially limited in major life activities, or be regarded as being so limited, is that it leaves open the possibility of "pure" discrimination, in which the adverse employment action is taken out of deep antipathy for the diagnosed condition rather than any mistaken perception of its effects on an individual's major life activities. This reaction is most likely to affect the very disabilities that are the subject of the greatest social disapprobation; perversely, the "substantial limitations" clause of the disability definition provides employers immunity to discriminate against the most stigmatized disabilities.

For example, in *Schwartz v. The Comex and New York Mercantile Exchange*,[27] an employee, Schwartz, who had worked for the defendant for five years, receiving promotions and raises, was terminated by the defendant after the plaintiff's supervisor, Jordan, learned that Schwartz had a psychiatric diagnosis.[28] Jordan remarked that the plaintiff would not have been hired had Jordan known of his mental illness. He ridiculed and harassed Schwartz because of his mental illness, culminating in the plaintiff's eventual termination. The court held that these allegations did not state a claim under the ADA. The reason for the court's holding was that

> Schwartz would have to allege facts that would indicate that because of Jordan's misperception of paranoid thought disorder, he treated plaintiff as unable to perform major life activities . . . Schwartz merely asserts that Jordan ridiculed and fired him, but he does not state that Jordan or COMEX regarded him as unable to work or perform any of the other major life activities described in the regulations. In fact, plaintiff alleges that COMEX rewarded him with raises and promotions throughout his five year tenure, in recognition of his capabilities . . . Schwartz cannot merely claim that his employer's perception of paranoid thought disorder was equivalent to a view that plaintiff was impaired in the performance of a major life activity.[29]

The equivalent of this logic in a race discrimination case would be a holding that an African American had not stated a claim because he alleged the employer had fired him solely because he was black, and not because the employer believed any associated stereotypes or misperceptions about blacks being lazy or unqualified. Schwartz did not request any kind of accommodation; he alleged that he was capable of doing his job well and was fired only because his employer learned he had mental illness. In fact, the wish of employers to exclude employees with the most stigmatized disabilities, such as mental illness or HIV seropositivity, may have nothing to do with the employer's assessment of employees' capacity to do the job and may not arise out of the employer's assumptions about the degree to which these people are substantially limited in major life activities.

---

at 1234. The First Circuit has both accepted it and rejected it. *Criado*, 145 F.3d at 442 (accepting); Soileau v. Guilford of Me., 105 F.3d 12 (1st Cir. 1997) (rejecting). The Third Circuit has recognized "thinking" as a major life activity, *Taylor*, 184 F.3d at 307. The Tenth Circuit has recognized "concentrating" as a life activity. *Pack*, 166 F.3d at 1305. The Ninth Circuit has recognized "engaging in sexual relations" as a major life activity, *McAlindin*, 192 F.3d at 1234.

[27] 1997 WL 187353 (S.D. N.Y. Apr. 15, 1997).

[28] Because this case was decided on the defendant's motion to dismiss, the court accepted the plaintiff's allegations as true.

[29] *Schwartz*, 1997 WL 187353, at *2.

These results, and many others like them, miss the crux of discrimination law. Discrimination law prohibits an employer from taking adverse action against an employee on the basis of an irrational antipathy toward his or her race, gender, or physical or mental condition *in addition to* taking actions based on a manifestly unjustifiable belief about the limitations that race, gender, or physical or mental condition place on the employee's abilities or performance. If an employer harbors an irrational discomfort, aversion, or antipathy toward a person on the basis of physical or mental condition, the employer's belief that the condition does not limit the employee's life activities should not excuse the employer, because his own antipathy limits the employee's working opportunities in a way the employee can do nothing to overcome.

Although the U.S. Supreme Court in *Nassau County v. Arline* and U.S. Congress in the ADA made clear their intention that someone excluded from a job because of an employer's irrational prejudice about his or her disability should be able to successfully claim that he or she was regarded as disabled, the Supreme Court recently retreated from this view in *Sutton v. United Airlines*. Both *Sutton* and the EEOC require a finding that an employer regard the employee as substantially limited across a class of jobs. This requirement has eviscerated most of the protection provided by the ADA to people discriminated against because they are regarded as being disabled.

The requirement that an employee be substantially limited in major life activities, or regarded to be substantially limited by the employer, is particularly problematic because it is often irrelevant to many disability-related prejudices, which arise primarily out of discomfort with difference. For example, the prejudice against psychiatric disabilities often takes the form of fear of violence[30]; perceiving someone to be violent does not necessarily mean perceiving them as substantially limited in one or more major life activities. Or, perversely, the prejudice often takes the form of an adamant belief that a person is not really limited in major life activities, but is simply self-indulgent and obnoxious[31] or prone to exaggeration of difficulty. A reporter for the *Washington Post* who returned to work after being hospitalized for depression reported the reactions of her coworkers: "Some people awkwardly changed the subject. Others tried to cover their discomfort with bluster. 'Well, snap out of it!' one person said cheerfully—implying, I guess, that feeling better was just a matter of trying harder."[32]

Psychiatric disabilities are not unique in this regard. Prejudice against conditions such as cancer and HIV infection is also not necessarily related to mistaken perceptions about limitations on major life activities.[33]

In fact, people with impairments, such as back conditions, heart conditions, and asthma, in which the principal question *is* whether an individual is erroneously perceived to be substantially limited in major life activities, are subject to a qualitatively

---

[30]In accounts in the popular media of opposition to the newly released EEOC guidelines on employer obligations to people with psychiatric disabilities under the ADA, lawyers and attorneys are quoted as worrying about workers who are violent or "going postal in the workplace," Terry Carter, "Unhappy to Oblige," *Am. Bar Ass'n J.* (July 1997): 37.

[31]One management lawyer accused the EEOC of promulgating regulations that would "permit jerks to claim disabling conditions," Carter, *id.* at n. 20.

[32]Tracy Thompson, *The Beast: A Reckoning With Depression* (New York: Putnam, 1990) at 206.

[33]Susan Sontag, *Illness as Metaphor* (New York: Farrar, Strauss & Giroux, 1978); *AIDS and Its Metaphors* (New York: Farrar, Strauss & Giroux, 1989).

different kind of discrimination than people whose conditions are perceived by others
to create such a difference as to be the primary aspect of the individual's identity.
The aversion and discomfort felt by employers and fellow employees toward people
with these disabilities transcend belief that a person is substantially limited in major
life activities. People's fear and discomfort in the presence of an individual with a
diagnosis of mental illness are not based on whether the individual can function but
on what he or she might do in the future, just as people's fear and discomfort in the
presence of someone diagnosed as HIV positive are not based on what that person
can or cannot do but on whether he or she is contagious.

It is precisely this sort of aversion that Congress repeatedly referred to and
intended to prohibit. In fact, in a study of professionals and managers in key decision-
making positions regarding employment, the extent of social distance[34] expressed
regarding various conditions and disabilities shows very little correlation between
unwillingness to work with an individual and the degree to which his or her condition
substantially limited one or more major life activities. Although these managers expressed a willingness to work with people who had heart disease, cancer, diabetes,
a stroke, polio, epilepsy, cerebral palsy, and paraplegia, they expressed an unwillingness to work with (in ascending order of their unwillingness) gay men or lesbians,
former convicts, people with mental illness, juvenile delinquents, alcoholics,[35] and
drug addicts.

Congress knew this. The repeated references in the legislative history to various
examples of discrimination bears it out. The woman with a master's degree in food
science and nutrition who ranked in the top 10% on the registered nutritionist examination was told that she would not be hired because her fellow employees would
not be comfortable with her cerebral palsy[36]; an auction house tried to forcibly remove a woman in a wheelchair not because the employees thought she could not
participate in the auction, but because she was "disgusting to look at"; the woman
with arthritis was denied a job "not because she could not do the work but because
'college trustees thought normal students shouldn't see her'."[37] In other words, these
people were discriminated against not because of other people's mistaken assessment
of their abilities or the degree to which their life activities were limited, but because
of other people's core discomfort with and aversion to their difference. Whether their
ability to undertake major life activities was substantially limited was not the cause
of the discrimination, but was at best a secondary attribute of the discriminatory
attitude and serves as a poor proxy to reflect it. More often than not, society has
preferred to think of its mistakes with disabled people as overcharitable paternalism
rather than loathing and contempt, but to articulate and follow an antidiscrimination
standard based on the former rather than the latter risks missing a lot of discriminatory activity.

The "substantial limitation" attributes too much rationality to the manner in
which people discriminate. In effect, it gives credit for a certain level of thought-

---

[34]The study asked the managers to rate a series of conditions: 2 (willingness to have the individual
as a regular friend), 3 (willingness to work beside the person), 5 (willingness to have the person as a
mere speaking acquaintance).

[35]The irony of these findings is, of course, that these managers probably work with more alcoholics
than any other group listed in the study.

[36]135 CONG. REC. S10720 (daily ed. Sept. 7, 1989) (statement of Sen. Harkin).

[37]Id.

fulness and analysis, when discrimination rarely proceeds past the level of noticing and recoiling from difference. Thus, it is no surprise that research has been showing for more than 30 years that people who are prejudiced against minorities or have a high level of ethnocentricity also tend to be prejudiced against people with disabilities.[38]

Conditions in which the disability is perceived to constitute a person's entire identity for the rest of society include blindness, deafness, paraplegia, and AIDS, which are easily recognized as disabilities by courts, as well as psychiatric disabilities, which are not.[39] Because blindness, deafness, and paraplegia form the unstated norm of disability law and because each often requires some form of reasonable accommodation, many courts have assumed that without a request for reasonable accommodation, a plaintiff somehow is not substantially limited in a major life activity. This is true despite the EEOC's admonition that limitations in work should be considered last, not first, in assessing limitations on major life activities.[40] Thus, an individual who is known to be diagnosed with one of the most socially despised conditions, such as mental illness or HIV seropositivity, may be excluded from the protections of the ADA, despite the adverse reactions of others because he or she did not ask for accommodations but simply for the opportunity to do the job.

Thus, in some ways, the requirement of substantial limitation on major life activities, or perception by others of such limitation, serves as a terrible punishment and disincentive to people with invisible disabilities, such as psychiatric disabilities, who by enormous efforts and courage have managed to function in spite of their disabilities[41] and are in effect told by the courts that their efforts prove they are not disabled at all. In *Olson v. General Electric,* the 3rd Circuit Court concluded that "Olson's ability to function normally despite what appear to be serious psychological and emotional problems defeats [his claim that he is disabled under the ADA]."[42] This is the same as telling Tom Dolan, the American swimmer with asthma who won a gold medal at the 1996 Olympics, that he could not have asthma because otherwise he would not have won the gold medal or telling Wilma Rudolph that she really did not have polio because she won a gold medal, at the Olympics. It is the

---

[38]For a thorough collection of the research supporting this, *see* Clark Freshman, "Whatever Happened to Anti-Semitism?: How Social Science Theories Identify Discrimination and Promote 'Coalition' Between 'Different' Minorities," *Cornell Law Rev.* 85 (Jan. 2000): 313.

[39]One useful (although hardly perfect) test for whether a disability is one that is perceived to overpower an individual's identity is to ask whether it is the sort of disability that makes strangers and acquaintances avoid talking to the individual. Another is to look at linguistic constructions to see whether people are identified in terms of the disability: those who are blind, deaf, have a mental illness, are mentally retarded.

[40]29 C.F.R. 1630 Pt. App. § 1630.2(j) (2000).

[41]The term *self-accommodation* has been coined to describe the efforts people make privately to deal with their disabilities. Examples of self-accommodation include both conscious and unconscious adaptations by the person with disabilities. Unconscious adaptations are exemplified by people with monocular vision. *See, e.g.,* Albertson's Inc. v. Kirkingburg, 527 U.S. 555 (1999); Wilson v. Pa. State Police Dep't, 964 F. Supp. 898 (E.D. Pa. 1997); Bartlett v. N.Y. State Bd. of Law Exam'r, 156 F.3d 321 (2d Cir. 1998) (finding that a person with a reading disability or dyslexia through self-accommodation achieved average reading skills when compared with the general population); Doane v. City of Omaha, 115 F.3d 624, 627 (8th Cir. 1997) (finding a police officer blinded in one eye self-accommodated or subconsciously adjusted himself to the impairment; his brain mitigated the effects of the impairment).

[42]101 F.3d 947, 953 (3d Cir. 1996).

•

very reverse of what Congress sought to accomplish in passing the ADA: to recognize people's transcendent abilities, not their disabilities.[43]

In a number of cases, courts have explicitly premised a finding that the plaintiff
was not disabled on the fact that he or she made it to work on time, did not take
leaves of absence, and asked for no accommodations. In one case, a plaintiff had
colitis and depression.[44] The plaintiff was hospitalized for two weeks for her depression, was in therapy, and took medication. However, the court found that

> while it is true that plaintiff missed two weeks of work because of her depression
> when she was admitted to Four Winds Hospital in 1994, there is no credible evidence
> on the record that her ability to perform her job was "substantially limited" because
> of her depression. Plaintiff alleges that her depression caused her to lose sleep and as
> a result she would be exhausted at work and cry. Plaintiff testified at her deposition,
> however, that apart from the two-week hospital stay, she never missed work because
> of her depression. The cases where depression has been held to substantially interfere
> with an individual's ability to work involve factual situations far more serious than
> the case at hand . . . plaintiffs were repeatedly hospitalized, took numerous or extended
> leaves of absence from work, and depression repeatedly interfered with the plaintiff's
> ability to get to work on time and perform effectively.[45]

In fact, in cases in which plaintiffs are tardy or take too many leaves of absence,
they are generally found to be unable to meet the essential elements of the job.[46] So
when a plaintiff's efforts to conceal a disability are reasonably successful, the plaintiff is not disabled. When a plaintiff's struggles to conceal a disability are less successful, or, in a specific case, when a plaintiff revealed her disability under the
mistaken impression that her employer would be sympathetic,[47] the plaintiff also
loses the case because he or she is considered not otherwise qualified for the position.[48]

Even when plaintiffs both perform the requirements of their jobs and manifest
their psychiatric disabilities, courts have found other ways of finding that they are
not disabled as a matter of law. For example, although the EEOC has made clear in
its *Compliance Manual* that "interacting with others" is a major life activity,[49] several
courts have questioned or rejected this interpretation.[50] It is particularly ironic for
courts to hold that interacting with others is not a major life activity, because a
substantial number of decisions finding plaintiffs with psychiatric disabilities not
otherwise qualified for employment do so on the grounds that "getting along with
others" is an essential function, not only of the job in question but also of employ-

---

[43] 135 CONG. REC. 19, 801 (1989).

[44] Johnson v. New York Medical College, 1997 U.S. Dist. LEXIS 14150 (S.D. N.Y. Sept. 18, 1997).
The colitis caused "cramping, rectal bleeding, lower back pain, diarrhea, mucous, explosive stool, tired-
ness and nausea," as well as "accidents" if she could not get to the bathroom on time.

[45] *Id.* at *17.

[46] Waggoner v. Olin Corp., 169 F.3d 481 (7th Cir. 1999); Scarborough v. Runyon, 1996 U.S. App.
LEXIS 19948 (7th Cir. Aug. 2, 1996). *See* further discussion in chapter 8.

[47] Doe v. Region 13 Mental Health-Mental Retardation Commission, 704 F.2d 1402 (5th Cir. 1983).

[48] Palmer v. Circuit Court, 117 F.3d 351 (7th Cir. 1997).

[49] *EEOC Compliance Manual*, 902.3(b) (Washington, DC: Bureau of Labor Statistics, 1999).

[50] Soileau v. Guilford of Maine, 105 F.3d 12, 15 (1st Cir. 1997); Breiland v. Advance Circuits, 1997
U.S. Dist. LEXIS 14424 (D. Minn. Sept. 16, 1997).

ment in general.[51] Therefore, courts hold that "getting along with others" is not a major life activity, so that a plaintiff who is substantially limited in this activity cannot be considered disabled but also hold that it *is* an essential element of employment, so that a person with this limitation is not "otherwise qualified" for work. This is an unfair paradox. A substantial limitation in any activity that is considered to be an essential element of employment generally must be a substantial limitation of the major life activity of work.

Origins of the Requirement of Substantial Limitation on Major Life Activities

Although race discrimination laws were written from the outset to prevent discrimination, the origin of the definition of disability used in the ADA was in legislation designed to provide vocational benefits and services on the basis of disability. This affected the definition of handicap in a way that disability discrimination law scholars and policy makers have not considered.

The main purpose of the Rehabilitation Act of 1973 was to redirect vocational rehabilitation services to people with the most severe impairments, because vocational rehabilitation services had been assisting less severely impaired people. The definition of *handicapped* that was adopted in 1973 ("any individual who (i) has a physical or mental disability which for such individual constitutes or results in a substantial handicap to employment and (ii) can reasonably be expected to benefit in terms of employability from vocational rehabilitation services"[52]) was written to define the class of people who could receive vocational rehabilitation benefits, but it did not fit well as a definition of people to be protected from disability discrimination. Definitions that demarcate a class to receive federal services and benefits are intended to be narrow; definitions to prohibit discrimination can be much broader.

Congress recognized as much. In 1974, in an attempt to clarify that not only did the antidiscrimination provision apply to people who were handicapped but to those with a history of a handicap or who were regarded as handicapped, Congress introduced the current definition, which applied only to the antidiscrimination provisions of the Rehabilitation Act. However, rather than writing a new definition entirely, the drafters of the 1974 amendments chose to revise the old standard to broaden it. At that time, Congress made clear that it intended to prohibit discrimination against any person who was handicapped, not just recipients of vocational rehabilitation services. Indeed, the legislative history explicitly indicated that people who were not handicapped at all, but only perceived as handicapped, were intended to be covered by the antidiscrimination provisions. The legislative history equated Section 504 with Title VI of the Civil Rights Act of 1964. Referring to the expansion of the definition of handicapped to include those who were regarded as being handicapped, the Senate Committee on Labor and Public Welfare stated that this definition was intended to

---

[51]McAlindin v. County of San Diego, 192 F.3d 1226, 1235 (9th Cir. 1999). *See also* Stauffer v. Bayer Corp., 1997 WL 588890 (N.D. Ind. 1997); *EEOC Enforcement Guidance: The Americans With Disabilities Act and Psychiatric Disabilities* at n. 15 (March 25, 1997).

[52]Section 706(8)(A) of the Rehabilitation Act of 1973.

include those persons who are discriminated against on the basis of handicap, whether
or not they are in fact handicapped, just as Title VI of the Civil Rights Act of 1964
prohibits discrimination on the grounds of race, whether or not the person discriminated against is in fact a member of a racial minority.[53]

In 1978, Congress underscored the connection with Title VI of the Civil Rights Act
by amending the Rehabilitation Act to make available "the remedies, procedures and
rights set forth in Title VI to *any person* aggrieved by any act or failure to act by
any recipient of federal assistance or Federal provider of such assistance under Section 794 of this chapter."[54]

As a practical matter, one of the reasons to require that an impairment substantially limit a plaintiff in one or more major life activities was because regulations to
the Rehabilitation Act, promulgated in 1977,[55] required that employers reasonably
accommodate the known disabilities of employees. Because reasonable accommodations required alterations and expenditures on the part of employers, there was an
understandable desire to limit the people who could claim those accommodations to
those who were substantially limited in one or more major life activities.[56]

Defendants in Section 504 cases rarely contested the issue of whether a plaintiff
was handicapped under the Act.[57] This was not because plaintiffs under Section 504
had more serious disabilities than did ADA plaintiffs. Plaintiffs were found to be
disabled under the Rehabilitation Act with disabilities identical to those found by
later courts to not constitute disabilities under the ADA: asbestosis,[58] asthma,[59] cancer,[60] rheumatoid arthritis,[61] diabetes,[62] heart attack and lumbar disc disease,[63] multiple sclerosis,[64] and having only one eye.[65]

---

[53] S. Rep. No. 93-1297, at 39 (1974).

[54] The Rehabilitation, Comprehensive Services, and Disability Discrimination Act of 1978 added
Section 794a(a)(2) (emphasis added).

[55] The administration was extremely reluctant to issue these regulations, and did so only after ac-
tivists occupied the office of the Secretary of Health, Education, and Welfare (HEW), Joseph Califano;
occupied the regional office of HEW in San Francisco for almost a month, *see* Joseph Shapiro, *No Pity:
People With Disabilities Forging a New Civil Rights Movement* (New York: Times Books, 1994), and a
federal court ordered HEW to issue the regulations, Cherry v. Mathews, 419 F. Supp. 922 (D. D.C.
1976).

[56] *See, e.g.,* "Excerpts From Secretary Joseph A. Califano's Preamble to Section 504 Regulations,
Title 45 Public Welfare," "Legal Rights of Mentally Disabled Persons," *Mental Health Law Project*
Vol. 2 (Washington, DC: Practicing Law Institute, 1979) at 1473, 1478.

[57] The most common defenses raised under the Rehabilitation Act centered on whether the act
provided a private right of action; whether the employer received federal funds as required under the
act; and whether liability depended on the federal funds being intended principally to assist employment.
The Supreme Court held that they did not in Conrail v. Darrone, 465 U.S. 624 (1984). It is telling that
the ALR Annotation, "Who Is an Individual With Handicaps Under the Rehabilitation Act of 1973?"
(97 A.L.R. Fed. 40) (1990) did not appear until 1990, and was preceded by several annotations related
to private right of action (60 A.L.R. Fed. 329) (1982) and the applicability of the Rehabilitation Act to
specified programs or activities (44 A.L.R. Fed. 148) (1979).

[58] *Cf.* Fynes v. Weinberger, 677 F. Supp. 315 (E.D. Pa. 1985), *with* Robinson v. Global Marine
Drilling, 101 F.3d 35, 36 (5th Cir. 1996) (the plaintiff with 50% reduction in lung capacity due to
asbestosis was not disabled under ADA).

[59] *Cf.* Jennings v. Alexander, 715 F.2d 1036 (6th Cir. 1983), *with* Ventura v. City of Independence,
1997 U.S. App. LEXIS 4102 (6th Cir. 1997) (the plaintiff with asthma was not substantially limited in
major life activities).

[60] *Cf.* Harrison v. Marsh, 691 F. Supp. 1223 (W.D. Mo. 1988) (the plaintiff with breast cancer

Courts have also increasingly ruled that severe, chronic illnesses, including cancer, are not disabilities under the ADA, and perceptions of serious illness that result in demotion or termination are not perceptions of disability under the ADA.[66] The 7th Circuit Court held that an employee who alleged that she was fired because she was perceived by her employer as having a serious medical condition did not state a claim under the ADA.[67] "If an employer discriminates against [employees] on account of their being (or being believed by him to be) ill, even permanently ill, but not disabled, there is no violation [of the ADA]." Although Judge Richard Posner was not explicit, his disjunction of "ill, even permanently ill" and "disabled" can only be explained by reference to the requirement of substantial limitation on major life activities, because permanent illness must surely be considered an impairment.[68]

It is difficult to exaggerate the extent to which courts are stretching the concept

---

had handicap), *with* Ellison v. Software Spectrum Inc., 85 F.3d 187, 189 (5th Cir. 1996) (the plaintiff with breast cancer was not disabled under ADA); Malewski v. Nationsbank of Florida, 978 F. Supp. 1095 (S.D. Fla. 1997) (the plaintiff with breast cancer was not disabled under ADA); Madjlessi v. Macy's West, 993 F. Supp. 736 (N.D. Cal. 1997) (the plaintiff with breast cancer was not disabled under ADA).

[61] *Cf.* Gelman v. Department of Education, 544 F. Supp. 651 (D. Colo. 1982) (the plaintiff with rheumatoid arthritis had handicap), *with* Sutton v. New Mexico Department of Children, Youth and Families, 922 F. Supp. 516 (D. N.M. 1996) (the plaintiff with degenerative arthritis requiring walker and surgery was not disabled under the ADA).

[62] *Cf.* Commonwealth DOT v. Tinsley, 564 A.2d 286 (Pa. 1989) (diabetes is a handicap under Section 504), *with* McCall v. Myrtle Beach Hospital, 1997 U.S. App. LEXIS 23745 (4th Cir. Sept. 10, 1997); Deckert v. City of Ulysses, 1995 U.S. Dist. LEXIS 14526 (D. Kan. Sept. 6, 1995) (diabetes is not a disability under the ADA).

[63] Kelly v. Metropolitan Atlanta Rapid Transit Authority, 1982 U.S. Dist. LEXIS 14308 (N.D. Ga. Mar. 31, 1982).

[64] *Cf.* Hutchings v. City and County Library, 516 F. Supp. 1265 (dormant multiple sclerosis is a handicap under the Rehabilitation Act), *with* Sorensen v. University of Utah Hospital, 12 N.D.L.R. 144 (D. Utah 1998) (active multiple sclerosis is not a disability under the ADA).

[65] *Cf.* Holly v. City of Naperville, 603 F. Supp. 220, 229 (N.D. Ill. 1985) (noting that the plaintiff who was blind in one eye was handicapped), *with* Hallums v. Coca Cola Bottling Co., 874 S.W.2d 30, 32 (Tenn. Ct. App. 1993) (finding the plaintiff's monocular vision did not constitute a handicap under the ADA); Santiago v. Temple Univ., 739 F. Supp. 974, 978 (E.D. Pa. 1990) (holding that partial loss of vision in one eye is not a handicap under the ADA); *and* Still v. Freeport-McMoran, Inc., 120 F.3d 50, 52 (5th Cir. 1997) (holding that the plaintiff who was blind in one eye was not disabled under the ADA).

[66] EEOC v. Gallagher, 959 F. Supp. 405 (S.D. Tex. 1997).

[67] Christian v. St. Anthony Medical Center, 117 F.3d 1051 (7th Cir. 1997). The plaintiff's alternate allegation, that she was fired because of the cost of the treatment to the employer's health plan was also held, without citation to any relevant ADA case law, regulation, or legislative history, not to state a claim. In fact, ADA case law, regulations, and legislative history all stand for the proposition that such an allegation states a claim under the ADA. 29 C.F.R. app. § 1630.15(a) (1999); H.R. Rep. No. 101-485, pt. 3, at 70 (1990); S. Rep. No. 101-116 at 85 (1989).

[68] Although the ADA does not define impairment, the regulations have defined impairment as: (a) any physiological disorder, or condition, cosmetic disfigurement, or anatomical loss affecting one or more of the following body systems: neurological, musculoskeletal, special sense organs, respiratory (including speech organs), cardiovascular, reproductive, digestive, genito-urinary, hemic and lymphatic, skin, and endocrine, or (b) any mental or psychological disorder, such as mental retardation, organic brain syndrome, emotional or mental illness, and specific learning disabilities. 29 C.F.R. § 1630.2(1) (2000).

of not being disabled. The *reductio ad absurdum* of the courts' insistence on finding plaintiffs not substantially limited in a major life activity is the number of cases in which plaintiffs are found not to be disabled under the ADA even though they died during the pendency of the litigation,[69] including plaintiffs with terminal cancer.[70] In spite of the U.S. Supreme Court's decision in favor of the plaintiff in *Arline,* courts have found people with tuberculosis not to be disabled for the purposes of the ADA,[71] in effect rejecting *Arline.* In fact, if anything, plaintiffs under the Rehabilitation Act had less severe impairments than ADA plaintiffs: a "very mild case of petit mal epilepsy,"[72] a "slight hearing loss and balance problem."[73]

This is equally true in the area of psychiatric disability. Under the Rehabilitation Act, a past history of "schizophrenic reaction"[74] sufficed to qualify the plaintiff as handicapped, because the focus was on whether the defendant discriminated against the plaintiff, not on whether the plaintiff was handicapped. Under the ADA, plaintiffs with depression, bipolar disorder, and even paranoid schizophrenia have been held to not be disabled because they are not substantially limited in a major life activity.[75]

Thus, Congress had little reason to believe when it passed the ADA that the "substantial limitation in major life activities" language would be used by courts to exclude claims of discrimination by individuals with virtually identical conditions under the ADA.[76] Although Congress did instruct that the ADA could not be read to grant less protection than Section 504 of the Rehabilitation Act,[77] it is clear that this is what is happening on a systemic level. The Supreme Court has recently reiterated the command that the ADA must not be read to give less protection than the Rehabilitation Act.[78] Yet because ADA cases are decided one at a time on a highly fact-specific basis, it is difficult to make this argument in any individual case. Nevertheless, the number of times a plaintiff found to be handicapped under the Rehabilitation Act can be "twinned" with a losing ADA case presenting the same disability is startling.

---

[69]Jerina v. Richardson Automotive, Inc., 960 F. Supp. 106 (N.D. Tex. 1997).

[70]Hirsch v. National Mall & Serv. Co., 989 F. Supp. 977, 980 (N.D. Ill. 1997); EEOC v. R. J. Gallagher, 959 F. Supp. 405, 409 (S.D. Tex. 1997).

[71]Lester v. Trans World Airlines, Inc., 1997 U.S. Dist. LEXIS 10857, at *20 n. 11 (N.D. Ill. July 23, 1997).

[72]Cain v. Archdiocese, 508 F. Supp. 1021 (D.C. Kan. 1981).

[73]Lemmo v. Willson, 583 F. Supp. 557 (D.C. Colo. 1984).

[74]Doe v. Syracuse School District, 508 F. Supp. 333 ("Plaintiff's ability to meet the definition of a handicapped individual is unchallenged.").

[75]Patterson v. Chicago Association for Retarded Citizens, 15 F.3d 719 (7th Cir. 1998) (a teacher with paranoid schizophrenia was not disabled).

[76]Madjlessi v. Macy's W, Inc., 993 F. Supp. 736 (N.D. Cal. 1997) (plaintiff with cancer undergoing treatment not disabled); Still v. Freeport-McMoran, 120 F.3d 50 (5th Cir. 1997) (plaintiff with one eye not disabled under the ADA); *in re* Hamilton, 122 F.3d 13 (7th Cir. 1997) (plaintiff with two heart attacks not regarded as disabled under the ADA). Interestingly, courts that find that an impairment amounts to a disability almost always cite to Rehabilitation Act precedent. However, in the wake of ADA cases, some judges are now deciding that plaintiffs are not disabled under the Rehabilitation Act, *see, e.g.,* McCarter v. West, 910 F. Supp. 519 (D. Kan. 1995) (individual with multiple sclerosis fibromyalgia, and chronic back pain not "disabled" under Section 501).

[77]S. Rep. No. 101-116, at 84 (1989).

[78]Bragdon v. Abbott, 524 U.S. 624 (1998).

Differences Between Congressional Intentions Regarding Substantial Limitations on Major Life Activities and Court Interpretations

It is true that under the ADA Congress intended to exclude plaintiffs with "minor" or "trivial" conditions from the protections of disability discrimination law. Unlike race and gender, disability can exist across a wide spectrum from trivial and minor to extremely severe, requiring some kind of line drawing to identify those who should be protected against discrimination. However, although Congress used infected fingers and the common cold as examples of "handicaps" that would not be covered by the law prohibiting disability discrimination,[79] courts have recently found plaintiffs with asbestosis, hemophilia,[80] HIV infection,[81] breast cancer,[82] and prostate cancer[83] not to be disabled because the plaintiff was not substantially limited in major life activities or not perceived to be limited in major life activities. An employee who was diagnosed with Hodgkin's disease underwent several surgeries, was treated with radiation, saw a psychologist for major depression, and could not stay at work full time after he returned because he was so ill was found not to be disabled.[84] This is obviously not what Congress intended in passing the ADA. The legislative history makes it clear that Congress considered many impairments to be per se disabilities, including blindness,[85] paraplegia,[86] mental retardation,[87] HIV infection,[88] cancer,[89] and perhaps epilepsy.[90]

Congress also made clear that an inquiry into whether a person was substantially limited in the major life activity of working should only take place if the individual was not substantially limited in any other major life activity. The EEOC followed congressional guidance when it promulgated regulations requiring courts to make findings of substantial limitations in working only if the individual was not substan-

---

[79] S. Rep. No. 101-116, at 23 (1989).

[80] Bridges v. City of Bossier, 92 F.3d 329 (5th Cir. 1996).

[81] Runnebaum v. NationsBank of Maryland, N.A., 123 F.3d 156 (4th Cir. 1997). (en banc).

[82] Ellison v. Software Spectrum, 1996 WL 284969 (5th Cir. May 30, 1996).

[83] Bumstead v. Jasper County, 931 F. Supp. 1323 (E.D. Tex. 1996).

[84] Nave v. Woolridge Construction of Pennsylvania, 10 N.D.L.R. 183 (E.D. Pa. 1997).

[85] "For example . . . a person who is blind is substantially limited in the major life activity of seeing." H.R. Rep. No. 101-485, pt. 3, at 28 (1990).

[86] "For example, a paraplegic is substantially limited in the major life activity of walking." H.R. Rep. No. 101-485, pt. 3, at 28 (1990).

[87] "For example . . . a person who is mentally retarded is substantially limited in the major life activity of learning." H.R. Rep. No. 101-485, pt. 3, at 28 (1990).

[88] "Persons infected with the Human Immunodeficiency Virus are considered to have an impairment which substantially limits a major life activity, and thus are considered disabled under the first test of this definition." See Memorandum of Arthur B. Culvahouse, Jr., Counsel to the President, from Douglas W. Kmiec, Acting Assistant Attorney General, Office of Legal Counsel, Department of Justice (Sept. 27, 1988) at 3, reprinted in Hearings on S. 933, the ADA, before the Committee on Labor and Human Resources, S. Rep. No. 101-156, at 346 (1990) and H.R. Rep. No. 101-485, pt. 3, at 28 n. 16 (1990).

[89] In describing the meaning of disability defined as "a record of an impairment" the House Judiciary Committee noted that "This test is intended to cover those who have a record of an impairment. This includes a person who has a history of an impairment that substantially limited a major life activity, such as those who have recovered from an impairment . . . Examples include a person who had, but no longer has, cancer." Id. at 29.

[90] "For example, a person with epilepsy, an impairment which substantially limits a major life activity." Id. at 28.

tially limited by his or her impairment in any other major life activity. Whereas many courts have explicitly recognized and followed this requirement, a growing number of courts are ruling against plaintiffs who cannot show that their substantial limitations, such as substantial limitations in sleep, affect their work performance.[91] This clearly misreads legal requirements. It is particularly perverse in that it punishes employees who struggle with loss of sleep and other limitations to still accomplish work objectives.

Congress flatly stated that "a person with an impairment who is discriminated against in employment is also limited in the major life activity of working."[92] The only exception recognized by Congress to this very explicit and broad instruction was a very narrow one:

> A person who is limited in his or her ability to perform a particular job, *because of circumstances unique to that job site or the materials used*, may not be substantially limited in the major life activity of working. For example, an applicant whose trade is painting would not be substantially limited in the major life activity of working if he has a mild allergy to a specialized paint used by one employer which is not generally used in the field in which the painter works.[93]

Note that even this narrow exception applies to a situation where the plaintiff claims an inability to work at a particular job (and therefore presumably a reasonable accommodation), not a situation where the plaintiff's position is that he or she *can* do the job with no accommodation whatsoever.[94]

In fact, in *Arline v. Nassau County School Board,* the Supreme Court noted that even if an individual's impairment did not substantially limit major life activities, the negative reactions of others "could nevertheless substantially limit that person's ability to work."[95] It underscored that "society's accumulated myths and fears about disability and disease are as handicapping as the physical limitations that flow from the actual impairment."[96] Congress cited *Arline* approvingly at several junctures in the legislative history of the ADA. The requirement that the employee be substantially limited in one or more major life activities, or be perceived as such by the employer, creates a difficulty that could be overcome by faithful adherence to *Arline* and the legislative history.

Conclusion

The courts' use of the "substantial limitations" language of the ADA to preclude consideration of disability discrimination cases has been criticized in legal scholar-

---

[91] Cody v. CIGNA Healthcare of St. Louis, Inc., 139 F.3d 595 (8th Cir. 1998).

[92] H.R. Rep. No. 101-485, pt. 3, at 29 (1990).

[93] *Id.*

[94] The continuation of the example makes it clear that Congress saw this example as a reasonable accommodation situation. *Id.*

[95] School Board of Nassau County v. Arline, 480 U.S. 273, 283 (1987).

[96] *Id.* at 284.

ship,[97] federal agency oversight, and congressional hearings, and by attorneys in the field. Several short- and long-term solutions to this problem are possible.

In the short term, plaintiffs' attorneys have to be ready for this argument and prepared to furnish evidence to defeat it. Plaintiffs' attorneys can maximize the chance that the client will be found disabled by showing that the plaintiffs' disability substantially limits their ability to care for themselves or to sleep, concentrate,[98] think, or interact socially. These limitations should be experienced in the plaintiffs' everyday life, not only in the workplace. They should show that the condition has affected past employment and past social interactions, and not only the current work environment. The plaintiff's expert should testify at length about the condition and how the nature of the condition will likely affect future employment and future life activities. Cases have survived motions for summary judgment when the plaintiff underscores the biological nature of the disability (often depression or bipolar disorder) and emphasizes that it is a long-term, if not a life-long, condition.[99]

Another possible solution is to resort more often to state antidiscrimination statutes, which have been proving more successful for plaintiffs claiming employment discrimination. In an increasing number of cases, plaintiffs who lose ADA claims because they are found not to be substantially limited in major life activities or regarded as such retain state claims under differently worded state antidiscrimination laws[100]; some plaintiffs choose to proceed under state laws alone. These state laws do not contain a substantial limitation clause, yet they appear to be successful at warding off claims based on broken fingers and bad colds. For example, the State of Washington requires proof that the plaintiff "1) had an abnormal condition and 2) was discriminated against because of the abnormal condition."[101] The State of New Jersey defines *handicapped* as meaning "suffering from any mental, psychological, physiological or neurological condition which prevents the normal exercise of any bodily or mental functions or is demonstrable, medically or psychologically, by accepted clinical or laboratory diagnostic techniques."[102]

---

[97]R. Bales, "Once is Enough: Evaluating When a Person Is Substantially Limited in Her Ability to Work," *Hofstra Labor Law J.* 11 (1993): 203; Steven S. Locke, "The Incredible Shrinking Protected Class: Redefining the Scope of Disability Under the Americans With Disabilities Act," *University of Colo. Law Rev.* 68 (1996): 107; Arlene Mayerson, "Restoring Regard for the 'Regarded As' Prong: Giving Effect to Congressional Intent," *Villanova Law Rev.* 42 (1997): 587; Robert Burgdorf, Jr., " 'Substantially Limited' Protection from Disability Discrimination: The Special Treatment Model and Misconstructions of the Definition of Disability," *Villanova Law Rev.* 42 (1997): 409.

[98]Although the 10th Circuit recently held that concentration was not a major life activity, Pack v. K-Mart, 166 F.3d 1300 (10th Cir. 1999), most courts have followed the EEOC's *Enforcement Guidance* in holding that it is, Glowacki v. Buffalo General Hospital, 2 F. Supp. 2d 346 (W.D. N.Y. 1998).

[99]*See, e.g.,* Krocka v. Bransfield, 969 F. Supp. 1073 (N.D. Ill. 1997)

[100]Olson v. G. E. Astrospace, 966 F. Supp. 312 (plaintiff with "dissociative condition" that "appears to be nearly life-long in duration and has been evidenced in his adult life by several acute psychiatric hospitalizations" is not disabled under the ADA because no substantial limitation in major life activities, but qualified under New Jersey's Law Against Discrimination); Reeves v. Johnson Controls World Services, 140 F.3d 144 (2d Cir. 1998) (plaintiff's panic disorder not a disability under the ADA because "everyday mobility" not a major life activity but plaintiff stated a claim under state law).

[101]Doe v. Boeing Co., 846 P.2d 531 (Wash. 1993) (construing the Washington State Discrimination Statute, RCW 49.60.010 et seq).

[102]N.J.S.A. 10:5–5(q). In interpreting this law, the New Jersey courts have explicitly ruled that it does not contain a "substantial limitations" requirement, Gimello v. Agency Rent-A-Car Systems, 594 A.2d 264 (N.J. App. Div. 1991).

Another solution is to amend the ADA to discard the substantial limitation in major life activity clause in "pure" employment discrimination cases, in which the employee is not asking for any accommodations. The substantial limitation requirement makes sense as a parallel to the reasonable accommodation requirement imposed on employers. If employers must spend money or readjust their policies and practices, then there is an understandable incentive to reasonably limit the number of people who can assert such claims. When an employee is not asking for accommodations, but simply to be treated like everyone else, it is illogical to require the employee to prove substantial limitations on major life activities, because the employee's argument in effect centers around the absence of any limitations relevant to the employment.[103]

---

[103] *E.g.*, in Ellison v. Software Spectrum, 85 F.3d 187 (5th Cir. 1996), the court refused to find that the plaintiff, who had been diagnosed with breast cancer and undergone radiation treatments, was disabled because "no special accommodations were necessary for Ellison, and that at all times, she had demonstrated the physical and mental ability to work . . . she never missed a day of work." The court also refused to find any material fact in dispute about whether her employer regarded her as disabled, in spite of the fact that "During a meeting in 1994 in which the departmental reduction was discussed, a member of the human resources department asked whether any of the potentially affected employees had special circumstances that needed to be considered, her employer responded 'Phyllis has cancer.' "

Chapter 5
"RECORD OF DISABILITY" AND "REGARDED AS HAVING A DISABILITY"

Many respondents to this book's survey echoed both social science research and case law when they concluded that the worst discrimination resulted from being labeled with a mental illness rather than from a reaction to any conduct or impairment on their part. As one respondent wrote, "some people assume that if someone was *ever* diagnosed as some kind of 'mental patient,' they must indeed be one *and* must be different all their life."[1] This respondent was rejected from a job "for no other reason except that I had been psychiatrically labeled."[2]

The response above shows the interconnected nature of having a history of disability and being regarded as disabled. Each of these provides a basis for protection under the Americans With Disabilities Act (ADA). The similarities and differences between these two provisions of the ADA and the way in which courts have interpreted them are discussed below.

Record of Disability

Both Section 504 of the Rehabilitation Act and the ADA protect people who have a record of disability or who have been misclassified as having a disability.[3] The Equal Employment Opportunity Commission (EEOC) has indicated that "this part of the definition is satisfied if a record relied on by an employer indicates that the individual has or has had a substantially limiting impairment."[4] Discrimination on the basis of a record of disability is greatly feared by people with histories of psychiatric hospitalization. In fact, Congress specifically had psychiatric and developmental disabilities in mind when it originally developed the idea of prohibiting discrimination on the basis of a record of disability.[5] The EEOC's *Technical Assistance Manual* echoes the association between psychiatric disability and discrimination on the basis

---

[1] Survey No. 8 (emphasis in original).

[2] *Id.*

[3] 42 U.S.C. § 12102(2)(B) (West 2000).

[4] 29 C.F.R. app. § 1630(2)(K).

[5] Both the legislative history of the ADA and the legislative history of the Rehabilitation Act specifically mention "people with histories of mental or emotional illness" as an example of the kind of people covered under the second prong of the definition of disability. *See, e.g.,* H.R. Rep. 101-485, pt. 2 at 52 and 53 (1990). When Congress first modified the definition of *handicap* in the Rehabilitation Act's prohibition of discrimination on the basis of handicap to include "record of handicap," the Senate Report noted that "Clause B [as a record of such an impairment] is intended to make clear that the coverage of Sections 503 and 504 extends to persons who have recovered—in whole or in part—from a handicapping illness, such as mental or neurological illness." S. Rep. No. 93-1297, at 40 (1974), *reprinted in 1974*, U.S.C.C.A.N. 6373.

of a record of disability.[6] Many people with serious psychiatric disabilities have been hospitalized, and before the passage of the ADA, employers routinely used questions about histories of hospitalization, especially psychiatric hospitalization, to screen out potential employees. This was recognized by Congress as one of the most potent forms of discrimination on the basis of a record of disability.

But what does it take to show a record of disability? Courts have made clear that a record of a diagnosis alone is insufficient to establish a record of disability under the ADA.[7] A record of treatment for an impairment is also insufficient.[8] One court has even held that taking leaves of absence for treatment of a psychiatric condition is insufficient to establish a record of disability.[9] The Supreme Court did state in *Nassau County v. Arline*[10] that "this impairment [tuberculosis] was serious enough to require hospitalization, a fact more than sufficient to establish that one or more of her major life activities were substantially limited by her impairment."[11]

It is ironic, then, that many courts have rejected hospitalizations, even extended hospitalizations with even longer recovery periods at home, as constituting a sufficient basis to establish a record of disability under the ADA.[12] This is particularly true in the 5th Circuit Court, where a ruling in favor of a plaintiff in an ADA case is as rare as a sighting of a whooping crane. The 5th Circuit has held as a matter of law that a plaintiff who had surgery to replace both hips and shoulders and missed more than a year of work while recovering did not establish a record of disability,[13] and that an injury and surgery that resulted in an inability to work for two years did not establish a record of disability.[14] The 2nd Circuit has held that a man who had a cerebral hemorrhage requiring 30 days in the hospital and 6 months bed rest at home did not establish a record of disability, calling it merely "a seven month impairment of his ability to work."[15] Following this opinion, a district court reluctantly held that hospitalization and treatment for breast cancer did not constitute a record of disability.[16]

---

[6]EEOC *Technical Assistance Manual,* 2.2(b) (1992) (referring to the "history of disability" prong as "also protect[ing] people with a history of mental illness").

[7]Davidson v. Midelfort Clinic, 133 F.3d 499, 510, n. 7 (7th Cir. 1998); Olson v. G. E. Astrospace, 101 F.3d 947 (3d Cir. 1996).

[8]Burch v. Coca-Cola, 119 F.3d 305, 321 (5th Cir. 1997).

[9]Mastio v. Wausau Service Corp., 948 F. Supp. 1396 (E.D. Mo. 1996) (two leaves of absence for posttraumatic stress disorder and clinical depression was insufficient as a matter of law to meet the requirement of a record of impairment that substantially limited one or more major life activities).

[10]480 U.S. 273 (1987).

[11]*Id.* at 281.

[12]Burch v. Coca-Cola 119 F.3d 305, 317 (5th Cir. 1997); Taylor v. U.S. Postal Service, 946 F.2d 1214, 1217 (6th Cir. 1991) (*Arline* should not be read for the "nonsensical proposition" that any hospital stay is enough to establish a record of impairment); Olson v. G. E. Astrospace, 101 F.3d 947, 952 (3d Cir. 1996); Horwitz v. L. and J. G. Stickley, 2000 U.S. Dist. LEXIS 17316 (N.D. N.Y. Nov. 30, 2000) (two psychiatric hospitalizations and 6 weeks of psychiatric center care do not create a record of disability); Taylor v. Phoenixville School District, 113 F. Supp. 2d 770 (E.D. Pa. 2000) (3 weeks of psychiatric hospitalization does not create a record of disability); Coghlan v. H.J. Heinz, 851 F. Supp. 808, 813 (N.D. Tex. 1994); Glidden v. County of Monroe, 950 F. Supp. 73 (W.D. N.Y. 1997); Glowacki v. Buffalo General Hospital, 2 F. Supp. 2d 346, 351 (W.D. N.Y. 1998).

[13]Ray v. Glidden Co., 85 F.3d 227, 229 (5th Cir. 1996).

[14]Pryor v. Trane, 138 F.3d 1024, 1027 (5th Cir. 1998).

[15]Colwell v. Suffolk County Police, 158 F.3d 635, 645-46 (2d Cir. 1998).

[16]Berk v. Bates Advertising, 25 F. Supp. 2d 265 (S.D. N.Y. 1998).

These decisions do not implement congressional intent in passing the ADA. Hospitalization, by itself, is insufficient to create a record of disability, because some people are hospitalized for reasons that do not involve impairments that substantially limit one or more major life activities. For example, hospitalization for liposuction or other cosmetic surgery would not create a record of a disability. However, extended hospitalization (especially in the days of managed care) for an impairment that substantially limited a major life activity, such as a cerebral hemorrhage or breast cancer, should create a record of disability, especially if an employer uses it to justify an adverse change in the terms and conditions of employment.

This is even more true for people who are hospitalized for psychiatric disabilities, especially those who are held involuntarily for observation or who are involuntarily committed. Because it is such a departure from the constitutional right to liberty to completely deprive a person of his or her freedom of movement, the behavioral threshold that justifies involuntarily holding a person for observation or treatment is very high. As the 3rd Circuit Court said, "when someone must be confined to a hospital because she is psychotic, increasingly agitated, and gripped by delusions, it is manifest that her abilities to think, care for herself, concentrate, and interact with others are substantially limited."[17] As a practical matter, people are held for observation when they seem to be either suicidal or psychotic, both of which are conditions that substantially limit a person's ability to care for himself or herself.

Thus, being detained for psychiatric observation entails at the very least that the examiners regard the individual as having an impairment that substantially limits a major life activity. It also creates a record of a disability, one which has traditionally formed the basis of a great deal of discrimination.

To summarize, what is necessary at the threshold to establish a record of disability is to show that an individual had, at one time in his or her life, an impairment that substantially limited one or more major life activities or was regarded as substantially limiting one or more major life activities. "Repeated and extensive inpatient treatments coupled with a history of outpatient treatment" have been deemed sufficient,[18] as have "three surgeries [followed by being] off work for over a year and a half.[19] Once a plaintiff clears this threshold, of course, he or she must still show that an employer discriminated on the basis of this record or history of disability. It is clear from all case law interpreting record of disability, as well as the EEOC regulations, that the defendant employer must be aware of the record at the time that the allegedly discriminatory decision was made,[20] although this appears to be more relevant to the question of whether an employer discriminated against a plaintiff than whether the record itself was sufficient to meet the first element of a Title I claim. It is less clear whether an employer must be aware of the specific way in which the impairment substantially limited a plaintiff's major life activities.[21] Other courts have suggested that an employer must rely on the record in the challenged employment action, but again, this seems to be relevant to the question of whether the employer discriminated rather than whether the record is sufficient.

---

[17]Taylor v. Phoenixville School District, 174 F.3d 142 (3d Cir. 1999).

[18]Testerman v. Chrysler, 1998 U.S. Dist. LEXIS 1882 (D. De. Feb. 11, 1998).

[19]Webner v. Titan Distribution, 101 F. Supp. 2d 1215, 1223 (N.D. Iowa 2000).

[20]Glidden v. County of Monroe, 950 F. Supp. 73 (W.D. N.Y. 1997); Glowacki v. Buffalo General Hospital, 2 F. Supp. 2d 346 (W.D. N.Y. 1998).

[21]Id. at n. 8.

Relatively few cases to date have relied on a record of disability in protecting people from disability discrimination. This could be because very few people voluntarily disclose their records of hospitalization and treatment. It could also be that the ADA's protection is meaningless because employers can and do discriminate on the basis of gaps in an applicant's resume. As one survey respondent noted, "I feel very fortunate to have not experienced overt discrimination. . . . It is possible that I have not attained employment due to the fact that I could not account for the gaps in my work history."[22] Another respondent wrote that "prospective supervisors and managers discriminate because if you've been sick for long periods of time, they don't understand why you have no job history."[23]

For the most part, plaintiffs who have a record of disability have filed claims in which they define themselves as having a disability or being regarded as having a disability. Plaintiffs defining themselves as disabled will have a more difficult time in the wake of the U.S. Supreme Court's decisions in *Sutton v. United Airlines,*[24] *Murphy v. United Parcel Service,*[25] and *Albertson's v. Kirkingburg.*[26] Some people who are precluded by these decisions from defining themselves as disabled because they are using mitigating medications or devices may have a premitigation record of an impairment that substantially limited one or more of their major life activities and may now choose to proceed on that basis.

Although the record of disability prong has been described as "a close sibling" of the "regarded as disabled" prong,[27] subtle but significant differences exist between them in terms of both proof and remedy. The record of disability prong requires a plaintiff to show that he or she once had a disability that substantially limited his or her major life activities. The regarded as disabled prong has repeatedly been interpreted to require a plaintiff to show that an employer believes that the employee is currently substantially limited in major life activities, a requirement that many plaintiffs with psychiatric disabilities cannot meet because that simply is not the source of the employer's discrimination.[28] In fact, the same court that made the "close sibling" comment found that the plaintiff could go forward on her record of disability claim, but not on her regarded as disabled claim, because although she could show that her learning disability had once substantially limited her learning, she could not show that her employer believed it did so at present.[29]

In addition, the record of disability prong may permit the plaintiff to request accommodations based on ongoing or recurrent limitations.[30] It is not clear whether

---

[22]Survey No. 109.

[23]Survey No. 6.

[24]Sutton v. United Airlines, 527 U.S. 471 (1999).

[25]Murphy v. United Parcel Service, 527 U.S. 516 (1999).

[26]Albertson's v. Kirkingburg, 527 U.S. 555 (1999).

[27]Davidson v. Midelfort Clinic, 133 F.3d 499, 509 (7th Cir. 1998). The interrelationship between the history of disability prong and the perceived disability prong would appear to be greatest when the plaintiff had been misclassified as disabled.

[28]*See* chapter 4 in this volume for a further discussion.

[29]Of course, the problem in the case, as in many psychiatric disability cases, was precisely that the employer did not believe she had a disability at all. Davidson v. Midelfort Clinic, 133 F.3d 499, 509 (7th Cir. 1998).

[30]Davidson, *id.* at n. 6, citing the EEOC's *Compliance Manual* P6887 at 907(a) at 5323, which refers to a possible obligation to accommodate ongoing limitations arising out of a history of disability.

people who argue that they are regarded as having a disability can ask for accommodations.[31]

Regarding an Individual as Having a Disability

Under the ADA and the Rehabilitation Act, plaintiffs can recover even if they are not disabled, if they can prove that they are regarded as disabled and discriminated against as a result. For people who are regarded as having psychiatric disabilities, this protection is crucial. People with physical disabilities need tangible accommodations, such as accessible transportation, TDD phones, and tapes and Braille to accomplish integration into the mainstream of employment and society. But for people with psychiatric diagnoses, the most important path to integration is for society to cease regarding them as disabled. People with psychiatric disabilities do not need tangible, material accommodations as much as they need respect, credibility, and acceptance. In other words, the central obstacle to integration into society revolves precisely around the way in which people with psychiatric conditions are regarded.

Although many ADA cases involving psychiatric disabilities are based on misconceptions or stereotypes, the cases involving claims that the plaintiff is regarded as having a psychiatric disability are probably the most confusing, chaotic, and unpredictable. There is absolutely no coherent judicial doctrine in this area. This is in part because hostility toward people who have psychiatric disabilities is often almost the mirror opposite of a stereotype that the disability substantially limits major life activities. Rather, coworker and supervisor harassment recounted in these cases repeatedly reflects the assumption that the employee is malingering and is perfectly able to do the job:

> In March 1991, store manager Randolph Maphis and district manager David Berkes took Mr. Lee for a ride in Mr. Berkes' car and asked him questions about his depression [citation to record omitted]. Both managers told him they did not believe he was depressed and urged him to tell them what his real problem was. Mr. Berkes told Mr. Lee, "you're within a gnat's ass of losing your job, what's really your problem?" [citation to record omitted]. Several times during the ride, the managers threatened him with termination and accused him of lying about the extent of his depression.[32]

Although the Supreme Court has held that a supervisor informed of sexual harassment who does nothing can be found liable for the harassment, a district court in Illinois held that when a person with a psychiatric disability claimed harassment based on disability, the supervisor's *failure* to intervene showed that he did not really perceive the employee as disabled because it demonstrated that the supervisor believed the employee could handle the matter on his own.[33]

---

[31]Deane v. Pocono Medical Center, 142 F.3d 138, 140–41 (3d Cir. 1998) (en banc).

[32]Lee v. Publix Supermarkets, 1998 U.S. Dist. LEXIS 8921 (N.D. Fla. Mar. 16, 1998).

[33]Mork v. Manpower, 1998 U.S. Dist. LEXIS 11312 at 14 (N.D. Ill. July 23, 1998), ("Mork also claims that his supervisors' failure to stop the harassment indicates that they regarded him as disabled. We disagree. If anything, their inaction suggests the opposite: that Mork's supervisors believed he was fully capable of taking care of himself and resolving any conflicts with his co-workers.")

But the confusion in the courts about what evidence is required to show that a defendant regarded an employee as psychiatrically disabled goes beyond these issues. Courts have no coherent idea of what behavior suffices to show that employees regard an employee as having a psychiatric disability.

Suggesting or Ordering Employees to Be Tested, Seek Counseling, Enter a Treatment Program, or Release Medical Records

The cases in this area present a continuum of employer pressure on employees to seek psychiatric evaluation and treatment—from making apparently sympathetic suggestions in the face of a death of a spouse or other traumatic event[34] to conditioning continued retention of employment on psychiatric or substance abuse evaluation or treatment[35] to being told not to return to the employment premises without a clearance from a physician.[36] Although it might seem to the logical reader that courts' holdings about whether an employer perceived an employee to be disabled fall along the same continuum, this is not the case. In some cases, just suggesting that an employee seek psychological counseling is considered evidence that the employee is perceived to be mentally disabled,[37] whereas in others, ordering an employee to submit to psychological counseling or be fired was not considered sufficient evidence that the employer perceived the plaintiff as disabled.[38]

Courts often appear to base their findings that an employer did not perceive an employee to be mentally disabled on a conclusion that the plaintiff simply should not prevail. Although this decision may be correct for other reasons, it leads to very confusing legal doctrine in the area of "regarded as being disabled." For example, in *Stewart v. County of Brown,* the 7th Circuit panel states that "the key missing evidence was any indication that Sheriff Donart thought that Stewart suffered from mental illness."[39] Yet, Sheriff Donart had "stated to third persons that he considered Stewart to be emotionally or psychologically unbalanced" and had "ordered a number of psychological evaluations for him."[40] The panel then admonishes the plaintiff, saying, "however sincerely Stewart may believe that Donart harbored a secret belief that he was mentally disabled, it was his job to show the existence of genuinely

---

[34] Johnson v. Boardman Petroleum, 923 F. Supp. 1563, 1566 (S.D. Ga. 1996); Vinson v. Cummins, 36 F. Supp. 2d 1085, 1094 (S.D. Ind. 1999).

[35] Miners v. Cargill, 113 F.3d 820 (8th Cir. 1997), *cert. denied,* 118 S. Ct. 441 (1997); Cody v. Cigna Health Care, 139 F.3d 595 (8th Cir. 1998); Walton v. City of Manassas, 162 F.3d 1158 (4th Cir. 1998); Jones v. Corrections Corp. of America, 993 F. Supp. 1384 (D. Kan. 1998).

[36] Duda v. Board of Education of Franklin Park, 133 F.3d 1054 (7th Cir. 1998).

[37] Pouncy v. Vulcan Materials Co., 920 F. Supp. 1566, 1580, n. 8 (N.D. Ala. 1996); Holihan v. Lucky Stores, 87 F.3d 362, 366 (9th Cir. 1996); Schnake v. Johnson County Community College, 961 F. Supp. 1478 (D. Kan. 1997).

[38] Webb v. Mercy Hospital, 102 F.3d 958 (8th Cir. 1996) (the plaintiff "was told she must participate in Employee Assistance Program counselling or she would be fired," the plaintiff was held not to have presented enough evidence that she was regarded as mentally disabled); Stewart v. County of Brown, 86 F.3d 107 (7th Cir. 1996); Linson v. Trustees of the University of Pennsylvania, 1996 U.S. Dist. LEXIS 12243 (E.D. Pa. Aug. 21, 1996); Cody v. Cigna Health-Care of St Louis, 139 F.3d 595 (8th Cir. 1998) (a nurse was offered medical leave and psychiatric evaluation, but this did not establish that the employer regarded her as having a substantially limiting impairment).

[39] 86 F.3d 107 (7th Cir. 1996).

[40] *Id.* at *4.

disputed facts."[41] In this case, there is clearly enough evidence that the sheriff considered Stewart to be mentally disabled to go to a jury. There is also significant evidence demonstrating that the sheriff's adverse employment decision was for nondiscriminatory reasons: Stewart used excessive force against residents of a community he identified as "sewer trash" and failed to show remorse. The basis on which the adverse outcome for Stewart was reached does matter to future cases. In another case, the court disregarded evidence that an employer was "continuously suggesting counseling" and stated that for a regarded as disabled claim to succeed, the plaintiff must show that "the employer regarded the employee as either unable to care for her or himself or unable to perform all the duties of the job."[42] Even under the U.S. Supreme Court's narrow reading of the regarded as disabled prong, this requirement clearly is too extreme.

The question of whether an employer should be held to regard an employee as having a mental disability may on first blush appear to be a difficult problem. First, it is desirable for employers to be concerned about the emotional well-being of their employees. Perhaps censoring an employer from suggesting that an employee may want to seek counseling is just another way of stigmatizing psychiatric disability.

However, rather than concluding that such a suggestion does not amount to regarding an employee as mentally disabled, a more tidy mode of legal analysis of these cases is to find that such a suggestion does not constitute discrimination, because, by itself, it does not qualify as an adverse job action. This interpretation would mean that cases in which an employer consistently pressured an employee to seek treatment, and, certainly, cases in which an employer ordered an employee to undergo a psychiatric examination or enter a treatment program as a condition of continued employment, qualify as both regarding the employer as disabled and an adverse job action.

Second, if an employee begins to act oddly, an employer may be motivated not only by concern for an individual employee, but for other employees or the business.[43] The EEOC regulations specifically permit an employer to require an employee to submit to a medical examination if it can be shown to be "job-related and consistent with business necessity."[44] Thus, if there are factual, documented incidents that would lead a reasonable employer to believe that an employee might no longer be capable of performing identifiable and essential elements of the job and examinations would resolve this issue, an employer may still insist on an examination if it has a justifiable, nondiscriminatory reason for doing so.[45] However, showing that the examination is "job-related and consistent with business necessity" is a defense to allegations of discrimination, not to the proposition that an employer regarded an employee as disabled. To insist on a psychiatric examination as a condition of continued employment, quite clearly, is something more than indicating concern for an employee's well-being. Threatening to fire an employee if he or she does not submit to a psychiatric examination or the release of its results does constitute "regarding

---

[41]*Id.*

[42]Vinson v. Cummins, 36 F. Supp. 2d 1085, 1094 (S.D. Ind. 1999).

[43]*See* Walton v. Manassas County, 162 F.3d 1158 (4th Cir. 1998).

[44]*See* chapter 8 for a further discussion.

[45]*See, e.g.,* Miller v. Champaign Community Unit School District, 938 F. Supp. 1201 (C.D. Ill. 1997) (after a specific series of incidents, the school district required a psychiatric examination; the court found that assuming the school district regarded the plaintiff as disabled, it had nondiscriminatory reasons for requiring the evaluation).

an employee as mentally disabled." Just because an employer may not have a diagnosis in mind does not make a difference. That is why the employer is seeking
the examination: to obtain expert confirmation or explanation for his lay intuitions.

It is equally important to emphasize that regarding someone as psychiatrically
disabled is not itself discriminatory; it simply places the employee in the protected
class of people who may not have unjustified adverse action taken against them on
that basis. For an employer to successfully defend a requirement that an employee
submit to a medical examination, it would have to show specific, concrete evidence
that the employee was failing to accomplish one or more essential elements of his
or her job or that there was evidence linked to substantial safety concerns to require
the examination; and that the examination was likely to be valid and reliable (a
major drawback of psychological or psychiatric testing as opposed to visual or
audiology examinations).[46]

Thus, a broader reading of the regarded as disabled prong does not necessarily
open the floodgates of litigation, but it does permit the court to examine the individualized, context-specific facts, as the ADA requires. Some courts have gone to
the other extreme, conceding that the employer regarded the employee as psychiatrically unsuited for the position but finding that because the employer only believed
the employee was unsuited for one particular position, not a range of jobs, that the
employer did not regard the employee as substantially limited in the major life
activity of working.[47] This is discussed more fully in chapter 4.

Arguably, a legal difference exists between ordering an employee to submit to
a psychiatric examination and conditioning employment on entering a treatment program. When balancing an employer's concerns and needs and an employee's privacy
concerns, there is historical precedent and legal recognition of the medical examination. There is none whatsoever for conditioning employment on entering into a
treatment program or requiring the employee to seek counseling, especially when
the counselor can, and often does, report back to the employer.[48]

It seems clear that an employer's requirement that an employee enter a treatment
program as a condition of employment is discrimination on the basis of perceived
disability. This issue has been raised in several cases. In one, the employer tried to
portray its actions as granting a reasonable accommodation to an employee, but the
court correctly pointed out that reasonable accommodations are asked for by employees, not unilaterally imposed by employers. In another case, a plaintiff charged
that his employer should have required him to enter a treatment program, and its
failure to do so constituted discrimination. The court dispatched this argument ve-
hemently:

> Indeed, force or coercion would contravene the ADA, which clearly states that an
> employee need not accept a proffered accommodation. Simply put, nothing in the
> ADA alters the sensible fact that legally competent adults, like Roberts, are responsible

---

[46] *See* Nichols v. American National Insurance Co., 154 F.3d 875, 882–884 (8th Cir. 1998) (striking
psychiatric testimony as unsupported under the standard of Daubert v. Merrell-Dow, 509 U.S. 579
[1993]).

[47] *See, e.g.,* Duncan v. Wisconsin Department of Health and Safety, 166 F.3d 930 (7th Cir. 1999).

[48] *See* Pouncy v. Vulcan, 920 F. Supp. 1566 (N.D. Ala. 1996) (the "career counsellor" told the
employee that their conversations were absolutely confidential, then called the employer and relayed
concerns about the employee on a speaker phone, which was overheard).

for making their own decisions concerning whether to seek counseling or other professional treatment for their problems . . . [for employers] to coerce employees to
obtain treatment . . . is unsupported and unsupportable. To rule otherwise would effectively countenance an erosion of personal responsibility that finds no basis in the
ADA or sound public policy.[49]

However, a court has also upheld an employer's requirement that an employee cease
taking a certain kind of psychotropic medication as permissible and not an action
adverse to the employee.[50]

Suggesting or Ordering That an Employee Take Leave Because of Psychiatric Disability

Cases frequently involve an employer suggesting or insisting that an employee take
leave to seek treatment for his or her emotional difficulties, or even refusing to let
employees return to work even though their treating physicians have cleared them
for employment.[51] One court suggested that if an employee was told to take disability
leave for mental health reasons, this constituted evidence of both a record of impairment and being regarded as being impaired.[52] Courts are clear that not permitting
an employee to return to work raises at least a jury issue that the employer regarded
the employee as being disabled.[53] For example, a case involving a police officer who
underwent psychological testing and was labeled as "severely disturbed" and not
permitted to return to work for two years was held to have created a genuine issue
of fact as to whether the officer was perceived as being mentally disabled.[54]

However, by the same token, courts are reluctant to find that an employer regards
an employee as disabled when the employer permits the employee to continue working, no matter what other evidence the employee presents that he or she was regarded
as being disabled. In another case, a police officer who was forced into a program
that intensively monitored him on a daily basis because he was taking Prozac was
not perceived as disabled because he continued to perform all the duties of a police
officer.[55]

Note that courts sometimes take this position in cases involving physical disabilities as well, for example, refusing to find that an employer regards an employee
as disabled, even if there is evidence of derogatory comments or actions in the record,
as long as the employee continues to earn the same salary and receive the same
benefits.[56] This is true even if the employee is transferred to another unit against his
or her will and specifically because of the disability. Courts reason that an employer

---

[49]Roberts v. County of Fairfax, 937 F. Supp. 541 (E.D. Va. 1996).

[50]Shiplett v. Amtrak, 1999 U.S. App. LEXIS 14004 (6th Cir. June 17, 1999), *cert. denied*, 528 U.S.
1078 (2000).

[51]Ralph v. Lucent Technologies, 135 F.3d 166 (1st Cir. 1998); Moore v. Board of Education, 134
F.3d 781 (6th Cir. 1998); Kvintus v. R. L. Polk, 3 F. Supp. 2d 788 (E.D. Mich. 1998).

[52]Pritchard v. Southern Co. Services, 92 F.3d 1130 (11th Cir. 1996).

[53]Motichek v. Buck Kreihs Co., 958 F. Supp. 266 (E.D. La. 1996) (an employee was not regarded
by the supervisor as disabled when the supervisor permitted the plaintiff to return to work as a ship
superintendent after making a statement that the plaintiff was mentally incapable of doing so).

[54]Dertz v. City of Chicago, 241997 WL 85169 (N.D. Ill. Feb. 24, 1997).

[55]Krocka v. Bransfield, 969 F. Supp. 1073, 1085 (N.D. Ill. 1997).

[56]Ellison v. Software Spectrum, 85 F.3d 187 (5th Cir. 1996).

that is willing to continue employing an individual cannot regard him as disabled, which is contrary to reason and says a lot about the underlying assumptions judges have about disability.

Remarks or Actions Relating to the Employee and Mental Disability

As seen at greater length in chapter 6, many workplace environments involve a substantial amount of harassing of workers with known or suspected psychiatric disabilities. Courts are reluctant to find that these remarks can support a finding that an employee is regarded as having a disability unless the plaintiff can point to remarks specifically made by a supervisor or the person charged with the adverse employment decision. Even when a supervisor makes the remarks, the majority of courts have found that this action is insufficient to support a holding that an employee is regarded as disabled.[57] Condoning the remarks or failing to address the issue is also not sufficient.

In one case in which it was clear that the employee should not recover under the ADA, the court reached the correct conclusion for the wrong reasons. An employee who had stalked another employee, sent her menacing letters, and struck her, resulting in criminal charges, was terminated. The terminated employee sued the employer, alleging that the employer regarded him as mentally ill: "Fenton contends that because defendants received reports from other employees that Fenton was 'unstable,' that he could 'go ballistic,' that he had a 'gun collection,' and that he was a 'Vietnam veteran'."[58] The court held that Fenton had not shown that the employer regarded him as mentally ill because "in his pleadings, Fenton never specifically alleges in clinical or diagnostic terms what psychological or physiological impairment Pritchard management believed him to be suffering."[59] It would be absurd to require plaintiffs to show that their employers thought they had a specific diagnosis to prove that they were regarded as psychiatrically disabled. Neither management nor anyone else except mental health professionals think in these terms. Few legitimate perceived mental disability cases would prevail under this standard. Management may well have perceived Fenton as mentally ill, but they had a legitimate and nondiscriminatory reason for firing him.

The confusion in legal doctrine is even more significant with the recent decisions by the U.S. Supreme Court in *Sutton v. United Airlines, Murphy v. United Parcel Service*, and *Albertson's v. Kirkingburg*. Although the Supreme Court in an earlier decision underscored that courts should not interpret the ADA to provide less protection than Section 504 of the Rehabilitation Act,[60] that is precisely what the Court did in its 1999 trilogy.

The Supreme Court had interpreted the "regarded as handicapped" prong of Section 504 at great length in *School Board of Nassau County v. Arline*.[61] This case

---

[57]*See, e.g.*, Webb v. Baxter Healthcare Corp., 57 F.3d 1067 (table case), 1995 WL 352485 (5th Cir. June 13, 1995) (the defendant won the summary judgment when the supervisor called the plaintiff "Sybil" after a movie character with multiple personalities and told the company's vice president that the plaintiff was "very much off her rocker").

[58]Fenton v. Pritchard, 926 F. Supp. 1437 (D. Kan. 1996).

[59]*Id.* at n. 6.

[60]Bragdon v. Abbott, 526 U.S. 1131 (1999).

[61]480 U.S. 273 (1987).

provided the principal guidance to courts in cases involving claims that the plaintiff was "regarded as" handicapped or disabled. The Court explained that a person might have an "impairment" or condition that did not

> diminish a person's physical or mental capabilities, but could nevertheless substantially limit that person's ability to work as a result of the negative reactions of others to the impairment ... By amending the definition of "handicapped" to include not only those who are actually physically impaired but also those *who are regarded as impaired and who, as a result, are substantially limited in a major life activity*, Congress acknowledged that society's accumulated myths and fears about disability and disease are as handicapping as the physical limitations that flow from actual impairment.[62]

This passage indicates that employers or prospective employers need only regard a person as impaired, and if that opinion or perception results in a substantial limitation on a major life activity, an employee is covered under the ADA. It is the employer who substantially limits the person by excluding him or her from work. It is "the negative reactions of others" that substantially limit the person. Those negative reactions need only exclude or limit a person from work to be substantially limiting; they do not have to encompass a carefully considered assessment of whether the impairment substantially limits the individual.

In drafting, debating, and passing the ADA, Congress repeatedly endorsed the reasoning in *Arline*,[63] and wrote its own language separately confirming that employers and prospective employers need only view a person as being impaired and not disabled for that person to be covered under the third prong.[64] One of the most significant passages in the legislative history is the following:

> A person who is rejected from a job because of the myths, fears and stereotypes associated with disabilities would be covered under this third test, *whether or not the employer's perception was shared by others in the field and whether or not the person's physical or mental condition would be considered a disability under the first or second part of the definition.*[65]

This passage emphasizes that even if a person is excluded from only one job, because "others in the field" do not share the employer's stereotype, the person excluded is still "covered under this third test." The Senate Labor and Human Resources Committee report stated that "[a] person who is excluded from *any activity* covered under this act . . . is being treated as having a disability which affects a major life activity"[66] and used exclusion from a restaurant as an example. There is no need to inquire whether "going to restaurants" is a major life activity or whether the maitre d' believed that the individual was substantially limited in a major life activity. It was clear that Congress intended for someone who was discriminated against in a par-

---

[62] 480 U.S. 273, 283–284 (1987) (citations omitted) (emphasis added).

[63] Senate Committee on Labor and Human Resources, S. Rep. No. 101-116, at 23 (1989); H.R. Rep. No. 101-485, pt. 3, at 30 (1990).

[64] Senate Committee on Labor and Human Resources, S. Rep. No. 101-116, at 24 (1989).

[65] H.R. Rep. No. 101-485, pt. 3, at 30 (1990).

[66] Senate Committee on Labor and Human Resources, S. Rep. No. 101-116, at 24 (1989).

ticular job to be protected from that discrimination and not have to show that many employers would discriminate against him or her in many different jobs.

Congress also endorsed the case of *Doe v. Centinela Hospital*,[67] in which a man who tested HIV-positive but was asymptomatic was rejected from a residential substance abuse treatment program solely on the grounds that he had tested positive for HIV. The defendant did offer Doe the option of entering its outpatient program. The defendant protested that it did not regard Doe as substantially limited in any major life activity and argued that "even under the 'perceived as handicapped' test, the perception must still relate to a substantial limitation on a major life activity."[68] The court rejected this argument, saying that the defendant "perceived plaintiff to have precisely the condition that he has, and treated him on that account as limited in his ability to learn how to deal with a dependency in the Life Starts program." As to the defendant's offer of the outpatient program, that went to reasonable accommodation rather than perception of disability. Evidence in the record shows that other residential substance abuse treatment programs did admit people who were HIV-positive. It seems clear from Congress's endorsement of *Doe* that blanket exclusions from programs or employment on the basis of an impairment do mean that the individual is "regarded as disabled" for the purposes of the ADA. Of course, a plaintiff must still show that he or she is otherwise qualified for the program or employment.

The EEOC promulgated regulations to the ADA that were substantially identical to the Section 504 regulations on which the *Doe* court relied.[69] The ADA regulations define an individual regarded as having a disability as one who (a) has a physical or mental impairment that does not substantially limit major life activities but is treated by an employer as such; (b) has an impairment that is substantially limiting only as a result of the attitudes of others; or (c) has no impairment but is treated as having a substantially limiting impairment.

The regulations make clear that a person who claims to be perceived as disabled may—but need not—have an impairment but that the impairment itself does not substantially limit the plaintiff in major life activities. If a plaintiff is substantially limited in major life activities, it is because of the attitudes and prejudices of others, not because of his or her impairment.

The Supreme Court's decisions in *Sutton* and *Murphy*, however, interpret the "regarded as" prong to require the plaintiff to show that the employer regarded him or her as having an impairment that substantially limited one or more major life activities.[70] This interpretation, which had been followed by many federal courts before the endorsement of the U.S. Supreme Court, shriveled the protection of the regarded as disabled definition so much that the case of a woman who was fired explicitly because she had experienced two momentary seizures was dismissed on the basis that the employer did not believe her to be substantially limited in a major life activity, even though there was no showing whatsoever that she could not do the job for which she had been hired.[71] Many courts have concluded that if the

---

[67] 1988 U.S. Dist. LEXIS 8401 (C.D. Cal. July 7, 1988).

[68] *Id.* at *13.

[69] Those regulations can be found at 45 C.F.R. § 84.3(j)(2)(iv) (2000).

[70] Murphy v. United Parcel Service, 527 U.S. 516 (1999); Sutton v. United Airlines, 527 U.S. 471 (1999).

[71] Deas v. RiverWest, 152 F.2d 471 (5th Cir. 1998).

defendant "only" believed the plaintiff could not fulfill the requirements of his or her position with the employer because of the perceived condition, the defendant did not regard the plaintiff as disabled, because the employer was prepared to believe that the plaintiff could perform any other job (with any other employer).[72]

As discussed in detail in the next chapter, this approach leaves defendants total freedom for the purest kinds of discrimination: discrimination based on sheer hostility toward a condition, not a mistaken assessment of its effect on a person's ability to perform major life activities.

Conclusion

The regarded as mentally disabled cases are a profound reflection of the confusion our society has regarding issues of psychiatric disability, personality, and conduct. Courts that have clear concerns about violence in the workplace have attempted to protect employer prerogatives by holding that an employee was not regarded as disabled in cases in which the evidence clearly points to a different conclusion. A better basis on which to decide these cases would be to find that the employer did indeed regard an employee who was told to get a psychiatric examination, seek psychiatric counseling, or take a leave of absence as disabled, and then go on to examine whether the employer's conduct constituted an adverse or discriminatory action, and if so, whether that action was justified.

---

[72]Duncan v. Wisconsin Department of Health and Safety, 166 F.3d 930 (7th Cir. 1999); Deas v. River West, 152 F.3d 471 (5th Cir. 1998).

Chapter 6
ABUSIVE WORK ENVIRONMENTS, STRESSFUL WORKING CONDITIONS, AND DISCRIMINATION

Despite widespread fear about extending the Americans With Disabilities Act (ADA) to protect people diagnosed with psychiatric disabilities, most employment discrimination lawsuits brought by people with psychiatric disabilities do not involve the kind of bizarre behavior associated with stereotypes of mental illness. Nor are these lawsuits brought by people of marginal qualifications seeking to retain employment by claiming discrimination. Nor are employers behaving in stereotypically discriminatory ways. Generally, employers do not fire people simply because they reveal a psychiatric diagnosis.

Rather, in the vast majority of employment discrimination cases involving people with actual or perceived psychiatric disabilities, the employees tended to be highly qualified. Most worked a considerable length of time, and their performances were "rated highly"[1] or "consistently rated as an above average to outstanding worker."[2] Some employees were "very successful, ... being named the company's all-time profit producer,"[3] "honored as Employee of the Month,"[4] or considered "exceptional"[5] and "fully successful."[6] In other cases, the employee "won numerous awards for his work,"[7] "performance evaluations were consistently good,"[8] or, at the least, the employee "received a 'meets standards' review on ... evaluations."[9]

Many employees filing suit had significant academic or professional expertise.[10] Some achieved promotions at a rapid pace, which occasionally precipitated the problems reflected in their respective litigation.[11] For others, problems arose due to a

---

Portions of this chapter are from Susan Stefan, "'You'd Have to Be Crazy to Work Here': Worker Stress, the Abusive Workplace, and Title I of the ADA," *Loyola Law Rev.* 31 (1998): 795.

[1] Simpkins v. Specialty Envelope, Inc., 94 F.3d 645 (table), No. 95-3370, 1996 WL 452858, at *1 (6th Cir. Aug. 9, 1996).

[2] DiGloria v. American Telegraph & Tel. Co., No. 92-1179-CIV-ORL-19, 1993 WL 735034, at *1 (M.D. Fla. Nov. 30, 1993).

[3] Holihan v. Lucky Stores, Inc., 87 F.3d 362, 364 (9th Cir. 1996).

[4] Mundo v. Sanus Health Plan, 966 F. Supp. 171 (E.D. N.Y. 1997).

[5] EEOC v. Amego, Inc., 110 F.3d 135, 138 (1st Cir. 1997).

[6] Gonzagowski v. Widnall, 115 F.3d 744, 746 (10th Cir. 1997).

[7] McCrory v. Kraft Food Ingredients, 98 F.3d 1342 (table), No. 94–6505, 1996 WL 571146, at *1 (6th Cir. Oct. 3, 1996).

[8] Hogarth v. Thornburgh, 833 F. Supp. 1077, 1080 (S.D. N.Y. 1993).

[9] Hunt-Golliday v. Metropolitan Water Reclamation District, 104 F.3d 1004, 1012 (7th Cir. 1997).

[10] *See, e.g.,* Misek-Falkoff v. IBM Corp., 854 F. Supp. 215, 218 (S.D. N.Y. 1994) (involving "a former college professor holding a PhD degree with a background in computers and linguistics who is now an attorney"). *See also* Fitzgerald v. Allegheny Corp., 904 F. Supp. 223, 225 (S.D. N.Y. 1995) (involving a plaintiff who was a senior vice president); Remine v. Deckers, 871 F. Supp. 1538, 1539 (D. Conn. 1995) (involving the director of the Connecticut Cancer Institute and vice-chair of the department of surgery); Robertson v. Neuromedical Center, 983 F. Supp. 669 (M.D. La. 1997) (involving a former neurologist).

[11] *See, e.g., Mundo,* 966 F. Supp. at 171-72; Lewis v. Zilog, Inc., 908 F. Supp. 931, 937 (N.D. Ga.

change in position[12] or a promotion to a supervisory position.[13] Most often, however, an excellent employee began to experience problems after the arrival of a new supervisor.[14] My survey of thousands of employment discrimination cases brought by employees with psychiatric disabilities shows that such cases fall into four principle categories:

1. Employees who had worked satisfactorily for an extended period of time until the appointment of a new supervisor and whose claims clearly arose from escalating interpersonal difficulties with their supervisors.[15]

2. Employees whose psychiatric disabilities arose from other work environment issues, including women who were sexually harassed[16]; individuals subjected to hostile work environments as a result of disability,[17] gender,[18] race,[19] or

---

1995); Wood v. County of Alameda, No. C 94 1557 TEH, 1995 WL 705139, at *1 (N.D. Cal. Nov. 17, 1995) (involving a plaintiff who had always received "satisfactory or better" evaluations until she was promoted to supervising clerk).

[12] See, e.g., Anderson v. General Motors Corp., 991 F.2d 794 (table), No. 92-2185, 1993 WL 94309, at *1 (6th Cir. Mar. 30, 1993).

[13] See, e.g., Wisniewski v. Ameritech, No. 95 C 2340, 1996 WL 501737, at *1 (N.D. Ill. Sept. 3, 1996).

[14] See, e.g., Simpkins, 1996 WL 452858, at *1; DiGloria, 1993 WL 735034, at *1. Criado v. IBM, 1998 U.S. App. LEXIS 11743 (June 18, 1998). This pattern is repeated in nondiscrimination cases as well, Edmonds v. Hughes Aircraft, 1998 U.S. App. LEXIS 9419 (4th Cir. May 8, 1998) (ERISA).

[15] See, e.g., Siemon v. American Tel. & Tel. Corp., 117 F.3d 1173, 1174 (10th Cir. 1997); Gonzagowski, 115 F.3d at 746; Weiler v. Household Financial Corp., 101 F.3d 519, 522 (7th Cir. 1996); Crawford v. Runyon, 37 F.3d 1338, 1339 (8th Cir. 1994); Johnson v. Merrell Dow Pharmaceutical, Inc., 965 F.2d 31, 32 (5th Cir. 1992); Barton v. Tampa Electric Co., No. 95-1986-CIV-T-17E, 1997 WL 128158, at *1 (M.D. Fla. Mar. 11, 1997); Soileau v. Guilford of Maine, Inc., 928 F. Supp. 37, 43 (D. Me. 1996), aff'd, 105 F.3d 12 (1st Cir. 1997); Hatfield v. Quantum Chem. Corp., 920 F. Supp. 108, 109 (S.D. Tex. 1996); Boldini v. Postmaster Gen., 928 F. Supp. 125, 128 (D. N.H. 1995); Voytek v. University of California, No. C-92-3465 EFL, 1994 WL 478805, at *1 (N.D. Cal. Aug. 25, 1994); DiGloria, 1993 WL 735034, at *1; Mancini v. General Electric Co., 820 F. Supp. 141, 143 (D. Vt. 1993). In other cases, the employee had been working for several years before problems arose with a new supervisor. See Pavone v. Brown, No. 95 C 3620, 1997 WL 441312, at *1 (N.D. Ill. July 29, 1997); McIntyre v. Kroger Co., 863 F. Supp. 355, 356, 359 n. 12 (N.D. Tex. 1994); Kent v. Derwinski, 790 F. Supp. 1032, 1035–37 (E.D. Wash. 1991).

[16] See, e.g., Iacampo v. Hasbro, Inc., 929 F. Supp. 562, 568 (D. R.I. 1996); Harrison v. Banque Indosuez, 6 F. Supp. 2d 224 (S.D. N.Y. 1998); Albert v. Runyon, 6 F. Supp. 2d 57 (D. Mass. 1998) (FMLA case in which a request for leave was based on psychiatric disability arising from sexual harassment); Wilson v. Chrysler, 172 F.3d 500 (7th Cir. 1999).

[17] This includes both physical and mental disabilities. It is not unusual for a psychiatric disability claim to arise out of a claim of harassment for physical disability. See Williams v. Kerr-McGee Corp., 110 F.3d 74 (table), No. 96-6090, 1997 WL 158176, at *1 (10th Cir. Apr. 1, 1997) (involving psychiatric problems related to exacerbation of lupus by job stress); Rivera-Flores v. Puerto Rico Tel. Co., 64 F.3d 742, 744–45 (1st Cir. 1995) (involving a plaintiff with cataracts and glaucoma being harassed by coworkers); Bryant v. Better Business Bureau, 923 F. Supp. 720, 727 (D. Md. 1996) (involving a woman who is deaf being harassed based on disability and sex); Mondzelewski v. Pathmark Stores, 162 F.3d 778 (3d Cir. 1998) (an employee suffers "nervous breakdown" because of harassment after injuring his back). Sometimes the harassment claim was related to the psychiatric disability itself. See McClain v. Southwest Steel Co., 940 F. Supp. 295, 300 (N.D. Okla. 1996); Henry v. Guest Servs., Inc., 902 F. Supp. 245, 251–52 (D.D.C. 1995) (involving a plaintiff harassed about his depression), aff'd mem., 98 F.3d 646 (D.C. Cir. 1996); Howard v. Navistar Int'l Trans. Corp., 904 F. Supp. 922, 932 (E.D. Wis. 1995) (involving a plaintiff whose supervisor called him a "wussy"), aff'd mem., 107 F.3d 13 (7th Cir. 1997); Haysman v. Food Lion, Inc., 893 F. Supp. 1092, 1098 (S.D. Ga. 1995) (involving a supervisor who told

      sexual preference[20]; whistleblowers[21]; and people whose disabilities were related to other claims of employer abuse or unfair treatment.[22]

3. Employees whose disabilities were related to increasing stress, increased hours on the job, or the demands of new positions or new responsibilities.[23] These people often requested, and were denied, accommodations considered reasonable by the Equal Employment Opportunity Commission (EEOC),[24] including modified work schedules involving limited overtime, no night shifts, transfers, or leaves of absence.[25]

4. Employees disciplined for misconduct, usually sexual harassment, who claimed that their behavior resulted from a mental disability or that being disciplined showed that their employer perceived them as being mentally disabled.[26]

---

the plaintiff that he thought the plaintiff was "a joke"). Plaintiffs whose psychiatric disability stems from harassment about a physical disability are more successful in their cases than are plaintiffs who claim to be harassed due to their psychiatric disability. *Cf. Rivera-Flores*, 64 F.3d 749, *with Henry*, 902 F. Supp. 251–252.

[18]*See, e.g., Hunt-Golliday*, 104 F.3d 1008; Webb v. Baxter Healthcare Corp., 57 F.3d 1067 (table), No. 94-1784, 1995 WL 352485, at *5 and n. 6 (4th Cir. June 13, 1995) (involving an ADA claim dismissed because "whatever emotional problems [the plaintiff] had were the result, rather than the cause, of her hostile work environment"); Boyce v. New York City Mission Society, 963 F. Supp. 290 (S.D. N.Y. 1997)

[19]*See, e.g.,* Barefield v. Chevron U.S.A., Inc., 1997 WL 9888, at *1 (N.D. Cal. Jan. 2, 1997) (noting that emotional distress stemmed from hostile work environment based on race); Sanders v. City of Chicago, 2000 U.S. Dist. LEXIS 1753 (N.D. Ill. Feb. 10, 2000) and 2001 U.S. Dist. LEXIS 3477 (N.D. Ill. Mar. 20, 2001).

[20]Usually the harassment is based on coworkers' or supervisors' assumptions about sexual preference. *See* Ralph v. Lucent Techs., Inc., 135 F.3d 166 (1st Cir. 1998); Kaufman v. Checkers Drive-In Restaurants, Inc., 122 F.3d 892, 893 (11th Cir. 1997); *Hatfield*, 920 F. Supp. 109.

[21]*See, e.g.,* Wagner v. Texas A&M Univ., 939 F. Supp. 1297 (S.D. Tex. 1996) (involving a retaliation in violation of the Texas Whistleblower Act).

[22]*See, e.g.,* Collins v. Blue Cross Blue Shield, 103 F.3d 35, 36 (6th Cir. 1996) (involving work-related stress); *Simpkins*, 1996 WL 452858, at *1, *8; *Mundo*, 966 F. Supp. at 171; Mears v. Gulfstream Aerospace Corp., 905 F. Supp. 1075, 1077 (S.D. Ga. 1995), *aff'd mem.,* 87 F.3d 1331 (11th Cir. 1996); *Anderson*, 1993 WL 94309, at *1.

[23]*See, e.g.,* Beck v. University of Wisconsin Board of Regents, 75 F.3d 1130 (7th Cir. 1996); Morton v. GTE North Inc., 922 F. Supp. 1169, 1173 (N.D. Tex. 1996) (involving an employee who began employment with the defendant company in 1969 and whose depression was attributed to increased job stress beginning in 1985), *aff'd mem.,* 114 F.3d 1182 (5th Cir.), *cert. denied,* 118 S.Ct. 205 (1997); *Wisniewski*, 1996 WL 501737, at *1 (involving an employee promoted to supervisor).

[24]*See* 29 C.F.R. § 1630.2(o) (1997).

[25]*See, e.g.,* Scott v. American Airlines, Inc., 1997 WL 278129 (N.D. Tex. May 15, 1997); Simmerman v. Hardee's Food System, Inc., No. CIV. A. 94-6906, 1996 WL 131948 (E.D. Pa. Mar. 22, 1996), *aff'd mem.,* 118 F.3d 1578 (3d Cir. 1997). The plaintiff in *Simmerman* requested an accommodation that his work hours be limited to 40 per week and he not be required to work night shifts. *See id.* at *1. However, the court found that working more than 50 hours a week and working both shifts was an "essential element" of managing the fast food restaurant. *See id.* at *5.

[26]*See, e.g.,* Graehling v. Village of Lombard, Ill., 58 F.3d 295, 298 (7th Cir. 1995) (involving an employee who alleged he was coerced into resigning because of, in part, bipolar depression and post-traumatic stress syndrome); Fenton v. Pritchard Corp., 926 F. Supp. 1437, 1441–1442 (D. Kan. 1996) (involving an employee who was fired after he stalked, harassed, and assaulted a coworker and who alleged that his employer perceived him as mentally disabled); Bunevith v. CVS/Pharmacy, 925 F. Supp. 89, 94 (D. Mass. 1996) (involving a plaintiff fired for violating sexual harassment policies); Biddle v. Rubin, 1996 WL 14001, at *11 (N.D. Ill. Jan. 9, 1996) (involving an employee charged with sexual

These cases undermine several assumptions held by the public and fostered by the media about ADA discrimination claims by employees with mental disabilities. First, although there has been widespread focus on employees in the fourth category as the primary beneficiaries of the ADA, case law reveals that employees in the first and second categories predominate.

Second, although the ADA is seen as a vehicle to open the workplace to people with pre-existing disabilities, in the vast majority of cases, the disability appeared to be triggered or greatly exacerbated by aspects of the workplace environment that could have been easily remedied, but were not. The majority of cases suggest that society is losing valuable, skilled, and dedicated employees because employers are unwilling to accommodate mental disabilities and courts have failed to enforce employers' obligation to do so. The employees who litigate these ADA cases could and did work for many years. Instead of an accommodation, many of them now receive disability benefits at enormous social and economic cost.

Third, only a few cases reflect employee behavior corresponding to social stereotypes of mental illness.[27] Likewise, few ADA cases reveal employers who exhibited stereotypical discriminatory attitudes toward individuals with mental disabilities, such as assuming that such individuals would be violent or dangerous or refusing to hire them because of their psychiatric diagnoses.[28]

Many of the cases, however, do reveal abusive or stressful work environments with very long hours and bullying supervisors. Employers' attitudes toward the impact of these conditions on employees with psychiatric disabilities mirrors past attitudes toward the employment of women and minorities: As long as such employees fit into the workplace culture and do not demand that it change, they will be accepted.

The employers in these cases are generally unwilling to grant employees with mental disabilities the kinds of workplace accommodations that would enable them to continue to work, such as transferring them away from an abusive supervisor. This unwillingness is particularly striking because the requested accommodations are

---

harassment who claimed his employer regarded him as disabled because he was called delusional); Miles v. General Services Administration, 1995 WL 766013, at *1 (E.D. Pa. Dec. 27, 1995) (involving an employee with carpal tunnel syndrome, diabetes, and depression who was fired for sexual harassment, intoxication at work, insubordination, and repeated absences); Mustafa v. Clark County School District, 876 F. Supp. 1177, 1179 (D. Nev. 1995) (involving a teacher accused of sexual misconduct); Gordon v. Runyon, 1994 WL 139411, at *1 (E.D. Pa. Apr. 21, 1994) (involving an employee discharged for assaulting a nurse, possessing mace and a stun gun, and exhibiting disruptive behavior); Klein v. Boeing Co., 847 F. Supp. 838, 843 (W.D. Wash. 1994) (finding an employee discharged because of a sex crime conviction and not because of a disability).

[27] See, e.g., Carrozza v. Howard County, Md., 45 F.3d 425 (table), 1995 WL 8033, at *1 (4th Cir. Jan. 10, 1995) (involving an employee emptying a trash bag on a table during a meeting); Solomon v. New York City Board of Education, 1996 WL 118541, at *1 (E.D. N.Y. Mar. 6, 1996) (involving a plaintiff claiming medical conspiracies against her); Lassiter v. Reno, 885 F. Supp. 869, 871 (E.D. Va. 1995), aff'd mem., 86 F.3d 1151 (4th Cir. 1996), cert. denied, 117 S.Ct. 766 (1997) (involving a plaintiff with delusional paranoid personality who believed his elderly neighbor was conspiring to burglarize his home); Hogarth, 833 F. Supp. 1080 (involving an FBI clerk who handed out blank doctors' notes that he signed in the name of a nonexistent doctor).

[28] But see McCrory, 1996 WL 571146, at *6 (noting that his supervisor stated he "was 'uncomfortable' with [the] plaintiff talking to customers while [the] plaintiff was on [antidepressant] medation"); Stradley v. LaFourche Communications, Inc., 869 F. Supp. 442, 444 (E.D. La. 1994) ("Based on his 'general life experiences,' [the plaintiff's supervisor] believed that [the plaintiff's] condition [of acute anxiety and depression] made him potentially violent and hostile in the workplace.").

common personnel practices routinely adopted in other circumstances. For example, transfer of employees is well established in sexual harassment cases; in several cases, transfers were accomplished when the supervisor, rather than the employee, requested it.[29] Moreover, some employers refused to permit employees to work "normal" 40- to 50-hour work weeks,[30] even though part-time work, especially for new mothers, is becoming commonplace.

Although management consultants increasingly counsel employers to treat workers with respect, few ADA cases involve employers who were willing to admonish abusive supervisors or insist on a civil workplace environment.[31] Employers' unwillingness to accommodate employees with mental disabilities is not a question of economics; many employers are far more willing to pay employees disability benefits than to transfer them to a new supervisor. Some employers, for example, have fought disability discrimination cases by arguing that the employee does not have a disability and then urged, encouraged, or forced the employee to retire on disability benefits.[32]

Employers' unwillingness to accommodate employees with psychiatric disabilities is also not the result of willful or malingering employees with diagnoses suggesting only mild impairments such as adjustment disorders. Most employees who file suit are in fact diagnosed with one of the so-called "serious mental illnesses" such as depression, bipolar disorder, or schizophrenia and its milder variants.[33]

---

[29]*See Misek-Falkoff*, 854 F. Supp. 219. (S.D. N.Y. 1994).

[30]Most requests for fewer work hours made by employees in ADA cases are requests to work 40-, 50-, and 60-hour work weeks instead of what they had been working. *See, e.g.,* Williams, 1997 WL 158176, at *2 (noting that the plaintiff's doctor recommended that the plaintiff "limit work days to ten hours including travel"); Brown v. Northern Trust Bank, 1997 WL 543098, at *1–2 (N.D. Ill. Sept. 2, 1997) (involving a plaintiff who requested to have her overtime hours reduced and that she be allowed to work "normal hours"); Kolpas v. G.D. Searle & Co., 959 F. Supp. 525, 527–528 (N.D. Ill. 1997) (involving a request that working time be reduced from 60–70 hours per week to 40 hours per week); Amy Stevens, "Boss's Brain Teaser: Accommodating Depressed Worker," *Wall St. J.* (Sept. 11, 1995): B1; "Long Hours Necessary in Many Jobs—But Is It an Essential Function?," *Disability Compliance Bull.* (Mar. 14, 1996): 3. Several newspapers reported the case of Santo Alba, a foreman at Raytheon who was working 70–80 hours a week when his supervisor told him his workload would increase again. That afternoon, Alba apparently stuck his head into a giant circular saw used to cut sheet metal and was decapitated. The family filed a complaint with the Massachusetts Commission Against Discrimination, claiming that the company knew Alba was diagnosed with manic depression and did nothing to reduce his hours. *See* Audrey Choi, "Family of Suicide Victim Claims Raytheon Drove Him to Death," *Wall St. J.* (Nov. 3, 1995): B14.

[31]For a rare example contra, *see* Siciliano v. Chicago Local 458, 3M and American Can, 1997 U.S. Dist. LEXIS 20519 (N.D. Ill. Dec. 18, 1997). This case involved a plant manager who investigated the plaintiff's complaints; warned coworkers that deliberately irritating the plaintiff would result in disciplinary action; issued written warnings emphasizing that no comments about the plaintiff would be tolerated; and sent written warnings to all employees requiring them to treat each other with respect, fairness, and dignity. Whether these actions reflect a unionized work force is not clear.

[32]*See, e.g.,* Cadelli v. Fort Smith School District, 23 F.3d 1295, 1297 (8th Cir. 1994) (noting that the principal told a teacher that his courseload could not be reduced without unduly disrupting the school but suggested at the same time that the teacher take sick leave for the rest of the year); *Misek–Falkoff*, 854 F. Supp. 221 (involving a plaintiff placed on mandatory disability retirement).

[33]*See, e.g.,* Blankenship v. Martin Marietta Energy System, Inc., 83 F.3d 153–55 (6th Cir. 1996) (involving a claim under state handicap discrimination statute by an employee with schizophreniform disorder); Tyler v. Runyon, 70 F.3d 458, 460 (7th Cir. 1995) (involving a claim under the Rehabilitation Act by a U.S. Postal Service employee diagnosed with paranoid schizophrenia); Breiland v. Advance Circuits, Inc., 976 F. Supp. 858, 859–62 (D. Minn. 1997) (involving a claim under ADA by an employee

Thus, the vast majority of ADA mental disability claims involve situations very different from employees exhibiting bizarre behavior or employers indulging in gross stereotypes. Instead, ADA cases involving mental disabilities raise issues at the heart of the employment relationship: the scope of permissible behavior of supervisors toward employees; the extent to which tolerance of stress is an "essential function"[34] of either a given job or employment in general; and the extent to which a worker is expected to tolerate insensitivity or abuse by supervisors or coworkers. ADA psychiatric disability claims focus increasingly on the balance between what employees must endure in a normal work environment (or risk being held unqualified for employment) and what employers must change about work environments (or risk being held not to have reasonably accommodated an employee with a psychiatric disability).

Although regulations and guidance promulgated by the EEOC require employers to permit employees to work fewer hours or work different shifts if feasible or to adjust supervisory methods,[35] plaintiffs with psychiatric disabilities who request these accommodations almost always lose ADA discrimination cases. This is because courts reflexively assume that conditions that preclude people with psychiatric disabilities from being successful are necessary elements of the workplace. Although courts understand that accessible workplaces may require teletypewriters or ramps, and that neither sexual harassment nor race discrimination is an employer prerogative, stress, punishing hours, overwork, unpleasant personality conflicts, and even worker abuse are much more commonly seen as intrinsic features of the workplace.[36] As Regina Austin noted,

> it is generally assumed that employers and employees alike agree that some amount of such abuse is a perfectly natural, necessary, and defensible prerogative of superior rank. . . . Workers for their part are expected to respond to psychologically painful supervision with passivity, not insubordination and resistance. They must and do develop stamina and resilience.[37]

But what about the worker who is exceptionally qualified to perform a given job, but who is not gifted with the "stamina and resilience" to cope with stress or abuse in the workplace? Numerous cases brought by employees with psychiatric disabilities raise issues such as being screamed at, assaulted, or treated unfairly by

---

diagnosed with major depression, schizoid personality disorder, and severe psychological stress); Kemer v. Johnson, 900 F. Supp. 677, 679 and n. 1 (S.D. N.Y. 1995) (involving a claim under ADA by employee diagnosed with depressive neurosis and schizotypal personality disorder), *aff'd mem.*, 101 F.3d 683 (2d Cir.), *cert. denied*, 117 S.Ct. 441 (1996); Patridge v. Runyon, 899 F. Supp. 291, 292 (N.D. Tex. 1995) (involving an employee diagnosed with schizophrenia).

[34]Under the ADA, a plaintiff must be a "qualified individual with a disability," 42 U.S.C. § 12112(a). A qualified individual is "an individual with a disability who, with or without reasonable accommodation, can perform the essential functions of the employment position that such individual holds or desires," *id.* at § 12111(8).

[35]See "Americans With Disabilities Act and Psychiatric Disabilities," in 2A *Americans With Disabilities Practice and Compliance Manual* (Supp. 1998) at 101–102 (hereafter *Practice and Compliance Manual*).

[36]See Regina Austin, "Employer Abuse, Worker Resistance, and the Tort of Intentional Infliction of Emotional Distress," *Stanford Law Rev.* 41(1) (1988): 1.

[37]*Id.* at 1, 2.

supervisors,[38] or continual mocking or mistreatment by coworkers.[39] In some cases, the complaints involve working conditions that most people, including the judges deciding the cases, would acknowledge as unfair,[40] a violation of standards of behavior in the workplace,[41] or even intolerable.[42] In other cases, work stress arises not from interpersonal conflicts but from an employee working either 50- to 70-hour weeks,[43] double shifts, or night shifts.[44]

---

[38] *See* Ralph v. Lucent Technologies, Inc., 135 F.3d 166 (1st Cir. 1998); Pavone v. Brown, 1997 WL 441312, at *2 (N.D. Ill. July 29, 1997); *Barton*, 1997 WL 128158, at *1 (involving a "plaintiff [who] allege[d] that she was not permitted to ask more than two (2) questions during training sessions, not allowed to use the restroom when needed, not allowed to take breaks so that she could take her medication, and constantly called into her supervisor's office and criticized"); Dewitt v. Carsten, 941 F. Supp. 1232, 1234 (N.D. Ga. 1996) (involving a supervisor who "scolded and yelled at [the] plaintiff"), *aff'd mem.*, 122 F.3d 1079 (11th Cir. 1997); Kotlowski v. Eastman Kodak Co., 922 F. Supp. 790, 800 (W.D. N.Y. 1996); *DiGloria*, 1993 WL 735034, at *1 (involving a plaintiff who alleged that her supervisor "repeatedly harassed her and on occasion verbally assaulted her in an aggressive and confrontational manner"); Kent v. Derwinski, 790 F. Supp. 1032, 1037 (E.D. Wash. 1991) (detailing that her supervisor would "lecture [the plaintiff] for up to two hours on getting along with co-workers . . .[,] order [her] to stand against the wall and not work, grab [her] arm in the restroom[,] . . . order her to keep silent about the conditions in the laundry, and criticize [her] for her behavior, which was due to her handicap"); Boyce v. New York City Mission Society, 963 F. Supp. 290, 292 (S.D. N.Y. 1997) (the chair of the Board of Mission Society was engaged in "yelling" and "cursing" at the plaintiff and called her into his office and locked the door so she could not leave).

[39] *See Ralph*, 135 F.3d 166 (1st Cir. 1998) (making the plaintiff the butt of sexually derisive jokes); *McClain*, 940 F. Supp. 300 ("Co-workers allegedly referred to Mr. McClain as 'crazy' and/or as 'a lunatic' and talked about people on Prozac or going to the mental health facility in Vinita, Oklahoma. Plaintiff further alleges that his supervisor . . . was 'hateful' and asked him 'what the f***'s wrong with you.' "); Muller v. Automobile Club, 897 F. Supp. 1289, 1291 (S.D. Cal. 1995) (inquiring of the plaintiff by a coworker as to her wearing her "target" and telling her that he had informed the threatening customer, whom others had seen earlier at the parking lot, where she lived and what kind of car she drove); *Kent*, 790 F. Supp. 1036 (involving the coworkers who called a woman with a mental disability "brain-dead" and "droolie"). *See also Howard*, 904 F. Supp. 932 (characterizing coworker harassment); *Henry*, 902 F. Supp. 252 (involving a plaintiff subjected to jokes about his depression, including the placement of a cartoon in his mailbox); *Haysman*, 893 F. Supp. 1098 (discussing the friction that developed as a result of a disability).

[40] *See Simpkins*, 1996 WL 452858, at *8.

[41] *See* Webb v. Baxter Healthcare Corp., 57 F.3d 1067 (table), No. 94-1784, 1995 WL 352485, at *5 (4th Cir. June 13, 1995).

[42] *See* Sedor v. Frank, 42 F.3d 741, 743 (2d Cir. 1994) (stating that "insensitivity on the part of fellow employees 'barely reached tolerable maturity levels for junior high students' ") (citation omitted); *Pavone*, 1997 WL 441312, at *8; *Hatfield*, 920 F. Supp. 109; *Kent*, 790 F. Supp. 1040–41.

[43] *See* Washington v. HCA Health Services of Texas, 1998 U.S. App. LEXIS 21551 (5th Cir. Sept. 3, 1998) (after working 12- to 16- hour days and 60- to 80-hour weeks, the plaintiff's doctor recommended a reduction to 10-hour days and 50-hour weeks); *Williams*, 1997 WL 158176, at *1 (involving a doctor who recommended that an employee limit her work days to 10 hours); Kolpas v. Searle, 959 F. Supp. 525, 527 (N.D. Ill. 1997) (requiring an employee to work at least 60- to 70-hour weeks); *Simmerman*, 1996 WL 131948, at *1 (involving an employee with depression who was not qualified to perform the essential functions of managing a fast food restaurant because he could work only the day shift and not more than 40 hours per week); Mazzarella v. United Postal Serv., 849 F. Supp. 89, 91–92 (D. Mass 1994) (noting that the plaintiff, by his own choice, worked 6 or 7 days a week, 8 hours a day, but testified "that such a schedule was probably not good for his 'balance' ").

[44] Webb v. Mercy Hospital, 102 F.3d 958, 959 (8th Cir. 1996) (involving a nurse who was unable to work the night shift). Because of the effects of some psychotropic medications, some workers who take these drugs find it extremely difficult to work night shifts or begin work early in the morning. *See Practice and Compliance Manual, supra* n. 35, at 101.

Courts cite three principle justifications for ruling against plaintiffs in these cases, corresponding to the elements of a prima facie case under the ADA. First, courts often conclude that a plaintiff is not disabled because his or her claimed disability results from stress, abuse, or difficulties with a supervisor. Even if the plaintiff is hospitalized—and despite EEOC enforcement guidance that interacting with others is a major life activity[45]—most courts hold as a matter of law that conditions arising from an interpersonal conflict at work or job-related stress cannot be considered a disability for the purposes of the ADA.[46]

Second, courts conclude that the ability to withstand stressful work conditions or the ability to get along with others is so essential to the job that a plaintiff cannot be considered a qualified individual with a disability.[47] Courts make abstract judgments that job stress and getting along with others are inherent to employment without examining each situation in the individualized terms required by the ADA. Courts, therefore, do not determine the source of the stress or interpersonal difficulties or whether, in the plaintiff's situation, that particular stressor is indeed essential to the plaintiff's actual job.[48]

Third, courts either refuse to consider or they simply deny plaintiffs' proffered reasonable accommodations.[49] Although the ADA requires courts to consider whether reasonable accommodations could render an employee qualified,[50] courts deem accommodations such as transfer or reduction in hours to be unreasonable in psychiatric disability cases, even though they are routinely granted in other disability cases. No court, however, has required an employer to show that abusive or stressful practices are so necessary to a job that eliminating them would "fundamentally alter" the actual job being done.

This chapter tracks the elements of an ADA claim, arguing that judicial assumptions about the nature of psychiatric disabilities and essential employment functions have resulted in the near-total failure of the ADA to protect individuals with psychiatric disabilities from employment discrimination. Solutions to this problem are discussed, focusing on the ADA's prohibition of practices that have a disparate impact on people with disabilities.

Defining Disability to Exclude Workers With Psychiatric Disabilities

To establish a claim under Title I of the ADA, a plaintiff must show that he or she is disabled, qualified for the job, and discriminated against on the basis of a disability.[51] The ADA defines disability as "[a] a physical or mental impairment that

---

[45] See *Practice and Compliance Manual, supra* n. 35, at 91. However, the EEOC notes that an individual "is not substantially limited just because [he or she] is irritable or has some trouble getting along with a supervisor or co-worker." *Id.* at 91, n. 15.

[46] See *infra* notes 95–121 and accompanying text. The only judge who appears to have a different understanding is Judge Richard Posner. See *infra* text accompanying notes 123–125.

[47] See *infra* notes 122–140 and accompanying text.

[48] See *infra* notes 144–186 and accompanying text.

[49] See *Ralph,* 135 F.3d 166 (1st Cir. 1998); *Lewis,* 908 F. Supp. 946 (finding that the "plaintiff's requested accommodation of a transfer [was] unreasonable as a matter of law"); *Mazzarella,* 849 F. Supp. 95; *Mancini,* 820 F. Supp. 148 (D. Vt. 1993) (involving an invalid request for transfer).

[50] See 42 U.S.C. § 12111(8).

[51] See *id.* at § 12112.

substantially limits one or more of the major life activities of such individual; [b] a record of such an impairment; or [c] being regarded as having such an impairment."[52]

The first and most common rationale used by courts in dismissing employment discrimination claims brought by employees claiming to have a psychiatric disability is that the employee is in fact not disabled under the ADA. The reason advanced by courts for this conclusion is not based on the absence of serious manifestations of disability—many plaintiffs are hospitalized, on medication, and under the care of one or more doctors or specialists. Rather, courts conclude as a matter of law that disabilities alleged by plaintiffs to be caused by workplace abuse, interpersonal conflicts, and job stress are not disabilities for purposes of the ADA.

Workplace Abuse and Interpersonal Conflicts on the Job

For many years, all law review articles written about abuse in the workplace focused specifically on abuse related to race or gender.[53] Vast compendia were written about labor law that did not contain a single word about abuse in the workplace. At the same time, case law and the popular press, books, and oral histories by and about workers[54] are filled with stories indicating both the extent to which workplace abuse is common and the toll it takes on workers. For example, every year the organization "9 to 5" sponsors a "worst boss" contest,[55] which receives thousands of entries, including,

> [a] manufacturing company [that] demand[ed] mandatory overtime, making some employees work 16 hours a day, seven days a week, then force[d] all employees to take their two-week vacations at the end of May, when most kids [were] still in school. The plant [was not] air-conditioned, but workers [were] forbidden to drink water unless on an authorized break.[56]

Other entries included a boss whose response to an employee's request for bereavement leave following a miscarriage late in her pregnancy was to demand the baby's death certificate[57] and an employee who "raced home [from work] to her hysterical children and found the baby sitter dead on the sofa" and was then ordered

---

[52]*Id.* at § 12102(2) (West 2000).

[53]Regina Austin provided one notable exception. *See* Austin, *supra* n. 36, at 1–5. A few authors have responded to her suggestion that the tort of intentional infliction of emotional distress be expanded to render employers more frequently liable for abuse in the workplace. *See* David P. Duffy, "Intentional Infliction of Emotional Distress and Employment at Will: The Case Against 'Tortification' of Labor and Employment Law," *Boston University Law Rev.* 74 (1994): 387, 390, 391. Other authors have written on workplace harassment based on a person's disability rather than on day-to-day abuse directed at all employees. *See, e.g.,* Frank S. Ravitch, "Beyond Reasonable Accommodation: The Availability and Structure of a Cause of Action for Workplace Harassment Under the Americans With Disabilities Act," *Cardozo Law Rev.* 15 (1994): 1475.

[54]*See, e.g.,* Rosalyn Baxandall and Linda Gordon, *America's Working Women: A Documentary History 1600 to the Present* (New York: Norton, 1995); Joe R. Feagin and Melvin P. Sikes, *Living With Racism: The Black Middle-Class Experience* (Boston: Beacon Press, 1994).

[55]*See* Tamara Jones, "A Real Piece of Work: 'Worst Boss' Contest Lets Employees Vent," *Washington Post* (Oct. 16, 1997): B1.

[56]*See id.*

[57]*See id.*

back to work by her employer, who said "she was of more use to him than to the nanny."[58]

These stories are extreme but not necessarily aberrant. Researchers have confirmed that workplace abuse is common. Despite losing a great deal of productivity, the American workplace is permeated with "an organizational perversity where abusers are often protected and the victims punished."[59] In a television show about mothers on welfare going back to work, one repentant woman explained why she had lost two jobs since returning to work and would now be able to retain the third because of the lessons she had learned:

> I guess I've been out of the work field too long to realize that if the boss screams at you for no reason or if he says something that's his way, whether you're right or wrong, it doesn't matter; it's the boss, and that's what I consider the business politics that I've learned on the past two jobs, so I'm ready for my third and my last.[60]

An article in *The Indiana Lawyer* noted casually, "Leadership styles vary greatly, of course. We've all had bosses who were screamers."[61] One article in the wake of the controversy surrounding basketball player Latrell Sprewell's attack on his coach[62] observed that

> one of the dirty little secrets of the American workplace—and a mostly overlooked wrinkle in the firing of basketball player Latrell Sprewell—is the so-called "screamer," a boss who feels at liberty to berate and belittle his employees even if he feels constrained by law or political correctness from making sexual advances or using racial epithets.[63]

Case law often describes harrowing workplace environments. One 3rd Circuit Court case is worth quoting in detail:

> Baccigalupi's [the supervisor] intent to inflict emotional distress can further be seen in his total lack of any vestige of compassion for any woman in the office. On one occasion Meyer told Baccigalupi that he "couldn't continue performing 'root canal' on woman agents on his staff because they broke down in tears." [The 3rd Circuit Court explained in a footnote that *root canal* is a term coined by Baccigalupi to describe intense and emotionally painful sessions in which he would berate and demean disfavored agents with the purpose of forcing them out of the company.] At that point, Baccigalupi simply selected a woman agent to abuse as a demonstration, saying, "Well, don't worry. I'll show you how to handle it." Appellant describes this contrived encounter as follows: He then called one of the woman agents in for review and

---

[58]*Id.* The story also detailed a boss who "in addition to routinely screaming insults and throwing trays of hot food at the employee . . . forced her to clean the floors with a toothbrush and crawl through a Dumpster to find a burned biscuit when she was seven months pregnant."

[59]*Id.* (quoting Dr. Harvey Hornstein of Columbia University, who studied more than 1,000 workers over 8 years).

[60]*The News Hour With Jim Lehrer* (Oct. 10, 1997) (New York & Washington, DC: Public Broadcasting Service) (comments of Renee Lawrence).

[61]George A. Buskirk, Jr., "Leadership in a Legal Organization," *Indiana Law Rev.* (Nov. 12, 1997): 17.

[62]*See* Jonathan Kirsch, "The Screamer and His Fire Within," *L. A. Times* (Dec. 14, 1997): M5.

[63]*Id.*

started the "root canal" and the intimidation on her until she broke down and started crying. R. Baccigalupi kept tearing and pressing into her and when it was over and she had left the office, he was holding out his suspender straps as if to say, this is how you handle it, don't let their emotions get in the way.[64]

The cases brought by plaintiffs with psychiatric disabilities under the ADA mirror these observations. Courts' generalizations that the ability to cope with virtually any level of stress is essential to maintaining employment in this country often insulate levels of abuse or extreme working conditions unnecessary to the essential functions of any job. The stories told by plaintiffs range from physical assault by supervisors[65] and limitations on use of the restroom[66] to repeated harassment and criticism.[67] *Kotlowski v. Eastman Kodak Co.*[68] is a fairly representative case in its seamless intertwining of gender and disability issues. Kotlowski's supervisor "berated her for her professional shortcomings and told her she had fallen through the cracks. [He] hovered around her cubicle, making her feel very nervous and pressured. He would sometimes tell her that stress was good for her."[69] When Kotlowski attempted to approach him with medical concerns, "he told [her] that she was a hypochondriac."[70] He also "repeatedly commented that the length of [her] skirts was too short, that she should dress more conservatively, and that people would perceive her in a negative way."[71]

Other cases arise out of workplace harassment over perceived homosexuality. One of the more extreme examples of these cases, which may now be prosecuted as sex discrimination cases,[72] is *Hatfield v. Quantum Chemicals*.[73] Hatfield's supervisor harassed him continually. In particular, the plaintiff alleged that his supervisor would sometimes summon [him] by calling him "pussy." In the spring of 1992, Hatfield had injured his back on the job. When he approached the supervisor about getting time off to see a chiropractor, the supervisor responded by telling Hatfield to get underneath his desk and perform oral sex on him. The supervisor then laughed and walked off. In May 1992, Hatfield was standing by a water fountain when the supervisor grabbed the back of his head and pulled it toward the supervisor's groin and asked if he was ready to perform oral sex on him.[74]

These kinds of stories are also found in ADA claims brought by people with physical disabilities[75] whose coworkers often taunt them by calling them mentally

---

[64]Subbe-Hirt v. Baccigalupi, 94 F.3d 111, 114, and n. 3 (3d Cir. 1996).

[65]*See* Hatfield v. Quantum Chemical Corp., 920 F. Supp. 108, 109 (S.D. Tex. 1996).

[66]*See* Barton v. Tampa Electric Co., 1997 WL 128158, at *1 (M.D. Fla. Mar. 11, 1997).

[67]*See* DiGloria v. American Telegraph & Tel. Co., 1993 WL 735034 (M.D. Fla. Nov. 30, 1993).

[68]922 F. Supp. 790 (W.D. N.Y. 1996).

[69]*Id.* at 800 (citations omitted).

[70]*Id.*

[71]*Id.*

[72]*See* Oncale v. Sundowner Offshore Services, Inc., 523 U.S. 75 (1998).

[73]920 F. Supp. 108 (S.D. Tex. 1996).

[74]*Id.* at 109.

[75]The difference is that plaintiffs with physical disabilities—even physical disabilities about which some are skeptical—often win their challenges of workplace abuse. *See, e.g.,* Goodman v. Boeing Co., 899 P.2d 1265, 1267 (Wash. 1995) (involving a plaintiff with carpal tunnel syndrome who won $1.1 million).

disabled.[76] In *Rivera v. Domino's Pizza*,[77] Rivera's coworkers and supervisors mocked his speech defect and cleft palate and lip by calling him "a numskull" and "retarded," and they told Domino's customers that he had been hired from a local facility for mentally handicapped people and that "the reason Rivera was 'so fucked up' was that he was a 'failed abortion.' "[78]

The cases often concern supervisors who curse, yell, or scream at their employees.[79] Neither the employer nor the courts, however, consider the screaming supervisor the problem in these situations.[80] As one author recently wrote,

> some bosses feel empowered to treat their subordinates with a degree of coarseness, contempt and cruelty that would be unthinkable in any other social setting. I observed that screamers are often coddled and even encouraged within the corporate culture if they are successful at making money for the company. . . . Screamers are still tolerated in workplaces where sexual advances and racial epithets are now forbidden.[81]

The reactions of psychiatrically vulnerable employees to this kind of treatment vary.[82] Some get angry and are fired for being "insubordinate"[83]; some break down and leave the premises, and they are then fired for leaving work without notifying their immediate supervisors.[84] As outlined in the next two sections, courts either find as a matter of law that plaintiffs cannot be disabled by the abusive treatment of supervisors or that their anger or breakdowns render them unqualified for employment. Courts reject outright any suggestion that the employer might have an obligation to either create a more respectful environment or, at least, transfer the employee.

In fact, one of the concerns addressed by the Supreme Court in *Oncale v. Sundowner Offshore Services*,[85] was the specter that the decision would create "a general

---

[76]Rivera-Flores v. Puerto Rico Tel. Co., 64 F.3d 742, 744 (1st Cir. 1995) (involving coworkers and supervisors who called a woman with cataracts and glaucoma "'little blind lady,' 'mentally retarded,' 'mutant,' cross-eyed, and physically repulsive, and hid or defaced her paperwork"); Williams v. Kerr-McGee Corp., 110 F.3d 74 (table), 1997 WL 158176 (10th Cir. Apr. 1, 1997) (involving psychiatric problems related to exacerbation of lupus by job stress).

[77]1996 WL 53802 (E.D. Pa. Feb. 9, 1996).

[78]*Id.* at *1 (citations omitted).

[79]*See, e.g.*, Curry v. Empire Berol, 134 F.3d 370 (table), 1998 WL 13407, at *1 (6th Cir. Jan. 7, 1998) (involving a supervisor who cursed at an employee); Dewitt v. Carsten, 941 F. Supp. 1232, 1234 (N.D. Ga. 1996) (involving a supervisor who "scolded and yelled at [the] plaintiff"), *aff'd mem.*, 122 F.3d 1079 (11th Cir. 1997).

[80]*See Curry*, 1998 WL 13407, at *4 (holding that the plaintiff failed to state a claim); *Dewitt*, 941 F. Supp. 1241 (granting the defendant's motion for a partial summary judgment).

[81]*Kirsch, supra* n. 62, at M5.

[82]Unfortunately for those who might have hoped that the advent of women in positions of authority might make for a kinder, gentler workplace, I have not been able to detect any gender-specific pattern of allegations of abuse or harassment at work. That is, although many of the cases are brought by women and minorities, both men and women are portrayed as abusive supervisors by employees of both genders. The stories seem to have far more to do with workplace cultures of hierarchy and authority than of gender.

[83]*See, e.g.*, Mancini v. General Electric Co., 820 F. Supp. 141, 143 (D. Vt. 1993) (involving a plaintiff who frequently had heated arguments with his supervisor, including one incident where he "lost his temper with his supervisor and directed abusive language at him").

[84]*See, e.g.*, Simpkins v. Specialty Envelope, Inc., 94 F.3d 645 (table), 1996 WL 452858, at *1–2 (6th Cir. Aug. 9, 1996).

[85]523 U.S. 75 (1998) (holding that Title VII covers same-sex harassment).

civility code for the American workplace."[86] The court was reassuring that this "risk" could be met by "careful attention to the requirements of the statute."[87] The court emphasized that "verbal or physical harassment" is not prohibited by Title VII and that it had "never held that workplace harassment, even harassment between men and women, is automatically discrimination."[88] Although concern about vague prohibitions of undefined behavior in the workplace is understandable, the vehemence with which the court rejected a "code of civility" in the workplace and rejected any prohibition on generalized workplace abuse only confirms the extent of the problem facing emotionally fragile workers today.

The Relationship Between Abuse and Interpersonal Conflicts and the Definition of Disability

One of the fundamental canons of psychiatry and the medical profession is that high levels of stress can cause, trigger, or exacerbate both physical illness and psychiatric disabilities.[89] These disabilities and illnesses, however, can diminish or even vanish if the stress is reduced.

Because courts, consciously or unconsciously, associate disability with the model of blindness, deafness, and severe mobility impairment, they construct disability as permanent, unchanging, and located totally within the individual. Although some courts have been able to understand that physical disability can manifest itself episodically[90] or as a result of a physical environment[91] or physical demands,[92] courts do not have the same understanding of psychiatric disabilities, which also manifest themselves episodically[93] and often as a result of environmental or psychological demands. Above all, courts cannot conceptualize disability as interactional or arising in an interpersonal context. Therefore, they cannot recognize many psychiatric disability claims, sometimes declaring that psychiatric disabilities of certain origins

---

[86] *Id.* at 80.

[87] *Id.*

[88] *Id.*

[89] *See* Linas A. Bieliauskas, *Stress and Its Relationship to Health and Illness* (Boulder, CO: Westview Press, 1982) at 22–23, 63, 81–87; Muhammad Jamal, "Relationship of Job Stress and Type-A Behavior to Employees' Job Satisfaction, Organizational Commitment, Psychosomatic Health Problems, and Turnover Motivation," 43 *Human Relations* 43 (1990): 727, 735. *See also* Simpson v. Chater, 908 F. Supp. 817, 822 (D. Or. 1995) (noting that the plaintiff's treating physician confirmed that "stress of working would exacerbate the progression of [the plaintiff's multiple sclerosis]").

[90] *See* Vande Zande v. Wisconsin Department of Administration, 44 F.3d 538, 544 (7th Cir. 1995) ("An intermittent impairment that is a characteristic manifestation of an admitted disability is, we believe, a part of the underlying disability, and hence a condition that the employer must reasonably accommodate. *Often the disabling aspect of a disability is, precisely, an intermittent manifestation of the disability rather than the underlying impairment.*") (emphasis added).

[91] *See* Fehr v. McLean Packaging Corp., 860 F. Supp. 198, 200 (E.D. Pa. 1994).

[92] *See* Valle v. City of Chicago, 982 F. Supp. 560, 565 (N.D. Ill. 1997) (finding that a police officer candidate with rhabdomyolysis [a physical disability that manifests itself under heavy physical exertion] stated a claim under the ADA when denied a requested accommodation of a relaxed running requirement in the police training program).

[93] *See Practice and Compliance Manual, supra* n. 35, at 93 ("Chronic episodic conditions may constitute substantially limiting impairments if they are substantially limiting when active or have a high likelihood of recurrence in substantially limiting forms.").

(primarily disabilities the plaintiff traces to difficulties with coworkers or supervisors) cannot even exist as a matter of law.[94]

In *Weiler v. Household Finance Corp.*,[95] the plaintiff asked to be transferred after her supervisor, who had decided to conduct her annual employment review in the cafeteria,

> got loud, sarcastic and abusive. He discussed her physical and mental disabilities in a loud voice and was critical of the various therapies she was undergoing. On numerous occasions during the evaluation, [he] allegedly lunged forward in his chair and put his face close to plaintiff's and got louder.[96]

This was apparently the culmination of a long campaign of abuse by the plaintiff's supervisor.[97] In a later decision granting the defendant's motion for summary judgment, the court noted,

> the ADA does not protect people from the general stresses of the workplace. Everyone has encountered difficult situations in the working environment. Being unwilling or even unable to work with a particular individual simply is not the equivalent of being "substantially limited" in the life activity of working ... The evidence shows that the plaintiff had a personality conflict with [her supervisor], albeit one which caused her to suffer anxiety and depression to an apparently significant degree. A disability is part of someone and goes with her to her next job. A personality conflict, on the other hand, is specific to an individual, in this case, [plaintiff's supervisor].[98]

In *Weiler*, the court, like subsequent courts in these cases, supported its decision by microanalyzing Weiler's situation as a personality conflict with her supervisor.[99] By definition, analyzing the situation in this way ensured that Weiler could not meet the EEOC regulatory requirement that her disability disqualify her from more than a single job.[100] The court did not frame her disability as an unusual fragility or vulnerability to interpersonal conflict or public humiliation[101] that she *would* carry

---

[94] *See* Siemon v. American Telephone & Tel. Corp., 117 F.3d 1173, 1176 (10th Cir. 1997) (stating that a "mental impairment merely prevent[ing a plaintiff] from working under a few supervisors within the organizational structure of one major corporation . . . is far too narrow to constitute a 'class of jobs'" under the ADA's interpretive guidelines); Weiler v. Household Finance Corp., No. 93 C 6454, 1995 WL 452977, at *5 (N.D. Ill. July 27, 1995) (holding that a conflict with an employer is not recognized as a disability under the ADA), *aff'd*, 101 F.3d 519 (7th Cir. 1996); Dewitt v. Carsten, 941 F. Supp. 1232, 1236 (N.D. Ga. 1996) (finding that job-related stress does not qualify as a disability under the ADA); Hatfield v. Quantum Chemical Corp., 920 F. Supp. 108, 110 (S.D. Tex. 1996) (holding that disability due to friction with a supervisor does not qualify as a disability under the ADA); Adams v. Alderson, 723 F. Supp. 1531, 1531 (D.D.C. 1989) (finding that an employee's reaction to a supervisor was a "transitory phenomenon" because it would disappear if the supervisor was removed).

[95] No. 93 C 6454, 1994 WL 262175 (N.D. Ill. June 10, 1994).

[96] *Id.* at *1.

[97] *Id.* at *1–2.

[98] *Weiler*, 1995 WL 452977, at *5.

[99] *See id.* at *4–5.

[100] *See* 29 C.F.R. § 1630.2(j)(3)(i) (1997). This section provides that with respect to the major life activity of working, "the term *substantially limits* means significantly restricted in the ability to perform either a class of jobs or a broad range of jobs in various classes as compared to the average person having comparable training, skills and abilities. The inability to perform a single, particular job does not constitute a substantial limitation in the major life activity of working."

[101] *See Weiler*, 1995 WL 452977, at *5.

with her to her next job and that, in fact, is replicated in many other psychiatric disability cases.[102]

It is important to underscore that psychiatric disabilities are the only disabilities in which courts look to etiology or cause rather than to manifestations of the disability itself to determine whether a plaintiff is a member of the protected class. Weiler was placed on disability leave and diagnosed with depression and anxiety after the incident with her supervisor.[103] The court acknowledged that she suffered "anxiety and depression to an apparently significant degree."[104] But it does not matter whether plaintiffs are institutionalized[105] or medicated with powerful psychotropic drugs,[106] courts are unmoved even if all testifying experts and physicians agree on their diagnosis. If the disability arises from interpersonal difficulties, it is not a disability under the ADA as a matter of law. Plaintiffs who claim that their psychiatric disability is related to a conflict with their supervisors do not win ADA cases.[107]

Meanwhile, physical disabilities that manifest themselves in interpersonal difficulties are protected, as are psychiatric disabilities that arise from various other sources. For instance, in *Gilday v. Mecosta County,*[108] the court held that an emergency medical technician who was fired because he was rude and could not get along with coworkers and patients stated a cause of action under the ADA because he was a diabetic.[109] The plaintiff had put forth sufficient evidence to overcome summary judgment by alleging that fluctuating blood sugar levels impaired his ability to work amiably with coworkers and others.[110] The court also noted that Gilday became "frustrated and irritable" when his blood sugar deviated from normal levels[111] and that "stress [could] also apparently cause his blood sugar to fluctuate wildly"[112]; therefore, the case was remanded so the district court could consider whether transfer to a less stressful and chaotic position would be a reasonable accommodation.[113] The court found that "the ability to get along with coworkers and customers is necessary for all but the most solitary of occupations"[114] and used this to support a finding of substantial limitation in Gilday's ability to work. This holding is in striking contrast to the legion of ADA cases where a plaintiff with a mental or emotional problem is found not to be disabled.

---

[102] *See* Mears v. Gulfstream Aerospace Corp., 905 F. Supp. 1075, 1077 (S.D. Ga. 1995) (noting that the precipitating event of a breakdown was the employee being escorted through the office by two security guards for a drug test after she had dropped files while suffering from a migraine), *aff'd mem.,* 87 F.3d 1331 (11th Cir. 1996).

[103] *See Weiler,* 1995 WL 452977, at *1.

[104] *Id.* at *5.

[105] *See* Miller v. National Casualty Co., 61 F.3d 627, 629 (8th Cir. 1995) (involving an employer held not to have been informed of the plaintiff's disability, despite a call from the plaintiff's sister saying that she "was mentally falling apart and the family was trying to get her into the hospital"); *Simpkins,* 1996 WL 452858, at *2; *Adams,* 723 F. Supp. 1531 note 1.

[106] *See Simpkins,* 1996 WL 452858, at *2.

[107] *See, e.g., id.;* Mundo v. Sanus Health Plan, 966 F. Supp. 171, 173 (E.D. N.Y. 1997); *Mears,* 905 F. Supp. 1075.

[108] 124 F.3d 760 (6th Cir. 1997).

[109] *See id.* at 765.

[110] *See id.*

[111] *Id.* at 761.

[112] *Id.*

[113] *See id.* at 766.

[114] *Id.* at 765.

Likewise, the very few psychiatric disability cases that survive motions to dismiss or for summary judgment are cases in which the disability either clearly does not arise from the work environment or arises from some physical and nonpersonal aspect of the employment. For example, courts have less difficulty accepting psychiatric disabilities such as posttraumatic stress disorder from service in Vietnam or from working search, rescue, and clean-up duty at an airplane crash site[115]; claustrophobia[116]; agoraphobia[117]; anxiety disorder related to commuting[118] stress related to working with nuclear energy[119]; and, occasionally, those related to the side effects of medication taken for mental disorders.[120]

Thus, the rejection of psychiatric disability is not so much a repudiation of the theory that disabilities can be triggered by environment or context as it is a visceral rejection of the specific contention that disabilities can be triggered by dealing with other people. The court in *Weiler* makes clear its belief that Weiler, who worked for Household Finance without difficulty for 7 years, is simply "unwilling" to work with her supervisor.[121] Whereas Gilday is excused from responsibility for monitoring his blood sugar level, Weiler is ousted from the legal system for failing to control her reaction to her supervisor, a man who conducted her performance evaluation in the cafeteria and yelled at her.[122] If Weiler's supervisor had sexually harassed her, the question would not be whether she could control her reactions, but why the supervisor was not controlling his actions. Her reaction to being yelled at is, however, her problem.

Of all judges to consider these ADA cases, only Judge Richard Posner has been willing to entertain the notion that disabilities may arise from interpersonal difficulties on the job. In *Palmer v. Circuit Court,* Judge Posner summarized the district court decision below:

---

[115] Sherback v. Wright Automotive Group 987 F. Supp. 433 (W.D. Pa. 1997).

[116] *See, e.g.,* Neveau v. Boise Cascade Corp., 902 F. Supp. 207 (D. Or. 1995) (denying a summary judgment because genuine issue existed whether claustrophobia caused by having to enter small enclosed "slusher" substantially limited the plaintiff's ability to perform her job).

[117] *See, e.g.,* Przybylak v. New York State Thruway Authority, No. 95-CV-0707E(F), 1997 WL 662346 (W.D. N.Y. Oct. 16, 1997) (denying a summary judgment because the genuine issue remained whether accommodation was reasonable); Ofat v. Ohio Civil Rights Commission, No. 94-J-31, 1995 WL 310051 (Ohio Ct. App. May 17, 1995) (affirming lower court's judgment against state for discrimination against an employee with panic disorder).

[118] *See, e.g.,* Poindexter v. Atchison, Topeka & Santa Fe Railway Co., 975 F. Supp. 1387 (D. Kan. 1997) (stating that the summary judgment was improper because a genuine issue existed whether plaintiff's anxiety disorder qualified as a disability), *rev'd and remanded,* 168 F.3d 1228 (10th Cir. 1999).

[119] *See, e.g.,* Pritchard v. Southern Co. Services, 102 F.3d 1118 (11th Cir. 1996) (reversing the summary judgment against the plaintiff on ADA and Rehabilitation Act claims).

[120] *Cf.* Overton v. Reilly, 977 F.2d 1190, 1195 (7th Cir. 1992) (finding that the summary judgment was precluded by a genuine issue of whether the plaintiff qualified for protection under the Rehabilitation Act due to depression medication that caused sleepiness at work) *and* Fehr v. McLean Packaging Co., 860 F. Supp. 198, 200 (E.D. Pa. 1994) (denying the summary judgment because a genuine issue remained whether shortness of breath caused by medication qualified as a disability under the ADA) *with* Gordon v. E. L. Hamm & Associates, 100 F.3d 907, 912 (11th Cir. 1996) (granting the summary judgment for the employer because the plaintiff failed to show that side effects resulting from chemotherapy treatments substantially limited his ability to work).

[121] *See Weiler,* 1995 WL 452977, at *4 ("It is clear that the plaintiff could work either in another position for this employer or for another employer—she simply could not (or would not) work under [her current supervisor].").

[122] *See id.* at *1.

The district judge determined, as a matter of law, that Palmer's depression and par-
anoia were not disabling because she testified in her deposition that she had never
had any problems at work before Clara Johnson became her supervisor. This meant,
the judge thought that Palmer had merely had "a personality conflict with her supervisor, Clara Johnson, and her co-worker, Nicki Lazzaro—although one which caused
her to suffer anxiety and depression to an apparently significant degree."[123]

Judge Posner at first appeared to support this conclusion:

The judge was certainly correct that a personality conflict with a supervisor or co-
worker does not establish a disability within the meaning of disability law . . . even
if it produces anxiety and depression, as such conflicts often do. Such a conflict is
not disabling; at most it requires the worker to get a new job.[124]

But then, in seeming contradiction to the previous two sentences, Judge Posner stated
what no other judge to date has understood:

But if a personality conflict triggers a serious mental illness that is in turn disabling,
the fact that the trigger was not itself a disabling illness is no defense. Schizophrenia
and other psychoses are frequently triggered by minor accidents or other sources of
normal stress . . . Our only point is to distinguish between the nondisabling trigger of
a disabling mental illness and the mental illness itself. On the record compiled in the
district court, it is not possible to negate the inference that Palmer has in fact a
disabling mental illness.[125]

Although people can differ over whether workplace abuse especially at the levels
seen in many of these cases constitutes a source of "normal stress" (with the accompanying assumption that normal stress conditions are acceptable), Judge Posner's
fundamental proposition that a disability should not be disqualified merely because
of its source in interpersonal conflict is sound. The key in psychiatric disability cases,
as in all other disability cases, is to look at the manifestations of disability rather
than the etiology of disability.

The Relationship Between Stress and the Definition of Disability

A number of ADA claims relate to difficulty in tolerating stress. Plaintiffs who allege
that their psychiatric disabilities arise from stress, like plaintiffs whose claims arise
from interpersonal difficulties, are regarded by courts as not being disabled as a

---

[123]Palmer v. Circuit Court, 117 F.3d 351, 352 (7th Cir. 1997). Although the description that the
personality conflict "caused her to suffer anxiety and depression to an apparently significant degree" is
identical to the phrase used in *Weiler*, the cases were decided by different judges, *id.*; *Weiler*, 1995 WL
452977, at *5. The *Weiler* decision predated, and obviously influenced, the judge in *Palmer*.

[124]*Palmer*, 117 F.3d 352 (citation omitted). The ease with which this circuit court judge with lifetime
tenure assumes that a clerical-level Black woman who has schizophrenia and major depression in Cook
County can simply "go out and get a new job" speaks volumes about the different worlds in which he
and the plaintiff live their lives.

[125]*Id.* It is, of course, not only schizophrenia that can be triggered in this way but also major
depression, anxiety disorders, and bipolar disorder. *See* Bieliauskas, *supra* n. 89, at 87; Peter C. Whybrow, *A Mood Apart: Depression, Mania and Other Afflictions of the Self* (New York: Basic Books,
1997) at 172–173, 182. However, the conditions Judge Posner described were only the ones principally
at issue in *Palmer*.

matter of law.[126] In one case, a plaintiff raised both job stress and interpersonal difficulties associated with her supervisor, a sheriff.[127] The court held that she could not be disabled as a matter of law:

> Indeed, the causal relationship between the job and her claimed "disability" distinguishes plaintiff's stress from other conditions that clearly constitute disabilities under the ADA. After all, a visually impaired person will be visually impaired no matter what job he holds; a quadriplegic will be unable to walk whether or not he is employed. Plaintiff's "disability," however, was triggered only when, out of the universe of hundreds of jobs, she held a very specific job in the jail that required a lot of interaction with inmates and with the Sheriff. According to plaintiff, this disability would not be triggered if plaintiff had a job that required less interaction with these individuals.[128]

Perhaps this plaintiff should not have won. Her inability to interact with prisoners in jail may have rendered her unable to perform an essential function of the job, and perhaps she could not be reasonably accommodated.[129] But the court found that she had not and could not demonstrate that she was disabled precisely because she alleged that her disability was triggered by personal interactions and because she referred to it as extreme stress and anxiety.[130]

The very essence of most psychiatric disabilities, however, is that they can be triggered or exacerbated by environmental stimuli, principally stress and stressful interactions with others.[131] In this respect, they are similar to many physical disabilities.[132] The very fact that psychiatric difficulties manifest themselves in certain contexts and relationships but not in others might be interpreted as making them easier to accommodate through transfer or reassignment. Instead, courts interpret this dichotomy to mean that they are not disabilities at all, at least for the purposes of Title I of the ADA. For example, in *Adams v. Alderson*,[133] the court noted that "Adams' present psychiatrist . . . describes his condition as a 'maladaptive reaction to a psychosocial stressor,' viz., the antagonizing supervisor, which is, however, a transitory phenomenon that can be expected to disappear when the 'psychosocial stressor' is

---

[126]*See, e.g.,* Mundo v. Sanus Health Plan, 966 F. Supp. 171, 173 (E.D. N.Y. 1997) ("An inability to tolerate stressful situations is not an impairment for purposes of the ADA."); Dewitt v. Carsten, 941 F. Supp. 1232, 1236 (N.D. Ga. 1996) (stating that stress triggered by only one job does not constitute a disability under the ADA), *aff'd mem.,* 122 F.3d 1079 (11th Cir. 1997).

[127]*See Dewitt,* 941 F. Supp. at 1234.

[128]*Id.* at 1237 (footnote omitted).

[129]The plaintiff had asked for a transfer to a position at the courthouse that apparently required less interaction with prisoners and the sheriff. *See id.* at 1234–1235. *But see* Sharp v. Abate, 887 F. Supp. 695, 699 (S.D. N.Y. 1995) (finding that the summary judgment was precluded because dealing with inmates may not be an essential function of a corrections officer in New York).

[130]*See Dewitt,* 941 F. Supp. at 1234.

[131]*See* Whybrow, *supra* n. 125, at 169–195.

[132]*See* Dwight Evans et al., "Severe Life Stress as a Predictor of Early Disease Progression in HIV Infection," *American J. Psychiatry* 154 (May 1997): 630 (finding that for every single severe stressor per 6-month study interval, the risk of early disease progression doubled, and for subjects in the study for at least 2 years, higher severe life stress increased the odds of developing HIV-disease progression nearly fourfold).

[133]723 F. Supp. 1531 (D.D.C. 1989) (involving the Rehabilitation Act).

removed."[134] This observation appears to indicate that Adams was capable of meeting the essential functions of the job with a transfer to a different supervisor. The next step would have been to inquire whether such a transfer was a reasonable accommodation under the circumstances. The court, however, used the psychiatrist's testimony to find that Adams was not disabled at all: "[The condition] is, therefore, hardly an 'impairment' which 'substantially limits one or more . . . major life activities.'"[135]

Most courts faced with claims of disability resulting from stress do not look at the results of the stress but simply hold as a matter of law that stress is not a disability under the ADA.[136] As with disabilities arising from interpersonal conflicts with supervisors and from workplace abuse, this conclusion misses the point. The question is not whether stress is a disability but whether the stress causes or is a symptom of a disability covered under the ADA.[137]

As in the case of interpersonal difficulties, courts have no problem understanding that job stress may cause physical disability.[138] But in a psychiatric disability case involving considerably greater manifestations of disability than reflected in the physical disability cases,[139] the court found that the plaintiff did not meet the definition of disability.[140]

Interestingly, although the definition of disability for purposes of receiving disability benefits is considerably more stringent than the definition of disability for purposes of the ADA[141]—and requires an inability to work in almost any job—many plaintiffs who lose ADA disability claims on the grounds that they are not disabled nevertheless receive disability benefits for the very disability at issue in the discrimination case.[142] Employers do not fight the disability benefits claim as rigorously as

---

[134] *Id.* at 1531.

[135] *Id.* [quoting 29 U.S.C. § 706(8)(B)] (defining *disability* for the purposes of the Rehabilitation Act).

[136] *See, e.g., Mundo,* 966 F. Supp. at 171; *Dewitt,* 941 F. Supp. at 1232.

[137] The EEOC, for example, has written that "'stress' . . . may or may not be considered [an] impairment, depending on whether . . . [it] result[s] from a documented physiological or mental disorder," *Technical Assistance Manual on the Employment Provisions (Title I) of the Americans With Disabilities Act,* 2.1(a)(i), II-3 (EEOC:1992). At least one court has followed this interpretation, *see* Paleologos v. Rehab Consultants, Inc., 990 F. Supp. 1460 (N.D. Ga. 1998).

[138] *See* Patterson v. City of Seattle, 97 F.3d 1460 (table), No. 95-35487, 1996 WL 528267, at *1–2 (9th Cir. Sept. 17, 1996) (indicating that job-related stress that exacerbated a plaintiff's Crohn's disease might require reasonable accommodation, but finding the requested accommodation not necessary for the plaintiff to perform essential functions of the job); Gonsalves v. J. F. Fredericks Tool Co., 964 F. Supp. 616, 621 (D. Conn. 1997) (acknowledging that hypertension or diabetes exacerbated by unreasonable work expectations may qualify as a disability under the ADA).

[139] Margeson v. Springfield Terminal Railway Co., No. CIV. A. 91-11475-Z, 1993 WL 343676, at *5 (D. Mass. Aug. 24, 1993) (stating that stress condition resulted in ongoing treatment, numerous trips to the emergency room, canceled family vacations, and absence from work).

[140] *See id.*

[141] To qualify for ADA protection, an employee "must show that she is a 'qualified individual with a disability' who can perform the essential functions of her position despite her disability or can perform the essential functions of her job with a reasonable accommodation." Lewis v. Zilog, Inc., 908 F. Supp. 931, 944 (N.D. Ga. 1995). However, to qualify to receive disability benefits, an employee must "be totally disabled to perform any job," *id.* at 945.

[142] *See, e.g.,* Hatfield v. Quantum Chemical Corp., 920 F. Supp. at 108, 111 (S.D. Tex. 1996); *Lewis,* 908 F. Supp. at 945.

the ADA claim; in fact, they often encourage and facilitate the disability benefits claim or even make it mandatory.[143]

Psychiatric Disability and the Requirement That Employees Be "Qualified Individuals"

In addition to requiring that plaintiffs demonstrate they are disabled in order to receive the protection of the ADA, courts require plaintiffs to establish that they are "qualified individual[s] with a disability."[144] To be a qualified individual, the plaintiff must be a person who can, "with or without reasonable accommodation, . . . perform the essential functions of the employment position."[145]

Interpersonal Conflicts and Being a "Qualified Individual"

Occasionally, a court will concede that a plaintiff is disabled and will examine the plaintiff's interpersonal difficulties in the context of being otherwise qualified for the job.[146] In determining whether a plaintiff is otherwise qualified for a job, courts undertake the very opposite mode of analysis to the one used in deciding whether a plaintiff has a disability. When courts consider whether a plaintiff is disabled, they conduct micro-analyses, examining the plaintiff's situation with great specificity. This typically leads to the determination that the inability to get along with one specific supervisor cannot constitute a disability because it leaves the plaintiff presumptively capable of performing every other job in which he or she does not report to the particular objectionable supervisor.[147]

When courts decide whether a plaintiff is "otherwise qualified," however, the inquiry is raised to a grand level of abstraction, with courts finding that "it is certainly 'a job-related requirement' that an employee, handicapped or not, be able to get along with co-workers and supervisors."[148] When deciding whether the plaintiff is disabled, courts assume that the plaintiff can get along with anyone but the supervisor in question.[149] When deciding whether the plaintiff is a "qualified individual with a disability," the plaintiff's inability to get along with one or a few people is

---

[143] See, e.g., Misek-Falkoff v. IBM Corp., 854 F. Supp. 215, 220 (S.D. N.Y. 1994), aff'd mem., 60 F.3d 811 (2d Cir. 1995).

[144] 42 U.S.C. § 12112(a) (1994).

[145] Id. at § 12111(8).

[146] Allen v. GTE Mobile Communications Service Corp., 6 A.D. Cases 1063, 1997 WL 148670 (N.D. Ga. Feb. 26, 1997); these concessions are usually made in the face of either defendant stipulations to the plaintiff's disability or overwhelming evidence of multiple hospitalizations and long histories of treatment. See, e.g., McCrory v. Kraft Food Ingredients, 98 F.3d 1342 (table), No. 94-6505, 1996 WL 571146 (6th Cir. Oct. 3, 1996); Misek-Falkoff, 854 F. Supp. at 218–219; Boldini v. Postmaster General, 928 F. Supp. at 125 (D. N.H. 1995); Lewis, 908 F. Supp. at 944.

[147] See Weiler v. Household Finance Corp., 1995 WL 452977, at *4 (N.D. Ill. July 27, 1995).

[148] Misek-Falkoff, 854 F. Supp. at 227 (S.D. N.Y. 1994).

[149] See, e.g., Hatfield v. Quantum Chemical Corp., 920 F. Supp. 108, 110 (S.D. Tex. 1996).

generalized into an inability to get along with anyone, thus rendering him or her unqualified for this or any other job.[150]

When courts analyze whether a plaintiff is disabled, the ability to get along with others is dismissed as not constituting a major life activity.[151] But when the question is whether a plaintiff is otherwise qualified to work, the ability to get along with others is deemed an essential function of the job, indeed, of any job.[152] Because social interactions are uniquely relevant in cases of psychiatric disability, this disparity sweeps into its net only people with psychiatric disabilities. Indeed, courts have enumerated a growing list of social skills as "essential" to employment.[153] Such skills include the ability to get along with supervisors and coworkers[154]; to accept and follow instructions[155]; to refrain from contentious arguments and insubordinate conduct with supervisors, coworkers, or customers[156]; to not cause or contribute to undue interruptions and hostility in the workplace[157]; and even to serve as a role model for other staff.[158] One court concluded that "plaintiff's behavior violated essential functions of her working environment" because she "conducted herself and her job as though she knew more about the particular business affairs than did her supervisors."[159]

In few of these cases do courts actually look at the specific functions of the particular job. For example, the ability to refrain from contentious arguments and insubordinate conduct with supervisors, coemployees, or customers was regarded as an essential function of the job of a mail carrier who delivered mail by herself in a rural area.[160]

In cases involving interpersonal difficulties, courts have deemed getting along

---

[150] See, e.g., Pesterfield v. Tennessee Valley Authority, 941 F.2d 437, 442 (6th Cir. 1991); Misek-Falkoff, 854 F. Supp. 227; Schmidt v. Bell, 1983 WL 631, at *14 (E.D. Pa. Sept. 9, 1983).

[151] See, e.g., Guilford of Maine, Inc., v. Soileau, 105 F.3d 12, 14–15 (1st Cir. 1997). This is true despite the fact that the EEOC has made it clear that interacting with others is, in fact, a major life activity. See Practice and Compliance Manual, supra n. 38, at 91.

[152] See, e.g., Grenier v. Cyanamid. Plastics, Inc., 70 F.3d 667, 675 (1st Cir. 1995).

[153] The district court judge in Palmer v. Circuit Court is one of the few exceptions. In dicta, he noted that "the non-essential functions of [the] plaintiff's job included working with Clara Johnson and Nicki Lazzaro." Palmer v. Circuit Court, 905 F. Supp. 499, 509 (N.D. Ill. 1995), aff'd, 117 F.3d 351 (7th Cir. 1997).

[154] See Pesterfield, 941 F.2d at 442; Misek-Falkoff, 854 F. Supp. at 227.

[155] See Boldini, 928 F. Supp. at 131.

[156] See id. (finding that the plaintiff failed to follow procedures and failed to accept authority).

[157] See Misek-Falkoff, 854 F. Supp. at 227. Under some circumstances, this could be seen as excluding union organizers from the realm of qualified employees.

[158] See EEOC v. Amego, Inc., 110 F.3d 135, 138 (1st Cir. 1997) ("The essential functions of that position included: supervising the day-to-day implementation of individual clinical, educational, and vocational programs and data collection for all programs; serving as a role model for staff in all areas of client programming, client services, and professional practice."). The court concluded that the plaintiff did not meet her burden of showing she was able to meet the essential function of overseeing and administering medication. See id. at 144.

[159] Boldini, 928 F. Supp. at 131. In this case, at the time of the events referred to by the court, Boldini had worked at the post office for almost 8 years, and her supervisor had been appointed in the previous year. See id. at 128.

[160] See id. at 131. Although there were allegations that she engaged in contentious arguments with customers and coworkers, these allegations arose for the first time 7 years after she began working, immediately after the appointment of a new supervisor. See id. at 128.

with bosses or coworkers an essential function of a job and the responsibility of the employee with a disability.[161] Cultivation of interpersonal relationships is rarely conceptualized as a shared responsibility.[162] Unfortunately, employers are not held to the slightest burden of training employees or supervisors on interpersonal skills or employee relations.[163] Like curb cuts, ramps, and other physical accommodations for people with disabilities, such training would probably benefit employees without disabilities as well.

Moreover, many courts do not appear to take very seriously plaintiffs' contentions that their difficulties in interpersonal relations stemmed from the actions of coworkers or supervisors. In one troubling case, a court declared that whether the plaintiff was correct when she stated she had not started the difficulties was irrelevant. The court noted that "where there are external indications of serious difficulties in the interaction between an employee and other employees and staff of the employer, as is the case here, the reality of perceptions of the supervisors, *regardless of the correctness of those perceptions,* presents a problem for the employer."[164]

The court is correct that supervisors' perceptions may present a problem for the employer, but the employer's problem may be one with the supervisors rather than with the plaintiff. If a supervisor perceived that cancer was contagious or that AIDS could be contracted from doorknobs, it is unlikely that a court would believe that the reality of the supervisor's perceptions, regardless of their correctness, was what counted in terminating an employee with cancer or AIDS. In *School Board of Nassau County v. Arline,*[165] the U.S. Supreme Court emphasized that disabilities could be constructed as much by the attitudes, interactions with, and reactions of others as by any inherent physical or mental limitations presented by the impairments themselves.[166] In interpreting the predecessor statute to the ADA,[167] the court disagreed with the assumption of the *Weiler* court that "a disability is part of someone that goes with her to her next job."[168] Rather, the court reasoned that disability can be

---

[161] *See id.* at 131; *Misek-Falkoff,* 854 F. Supp. at 227.

[162] *See* Wernick v. Federal Reserve Bank, 91 F.3d 379, 384 (2d Cir. 1996) ("one of the essential functions of [*her*] job was to work under her assigned supervisor") (emphasis added).

[163] Although some employers have undertaken such efforts voluntarily, the EEOC has reserved judgment on whether such training could be required as a reasonable accommodation for an individual with a disability. *See* Office of Technology Assessment, U.S. Congress, *Psychiatric Disabilities, Employment, and the Americans With Disabilities Act* (Washington, DC: Government Printing Office, 1994) at 80, n. 7.

[164] *Misek-Falkoff,* 854 F. Supp. at 228 (emphasis added).

[165] 480 U.S. 273 (1987).

[166] *See id.* at 282 and 283 ("That history [of 504] demonstrates that Congress was as concerned about the effect of an impairment on others as it was about its effect on the individual. . . . Such an impairment might not diminish a person's physical or mental capabilities, but could nevertheless substantially limit that person's ability to work as a result of the negative reactions of others to the impairment.")

[167] *See* the Rehabilitation Act of 1973, 29 U.S.C. § 791, 793–794 (1994). Congress intended interpretation of the Rehabilitation Act to conform to interpretation of the ADA and referred specifically and approvingly to the U.S. Supreme Court's interpretation of the definition of *disability* in *Arline* at several points in the legislative history of the ADA. *See* S. Rep. No. 101-116, at 23–24, 27 (1989); H.R. Rep. No. 101-485, pt. 2, at 53 (1990), *reprinted in* 1990 U.S.C.C.A.N. 303, 335; H.R. Rep. No. 101-485, pt. 3, at 30 (1990), *reprinted in* 1990 U.S.C.C.A.N. 445, 453.

[168] *Weiler,* 1995 WL 452977, at *5.

created by one's environment.[169] In fact, Congress made clear in a variety of ways, including the legislative history, comments from the floor of both the House and Senate, and through reprinting of testimony at hearings, that the reactions of others could create disabling obstacles as much or more than an individual's impairment.[170]

Stress and Being a "Qualified Individual"

In cases involving the determination of whether an employee who has difficulty withstanding stress is a qualified individual, courts also use reasoning that contradicts their assumptions when making decisions about whether people who have difficulty dealing with stress have a disability. Courts conclude in one of two ways that people whose alleged psychiatric disabilities are caused by stress are not disabled under the ADA. Either the court assumes that the stress is associated with the specific job and that the plaintiff could do any job except the one at issue,[171] or the court concludes that stress does not qualify as a disability.[172] In deciding whether a plaintiff who experiences stress in the workplace is qualified for employment, courts rely on the generalization that all employees must be able to endure stress in general; otherwise, they are not qualified for employment.[173] This contradicts Congress's instructions on interpreting the ADA on a case-by-case basis.[174]

Distinctions regarding the source of stress in the workplace are vital to understanding the requirements of Title I in the context of individuals with psychiatric disabilities. Stress in the workplace is caused by a variety of factors. The only court to parse the causes of stress noted the following:

> Sometimes . . . the job is inherently stressful. (Dealing with inmates would be a good candidate for an inherently stressful job.) Sometimes, the job is stressful because one's boss is unpleasant or demanding or yells at his employees or because the employee just does not hit it off with her boss or co-workers. Other times, the employee simply may be ill-suited in temperament or skill for the job and this poor fit will necessarily create stress as the employee endeavors to perform a job whose demands are simply too much for her.[175]

These different sources of stress have markedly different meanings under the ADA, and may lead to markedly different outcomes.

---

[169] See Arline, 480 U.S. at 283 n. 10 ("The effects of one's impairment on others is as relevant to a determination of whether one is handicapped as is the physical effect of one's handicap on oneself.").

[170] See H.R. Rep. No. 101-485, pt. 2, at 35 (1995), reprinted in 1990 U.S.C.C.A.N. 317 (quoting Senator Weicker's testimony that "people with disabilities have been saying for years that their major obstacles are not inherent in their disabilities, but arise from barriers that have been imposed externally and unnecessarily"); Cong. Rec. 135(10) (1989): 711 ("But ask any person with a disability: most often it is not his or her own disability that is limiting; it is the obstacles placed in the way by an independent society.") (statement of Senator Harkin).

[171] See, e.g., Dewitt v. Carsten, 941 F. Supp. 1232, 1235–1236 (N.D. Ga. 1996).

[172] See, e.g., id.

[173] See, e.g., id. at 1237.

[174] See, e.g., Ennis v. National Association of Business & Education Radio, Inc., 53 F.3d 55, 59–60 (4th Cir. 1995) [construing 42 U.S.C. § 12102(2)].

[175] Dewitt, 941 F. Supp. 1235.

The Job Is Inherently Stressful

The ADA requires that a plaintiff be able to perform the essential functions of a job with or without reasonable accommodation.[176] If the stress causing or exacerbating an employee's psychiatric disability is fundamentally intertwined with the essential functions of the job, and cannot be reasonably accommodated, an employer cannot be required to alter the essential functions of the job.[177]

Some courts have characterized either a particular job or all employment as "inherently stressful."[178] However, the interaction of psychiatric disability and stress is far more complicated and contextual than courts have considered. For example, as one woman with a psychiatric diagnosis wrote,

> for a decade, I functioned in the high-stress world of urban policing. Fortunately, when I got really down, there were an abundance of mental health professionals to whom I could turn for discussion and medication. Unfortunately, aberrant behavior is not easily detected among urban police professionals. Because of their independence in a patrol car and little or no supervision while on duty, they have a cult-like environment that almost encourages and rewards aggression and other violent attitudes toward street criminals. For this reason, my dark, irascible nature could sneak up on me and envelop me before anyone around me might notice. At one point I developed a reputation on the street of being the "lady cop who wouldn't take no lip off nobody." I actually considered it a compliment at the time.[179]

This woman functioned well in the stressful life of a police officer on the street but poorly in a job that was apparently less stressful. The second job required her to be "cooped up in a little room with a bunch of chattering women. [She] thought [she] would strangle more than one of them."[180] In another case, "an individual who was expert in cold stress and survival found crossing the polar ice cap considerably less demanding than giving an important lecture at the Edinburgh Medical School."[181]

Case studies show there is no single set of circumstances that employees with psychiatric disabilities identify as stressful. For example, although case law suggests that, for many people, working at home is considered less stressful,[182] in a study of workers with psychiatric disabilities, one woman stated she did not like to work at home because she "can go days without saying a word to anybody and that tends to make things more stressful."[183] One person interviewed for the study recalled a period in which he and his colleagues worked 80 hours each week. This employee stated that "it was constant intense hours, not just being there for 80 hours. . . . And I didn't get any more symptomatic because I was purposeful, and I was getting

---

[176] See 42 U.S.C. § 12112(b)(5).

[177] See, e.g., Boldini v. Postmaster General, 928 F. Supp. 125, 131 (D. N.H 1995). The employer may have to transfer the employee to an available, open position. See 29 C.F.R. § 1630.2(o)(2)(ii) (1997).

[178] Schmidt v. Bell, No. CIV. A. 82-1758, 1983 WL 631, at *14 (E.D. Pa. Sept. 9, 1983) (holding that the position of student loan collector was inherently stressful under the Rehabilitation Act).

[179] Tammy D. Clevenger, "Where Do I Fit In?" Psych. Services 48 (Aug. 1997): 1007.

[180] Id.

[181] Whybrow, supra n. 125, at 170.

[182] See, e.g., Paleologos v. Rehab Consultants, Inc., 990 F. Supp. 1460 (N.D. Ga. 1998); Hernandez v. City of Hartford, 59 F. Supp. 125, 128 (D. Conn. 1997).

[183] Laura Mancuso, Case Studies on Reasonable Accommodations for Workers With Psychiatric Disabilities (Sacramento: California Department of Mental Health, 1993) at 35.

somewhere, had a sense of accomplishment. I got much more symptomatic when I had a lot of time on my hands."[184]

Thus, whether a job is inherently stressful requires a far more individualized determination than courts have previously conducted. Similarly, the relationship between stress and psychiatric disability is more complex. However, trying to parse out whether the stress complained of is inherent to the essential functions of the job would be a useful first step for most courts.

The Job Is Stressful Because the Boss Is Unpleasant, or Demanding or Yells at the Employees

Although workplace harassment or hostile work environment claims are presumably covered by the ADA,[185] the courts have made it clear that standards for establishing such a claim are extraordinarily high. "No matter how severe the abuse, [the employer] is only liable under the ADA if the harassment was because of [the employee's] disability."[186] In *Casper v. Granite Corporation,* the plaintiff, who was mildly retarded, was called "Rick Retardo," "dumb ass," and "a tax write-off because he's handicapped and belongs to the [*sic*] government property."[187] The 7th Circuit Court found that the plaintiff had failed to demonstrate a hostile work environment because most of the hostile incidents he described, namely, his supervisors' "yelling, use of foul language, and questioning of [him]," did not directly relate to his mental condition; the supervisors yelled and swore at nondisabled employees as well.[188]

Nor does displaying anger at a plaintiff's illness or request for accommodations suffice to create a hostile work environment under the courts' current interpretation of the ADA. The behavior of a supervisor who "became angry when the plaintiff needed surgery and told her that she 'better get well this time' and that he would 'no longer tolerate her health problems'" and "told staff to avoid communication with the plaintiff, ignored her[,] and excluded her from meetings,"[189] was described

---

[184]*Id.*

[185]Every district court that has decided the issue has held that the ADA covers hostile environment claims. *See, e.g.,* McClain v. Southwest Steel Co., 940 F. Supp. 295, 301–302 (N.D. Okla. 1996); Rodriguez v. Loctite Puerto Rico, Inc., 967 F. Supp. 653, 663–664 (D. P.R. 1997); Rio v. Runyon, 972 F. Supp. 1446, 1459 (S.D. Fla. 1997); Henry v. Guest Services, Inc., 902 F. Supp. 245, 250 (D. D.C. 1995), *aff'd mem.,* 98 F.3d 646 (D.C. Cir. 1996); Haysman v. Food Lion, Inc., 893 F. Supp. 1092, 1106–1107 (S.D. Ga. 1995). However, only one circuit court has definitively held that a cause of action exists for a hostile work environment under the ADA, Flowers v. Southern Regional Physician's Services, 2001 U.S. App. LEXIS 5288 (5th Cir. Mar. 30, 2001), and one appears to have implicitly accepted such a cause of action, Keever v. Middletown, 145 F.3d 809, 813 (6th Cir. 1998). The remainder of the circuit courts, although hinting strongly that they would rule that the ADA creates a cause of action for a hostile work environment, have not found it necessary to decide the question, Walton v. Mental Health Association, 168 F.3d 661, 667 (3rd Cir. 1999); Conley v. Village of Bedford Park, 2000 U.S. App. LEXIS 11959 at *23 (7th Cir. May 31, 2000); Cannice v. Norwest Bank of Iowa, 189 F.3d 723 (8th Cir. 1999).

[186]Haysman v. Food Lion, 893 F. Supp. 1092, 1108 (S.D. Ga. 1995).

[187]2000 U.S. App. LEXIS 16241 (7th Cir. 2000), *cert. denied,* 121 S.Ct. 1410 (Mar. 26, 2001).

[188]*Id.*

[189]McConathy v. Dr. Pepper, 131 F.3d 558, 560 (5th Cir. 1998).

as merely "insensitive and rude" by the court, which held that these allegations did not state a claim of hostile work environment.[190]

Although it is hard to imagine that it is essential to the function of any job for a supervisor to yell at employees or to behave in the variety of abusive ways chronicled in the cases above, attempting to stem the tide of disabling workplaces abuse creates precisely the issues that employees fear the most: uncertain, unpredictable, and unquantifiable costs. Changing workplace culture does, of course, implicate these costs.[191] If an employer wishing to avoid liability under the ADA wants to know what the law requires and what it prohibits, the employer may be frustrated by discussions of transforming "workplace culture" and by the individualized approach of the ADA. When does a raised voice become yelling? When does swearing create a hostile work environment? Is the rule the same in New York City as it is in Minneapolis? The employer might aspire to create a workplace where individuals are treated with respect and dignity, but the employer may equally wish to know as specifically as possible the point at which abuse, stress, or failure to discipline or terminate an abusive supervisor becomes illegal. Perhaps because of the fears of subjectivity and of government enforcement of indeterminate civility codes, courts rarely grant claims relating to hostile work environments under the ADA.

These issues are virtually identical to the questions raised by sexual harassment law; indeed, many ADA cases brought by women include claims of sexual harassment, and many ADA claims brought by African Americans include claims of race discrimination. It is rare for a court to demonstrate an understanding of how race and sexual harassment claims are often inextricably intertwined with disability discrimination cases. These issues are discussed in the next section.

The Job Is Stressful Because the Employee Just Does Not Hit It Off With His or Her Boss or Coworkers

Stress caused by failing to "hit it off" with one's boss or coworkers covers a multitude of situations, some of which, such as workplace harassment or hostile environment, are presumably covered by the ADA. In fact, stress caused by failing to hit it off with one's boss or coworkers may be the result of any number of factors. An examination of cases brought under the ADA suggests that race and gender discrimination may constitute a considerable cause of the stress generated in a situation in which an employee does not hit it off with the boss or coworkers. It is no coincidence that employees raise a substantial number of psychiatric disability claims under the ADA or the Rehabilitation Act of 1973[192] in conjunction with claims of gender discrimination,[193] sexual harassment,[194] race discrimination,[195] or racially hostile work environments.[196]

---

[190] Id. at 563–564.

[191] I am grateful to Professor Michael Kelly of the University of San Diego School of Law for taking the time to discuss this issue with me.

[192] 29 U.S.C. §§ 701–797 (1994).

[193] See Hunt-Golliday v. Metropolitan Water Reclamation District, 104 F.3d 1004, 1006 (7th Cir. 1997); Hazeldine v. Beverage Media, Ltd., 954 F. Supp. 697–699 (S.D. N.Y. 1997); Kotlowski v. East-

Many ADA claims, both psychiatric and physical, involve the intersection between race or gender discrimination and disability. In one kind of case, race or gender discrimination is alleged to cause or aggravate physical[197] or psychiatric[198] problems. In another kind of case, African American plaintiffs with disabilities allege that because of their race, they are granted fewer accommodations than white employees with disabilities.[199] In yet another kind of case, plaintiffs allege that a combination of race and disability discrimination drives employers to treat them disadvantageously.[200] A study conducted of complaints involving psychiatric disability discrimination filed with the EEOC showed that although African American women who filed disability discrimination charges based on physical disability had the highest percentage of beneficial outcomes (24.6%), African American women who filed discrimination charges based on psychiatric disability had strikingly low rates of beneficial outcomes (7.4%). White men had similar rates of beneficial outcomes whether they filed physical or psychiatric disability complaints (16.5% for physical disabilities and 17.6% for psychiatric disabilities).[201] The same study found that complaints filed by Hispanics were four times less likely to result in beneficial outcomes than complaints filed by non-Hispanics.[202]

The interaction of race and gender discrimination, abusive work environments, and severe emotional debilitation has been evident in case law and research literature for more than 25 years.[203] Before the ADA, many claims of race and gender dis-

---

man Kodak Co., 922 F. Supp. 790, 794–795 (W.D. N.Y. 1996); Lewis v. Zilog, Inc., 908 F. Supp. 931, 936 (N.D. Ga. 1995).

[194] See Kaufman v. Checkers Drive-In Restaurants, Inc., 122 F.3d 892, 893 (11th Cir. 1997); *Hunt-Golliday*, 104 F.3d at 1006; Bryant v. Better Business Bureau, 923 F. Supp. 720, 727 (D. Md. 1996); Dunegan v. City of Council Grove, 77 F. Supp. 2d 1192 (D. Kan. 1999); Smith v. First Union National Bank, 202 F.3d 234 (4th Cir. 2000).

[195] See *Hunt-Golliday*, 104 F.3d at 1006; Guice-Mills v. Derwinski, 967 F.2d 794, 796 (2d Cir. 1992); Brown v. Northern Trust Bank, No. 95 C 7559, 1997 WL 543098, at *7 (N.D. Ill. Sept. 2, 1997).

[196] See Palmer v. Circuit Court, 117 F.3d 351, 351–352 (7th Cir. 1997); Contreras v. Suncast Corp., No. 96 C 3439, 1997 WL 598120, at *1–2 (N.D. Ill. Sept. 19, 1997); Prince v. Suffolk County Dept. of Health Services, Nos. 89 Civ. 7243 (LAP), 89 Civ. 8085 (LAP), 1996 WL 393528, at *1–3 (S.D. N.Y. July 12, 1996); Rivera v. Domino's Pizza, Inc., No. CIV. A. 95–1378, 1996 WL 53802, at *1–2 (E.D. Pa. Feb. 9, 1996).

[197] Williams v. Dairy Fresh Ice Cream Inc., No. CIV. A. 2:95-1041-RV, 1997 WL 834163, at *1 (S.D. Ala. Oct. 10, 1997) (involving an aggravation of the plaintiff's epilepsy due to poor treatment by supervisor, including the use of racial epithets).

[198] Webb v. Baxter Healthcare Corp., 57 F.3d 1067 (table), No. 94-1784, 1995 WL 352485, at *5 (4th Cir. June 13, 1995); *id.,* Smith v. First Union National Bank.

[199] Crawley v. Runyon, 1998 U.S. Dist. LEXIS 9603 at *2; Harris v. City of Chicago, 1998 U.S. Dist. LEXIS 1466 at *19–20 (N.D. Ill. Feb. 9, 1998).

[200] See Kathryn Moss, *Psychiatric Disabilities, Employment Discrimination Charges, and the ADA* (Final report for the Mary E. Switzer Distinguished Research Fellowship, Project H133F50029; Washington, DC: U.S. Department of Education, Office of Special Education and Rehabilitative Services, National Institute on Disability and Rehabilitation Research, 1996) at 23 (a sample EEOC psychiatric discrimination case includes "charging [a] party alleged that he was discriminated against because of his race (African American) and disability (schizophrenia). He claimed that he was provided with less training than his White coworkers without disabilities.")

[201] *Id.* at 40, Table 6.

[202] *Id.*

[203] See, e.g., Austin, *supra* n. 39, at 1-5, 8-17, 51-55; Ezra E. H. Griffith and Elvin J. Griffith,

crimination included descriptions of psychiatric disability suffered by the plaintiff.[204] Such claims, especially those related to a hostile environment, also included allegations that the employer's actions caused the employee "severe and substantial emotional distress."[205] Despite evidence of the interaction between race and gender discrimination claims and claims of severe emotional distress in the workplace, the courts have not generally appreciated the intersection of these claims.

In fact, if employees sue for disability discrimination in addition to race, gender, or age discrimination, the court may accuse the plaintiff's attorney of adopting a "kitchen sink" approach to the litigation.[206] Thus, each claim is delegitimized simply because of the presence of others. More often, courts consider the claims in a conceptual vacuum, separating various kinds of discrimination and ignoring the interrelationship among them.

The relationship between discrimination on the basis of psychiatric disability and race or gender discrimination may be concurrent. For more than 20 years, studies have confirmed "significant correlations between negative attitudes toward different racial groups and the mentally ill."[207] Recent studies conclude that

> the social and demographic characteristics which place some people at severe disadvantage in the labor market [e.g., age, race, and gender] operate even more strongly among those with mental conditions, suggesting that the presence of a mental condition makes a bad employment situation much worse than would be indicated by either the mental condition or the social or demographic characteristics alone.[208]

Case law suggests that members of racial minority groups who have disabilities work in environments where they must contend with hostility toward both their racial status and their disability.[209]

"Racism, Psychological Injury, and Compensatory Damages," *Hospital & Community Psychiatry* 37 (Jan. 1986): 71.

[204] *See* Bundy v. Jackson, 641 F.2d 934, 944–946 (D.C. Cir. 1981); Xieng v. Peoples National Bank, 821 P.2d 520, 523 (Wash. Ct. App. 1991).

[205] Green v. American Broadcasting Co., 647 F. Supp. 1359, 1361 (D.D.C. 1986).

[206] *See Hunt-Golliday*, 104 F.3d at 1006 ("In this lawsuit, [the plaintiff] tossed everything in the kitchen, including the sink, at her former employer.").

[207] Clifford R. Schneider and Wayne Anderson, "Attitudes Toward the Stigmatized: Some Insights From Recent Research," *Rehabilitation Counseling Bull.* (June 1980): 299, 301 [citing Robert Harth, "Attitudes Towards Minority Groups as a Construct in Assessing Attitudes Towards the Mentally Retarded," *Education & Training of the Mentally Retarded* 6 (1971): 142; Charles L. Mulford, "Ethnocentrism and Attitudes Toward the Mentally Ill," *Soc. Q.* 9 (1968): 107].

[208] Edward H. Yelin and Miriam G. Cisternas, "Employment Patterns Among People With and Without Mental Conditions," in Richard J. Bonnie and John Monahan, eds., *Mental Disorder, Work Disability and the Law* (Chicago: University of Chiago Press, 1997) at 25, 27.

[209] *See Rivera*, 1996 WL 53802, at *5. In *Rivera*, the coworkers of a Puerto Rican plaintiff with a speech impediment called him, among other things, "retarded," "hired from . . . a facility for mentally handicapped people," "Mexican tamale," "a dumb Puerto Rican," "a dumb Mexican," and "shit for brains" and said Puerto Ricans were not worth a damn; *id.* at *1. When the plaintiff complained to the regional manager, he was told "that's the way they joke around" and that he "should not take it so seriously"; *id.* at *2. *See also* Rivera v. Heyman, 982 F. Supp. 932, 933–34 (S.D. N.Y. 1997) (involving an HIV-positive employee who complained of racial and religious slurs in addition to harassment based on his disability); Chua v. St. Paul Federal Bank for Savings, No. 95 C 2463, 1996 WL 34458, at *4 (N.D. Ill. Jan. 26, 1996) (involving an Asian American man who was subjected to racially derogatory names and was imitated and mocked because of a limp).

Other cases suggest a cause-and-effect situation. In these situations, race discrimination or gender harassment may lead to massive stress for the employee who, in turn, will seek professional assistance and receive a diagnosis arguably requiring an accommodation.[210]

For example, in one case, an African American research analyst for Suffolk County (New York) alleged that when he tried to use his research regarding the statistically significant number of low-birthweight babies born to African American women in Suffolk County as the basis for his PhD thesis, he was transferred and demoted because his supervisor was concerned that these facts would become public.[211] His complaint alleged that this demotion caused his psychological disability, which in turn resulted in his discriminatory termination.[212] Ultimately, he applied for and received disability benefits.[213] The defendant argued that it terminated the plaintiff because he could not do his job and that his receipt of disability benefits estopped him from arguing that he was a "qualified individual."[214] The court rejected this argument, finding that the plaintiff alleged that "'the transfer and the surrounding facts of the transfer' and 'the intense level of harassment' by [the defendant] caused his mental disability."[215] The court continued: "[Defendant], therefore, may not profit from its wrongdoing by relying on the very disability which its discriminatory conduct created (assuming [plaintiff's] allegations are true) to terminate [plaintiff's] employment."[216]

This court did what courts rarely do. It understood the interrelationship of the race and disability discrimination charges. In cases involving work environments where hostility is expressed based on both race and disability, however, courts rarely aggregate both forms of harassment in considering the hostile environment claims.[217] In fact, contrary to the language of the ADA and its regulations, a few courts have even held that people with disabilities caused by workplace harassment and sex discrimination are somehow not covered by the ADA.[218] More often, courts disjoin

---

[210] See Webb, 1995 WL 352485, at *5; Prince, 1996 WL 393528, at *2–3, *5 (involving race discrimination by an employer that led to mental disability); see also Jeanine Grobe, ed., Beyond Bedlam (Chicago: Third Side Press, 1995) at 167 ("Despite the popular belief that 'madness' is biological in origin, the survivors in this section [of the book] have a different story. From our experiences, 'madness' has to do with homelessness, poverty, sexism, racism, ableism, mentalism, ageism, homophobia, ethnocentrism, and child abuse, to name a few."). In one case, the employer's response to an employee's complaint of harassment based on gender and national origin was to write a memorandum to the company's human resources department stating that she was paranoid and to require her to undergo counseling as a condition of her job; see Kohn, 1998 WL 67540, at *1.

[211] See Prince, 1996 WL 393528, at *2. Ironically, far more people are privy to this research (at least as allegations) because of this litigation than would have been the case if Prince had simply been permitted to write his PhD thesis.

[212] See id. at *2–3.

[213] See id. at *5.

[214] See id.

[215] Id. at *5 n. 8.

[216] Id.

[217] See Rivera, 1996 WL 53802, at *4 n. 3.

[218] See Williams, 1997 WL 834163, at *1 (holding that the employee's claim that his employer's racial discrimination and harassment aggravated his epilepsy did not state a claim under the ADA); see also Krocka v. Bransfield, 969 F. Supp. 1073, 1083 (N.D. Ill. 1997) (denying the employee's summary judgment motion on grounds that he was not disabled under the ADA); Mears v. Gulfstream Aerospace Corp., 905 F. Supp. 1075, 1082 (S.D. Ga. 1995) ("If Gulfstream's conduct did cause [the] Plaintiff's

race or sex discrimination and disability discrimination claims, treating each in an immaculate evidentiary vacuum.[219]

To be fair, the law is structured to make it very difficult for courts to avoid this response.[220] Section 504 of the Rehabilitation Act, which limits recovery for discrimination to situations in which the worker's handicap is the "sole" reason for discrimination, provides the classic example.[221] Thus, as Congress noted when it eliminated this requirement from the ADA,[222] an individual discriminated against on the grounds of both race and disability could not recover under the law prohibiting disability discrimination until the early 1990s.[223]

However, other structures are still in place that present more conceptually challenging obstacles. For example, the interrelationship between disability discrimination law and employee disability benefits law has presented difficulties in several cases.

If an employer, by racist acts or gender discrimination, causes an employee's mental disability, many courts still struggle with whether the case should be framed as a civil rights case or a medical problem appropriately dealt with under the rubric of worker's compensation or disability benefits.[224]

The difficulty of formulating an appropriate approach is caused in part by conceptual distinctions between race and gender discrimination on the one hand and disability discrimination on the other. Disability has only recently evolved from a totally medical concept to one with political, social, and civil rights ramifications.[225] Thus, disability discrimination law coexists with disability benefits law, ranging from worker's compensation to the Employment Retirement Income Security Act,[226] which may help shape outcomes in ADA cases, even when not explicitly addressed.[227]

For example, the maintenance of abusive and stressful workplaces, and the consequent exclusion of more psychiatrically fragile workers, has arguably been facilitated by the existence of disability benefits. Granting disability benefits to workers who are particularly vulnerable to workplace abuse reinforces the notion that the problem lies with the worker and not the working environment. Thus, the existence

---

disability, her remedy is under Georgia's worker compensation laws, not the ADA."), aff'd mem., 87 F.3d 1331 (11th Cir. 1996).

[219] See Leisen v. City of Shelbyville, 968 F. Supp. 409 (S.D. Ind. 1997).

[220] See id. at 417–422.

[221] See 29 U.S.C. § 794 (1994).

[222] See S. Rep. No. 101-116, at 44–45 (1989).

[223] See id.

[224] See Mears, 905 F. Supp. at 1082; Webb, 1995 WL 352485, at *6 n. 6. This issue is similar to the tort–civil rights–worker's compensation trilemma raised by sexual harassment suits. See, e.g., Jean C. Love, "Actions for Non-Physical Harm: The Relationship Between the Tort System and No-Fault Compensation (With an Emphasis on Workers' Compensation)," Cal. Law Rev. 73 (1985): 857. However, it is more difficult in the context of disability discrimination because, unlike gender, disability has been historically a medical concept.

[225] See Matthew B. Schiff and David L. Miller, "The Americans With Disabilities Act: A New Challenge for Employers," Tort & Ins. Law J. 27 (1991): 44–48.

[226] 29 U.S.C. §§ 1001-1461 (1994).

[227] See Ilana De Bare, "Making Accommodations: Employers Dealing With Mental Illness in Wake of Federal Disability Law," S. F. Chron. (Sept. 8, 1997): B1 (quoting one attorney as saying "we've got to integrate as many as five different laws—the ADA, workers' comp, long-term disability leave, voluntary paid leave policies, and the Family and Medical Leave Act.").

of these disability benefit programs allows employers and society to continue to characterize the abusive workplace as "normal" and its casualties as "abnormal" in a way that has not been possible with sexual harassment, sex discrimination, and hostile racial environments.

The 9th Circuit's predicament in *Nichols v. Frank*[228] vividly reflects the dilemmas created by this approach. Nichols, a woman who is deaf and mute,[229] was forced by her supervisor—the only supervisor who knew sign language—to perform sexual acts.[230] The forced sexual acts and her fear of communicating with anyone at work about them resulted in Nichols experiencing severe emotional distress.[231] The emotional distress and her aversion to sex because of the harassment caused her marriage to deteriorate.[232] Her supervisor forced her to perform oral sex before he would give her a two-week leave of absence when her husband began divorce proceedings.[233] Nichols was subsequently diagnosed with posttraumatic stress disorder for which she received disability benefits under the Federal Employees Compensation Act (FECA),[234] the federal equivalent of worker's compensation.[235] When she sued her employer for sex discrimination and won, the employer appealed on the grounds that her disability benefits were the exclusive remedy under FECA for her workplace injuries.[236]

The 9th Circuit Court rejected this argument with somewhat strained legal reasoning, finding that Nichol's posttraumatic stress disorder was distinguishable from the impact of sex discrimination.[237] The court found that the former was "a disease proximately caused by her employment," but it underscored that the latter was not.[238] The court pointed out that it would be inequitable to restrict Nichols to her disability benefits (which were 75% of her pay) while awarding a claimant under identical circumstances who did not suffer from posttraumatic stress disorder full back pay.[239] This is certainly true, but it still results in the court explicitly constructing the plaintiff's extreme distress at being forced to have sex into a "disease," which was somehow separable from the injury of sex discrimination. The problem with this case is that Nichol's experience as she lived it could not be parsed into separate categories: Being deaf and mute was integral to her sexual harassment; her emotional anguish at being forced to have sex was intensified by the fact that the only person she could communicate with at work was the supervisor who was forcing her to have sex.

---

[228] 42 F.3d 503 (9th Cir. 1994).

[229] *See id.* at 506. The intersection of disability and sexual harassment and abuse is one that has escaped attention, although it is clear that disabled women disproportionately suffer sexual assault, abuse, and harassment. *See* Judith I. Avner, "Sexual Harassment: Building a Consensus for Change," *Kansas J. of Law & Public Policy* 3 1994): 57, 64, 65.

[230] *See Nichols*, 42 F.3d at 506.

[231] *See id.*

[232] *See id.*

[233] *See id.*

[234] 5 U.S.C. §§ 8101-8193 (1994).

[235] *See Nichols*, 42 F.3d at 506.

[236] *See id.* at 515.

[237] *See id.* at 515, 516.

[238] *Id.* The 9th Circuit Court based its conclusion that posttraumatic stress disorder was a disease on the fact that it is a diagnosis in the fourth edition of the *Diagnostic and Statistical Manual* (Washington, DC: American Psychiatric Association, 1994).

[239] *See id.* at 515–516.

These types of cases implicate intersectionality concerns[240] and are more complex than the current structure of legal claims permits. The intersectionality implicates both the experience of the individual and the discriminating attitudes faced by the individual. For example, harmful and mistaken stereotypes about African Americans may include laziness or, in the case of males, violence. Harmful and mistaken stereotypes about people with learning disabilities or mental illness may also include assumptions that people with these disabilities are lazy or violent. Thus, the kind of discrimination that an African American with a learning disability or a mental illness experiences may be either more easily triggered or more intense because the two stereotypes operate to reinforce each other. The kinds of stereotypes that operate against women in general include assumptions about irrationality and emotionalism. Therefore, employers may regard women more readily as having a psychiatric disability, but they may take women's reports of psychiatric disability less seriously.

Whether concurrent or cause and effect, it is clear that in the real life of workers, sexual or racial harassment is inextricably intertwined with stress, anxiety, and depression in a dynamic that drains the worker and whose accumulated effects may drive him or her into temporary or permanent psychiatric disability. Any claim for disability benefits, however, may erase or at least threaten the discrimination claim.[241]

Thus, discrimination law as it currently exists has no mechanism for dealing with the cumulative or synergistic effects of different kinds of discrimination, and, in fact, further disadvantages individuals who suffer several kinds of discrimination. An individual with a disability who is a member of an ethnic minority may not even know the source of adverse treatment by an employer and, indeed, to assume that this is knowable, identifiable, or separable into distinct categories is an assumption that may be mistaken.

---

[240] *Intersectionality* describes the way in which the experiences of individuals who belong to two or more marginalized or minority groups are not reflected in the paradigms that describe discrimination for any of the groups. These individuals are doubly or triply burdened by being subjected to the dominant practices of several different hierarchies, without legal recourse or even narrative description of their experiences. For example, as conceptualized by Kimberle Crenshaw, Black women find themselves at the intersection of race and gender discrimination. *See* Kimberle Crenshaw, "Mapping the Margins: Intersectionality, Identity Politics, and Violence Against Women of Color," *Stanford Law Rev.* 43 (1991): 1241, 1242–1244; Kimberle Crenshaw, "Demarginalizing the Intersection of Race and Sex: A Black Feminist Critique of Antidiscrimination Doctrine, Feminist Theory and Antiracist Politics," *U. of Chicago Legal F.* (1989): 139, 140. In this case, Nichols was subject to the intersection of gender, physical, and psychiatric disability; there is no legal structure available that encompasses the damage and injuries she suffered.

[241] For some time, courts appeared to be heading toward a per se rule that any claim for disability benefits created an irrefutable presumption that a plaintiff was not a qualified employee. *See, e.g.,* McNemar v. Disney Store, Inc., 91 F.3d 610, 619 (3d Cir. 1996). However, carefully written court decisions and EEOC policy guidance explaining the difference between the definition of *disability* for disability benefits purposes and ADA purposes appear to have slowed down this general trend. *See, e.g.,* Talavera v. School Board, 129 F.3d 1214, 1216–1221 (11th Cir. 1997); Weigel v. Target Stores, 122 F.3d 461, 463–469 (7th Cir. 1997); Swanks v. Washington Metropolitan Area Transit Authority, 116 F.3d 582, 584-87 (D.C.C. 1997); Robinson v. Neodata Services. Inc., 94 F.3d 499, 502 n. 2 (8th Cir. 1996); Equal Employment Opportunity Commission, "Enforcement Guidance on the Effect of Representations Made in Applications for Benefits on the Determination of Whether a Person Is 'a Qualified Individual With a Disability' Under the Americans With Disabilities Act of 1990," *EEOC Compliance Manual* (Washington, DC: Bureau of National Affairs, 1997) at 3 (N:2281).

The Employee Is Ill-Suited in Temperament or Skill for the Job, and This Poor Fit Will Necessarily Create Stress

A lack of suitability for a job clearly brings about the stress that many people feel in their jobs, but it appears to describe only a few of the cases brought by people with psychiatric disabilities under the ADA.[242] As noted at the beginning of this chapter, most of the plaintiffs in ADA cases are well-qualified to perform the technical aspects of their jobs. The problem presented in cases involving people with psychiatric disabilities, unlike in cases involving people with physical disabilities, is rarely whether they can do the job itself.[243] As stated by one court in a case involving psychiatric disability: The plaintiff "incorrectly assumes that the essential functions of the job of shift electrician require only technical ability and experience as an electrician."[244] Under most circumstances, people with psychiatric disabilities choose jobs carefully, precisely to get "a good fit."[245] Therefore, it is rarely the case that the stress felt by these plaintiffs arises from their lack of skill. It arises, rather, from interpersonal difficulties or from being asked to work for too many hours.

The court in *Dewitt v. Carsten*[246] opened its opinion by laying out all possible sources of stress on the job but ultimately did not pursue this line of reasoning. The plaintiff claimed that the yelling by her boss and working with jail inmates caused her stress,[247] two very distinct sources of stress according to the court's own rubric. However, the court concluded that stress was not a disability and that "an employer may not be required to transfer a stressed, dissatisfied employee."[248] Thus, in *Dewitt,* the court joined all other courts, which treat "stress" as a macroconcept, without regard to its origin, cause, or interaction with disability. The court effectively declared that tolerating stress was an essential function of all jobs and that transfer to ameliorate stress would never be a reasonable accommodation.

Using the ADA to Attack Objectively Abusive or Unreasonably Stressful Workplace Environments

Employment discrimination against persons with psychiatric disabilities is not primarily about exclusion from job opportunities as a result of myths about mental illness. It is about the disparate impact of the *extremes* of abuse and stress in the

---

[242] *See* Johnston v. Morrison, 849 F. Supp. 777, 778–779 (N.D. Ala. 1994) (noting that a waitress who could not handle the pressure of working on crowded nights or memorizing frequent menu changes was not qualified to perform essential functions of the job).

[243] Allen v. GTE Mobile Communications Unit, 6 A.D. Cases 1063, 1997 WL 148670 at *2 (N.D. Ga. Feb. 26, 1997) (the "Defendant and the Court agree that [the] plaintiff has the requisite skill, experience, and education to perform her position at GTE.")

[244] Grenier v. Cyanamid Plastics, Inc., 70 F.3d 667, 674 (1st Cir. 1995).

[245] Mancuso, *supra* n. 183, at 35.

[246] 941 F. Supp. 1232 (N.D. Ga. 1996), *aff'd mem.,* 122 F.3d 1079 (11th Cir. 1997).

[247] *See id.* at 1234.

[248] *Id.* at 1237.

American workplace on people with psychiatric disabilities.[249] Just as an employer's failure to have an elevator or an accessible bathroom hinders a person in a wheelchair from performing a job, an employer's antagonistic, hostile, or extremely stressful work environment prevents a person with a psychiatric disability from performing a job that the person is qualified to perform and is completely capable of performing.

Neither the absence of an accessible bathroom nor the presence of a hostile and abusive environment necessarily indicates intentional hostility toward people with disabilities. However, the ADA prohibits actions with a disparate impact on people with disabilities.[250] Both the failure to provide accessible bathrooms and the presence of an abusive environment operate to exclude people with particular disabilities.

Abusive Workplaces Have a Disparate Impact on Individuals With Psychiatric Disabilities

Disparate impact discrimination is prohibited under the ADA. The statute defines discrimination to include "utilizing standards, criteria, or methods of administration that have the effect of discrimination on the basis of disability ... or that perpetuate the discrimination of others who are subject to common administrative control."[251]

The legislative history of the ADA confirms that Congress fully intended to prohibit disparate impact discrimination. The legislative history of the ADA states that "discrimination results from actions or inactions that discriminate by effect as well as by intent or design."[252] Specifically, the Senate Judiciary Committee report explaining the meaning of "discrimination" for Title I declared that "subparagraphs (B) and (C) incorporate a disparate impact standard to ensure that the legislative mandate to end discrimination does not ring hollow. This standard is consistent with the interpretation of section 504 by the U.S. Supreme Court in *Alexander v. Choate*."[253] If there were any doubt remaining as to the viability of a disparate impact cause of action under Title I of the ADA, it was removed by the passage of the Civil Rights Act of 1991,[254] which, in providing for compensatory and punitive damages for intentional discrimination under Title I of the ADA, specifically distinguishes such a claim from "an employment practice that is unlawful because of its disparate impact."[255]

---

[249]By italicizing *extremes*, I am emphasizing that I am not discussing a plaintiff who perceives slights and takes offense where others would not. I am discussing an individual whose reaction to conduct and conditions that all employees would characterize as upsetting and offensive is disabling to that individual.

[250]*See infra* text accompanying notes 243–263.

[251]42 U.S.C. § 12112(b)(3) (1994).

[252]S. Rep. No. 101-116, at 6 (1989). The equivalent House report contains identical language. *See* H.R. Rep. No. 101-485, pt. 2, at 29 (1990), *reprinted in* 1990 U.S.C.C.A.N. 303, 310.

[253]S. Rep. No. 101-116, at 30 (1989). The equivalent House report contains identical language. *See* H.R. Rep. No. 101-485, pt. 2, at 61 (1990), *reprinted in* 1990 U.S.C.C.A.N. 343. In Alexander v. Choate, the U.S. Supreme Court "reject[ed] the boundless notion that all disparate impact showings constitute prima facie cases under 504"; 469 U.S. 287, 299 (1985).

[254]Pub. L. No. 102-166, 105 Stat. 1071 (1991) (codified as amended in scattered sections of 2 U.S.C., 16 U.S.C., 29 U.S.C., and 42 U.S.C.).

[255]42 U.S.C. § 1981a(a)(2) (1994).

In addition, most circuit courts acknowledge the existence of a cause of action under the ADA based on disparate impact,[256] although it is rarely invoked, and it is even more rarely invoked in employment discrimination cases.[257] However, it is clear that "[the ADA] requires employers to eliminate ostensibly neutral barriers that disparately impact the disabled."[258]

If a facially neutral practice, such as an objectively abusive work environment, operates to exclude employees with psychiatric disabilities, and an employee requests that abusiveness be minimized as a reasonable accommodation, the law requires employers to reasonably accommodate individuals with disabilities unless such accommodation imposes an undue hardship.[259] Furthermore, employers must eliminate qualification standards or job requirements that disparately disadvantage those with disabilities unless such requirements are job-related and consistent with business necessity.[260]

Although this is a claim about hostile work environments, it is not, in this particular iteration,[261] a hostile work environment claim in the technical sense. Although the Supreme Court has recognized the right to work in an environment free from intimidation, insult, and ridicule based on one's membership in a protected class,[262] this is a far cry from recognizing a right to work in an environment free from free-ranging, universally applicable intimidation, insult, and ridicule.[263] Hostile environment claims are another form of the intentional discrimination, or disparate treatment, claim. Although hostile environment claims have been recognized under the ADA,[264] they require animus against people with disabilities, or against a plaintiff individually because of his or her disability.

Yet although cases exist in which a supervisor is explicitly hostile to a disability, they are far less frequent than cases in which a supervisor is exempt from liability precisely because he or she exhibits hostility indiscriminately. As one court noted, the plaintiff's supervisor "denies ever having harassed the plaintiff or having discriminated against him in any way. The record indicates that [the supervisor] did express hostility toward her subordinates, but that she did so indiscriminately."[265] Another court wrote that "the fact that black employees and nonhandicapped employees complained of the same kind of bullying and harassment makes it difficult

---

[256] *See, e.g.,* Matthews v. Commonwealth Edison Co., 128 F.3d 1194, 1195–96 (7th Cir. 1997); Monette v. Electronic Data Systems Corp., 90 F.3d 1173, 1178 n. 5 (6th Cir. 1996); Helen L. v. Didario, 46 F.3d 325, 335 (3d Cir. 1995).

[257] When disparate impact cases are brought under the ADA, they are almost always brought as Title II or Title III cases against state or local governments. *See, e.g.,* Crowder v. Kitagawa, 81 F.3d 1480, 1483–1484 (9th Cir. 1996); Inmates of Allegheny County Jail v. Wecht, 93 F.3d 1124, No. 95-3402, 1996 WL 474106, at *5 (3d Cir. Aug. 22, 1996), *vacated,* 93 F.3d 1146 (3d Cir. 1996); Helen L., 46 F.3d 331–332; Wolford v. Lewis, 860 F. Supp. 1123, 1134 (S.D. W.Va. 1994) (involving claims under section 504 of the Rehabilitation Act).

[258] *Monette,* 90 F.3d at 1178 n. 5.

[259] *See* 42 U.S.C. § 12112(b)(5)(A); *Monette,* 90 F.3d at 1179.

[260] *See* 42 U.S.C. § 12112(b)(6); *Monette,* 90 F.3d at 1179.

[261] *See infra* text accompanying notes 259–262.

[262] *See* Meritor Savings Bank v. Vinson, 477 U.S. 57, 65–66 (1986).

[263] Indeed, the U.S. Supreme Court just underscored that Title VII provides no constraints against such environments. *See* Oncale v. Sundowner Offshore Services, Inc., 523 U.S. 75 (U.S. Mar. 4, 1998).

[264] *See* Haysman v. Food Lion, Inc., 893 F. Supp. 1092, 1106–1107 (S.D. Ga. 1995). *See also* cases cited *supra* n. 185.

[265] Mazzarella v. U.S. Postal Service, 849 F. Supp. 89, 91–92 (D. Mass. 1994) (citations omitted).

for the court to find a discriminatory motivation behind the undeniably bad treatment [plaintiff] received."[266] In yet another decision, the court dismissed a claim of discrimination on the basis of psychiatric disability, in part because

> Mr. Lee alleges that . . . Mr. Maphis began making disparaging remarks about disabilities and mental illness. The example Mr. Lee cites, however, was a remark about blacks and women. [citation to record omitted] According to other documents in the record, the scope of Mr. Maphis's rude remarks was by no means confined to mental health issues.[267]

Although judges in some of these cases have indicated that the plaintiff produced clear evidence that the abusive work environment had a much greater impact on him or her than on other employees because of his or her disability, at least one judge required the plaintiff to specifically request that the abuse be curtailed as a reasonable accommodation to his disability.[268] This was required even though the employer was particularly—even uniquely—well situated to be aware of the disparate impact of its treatment on the plaintiff:

> It is clearly the case that plaintiff, because of his [posttraumatic stress disorder], was unusually sensitive to the bullying management style of his . . . supervisors. This might be viewed as raising an issue of accommodation. While one would expect management at a veterans hospital to be aware of and sensitive to the difficulties experienced by veterans with Post-Traumatic Stress Disorder, the record suggests that at no time did plaintiff and his doctors make a real effort to educate management adequately about PTSD. . . . Given the difficulties of trying to accommodate an employee whose disability is aggravated by job-related stress, the court believes more was required of [the plaintiff] than a generalized complaint about working conditions to immediate supervisors to trigger an obligation on defendant's part to accommodate.[269]

However, as will be discussed, even employees' specific requests to lower the level of hostility at work because of its deleterious effect on a disability have not succeeded with some courts.

Disparate Treatment: Ending Workplace Abuse as a Reasonable Accommodation

The disparate impact model shades quickly into the disparate treatment model if an employee requests a less abusive workplace as a reasonable accommodation to his or her disability and is denied that request. Although an employer may not intentionally discriminate against people with psychiatric disabilities by maintaining an abusive or unnecessarily stressful work environment, intentional discrimination may come into play if an employer is made aware of the impact of workplace abuse on an employee—and the nexus between workplace conditions and the employee's disability—and refuses to make any changes.

In a few cases in which plaintiffs have identified themselves as being disabled

---

[266]Pavone v. Brown, No. 95-C-3620, 1997 WL 441312, at *9 (N.D. Ill. July 29, 1997).

[267]Lee v. Publix Supermarkets, 1998 U.S. Dist. LEXIS 8921 (N.D. Fla. Mar. 16, 1998).

[268]See id. at *8.

[269]Id.

and have asked for accommodations such as "a nonhostile working environment"[270] or "softer management approaches,"[271] courts have not shown that they comprehend the connection between psychiatric disability and a hostile work environment. For example, one court noted that the plaintiff:

> has provided nothing to show that even if she were a qualified individual with a disability [the defendant] failed to make reasonable accommodations for her. . . . In regard to her second request for accommodation, the record shows that at the civil service hearing she *merely* asked for a non-hostile working environment. Even if this could be considered a genuine request for accommodation for her mental condition involving panic attacks and stress, it occurred about 1/2 years after her suspension and long after she filed this complaint—and that was way too late.[272]

Although race discrimination and gender discrimination laws have not eliminated racism and sexism from the workplace, they have established a common understanding that such behavior is unacceptable. Because of public education and litigation, employers now perceive that the employee who sexually harasses another employee or makes racist remarks or jokes is the problem employee, not the employee who is harassed or is the butt of the racist jokes.

The same transformation of understanding must take place with regard to the supervisor who is harsh or abusive to his or her employees. At present, it is the employees who are viewed as having the problem, as being "too fragile" to work, even in the face of extensive and excellent work histories. The stressful or abusive workplace is still commonly defended as the employer's prerogative.

Making working conditions more pleasant or less abusive may appear to be far less expensive than the accommodations required for employees with physical disabilities. However, any suggestion that the ADA requires these ameliorative measures is fiercely resisted by employers and dismissed out of hand by courts. Requiring such changes in working conditions threatens deeply held beliefs about employer prerogatives far more than building ramps or installing TTY telephones. As has been aptly noted by the foremost empirical researcher into the costs and consequences of the ADA, resistance to the ADA is far more a matter of the culture of the employment environment than it is a matter of expense.[273] Rather than protect workers with psychiatric disabilities, courts have wholeheartedly protected employer prerogatives in this area. As one court stated, "forcing transfers of employees under the guise of reasonably accommodating employees under the ADA inherently would undermine an employer's ability to control its own labor force."[274] Yet disparate impact of objectively abusive supervisors on people with psychiatric disabilities exists and can be established fairly easily through empirical literature and expert testimony.

Furthermore, the remedies requested—either the cessation of supervisor abuse or the transfer of the employee—already comport with good management practice. Controlling the abusive supervisor is an accommodation that will benefit all employees in the workplace and is unlikely to create resentment among the coworkers

---

[270]Hunt-Golliday v. Metropolitan Water Reclamation District, 104 F.3d 1004, 1013 (7th Cir. 1997).

[271]Boldini v. Postmaster General, 928 F. Supp. 125, 131 (D. N.H. 1995).

[272]*Id.* at 1012–1013 (emphasis added).

[273]*See, e.g.,* Barbara Presley Noble, "A Level Playing Field for Just $121," *N.Y. Times* (Mar. 5, 1995): 21.

[274]Lewis v. Zilog, Inc., 908 F. Supp. 931, 948 (N.D. Ga. 1995).

of the employee with a disability. It is difficult to justify refusal to transfer a qualified person with a disability, a remedy routinely granted for others (such as victims of sexual harassment) as anything but discrimination. Because courts routinely order transfer as a reasonable accommodation for people with physical disabilities, the reluctance of the courts to order transfer in psychiatric disability cases cannot simply be characterized as unwillingness to interfere with managerial prerogatives in this area.

Unnecessarily Stressful Environments and Disparate Impact on People With Psychiatric Disabilities

As noted previously, stress is a far more complex subject than workplace abuse. First, workplace abuse in its most extreme forms is concrete and tangible (e.g., supervisors screaming, throwing things, or hitting employees) and is universally experienced as unpleasant and offensive by workers. Stress, however, is rarely tangible in a similar way. Most sources of stress, even long working hours, are experienced differently by different workers. Different workers with psychiatric disabilities will find different experiences stressful and require different accommodations.

Second, it is difficult for an employer to point to any benefit that abusive supervisors provide for his or her enterprise. To the extent that stress results from causes other than workplace abuse, it more directly implicates core business functions. Because of downsizing, employees are being asked to take on more responsibility and work longer hours, and this is directly connected to some of the difficulties experienced by employees with psychiatric disabilities.

Furthermore, few existing legal principles tell us the threshold beyond which no one should be expected to work. Nonprofessional employees may be entitled to overtime pay, but they may also be forced to work overtime. Union agreements tend to focus on how much notice must be given before an employee is required to work overtime and on whether the extra pay should be time and a half or double time.[275] Very few cases have dealt directly with the amount of work an employer can expect of an employee with a psychiatric disability. In one case involving claims under a state disability discrimination law, an attorney with depression won $300,000 in damages and $800,000 in attorney fees in an arbitration award after his employer refused his request for a one half day off a week every time he worked two consecutive weeks in a row of more than 45 hours a week.[276]

To prove an employment discrimination case based on disparate impact under the ADA, a plaintiff must show "that the employer has fixed a qualification that bears more heavily on disabled than on other workers and is not required by the necessities of the business or activity in question."[277] An employer may maintain discriminatory practices only if it can be proven that to change these practices would "impose an undue hardship."[278] It is difficult to imagine courts conducting the kind of review necessary to determine whether employers' specific downsizing decisions

---

[275] See, generally, Bureau of National Affairs, *2000 Sourcebook on Collective Bargaining: Wages, Benefits and Other Contract Issues* (Washington, DC: Author, 1995).

[276] See Choi, *supra* n. 30, at B14.

[277] Matthews v. Commonwealth Edison Co., 128 F.3d 1194, 1195–96 (7th Cir. 1997).

[278] 42 U.S.C. § 12112(b)(5)(A) (1994).

or massive layoffs leading to greatly increased hours and responsibilities for the remaining workers, were "necessary." In addition, unlike the case of controlling the abusive supervisor, accommodations in the form of requiring fewer hours of work from employees with psychiatric disabilities will likely lead to resentment on the part of coworkers who do not receive this accommodation. That resentment itself may trigger more stress for the employee than working excessive hours. The task of formulating an appropriate conceptual approach to workplace stress caused by excessive hours is beyond the scope of this chapter, but it must be done.

In the past, an employee's vulnerability to stress or highly unpleasant workplace conditions established only that the employee could not work, and he or she was fired or quit. The lucky people received disability benefits. The advent of the ADA requires a reexamination of who should take responsibility for readjustment of the workplace.

Conclusion

The past decade has seen massive corporate mergers and downsizing, with escalating work hours and increasing stress on the job. Managers and supervisors may be more likely to take out their own work pressures on employees. Workers who are dependent on employment in a particular location or who are trying to vest pensions may be relatively powerless to change their circumstances, and the powerlessness itself is a cause of even greater stress. All of this is happening in workplaces that are increasingly less unionized; unions are in any event more concerned with preserving employment security and benefits than in eliminating workplace stress and abuse.

Against this backdrop of the American workplace in the 1990s, it should not come as a surprise that employment discrimination claims involving psychiatric disabilities are growing rapidly. Skilled and talented workers are being pushed beyond the limits of their endurance and are fighting back in the only way left to many of them. These workers embody the purposes of the ADA in some ways: They are qualified for their jobs, and the accommodations they request do not cost money and would lead to a more productive work force in general if implemented.

But these employees are losing their ADA cases because abuse and stress are seen as intrinsic to employment, as invisible and inseparable from conditions of employment as sexual harassment was 20 years ago. The notion that employers are entitled to create a hostile, abusive environment as long as the hostility is generalized and the abuse is universal still predominates. However, a more careful examination and articulation of the principles of the ADA suggest that such environments have a substantial disparate impact on people with psychiatric disabilities, who are losing opportunities for employment as a result of practices that have no productive value for the employer.

Although extremely abusive environments, for example, constantly screaming or assaultive supervisors, are easy to identify and difficult to justify, stress in the workplace represents an entirely different and more complex set of issues for disability law. It is clear that except for abusive work environments, no single set of circumstances (not even extremely long hours) is uniformly experienced as stressful by workers. Indeed, an environment of respect and collegiality probably would cushion some of the stress associated with long hours. What is clear from examining the cases brought under the ADA is that courts must begin to parse out the source of stress in deciding whether a worker's ability to withstand it is indeed an "essential function" of the specific job the worker is being asked to do.

Likewise, courts should follow the lead of Judge Posner in looking to the manifestations rather than to the etiology of disability in determining whether a plaintiff has a disability under the ADA. People can drive each other crazy; hostile, abusive treatment can trigger underlying vulnerabilities; and stress can be the final stinging straw on the trembling camel's back.

Ultimately, integrating skilled people with psychiatric disabilities in the workplace may require that employers have more responsibility to ensure a respectful and nonabusive workplace that is free of unnecessary stress. Almost all of the accommodations required by people with psychiatric disabilities are uncontroversially accepted as good managerial and personnel practice in the business world. Treating employees with dignity and respect, curbing unnecessary stress, resolving supervisor–employee friction, and promoting flexibility in response to the individual needs of employees will not only accommodate people with psychiatric disabilities, but it will also work to the advantage of everyone in the workplace.

Chapter 7
WHAT IS DISCRIMINATION?

Even if a plaintiff is a member of the class of people protected by the Americans With Disabilities Act (ADA), he or she must still prove discrimination on the basis of disability to prevail in litigation under the ADA. The last chapter discussed the abusive work environment and excess hours as forms of disparate impact discrimination against people with psychiatric disabilities. This chapter explores other forms of discrimination under the ADA. It examines such policies as pre-employment inquiries, pre-employment testing, and requiring employees to submit to individual psychiatric examinations. It also looks at the ADA's requirement that employers keep all information about their employees' health confidential. The ADA prohibits discrimination based on association with a disabled person as well as retaliation for engaging in protected activities under the ADA. Finally, the chapter examines the characteristics of successful cases under the ADA.

Adverse Employment Action

Not all employer actions taken on the basis of disability, no matter how upsetting to an individual employee, constitute an "adverse employment action" prohibited by the ADA. For example, requiring an employee to cease taking Xanax was held by one court not to constitute an adverse employment action.[1] In another case, a court found a factual dispute as to whether a demotion was an adverse employment action or a voluntary and uncoerced decision on the part of the employee.[2] Courts have uniformly held that requiring an employee to submit to a psychiatric examination is not, by itself, an adverse employment action.[3] Other courts have held that telling an employee to seek psychiatric counseling does not constitute adverse employment action; therefore, it is not actionable as discrimination under the ADA. Ostracism at the workplace[4] and delay in a promised transfer[5] have also been held to not constitute adverse employment actions. In general, an employer must change the salary or the terms and conditions of employment in a way that is detrimental to the employee to constitute an adverse employment action. Of course, to be illegal under the ADA, the adverse action must be taken as a result of the employee's disability.

---

[1] Shiplett v. Amtrak, 1999 U.S. App. LEXIS 14004 (6th Cir. June 17, 1999).

[2] Berry v. City of Savannah, 1999 U.S. App. LEXIS 6278 (6th Cir. Apr. 1, 1999).

[3] Yin v. California, 95 F.3d 864 (9th Cir. 1996); Deckert v. City of Ulysses, 1995 WL 580074 (D. Kan. Sept. 6, 1995); Sullivan v. River Valley School District, 197 F.3d 804 (6th Cir. 2000).

[4] Strother v. Southern California Permanente Medical Group, 79 F.3d 859, 869 (9th Cir. 1996) ("mere ostracism in the workplace is not enough to show an adverse employment decision") (quoting Fisher v. San Pedro Peninsula Hospital, 214 Cal. App. 3d 590, 615 [1989]).

[5] Amro v. Boeing Co., 2000 U.S. App. LEXIS 28958 (10th Cir. Nov. 14, 2000).

Blanket Exclusions on the Basis of Disability

The classic example of discrimination on the basis of disability is the blanket exclusion: People who are blind cannot be jurors,[6] people who have AIDS cannot marry,[7] people with one arm cannot be police officers,[8] and people who are HIV positive cannot be accepted by drug rehabilitation programs.[9] Courts have struck down these kinds of statutory and policy pronouncements, which are clearly examples of intentional discrimination. These blanket exclusions are highly disfavored under the ADA, whose very premise is that discrimination against people with disabilities arises from just such generalizations and that every individual ought to be given a chance to prove what he or she can do.

Some courts have permitted blanket exclusions from employment on the basis of eyesight,[10] blood pressure,[11] diabetes,[12] and, most recently, history of alcoholism or substance abuse.[13] These blanket policies usually arise in the law enforcement firefighting context. Some courts have sidestepped the discriminatory nature of the policies by finding that the plaintiffs are not disabled. These findings are based on the dubious rationale that exclusion from law enforcement or firefighting does not amount to a substantial limitation on employment opportunities or that bad eyesight and high blood pressure are so commonplace that they impose no general employment disadvantage and thus do not rise to the level of an ADA disability. This second argument is sure to gain additional ground in light of the recent trilogy of Supreme Court decisions in *Sutton v. United Airlines, Vaughn v. United Postal Service,* and *Albertson's v. Kirkingburg.*[14]

For people with psychiatric disabilities, the blanket exclusions that have the most significance are those based on taking psychotropic medications or having a history of mental health treatment. Although the biological model of mental illness carries a message that people diagnosed with mental illness can successfully be treated with medication, the truth is that taking medication for mental health problems can have more adverse impact on employment opportunities than on moods or even the behaviors that the medication is intended to treat.

This is because of the numerous examples of blanket exclusions from employment or adverse actions arising solely on the basis of taking medication. Although there is enormous encouragement for people to take certain medications (e.g., Prozac)[15] or to give medications to their children (e.g., Ritalin), there is little concurrent disclosure of the punitive or unpleasant employment consequences of taking these

---

[6]Galloway v. Superior Court of the District of Columbia, 816 F. Supp. 12 (D.D.C. 1993).

[7]T. E. P. v. Leavitt, 1993 U.S. Dist. LEXIS 19099 (D. Utah Nov. 22, 1993).

[8]Stilwell v. Kansas City Board of Police Commissioners, 872 F. Supp. 682 (W.D. Mo. 1995).

[9]Doe v. Centinela Hospital, 1988 U.S. Dist. LEXIS 8401 (C.D. Cal. July 7, 1988).

[10]Joyce v. Suffolk County, 911 F. Supp. 92 (E.D. N.Y. 1996).

[11]*Id.*

[12]Davis v. Meese, 692 F. Supp. 505 (E.D. Pa. 1988) (Rehabilitation Act case). *But see* Bombrys v. City of Toledo, 849 F. Supp. 1210 (N.D. Ohio 1993) and EEOC v. Chrysler, 917 F. Supp. 1164 (E.D. Mich. 1996), holding respectively that blanket discrimination on the basis of a diagnosis of diabetes or on the basis of a certain blood sugar level was discriminatory under the ADA.

[13]EEOC v. Exxon Corp., 203 F.3d 871 (5th Cir. 2000).

[14]*See* the discussion of these decisions in chapter 2 of this volume.

[15]*See, e.g.,* Peter Kramer, *Listening to Prozac* (New York: Penguin, 1997) about health maintenance organizations conducting patient profiles of heavy users and encouraging them to take Prozac.

medications. The U.S. Army, for example, currently refuses to accept anyone for enlistment who has taken Ritalin in the past 10 years.[16] The City of Chicago Police Department had a policy that any officer taking Prozac would be placed in a program called the Personnel Concerns Program to "correct an officer exhibiting unacceptable behavior that is contrary to the goals of the CPD."[17] Officers with no record of adverse behavior were subject to the program, which required intensive supervision of the officer, because taking Prozac was considered a "significant deviation from [the officer's] normal behavior."[18]

Pre-Employment Inquiry or Testing for Mental Disabilities

The ADA makes it clear that an employer may not inquire into the current mental health or past diagnoses or hospitalizations of an applicant for employment.[19] The ADA prohibits the well-known "application form that lists a number of potentially disabling impairments and asks the applicant to check any of the impairments he or she may have."[20] Nor may an employer make inquiries about an applicant's past history of job-related injuries or worker's compensation claims before extending an offer of employment.[21] However, an employer subject to the affirmative action requirements of Section 503 of the Rehabilitation Act may invite applicants to identify themselves as disabled if the applicant is informed that disclosure is not required and, if given, is used solely for affirmative action purposes.[22]

An employer can, however, ask an applicant whether he or she can perform job-

---

[16] "Ritalin Use Barred for Many Athletes, Military," Scripps Howard News Service, *Knoxville-News Sentinel,* June 23, 1997; Federal Document Clearinghouse Congressional Testimony, Mar. 12, 1998, Lieutenant General Frederick E. Vollrath, Deputy Chief of Staff, Personnel, U.S. Army House National Security, Military Personnel, Military Recruiting, and Personnel Policies.

[17] Krocka v. Bransfield and the City of Chicago, 969 F. Supp. 1073 (N.D. Ill. 1997), *aff'd,* Krocka v. City of Chicago, 203 F.3d 507 (7th Cir. 2000).

[18] *Id.* Having required the plaintiff to be subject to such intense supervision under this program that other police officers did not want to work with him because he was taking Prozac, the Chicago Police Department also required him to take a blood test because it did not believe he was actually on Prozac and then defended itself in the ensuing litigation by claiming (successfully) that it did not perceive the plaintiff as being disabled. The plaintiff did survive the defendant's motion for summary judgment on whether he actually was disabled under the ADA, was granted summary judgment on his 4th Amendment claim regarding the blood test, and was permitted to go to trial on the policy requiring his participation in the Personnel Concerns Program.

[19] The ADA itself provides that "except as provided in paragraph (3), a covered entity shall not conduct a medical examination or make inquiries of a job applicant as to whether such applicant is an individual with a disability or as to the nature or severity of such disability." 42 U.S.C. § 12112(d)(2)(A). Paragraph 3 provides that an employer may require a medical examination after an offer of employment has been made and before commencement of employment and may condition the job on the results of the examination as long as all entering employees are subjected to the examination and its results are kept confidential. 42 U.S.C. § 12112(d)(3). The language of the statute is reproduced in the regulations at 29 C.F.R. § 1630.13.

[20] 29 C.F.R. § 1630.14(a) (Appendix).

[21] 29 C.F.R. § 1630.13(a).

[22] Although the Rehabilitation Act requires companies that contract with the federal government to make affirmative efforts to hire people with disabilities, this requirement is not enforced in practice. Jonathan S. Leonard, "Disability Policy and the Return to Work," in Carolyn S. Weaver, ed., *Disability and Work* (Washington, DC: American Enterprise Institute Press, 1991) at 46, 51–54.

related functions and even to explain or demonstrate how the applicant would perform the job. In addition, if a disability is already known or obvious and an employer
could reasonably believe that the disability would interfere with a job-related function, the employer may inquire as to how the applicant will perform this function.
An employer may also inquire into a disability for which an applicant requests
reasonable accommodation.

A frequent area of controversy in the courts is whether an employee who responded falsely to an illegal disability-related inquiry may be terminated without
violating the ADA on the basis of his or her misconduct in falsifying an application
form. Several state and federal courts have held that to permit an employer to terminate an employee under these circumstances "at best would have ignored the
employer's unlawful inquiries, and at worst would have rewarded the employer for
them."[23] Another court noted that the illegal inquiries "set up a situation that is
likely to 'trap' a disabled applicant into making false statements that a non-disabled
applicant has no incentive to make."[24]

Despite the clear requirements of the ADA, Congress' intention is not being
completely realized. First, some employers continue to use blatantly illegal employment application forms.[25] Courts disagree about whether a person without disabilities
has a cause of action to challenge such forms.[26] Second, the Equal Employment
Opportunity Commission (EEOC), receiving heavy pressure from employers to relax
the prohibitions of the ADA, has redrafted its *Enforcement Guidance* on permissible
pre-employment inquiries twice, each time giving employers more and more room
to ask disability-related questions. Third, employers have several ways in which they
can legally sidestep the ADA's intention that they make hiring decisions without
awareness of hidden disabilities.

Use of Permissible Drug Tests to Detect Psychotropic Drugs

The ADA does permit employers to screen applicants for illegal use of drugs. These
drug screens detect the presence of any number of prescription drugs, of course,
including drugs used to treat migraine headaches,[27] as well as psychotropic drugs;
several respondents to my survey believed that they had been subject to discrimi-

---

[23]Lysak v. Seiler Corp., 415 Mass. 625, 614 N.E.2d 991 (Mass. 1993); Kraft v. Police Commissioner
of Boston, Mass. 155, 571 N.E.2d 380 (Mass. 1991) (involving an inquiry about hospitalization for
mental illness); Huisenga v. Opus Corp., 494 N.W.2d 469, 473–474 (Minn. 1992).

[24]Downs v. MBTA, 13 F. Supp. 2d 130, 140 (D. Mass. 1998).

[25]*See, e.g.,* Adler v. I & M Rail Link, 13 F. Supp. 2d 912 (N.D. Iowa 1998), (a rail employment
application form asked about "physical problems," whether applicants had ever been injured on the job,
and claims under Workman's Compensation and disability insurance they had made against the railroad's
predecessor in interest).

[26]The 10th Circuit Court answered this question in the affirmative, Griffin v. Steeltek, 1998 U.S.
App. 27682 (10th Cir. Oct. 29, 1998). *See also* Roe v. Cheyenne Mountain Conference Resort, 124 F.3d
1221 (10th Cir. 1997) and Gonzales v. Sandoval County, 2 F. Supp. 2d 1442, 1444 (D. N.M. 1998).
Although explicitly not deciding the question and leaving the possibility open that a person without a
disability could show some injury from such a question, the 5th Circuit Court exhibited a more skeptical
approach, Armstrong v. Turner Industries, 141 F.3d 554, 562 (5th Cir. 1998). *See also* Adler v. I & M
Rail Link, L. L. C., 13 F. Supp. 3d 912 (N.D. Iowa 1998) (adopting the position that only people with
disabilities can challenge prohibited questions on applications).

[27]*See* Castro v. Child Psychiatry Center, 1997 U.S. Dist. LEXIS 3495 (E.D. Pa. Mar. 25, 1997).

nation as a result of these drug tests. Others had been deterred from applying for jobs that required drug tests because of concerns that their use of psychotropic drugs would be detected and misunderstood.

Preoffer Psychological Testing[28] – "Profiles"

The EEOC has ruled that although employers are not permitted to ask about or test for mental or emotional disorders, they may test for "personality traits" such as "honesty, tastes, and habits."[29] This leads to the question of how personality tests differ from the prohibited examinations. The EEOC has issued extensive interpretation on these questions.[30] In these documents, the EEOC takes the position that the kinds of tests that are precluded are those that "seek information about an individual's physical or mental impairments or health" or that "provide evidence that would lead to identifying a mental disorder or impairment."[31] The following factors are significant in deciding whether a given test is illegal under the ADA:

- whether it is administered and/or interpreted by a health care professional;
- whether it was designed to reveal an impairment in physical or mental health;
- whether it is invasive (i.e., requires drawing of urine, blood, or breath);
- whether it measures an applicant's performance of a task or an applicant's physiological response to performing the task;
- whether it is normally given in a medical setting; and
- whether medical equipment is used.[32]

The EEOC illustrates its points with hypotheticals about psychological examinations: They are forbidden if they lead to diagnoses in the fourth edition of the *Diagnostic and Statistical Manual* (*DSM-IV*), such as depression, excessive anxiety, or certain compulsive disorders, but are permissible if they test whether an applicant is likely to lie.

The difficulty of making a distinction between permitted and prohibited tests was highlighted in *Thompson v. Borg-Warner Protective Services*,[33] in which a test that concededly screened for "behavior problems" and "emotional instability" was

---

[28] For a discussion of psychological testing and profiles as a condition of receiving welfare services or housing, *see* Susan Stefan, *Unequal Rights: Discrimination Against People With Mental Disabilities and the Americans With Disabilities Act* (Washington, DC: American Psychological Association, 2000).

[29] *EEOC Enforcement Guidance: Preemployment Disability-Related Questions and Medical Examinations* (Washington, DC: Oct. 10, 1995) at 16–17.

[30] *See, e.g., Enforcement Guidance.* This *Enforcement Guidance* replaced, and considerably revised, a prior *Enforcement Guidance* that had been the subject of considerable disgruntlement and protest from employers. *See also Technical Assistance Manual on the Employment Provisions of the Americans With Disabilities Act* (1992). The EEOC and the U.S. Department of Justice also responded by a letter to inquiries about whether questions can be asked regarding mental or psychological conditions in a variety of employment circumstances, including applications for employment as a state judge; letter from Elizabeth M. Thornton, EEOC, to David L. Withey, quoted in Joan Goldschmidt, "Merit Selection, Current State, Procedures and Issues," *U. of Miami Law Review* 49 (1994): 1, 60–61.

[31] *EEOC Enforcement Guidance, supra* n. 28, at 14.

[32] *Id.*

[33] Thompson v. Borg-Warner Protective Services, 1996 U.S. Dist. LEXIS 4781 (N.D. Cal. Mar. 11, 1996).

found as a matter of law not to implicate the ADA because "emotional instability" was not the same as a clinical diagnosis under the *DSM-IV*.[34] The court held that

> there is no evidence in the record that "behavioral problems" or "emotional insta-
> bility" as those are revealed in the Plan for Achieving Self Support-III (PASS-III)
> survey, are either themselves disabilities or are characteristics that can lead to iden-
> tifying whether an applicant has an impairment, whether defined by the *DSM* or some
> other parameter.[35]

Interestingly, the EEOC does not include any requirement that an employer show that the test is actually valid, that is, that it successfully discriminates between honest and dishonest people, assuming that this is a stable personality trait and not one that varies from situation to situation (a major assumption). Of course, employers may use invalid tests as long as those tests are not discriminatory, but it is very likely that these "personality trait" tests have a significantly disparate impact on people with mental disabilities. If the tests *have* been validated, it is likely that they have been validated through comparison with a test that is not permitted by the EEOC. This area could benefit from a great deal of further research: How many employers use these "personality tests?" How determinative are they in hiring decisions? How valid are they? Do they disparately impact people with mental disabilities?

Referring an applicant for a pre-employment examination by a psychologist is clearly forbidden by the ADA.[36] However, the distinction with personality tests may be illusory if a nonexpert is administering a test created by experts, following their instructions, and interpreting the test according to their expertise. If the personality tests are only, as the EEOC puts it, "to measure things such as honesty, tastes, and habits," it is not clear why a standardized test is needed. Presumably, a personal interview serves the function of assessing personality.

Several specific tests given to applicants for jobs such as corrections officer, fire fighter, and security guard have been challenged in court under the ADA. These include the Minnesota Multiphasic Personality Inventory and the Pass-III D.A.T.A. Survey.[37] In more than one case, the courts have suggested that subjecting an appli-cant to a battery of these tests also runs afoul of the ADA.[38]

Several cases involving applicants turned down for positions with police de-

---

[34] *Id.* at *6, *7.

[35] *Id.* The court denied the summary judgment to the defendant on the plaintiff's claim under Cal-ifornia labor law, which protects job applicants from "coercion" by employers to "adopt or follow or refrain from adopting or following any particular course or line of political action or political activity." *California Labor Code* Section 1102. Because the PASS-III required the applicant to respond to state-ments such as "marijuana should be legalized," "the drinking age should be lowered," and "the police and courts are lenient on drug users," the court found that the test implicated this provision of California law. *Id.* at *9.

[36] Barnes v. Cochran, 944 F. Supp. 897 (S.D. Fla. 1996).

[37] Thompson v. Borg-Warner Protective Services, 1996 U.S. Dist. LEXIS 4781 (N.D. Cal. Mar. 11, 1996).

[38] Doe v. District of Columbia, 796 F. Supp. 559 (D.D.C. 1992) (the use of the Minnesota Multi-phasic Personality Inventory on applications to be a firefighter); Barnes v. Cochran, 944 F. Supp. 897 (S.D. Fla. 1996) ("Finally, Dr. Stock performed the Minnesota Multiphasic Personality Inventory, the Inwald Personality Inventory, the Otis Lennon School Ability Test, the Hilson Profile/Success Quotient Test, and the California Psychological Inventory. Such an extensive examination constitutes a prohibited pre-employment medical examination"). *Id.* at 905.

partments because of unsatisfactory psychological evaluations by a psychologist, which would appear to be illegal under the EEOC guidelines, have been short circuited by the courts' ruling that the applicants were neither disabled nor regarded by the police departments as disabled.[39] The courts reasoned that the police departments only regarded the applicants as having personality traits that rendered them unsuitable to be police officers.

Postoffer Psychological Testing

Once an applicant is offered employment, he or she may be asked to take a standard medical examination, which is legal under the ADA as long as all employees are asked to take the same examination and the results are kept in a confidential file that is separate from an employee's personnel file.[40] The ADA provides that "a covered entity may require a medical examination after an offer of employment has been made to the job applicant and prior to the commencement of employment duties of such applicant" if "(A) all entering employees are subjected to such an examination regardless of disability; (B) information obtained regarding the medical condition or history of the applicant is collected and maintained on separate forms and in separate medical files and is treated as a confidential medical record"[41]; and "(C) the results of such examination are used only in accordance with this title."[42] This examination includes mental health examinations. The EEOC recognizes that some jobs have (presumably legitimate) "psychological criteria" requirements.

Requiring Employees to Undergo Psychiatric Examinations

The ADA also provides that an employer shall not require a medical examination and shall not make inquiries of an employee as to whether such employee is an individual with a disability or as to the nature or severity of the disability, unless

---

[39] Greenberg v. New York State, 919 F. Supp. 637 (E.D. N.Y. 1996) (the failure to hire a correctional officer based on his performance on a psychological examination indicating that he lacked the ability to make decisions in emergency situations, perform well under stress, and identify with disruptive situations was found not to violate the ADA because the officer did not prove that he was regarded as having a mental disability and did not allege that he was substantially impaired in a major life activity.)

[40] The law does not require that these postoffer medical examinations be job related. Four percent of employers test for HIV infection, sexually transmitted diseases, or both, Kirstin Downey Grimsley, "Pre-Hiring Medical Screening Put to the Test," *The Washington Post* (Oct. 27, 1998): C1. Fewer than 1% conduct genetic testing for the likelihood of developing breast cancer, colon cancer, and Huntington's disease. In one case, employees sued after finding that their "routine" pre-employment physicals included pregnancy tests, screening for syphilis, and, in the case of a Black employee, sickle cell anemia. The 9th Circuit Court permitted a Title VII claim but rejected an ADA claim because the "ADA imposes no restriction on the scope of entrance examinations" and does not limit the examinations to matters that are "job-related and consistent with business necessity"; Norman-Bloodsaw v. Lawrence Berkeley Laboratory, 135 F.3d 1260, 1273 (9th Cir. 1998). Although the medical tests need not be job related, if the applicant is rejected for the job postoffer, the employer must give a job-related reason.

[41] Violations of this requirement of confidentiality are discussed *infra* at 152–153.

[42] 42 U.S.C. § 12112(d)(3). The law provides that supervisors and managers may be informed regarding restrictions on the work and duties of the employee and necessary accommodations, 42 U.S.C. § 12112(d)(3)(B)(i).

such examination or inquiry is shown to be job-related and consistent with business necessity.[43]

The regulations of the EEOC essentially reproduce the statutory language, but the *Interpretive Guidance* to the regulations amplifies substantially on what is prohibited and what is permissible. An employer is not permitted to require a test for AIDS, HIV infection, or cancer if an employee "suddenly starts to use increased amounts of sick leave or starts to appear sickly," unless the employer can demonstrate that such testing is job-related and consistent with business necessity.[44] However, the *Interpretive Guidance* to 29 C.F.R. § 1630.14(c), the provision on permissible examinations of employees, gives employers so broad a scope for investigation as to virtually nullify the statutory protection: "This provision permits employers to make inquiries or require medical examinations (fitness for duty exams) when there is a need to determine whether an employee is still able to perform the essential functions of his or her job."[45]

The provision permits employers or other covered entities to make inquiries or require medical examinations necessary to the reasonable accommodations process described in this part. This provision also permits periodic physicals to determine fitness for duty or other medical monitoring if such physicals or monitoring are required by medical standards or requirements established by federal, state, or local law that are consistent with the ADA and this part (or in the case of a federal standard, with section 504 of the Rehabilitation Act) in that they are job-related and consistent with business necessity. The EEOC goes on to give examples of such "medical standards" and "monitoring": requirements for bus and truck drivers, medical requirements for pilots, Occupational Safety and Health Administration standards, and Federal Coal Mine Health and Safety Act standards.[46]

Case law indicates that employers frequently require their employees to have medical and psychiatric examinations.[47] Despite the significant intrusiveness of psychiatric examinations, especially compelled examinations, the few courts to have considered the question have ruled that, by themselves, such examinations do not

---

[43]42 U.S.C. § 12112(d)(4)(A) (LEXIS 2000).

[44]*EEOC Interpretive Guidance* to 1630.13(b) (current through Sept. 4, 2000).

[45]If an employer cannot do this to determine whether a job applicant may perform the essential functions of the job, it is not clear why an employer may require it of an existing employee. Presumably, the explanation is that it is more difficult for an applicant to prove that the test results were the reason for the failure to hire, but it seems equally plausible that an adverse employment action taken after a required examination may be attributed to other factors, as indeed case law has proven true, Palesch v. Missouri Commission on Human Rights, 2000 U.S. App. LEXIS 29545 (8th Cir. Nov. 21, 2000) (the employee was initially terminated for refusing to release her psychiatric records to her employer's physician; after she released her records, the employer's physician concluded that she could not perform the essential elements of the job and she was terminated again).

[46]*Id.*

[47]Duda v. Board of Education, 133 F.3d 1054 (7th Cir. 1998); Dockery v. City of Chattanooga, 1997 U.S. App. LEXIS 36763 (6th Cir. Dec. 23, 1997); Hoffman v. Brown, 1997 U.S. Dist. LEXIS 18800 (W.D. N.C. Oct. 24, 1997); Miller v. Champaign School District, 983 F. Supp. 1201 (C.D. Ill. 1997). For a particularly egregious example of employer-required medical examinations, *see* EEOC v. Prevo's Family Market, 135 F.3d 1089 (6th Cir. 1998), in which the 6th Circuit Court reversed a jury damage verdict on behalf of an HIV-positive produce clerk who was placed on involuntary leave with pay after revealing his diagnosis and told he could return to work only after undergoing a medical examination.

constitute adverse employment action amounting to discrimination.[48] Rather, a refusal to submit to such examinations has been held to be insubordination and to constitute legitimate, nondiscriminatory grounds for terminating.[49] Nor does the employer's requirement of a psychiatric examination establish that the employer regards the employee as disabled.[50]

Employers' Requirement That Employees Returning From Leave of Absence for Medical Reasons Submit Medical Certification of Fitness

If an employee has disclosed that he or she has a psychiatric condition and has been given leave on that basis, several courts have held that the employer may require the employee to submit certification from a mental health professional prior to permitting him or her to return to work or after reinstatement.[51] This does not mean that the employer can have blanket access to all the employee's psychiatric records; in fact, a statement that the employee can perform his or her job is the only documentation an employer can request.

The ADA appears to permit the employer to require that an employee returning from leave obtain certification of fitness to return to duty from the employer's medical department rather than his or her own mental health professional. However, depending on the nature of the leave and the nature of the request for certification, such a request may violate the Family and Medical Leave Act (FMLA),[52] which allows an employer to request a certification of an employee's ability to return to work only from the employee's health care provider.[53] Although the employer's health care provider may, with the employee's permission, contact the employee's health care provider "for purposes of clarification of the employee's ability to return to work,"[54] the employer may not request additional information, may not request any information about any condition that was not the subject of the FMLA leave, or delay the employee's return to work during this time.[55] At least one court has held that the FMLA prohibits an employer from requiring an employee who has been on leave for depression to submit to a separate psychiatric examination before returning to work.[56] The court found that the ADA permitted such an inquiry but that the FMLA did not, and it found no incongruity in this:

---

[48] Yin v. California, 95 F.3d 864 (9th Cir. 1996); Deckert v. City of Ulysses, 1995 WL 580074 (D. Kan. Sept. 6, 1995); Sullivan v. River Valley School District, 197 F.3d 804 (6th Cir. 2000).

[49] Fritsch v. City of Chula Vista, 2000 U.S. Dist. LEXIS 14820 (C.D. Calif. Feb. 23, 2000); Moore v. Board of Education of Johnson City Schools, 134 F.3d 781, 783 (6th Cir. 1998).

[50] See Sullivan v. River Valley School District, n. 48, and discussion later in this chapter.

[51] Virginia Department of Taxation v. Daughtry, 250 Va. 542; 463 S.E.2d 847 (V. 1995); Moore v. Johnson City School District, 134 F.3d 781 (6th Cir. 1998); Brumley v. Pena, 62 F.3d 277, 278–279 (8th Cir. 1995) (Rehabilitation Act); Pesterfield v. TVA, 941 F.2d 437, 437–438 (6th Cir. 1991) (Rehabilitation Act).

[52] 29 U.S.C. § 2601 et seq. (LEXIS 2000).

[53] 29 U.S.C. § 2614(a)(4). The regulations implementing the Family and Medical Leave Act indicate that this certification "need only be a simple statement of the employee's ability to return to work," 29 C.F.R. § 825.310(c) (LEXIS current through Sept. 4, 2000).

[54] Id.

[55] Id.

[56] Albert v. Runyon, 6 F. Supp. 2d 57 (D. Mass. 1998).

It would be far more surprising if the juxtaposition of these statutes (each of which seeks to safeguard employees' rights in different ways) were to deprive employees of a right so explicitly granted in the FMLA—the right to be reinstated upon submitting a "simple statement" of fitness to return.[57]

Thus, it appears that the FMLA may give employees with mental disabilities greater rights than does the ADA in this area, and both employees and their attorneys should be aware of the FMLA provisions. The FMLA does not specifically require that an employee invoke it when requesting a leave of absence,[58] and nothing in either statute indicates that a leave given as an accommodation under the ADA may not also be subject to the FMLA.

Medical Examinations for Rehired Employees

A further erosion of the protection against preoffer inquiries into disability has taken place as courts increasingly hold that the requirement does not apply to employees who are being rehired after leaving their employment for disability-related reasons.[59] In some cases, employers seek a medical release rather than a full medical examination, and some courts have held that this distinction is crucial in upholding an employer's actions.[60]

Breach of Confidentiality as a Violation of the ADA

Despite the requirement that records of a disability obtained through medical examinations be kept confidential, case law reflects that this confidentiality protection is subject to several exceptions. For example, the confidentiality provisions of the ADA are not applicable to disability information obtained before the ADA took effect.[61] Courts have also held that the confidentiality provisions do not apply to information obtained from employees in order to get group health insurance,[62] nor are they immune from discovery in ADA claims by other employees.[63] The EEOC ruled that an employer may divulge information about an employee's medical condition to a union if the employee's accommodations implicate a collective bargaining

---

[57]*Id.* at *32, n. 6.

[58]29 C.F.R. § 825.302, 825.303 (LEXIS, current through Sept. 4, 2000).

[59]Grenier v. Cyanamid Plastics, 70 F.3d 667 (1st Cir. 1995); Harris v. Harris & Hart, 206 F.3d 838 (9th Cir. 2000).

[60]*Harris, supra* n. 59.

[61]Buchanan v. City of San Antonio, 85 F.3d 196 (5th Cir. 1996) (citing the EEOC notice No. 915.002, May 19, 1994).

[62]Barnes v. Benham Group, 22 F. Supp. 2d 1013 (D. Minn. 1998).

[63]Scott v. Leavenworth Unified School District, 190 F.R.D. 583 (D. Kan. 1999) (a school psychologist with depression sought the personnel files of other employees that she claimed had been given accommodations that she had been denied).

agreement.[64] In any event, case law indicates that confidentiality is breached without apparent justification quite regularly.[65]

Several circuits have held that a plaintiff need not prove that he or she is disabled to prevail on a claim under the ADA that the employer violated the confidentiality provision of the ADA.[66] Another case suggests that when an employer requires an employee to submit to a psychiatric examination or to release mental health records, addressing the employee's concerns about confidentiality is a required part of the interactive process mandated by the ADA.[67]

"Misconduct" and Disability Discrimination

The issue of when an employer can discipline or fire an employee with a disability for misconduct raises a variety of complex issues. Although courts have agreed that employers do not have to tolerate misconduct in the workplace, no consistent jurisprudence addresses the underlying welter of issues.

The first step toward coherent doctrine in this area is to avoid the use of the word "misconduct." If an employee's conduct is framed at the outset as misconduct, the deck is stacked against a careful examination of the facts of a case. Calling behavior "misconduct" predetermines outcomes because it assumes both intentionality and choice and has connotations in our society that make it utterly opposed to "disability." It is easy for a court to hold that an employer should not have to tolerate misconduct in the workplace. This is simply another way of phrasing the conclusion that the employee loses the case.

First of all, what is "misconduct"? Cases involving misconduct run the gamut from employees who commit battery and sexual harassment (often by doctors, lawyers, and professors who "discover" their disabilities in the aftermath of professional discipline[68]) to employees with brain damage or mental retardation being fired for failing to follow complex written policies,[69] quacking at fellow employees,[70] or not paying 27 cents due for a salad[71] to an employee (a doctor) falling asleep because of sleep apnea.[72] They include conduct ranging from bringing a gun to work[73] to the

---

[64]Letter Re: Confidentiality and Unions, 10 N.D.L.R. ¶ 385, *Disability Compliance Bull.* 10 (Nov. 27, 1997): 10, 24.

[65]Buchanan v. City of San Antonio, 85 F.3d 196 (5th Cir. 1996) (an applicant with depression); Keene v. TECO Energy Corp., 2000 U.S. Dist. LEXIS 2271 (M.D. Fla. Mar. 1, 2000); Fredenberg v. Contra Costa County, 172 F.3d 1176 (9th Cir. 1999), *see* cases in n. 100.

[66]Fredenberg v. Contra Costa County, 172 F.3d 1176, 1182 (9th Cir. 1999); Cosette v. Minnesota Power and Light, 188 F.3d 964, 969 (8th Cir. 1999); Mack v. Johnstown America Corp., 1999 U.S. Dist. LEXIS 6917 (W.D. Pa. May 12, 1999).

[67]Hrobowski v. Henderson, 2000 U.S. Dist. LEXIS 7293 (N.D. Ill. May 23, 2000).

[68]Ramachandar v. Sobol, 838 F. Supp. 110 (S.D. N.J. 1993); Doe v. Connecticut Department of Health Services, 75 F.3d 81 (2d Cir. 1996).

[69]Fernbach v. Dominick's Finer Foods, 936 F. Supp. 467 (N.D. Ill. 1996).

[70]Gasper v. Perry, 1998 U.S. App. LEXIS 14933 at *5 (4th Cir. July 2, 1998) (Gasper also engaged in other inappropriate behavior, such as demanding to lick his colleague's ice cream cones and inquiring about the differences in their brassieres).

[71]" 'Misconduct' Questioned in the Discharge of Worker With Down's Syndrome," *Disability Compliance Bull. 12* (June 4, 1998): 4, 1.

[72]Brohm v. J. H. Properties, 947 F. Supp. 299 (W.D. Ky. 1996), *aff'd,* 149 F.3d 517 (6th Cir. 1998).

[73]Hindman v. GTE, 1994 WL 371396 (M.D. Fla. June 24, 1994).

"conduct" of thinking hostile thoughts.[74] Disabilities raising "misconduct" issues range from diabetes[75] to Tourette's syndrome[76] to alcoholism[77] and drug abuse[78] to psychiatric disabilities.[79]

One crucial point to note at the outset is that the ADA itself permits differential treatment in this area of employees with two kinds of disabilities: those who are alcoholics or are using illegal drugs. Thus, the statute permits an employer to

> hold an employee who engages in the illegal use of drugs or who is an alcoholic to the same qualification standards for employment or job performance and behavior that such entity holds other employees, even if unsatisfactory performance or behavior is related to the drug use or alcoholism of such employee.[80]

Several courts have explicitly noted the different standards in the ADA for "misconduct" claims attributable to alcohol and illegal drug use and those attributable to other disabilities.[81] This still leaves room for a discrimination claim if the alcoholic employee is subject to adverse action for behavior if other employees without disabilities engage in the same behavior but are not punished or receive lesser punishments.

People with disabilities other than alcoholism or illegal drug use may also have a discrimination claim if their conduct is treated differently than that of other employees. But, in addition, the statutory provision quoted previously suggests that for employees with disabilities other than alcoholism or illegal drug use, "conduct caused by a qualifying disability is protected by the ADA."[82] Many disabilities manifest themselves in forms of behavior or conduct, and psychiatric disability is manifested almost completely in this way.

The 2nd Circuit,[83] the 4th Circuit,[84] and the 10th Circuit[85] have refused to recognize a sharp dichotomy between a disability and the manifestations of that disability for ADA purposes.[86] For example, in a carefully reasoned opinion, the 10th Circuit rejected an employer's argument that discrimination based on disability is prohibited by the ADA but that discrimination based on misconduct by the disabled

---

[74]Collins v. Blue Cross Blue Shield, 228 Mich. App. 560, 579 N.W.2d 435 (1998); Layser v. Morrison, 935 F. Supp. 562 (E.D. Pa. 1995).

[75]Gilday v. Mecosta County, 124 F.3d 760 (6th Cir. 1997).

[76]Purcell v. Pennsylvania Department of Corrections, 1998 U.S. Dist. LEXIS 105 (E.D. Pa. Jan. 9, 1998) (a Title II case involving a prisoner).

[77]DeSpears v. Milwaukee County, 65 F.3d 635 (7th Cir. 1995).

[78]Teahan v. Metro-North C. R. Co., 951 F.2d 511 (2d Cir. 1991) .

[79]Deberry v. Runyon, 1998 U.S. Dist. LEXIS 12532 (M.D. N.C. Apr. 20, 1998); Hamilton v. Southwestern Bell, 136 F.3d 1047 (5th Cir. 1998) (posttraumatic stress disorder).

[80]42 U.S.C. § 12114(c)(4). Illegal drug users are, in any event, not covered by the ADA unless they have been or are in a supervised rehabilitation program and are no longer engaged in such use, 42 U.S.C. § 12114(a) and (b).

[81]Nielsen v. Moroni Feed Co., 162 F.3d 604 (10th Cir. 1998).

[82]Id.

[83]Teahan v. Metro-North C.R. Co., 951 F.2d 511 (2d Cir. 1991). The second time the case came up for appellate review, however, the 2nd Circuit affirmed the district court's holding that Teahan was not "otherwise qualified" for his position, 80 F.3d 50 (2d Cir. 1996).

[84]Martinson v. Kinney Shoes Corp., 104 F.3d 683 (4th Cir. 1997).

[85]Den Hartog v. Wasatch Academy, 129 F.3d 1076 (10th Cir. 1997).

[86]The 5th Circuit Court, in a particularly unthoughtful decision, appears to have adopted the rule that an employee who has committed an act of misconduct cannot "hide behind the ADA," Hamilton v. Southwestern Bell, 136 F.3d 1047 (5th Cir. 1998).

person is permitted by the ADA. Noting that the ADA specifically permits employers to hold an employee who engages in the illegal use of drugs or who is an alcoholic to the same standards of conduct as any other employee, even if unsatisfactory behavior or performance is related to alcoholism or drug use, the 10th Circuit held that "Congress implicitly did not intend to extend the same employer prerogative to employees with other disabilities."[87] The court also noted that Congress had provided defenses to employers such as "direct threat" and "undue hardship," implying that "there are certain levels of disability-caused conduct that need not be tolerated or accommodated by the employer. However, the necessary corollary is that there must be certain levels of disability-caused conduct that have to be tolerated or accommodated."[88]

Therefore, "as a general rule, an employer may not hold a employee with a disability to precisely the same standards of conduct as an employee without a disability unless such standards are job-related and consistent with business necessity."[89] If those conduct standards are consistent with business necessity, the employer must provide reasonable accommodations to enable the employee to meet them. The court stated clearly that "the employer must tolerate eccentric or unusual conduct caused by the employee's mental disability, so long as the employee can satisfactorily perform the essential functions of his job."[90] This language is extremely important because it precludes employers from devising rules of workplace behavior that, although neutral on their face, have an enormously disparate impact on employees with psychiatric disabilities. These seemingly neutral rules may be devised precisely to ensure the removal of employees whose job performance gives no cause for complaint, and who are not in the least threatening, but whose disability-related behavior nevertheless makes fellow employees uncomfortable. "Thus," the court concluded, "appellees' effort to put all disability-caused conduct beyond the pale of ADA protection cannot be correct" because "to permit employers carte blanche to terminate employees with mental disabilities on the basis of any abnormal behavior would largely nullify the ADA's protection of the mentally disabled."[91]

But what is "conduct caused by a qualifying disability"? At either end of the spectrum, this question is easy to answer. Generally speaking, for example, Tourette's syndrome "causes" tics and barks[92] and epilepsy "causes" the flailing gestures of a seizure,[93] but depression does not "cause" sexual harassment.[94] An employee with Tourette's syndrome who is fired for tics and barks would be fired because of the

---

[87]*Hartog, supra* n. 85.

[88]129 F.3d 1076, 1087 (10th Cir. 1997).

[89]*Id.*

[90]*Id.* at 1088.

[91]*Hartog, supra* n. 85, at 1087.

[92]*But see* Oliver Sacks, *An Anthropologist on Mars* (New York: Knopf, 1995) (telling the story of a Canadian surgeon with Tourette's syndrome, who "barks" and "tics" with considerable frequency, except when he is operating).

[93]Martinson v. Kinney Shoe Co., 104 F.3d 683 (4th Cir. 1997) (a person having seizures is fired because of his disability). *But see* some criminal cases expressing skepticism about the degree of control an individual with "psychomotor epilepsy" has over his behavior, People v. Grant, 1979 U.S. Dist. LEXIS 13190 (N.D. Ill. Apr. 1, 1979).

[94]Maes v. Henderson, 33 F. Supp. 2d 1281 (D. Nev. 1999); Motzkin v. Trustees of Boston University, 938 F. Supp. 983 (D. Mass. 1996).

disability, and an employee who is fired for having seizures would be fired because of the disability.

But what about conduct one or two steps away in the chain of causation from the disability? Judge Posner suggested in *DeSpears v. Milwaukee* that alcoholism might "cause" drinking, but not drunk driving.[95] However, the 2nd Circuit Court in *Teahan* considered that alcoholism "caused" absenteeism. Although depression clearly does not cause sexual harassment, the loss of judgment attendant on the manic phase of bipolar disorder might be a causal factor in behavior in which an employee might not otherwise engage.[96]

Some plaintiffs have alleged that side effects of the medication taken for the disability caused the misconduct precipitating their termination or discipline.[97] Should side effects of medication be considered separately from the disability or as indistinguishable from the disability?

In addition, the framing of the conduct in question can predetermine the outcome of the case. Consider the case of a young man with mental retardation who had worked at Lucky Stores for 5 years and had been accustomed to asking whether he had enough money for his lunch. One day, he was told he was 27 cents short, but he took his salad to the parking lot and ate it anyway, whereon he was promptly fired, apparently at the behest of a new manager.[98] If his conduct were framed as stealing, the plaintiff would lose the case because theft is obviously not a manifestation of mental retardation. If his conduct were framed as failing to pay for a salad because of an inability to do the mathematics involved in comparing the cost of the salad to the money in his pocket, the plaintiff wins. What is most likely true in this case shows just how complex the issue is: It was probably the case that Colin Turrin knew he was not entitled to the salad and was not supposed to eat the salad but because of his mental retardation could not foresee that the consequence of disobeying the rule would be the loss of the job he had prized for 5 years. Other questions include whether the rule being enforced by the employer is a necessary rule, whether it has a disparate impact on individuals with disabilities, and whether an individual employee could be accommodated before adverse action was taken.

Sometimes the behavior for which the employee is disciplined or terminated occurred off the job. In some cases, the adverse action is justified, such as criminal conviction for molesting a child or shooting up a bar with an automatic weapon, but in other cases, it is not so clear. For example, in *Doe v. Region 13 Mental Health-Mental Retardation Commission,*[99] a mental health professional, who was increasingly depressed and talked of suicide off the job, was fired, even though her work record and performance were unquestionably excellent. The 5th Circuit Court held that her termination was justified because of the consequences that her suicidal behavior or gestures might have on her clients, although there was no evidence she ever betrayed her mood to her clients.

Thus, the intersection of "off-the-job" behavior with concerns about future conduct based on current problematic behavior poses issues of particular interest to

---

[95]DeSpears was arguably wrongly decided because there was no showing that driving was an essential function of DeSpears's job.

[96]Mawson v. U.S. West, 23 F. Supp. 2d 1204 (D. Colo. 1998).

[97]Taylor v. Dover Elevator Systems, 917 F. Supp. 455 (N.D. Miss. 1996).

[98]"'Misconduct' Questioned in the Discharge of Worker With Down's Syndrome," *supra* n. 71.

[99]704 F.2d 1402 (5th Cir. 1983) (a Rehabilitation Act case).

people with psychiatric disabilities. Courts must proceed with particular care in this area if they are to ensure that the protections of the ADA remain meaningful when there is no job-based misconduct at all, only concerns about what might happen in the future. Sometimes, for example, an employee reveals his or her angry or violent feelings about work to an employee behavioral assistance plan therapist.[100] Other times, an employee may exhibit odd behavior. Courts are often very quick to grant an employer carte blanche to take corrective action, including termination of employees who have psychiatric disabilities or potential psychiatric disabilities from jobs involving security, police work, or carrying a weapon,[101] which may be an expression of some of the most common stereotypes about people with psychiatric disabilities.

Sometimes the employee breaks no "rule" but behaves in a way that makes other employees or customers uncomfortable; this raises a difficult question. Accommodations are typically discussed as though the employer and employee exist in a vacuum. It is clearly true that other employees' irrational fears, for example, of contagion from AIDS, cannot excuse an employer's discrimination.[102] It is also true that an employee's behavior that might, out of context, be considered to reflect psychiatric disability looks different when it turns out everyone in the office engages in the same behavior.[103] Nevertheless, some behavior, which clearly does not constitute a "direct threat," makes other employees uncomfortable.

These issues provoke questions unanswered by the ADA about the extent to which workplace norms should be altered to accommodate people who are "different" but can do the job. Almost everyone agrees that someone who stutters painfully should not be fired and that fellow employees should deal with their discomfort related to the stuttering. Most people feel similarly about someone who weeps at the office or someone who speaks too loudly because of a disability. One case that illustrates this issue is *Gasper v. Perry,* which involved a man with brain damage that left him unable to readily respond to social cues. He asked embarrassing questions, such as how "racer-type" bras differed from regular bras; he refused to let a fellow employee pass through a door unless she gave him a lick of her frozen yogurt cone; on encountering a colleague with a duck head umbrella, he grasped it, pointed it at her face, and quacked loudly; and he dropped to his knees and begged a female colleague never to cut her "long, beautiful hair."[104] The court upheld the firing of the employee in *Gasper v. Perry* as a firing for misconduct, without much discussion of the difficult issues involved.

Misconduct seems at the least to involve an appreciation of the inappropriate or

---

[100]Collins v. Blue Cross Blue Shield, 103 F.3d 35 (6th Cir. 1996) (vacating the lower court's decision in favor of the employee who was terminated after a psychiatrist reported the employee's threats, even though the psychiatrist did not think the threats were serious); Layser v. Morrison, 935 F. Supp. 562 (E.D. Pa. 1995) (security guard with violent dream sought help immediately from psychiatrist, who "promptly warned [employer]").

[101]Lassiter v. Reno, 1996 U.S. App. LEXIS 13138 (4th Cir. May 29, 1996) (a deputy marshal was terminated after he began to show signs of paranoid personality disorder).

[102]School Board of Nassau County v. Arline, 480 U.S. 273 (1987). Note that the U.S. Department of Justice under President Reagan made precisely that argument to the U.S. Supreme Court, *id.* at 282.

[103]Cody v. Cigna Health Care 139 F.3d 595 (8th Cir. 1998) (the plaintiff's carrying a voodoo doll must be taken in the context that her supervisor made voodoo dolls as gifts for everyone in the office).

[104]Gasper v. Perry, 1998 U.S. App. LEXIS 14933 at *8–10 (4th Cir. July 2, 1998).

violative nature of the workplace behavior, a factor that appeared to be lacking in *Gasper v. Perry.* In addition, if misconduct is defined as an infraction of a company rule, the rule should be explicit, clear, and applicable to all employees. Often, a close reading of a case purportedly involving misconduct reveals that an odd or eccentric employee worked without disciplinary incident for years until a new supervisor was appointed.[105] Employers and supervisors can set a tone of tolerance and supportiveness, which is picked up by other workers, or they can covertly encourage complaints about the behavior of a particular worker. Another helpful step is to determine whether reasonable accommodation is possible and whether an employer made any efforts to reasonably accommodate an employee.

In some ways, the misconduct dilemma is easy to solve, because the people who misuse the law's protections against disability discrimination to attempt to insulate their own misconduct frequently "discover" their diagnosis in the wake of disciplinary action. The common doctrine that the employer cannot be liable for discriminating on the basis of a disability that was unknown at the time of the adverse action should largely take care of this problem.

Courts should insist on a nexus between the alleged disability and the conduct for which an employee is disciplined. Very few covered disabilities can be said to cause sexual harassment, for example. Is the rule reasonable? Does it have a disparate impact on people with the kind of disability the plaintiff has? The court should look at how long the person has been working without problems and look in particular for the appearance of a new supervisor on the scene. The court should also examine how other employees who behave similarly are treated and look to see whether an attempt to accommodate the behavior has been made.

Associational Discrimination

The ADA also prohibits discrimination against a qualified person without a disability on the basis of his or her known relationship or association with a person with a disability.[106] This provision was apparently prompted by the situation of a woman who was fired from a long-held job after her son, who was diagnosed with AIDS, came to live with her.[107]

Congress gave several examples of the actions it intended to prohibit by enacting this provision of the ADA: firing an employee for doing volunteer work with people who have AIDS, or refusing to hire someone with a spouse who has a disability because of the fear that the employee would often miss work to care for the spouse. The legislative history of the ADA makes clear that employees without disabilities are to be protected from adverse employment actions based on myths and stereotypes about the disabilities of their family members and friends. In addition, the associational discrimination provision was also intended to prohibit employers from taking adverse actions against employees on the basis of presumptions—or facts—about

---

[105]*Id.* at n. 104. *See also* "'Misconduct' Questioned in the Discharge of Worker With Down's Syndrome," *Disability Compliance Bull.* (June 4, 1998) p. 1.

[106]42 U.S.C. § 12112(b)(4) (West 2000).

[107]H.R. Rep. No. 101-485, pt. 2, at 30 (1990), *reprinted in* 1990 U.S.C.C.A.N. 303, 312.

increases in health insurance costs associated with spouses or children with disabilities.

The "association" provision does not apply only to family members and friends. It also includes discrimination against employees who do volunteer work with people with disabilities as well as operators of group homes and facilities that provide care for people with disabilities. However, the association must be with specific disabled people: The 1st Circuit upheld the dismissal of a case charging that employees had been fired for doing unpopular AIDS advocacy work. The court held that the "provision was intended to protect qualified individuals from adverse job actions ... arising from the employees' relationships with particular disabled persons."[108]

However, an employer need not make any reasonable accommodations for an employee who does not have a disability but who has a relative with a disability. For example, such an employee is not entitled under the ADA to additional leave or a flexible work schedule,[109] although the employee might be entitled to such leave under the Family Medical Leave Act.[110]

To state a claim of associational discrimination, a plaintiff must show that

- he or she was subjected to adverse employment action
- he or she was qualified for the job
- he or she was known to have a relative or an association with a person with a disability
- the adverse employment action occurred under circumstances that raised a reasonable inference that the disability of the relative or associate was a determining factor in the action.[111]

Compared with other employment discrimination allegations, relatively few cases of employment discrimination based on association have been brought under the ADA. Although the cases have been few, they are sufficient in number to permit certain conclusions.

Courts have interpreted the associational discrimination claim very narrowly, refusing to consider claims that seem intuitively to fit into the associational discrimination framework. Associational discrimination claims tend to fall into several identifiable categories:

- employees, always women, who are fired for taking too much time off to care for sick children or spouses (in these cases, the employees always lose their associational discrimination claims)[112]
- homes or facilities for people with substance abuse or other disabilities that are denied permits by the neighborhoods in which they seek to locate (in

---

[108]Oliveras-Sifre v. Puerto Rico Department of Health, 214 F.3d 23, 26 (1st Cir. 2000).

[109]See 28 C.F.R. § 1630.8, *Interpretive Guidance.*

[110]See chapter 2, this volume.

[111]Den Hartog v. Wasatch Academy, 129 F.3d 1076 (10th Cir. 1997).

[112]Tyndall v. National Education Centers, 31 F.3d 209 (4th Cir. 1994); Ennis v. National Association of Business & Education Radio, 53 F.3d 55 (4th Cir. 1995); Padilla v. Buffalo State College Foundation, 958 F. Supp. 124 (W.D. N.Y. 1997); Rocky v. Columbia Lawnwood Regional Medical Center, 54 F. Supp. 2d 1159 (S.D. Fla. 1999); Walthall v. Fulton County School District, 18 F. Supp. 2d 1378 (N.D. Ga. 1998), *aff'd,* 102 F.3d 131 (11th Cir. 1999).

these cases, the homes or facilities always win their associational discrimination claims)[113]

- employees who are fired because of concerns about health insurance costs of employees' spouses or children with disabilities (in these cases, the courts tend to favor the employees)[114]

- challenges to inequities in employer health benefit programs that fail to provide coverage for the conditions of a spouse or child with a disability (these claims always lose)[115]

- married couples who work as a unit and are terminated when one spouse becomes disabled, or variations on this theme (these cases have mixed outcomes and are very fact specific)[116]

- an interesting mixed bag of miscellaneous cases that present situations not explicitly described by Congress or the EEOC (in these cases, employees always lose).[117]

Although many associational discrimination cases lose, not all of them do. A few stray cases that are paradigm examples of Congress's intent have been won: an employer who fired an employee when the employee's son developed an expensive liver disease[118]; an employer who refused to hire a woman because her spouse had a disability and the employer worried that she would take too much time off[119]; and an employer who fired a waiter because the waiter's partner had AIDS.[120] In another early case, a court denied summary judgment to an employer that fired an employee who could not attend work-related social events because of his wife's disability.[121]

However, the classic associational discrimination case (the principal case that is

---

[113]Oak Ridge Care Center v. Racine Co., 896 F. Supp. 867 (E.D. Wisc. 1995); Innovative Health Systems v. City of White Plains, 117 F.3d 37 (2d Cir. 1997); Discovery House Inc. v. Indianapolis, 43 F. Supp. 2d 997 (N.D. Ind. 1999).

[114]Le v. Applied Biosystems, 886 F. Supp. 717 (N.D. Ca. 1995); Pater v. Deringer Manufacturing Co., 1995 U.S. Dist. LEXIS 12942 (N.D. Ill. Sept. 7, 1995); Potts v. National Health Care, 961 F. Supp. 1136 (M.D. Tenn. 1996); Jackson v. Service Engineering, 96 F. Supp. 2d. 873 (S.D. Ind. 2000).

[115]Niemeier v. Tri-State Fire Protection District, 2000 U.S. Dist. LEXIS 12621 (N.D. Ill. Aug. 24, 2000); Micek v. City of Chicago, 1999 U.S. Dist. LEXIS 16263 (N.D. Ill. Oct. 4, 1999); Moresi v. AMR Corp., 1999 U.S. Dist. LEXIS 13644 (N.D. Tex. 1999).

[116]Sedlacek v. Hillis, 3 P.3d 767 (Wash. App. 2000), *review granted*, 21 P.3d 1150 (Wash. 2000); Beck v. Dahn Corp., 1998 U.S. App. LEXIS 9709 (10th Cir. May 12, 1998); Deghand v. Walmart, 926 F. Supp. 1002 (D. Kan. 1996) (a husband had a mental breakdown and was well treated by the employer, but the wife's claim for associational discrimination survived because nothing in the statute required that the person with a disability be the subject of discrimination to sustain an associational discrimination claim).

[117]Braverman v. Penobscot Shoe Co., 859 F. Supp. 596 (D. Me. 1994) (the associational discrimination provision was not meant to cover firing because the employee kept other employee's cancer secret); O'Connell v. Isocor Corp., 56 F. Supp. 2d 649 (E.D. Va. 1999) (no associational discrimination claim stated by employee who was fired after the disabled employee she replaced sued the company for employment discrimination); Oliveras-Sifre v. Puerto Rico Dept. of Health, 214 F.3d 23 (1st Cir. 2000) (AIDS advocates who claimed they were fired because they advocated on behalf of disabled individuals failed to allege any specific association with a disabled individual and thus failed to state a claim).

[118]Le v. Applied Biosystems, 886 F. Supp. 717 (N.D. Ca. 1995).

[119]Reddinger v. Hospital Central Services, 4 F. Supp. 2d 405 (E.D. Pa. 1998).

[120]Saladin v. Turner, 936 F. Supp. 1571 (N.D. Okla. 1996).

[121]Wilson v. Association of Graduates of the U.S. Military Academy, 946 F. Supp. 294 (S.D. N.Y. 1996).

always cited in other cases) involved an employee with a child who had a psychiatric disability. Howard Den Hartog had been a teacher at Wasatch Academy for more than 25 years when he was fired because of the behavior of his adult son Nathaniel, who was diagnosed with bipolar disorder.[122] The struggle between the Wasatch Academy and the Den Hartog family took place over several years and is a heart-wrenching story with few easy answers. The legal holdings of the *Den Hartog* case do, however, lay out some principles in deciding associational discrimination cases involving people with psychiatric disabilities.

Wasatch Academy is a boarding school and requires full-time faculty members to live on campus. In 1992, Den Hartog's 21-year-old son Nathaniel was diagnosed with bipolar disorder and was hospitalized. After his hospitalization, he returned to live with his parents on the campus of Wasatch Academy. The headmaster, aware of his diagnosis, offered him part-time employment at the academy. However, in early 1993, Nathaniel "developed close ties" with the headmaster's 16-year-old son Travis. Possibly at Travis's request,[123] Nathaniel took him to a psychiatric hospital and later called the headmaster's house to see how Travis was doing. He said he would slit his wrists if he could not speak to Travis, which he later explained he did not mean literally but simply to express the urgency of his desire to speak to Travis.

Nathaniel's telephone calls became more threatening; the police were called, and Nathaniel was institutionalized in early 1993. At that point, the headmaster told the Den Hartogs that "if Nathaniel's condition resulted in the Den Hartogs' being unable to live at Wasatch, then Den Hartog might be terminated." Mrs. Den Hartog informed the headmaster that she would not exclude her son from home at Christmas: "we would not say, Nathaniel, you cannot come home because Joe Loftin says you cannot be here."[124] The school paid for an apartment in a nearby city for Nathaniel to live in with his mother. Nevertheless, Nathaniel continued to come back and visit Wasatch Academy. After Nathaniel beat a former schoolmate (not on Wasatch Academy grounds) and told the schoolmate that he planned to attack the headmaster next, Howard Den Hartog was fired.

Den Hartog was clearly fired because of his association with his son. However, he lost his case. He demonstrated to the court's satisfaction that his son was disabled: The court held that bipolar disorder was a disability under the ADA, "at least if it is sufficiently severe, as was the case here."[125] The court cited several other appellate decisions holding bipolar disorder to be a disability for ADA purposes.

The court noted that "Wasatch does not claim that Den Hartog's performance as a schoolteacher was in any way deficient, except inasmuch as his presence on the campus may have attracted Nathaniel to the campus."[126] In addition, the court stated that "although Loftin told Den Hartog that the reason for non-renewal was the elimination of his position, Loftin testified in his deposition that absent Nathaniel's behavior, Den Hartog 'very possibly' would still be employed by Wasatch."[127] The

---

[122]Den Hartog v. Wasatch Academy, 129 F.3d 1076 (10th Cir. 1997).

[123]Although it is unclear whether the trip to the hospital was made at Travis's request or on Nathaniel's initiative, when a case is decided on summary judgment, the court must resolve all factual ambiguities in favor of the nonmoving party, in this case, Den Hartog; 129 F.3d 1076 (10th Cir. 1997).

[124]129 F.3d 1076, 1079 (10th Cir. 1997).

[125]*Id.* at 1080–1081.

[126]*Id.* at 1082.

[127]*Id.* at 1079.

court also disagreed with Wasatch Academy's argument that its discrimination was based on Nathaniel's misconduct rather than his disability, which Wasatch argued was not discrimination prohibited by the ADA.[128]

In fact, the court agreed that Den Hartog had made out a prima facie case of discrimination on the basis of association. However, it held, as a matter of first impression, that the employer's affirmative "direct threat" defense could be applied to persons with disabilities who associated with the plaintiff employee. It also held that the employer's duty to provide reasonable accommodations did not extend either to employees' relatives with disabilities or to an employee who is not disabled but who has a relative with a disability.

The court found that Nathaniel was a direct threat, based on his repeated and direct threats to members of the Wasatch community and his propensity to carry them out. "The threat Nathaniel posed to the Wasatch community objectively appeared to Wasatch and Loftin to be grave in nature, likely to result in harm severe in magnitude, and both imminent and ongoing in duration, thereby satisfying all the factors under 29 C.F.R. 1630.2(r)."[129]

Although *Den Hartog v. Wasatch Academy* is the principal case on associational discrimination, no further cases have been reported involving associational discrimination based on a family member's or friend's mental illness or perceived mental illness and no cases have been reported in the media of firing or termination on this basis.

Retaliation for Protected Activity

The ADA also specifically prohibits employers from retaliating against employees for engaging in protected activity under the ADA.[130] This prohibition, taken from Title VII of the Civil Rights Act, protects individuals who have "opposed any act or practice made unlawful" by the ADA or who have "made a charge, testified, assisted or participated in any manner in an investigation, proceeding or hearing" to enforce any provision of the ADA.[131]

Retaliation claims have succeeded where disability discrimination claims have failed because, unlike disability discrimination, a plaintiff does not need to prove that he or she is disabled to recover on a retaliation claim. The plaintiff need only prove that he or she engaged in protected activity and suffered an adverse employment action and then show a causal connection between the protected activity and the adverse employment action.

Proving a causal connection is often difficult, and many courts look to the timing of the adverse employment action in relation to the protected activity. A lapse of seven weeks between filing a complaint with the EEOC and termination raises suspicions[132]; a gap of 1 year has been held by many courts to be too long to raise any inference of retaliation.[133]

---

[128]*Id.* at 1084. *See* a discussion in this book about misconduct at 65–69.

[129]*Id.* at 1089.

[130]42 U.S.C. § 12203(a).

[131]29 C.F.R. § 1630.12(a).

[132]Farley v. Nationwide Mutual Insurance Co., 197 F.3d 1322, 1337 (11th Cir. 1999).

[133]Linser v. Ohio Department of Mental Health, 2000 U.S. App. LEXIS 25644 (6th Cir. Oct. 6, 2000); Jackson v. Pepsi-Cola Co., 783 F.2d 50, 54 (6th Cir. 1986).

Characteristics of Successful Employment Discrimination Cases

Successful employment discrimination cases on behalf of people with mental disabilities are so rare that the successful ones must have something to teach us—from broad lessons about social values to relatively narrow lessons about successful lawyering. "Successful" cases can be defined in various ways. Obviously, a case in which a verdict for the employee is sustained at the appellate level represents one manifestation of success; a successfully negotiated settlement represents another kind of success. In studying successful cases, I looked at all cases in which some kind of beneficial outcome to the plaintiff was reported, from settlement to litigation victory. In effect, a successful case is one in which the plaintiff's action, whether filing an EEOC complaint or a court case, results in an improvement of the situation that led to the action.

Plaintiffs whose psychiatric disabilities clearly predated their employment with the defendant[134] do far better than those whose disabilities have arisen in the course of their employment with the defendant.[135] This outcome reflects the continuing (and discriminatory) suspicion that people "make up" or pretend to have mental disabilities to gain advantages in society.

Successful cases on behalf of people with psychiatric disabilities or perceived disabilities tend to cluster in certain kinds of employment, such as situations in which the employer is a provider of mental health services.[136] Plaintiffs whose employment involves areas perceived as relating to public safety (e.g., police,[137] pilots,[138] and bus drivers[139]) generally do very badly. Thus, the outcome of case law itself is a reflection of the continuing stereotype that people with psychiatric disabilities are unsafe and unpredictable.

Successful cases tend to revolve around certain kinds of claims. Retaliation claims, which do not require proof of the plaintiff's disability, have done well.[140] Claims brought under state statutes analogous to the ADA, but sometimes more generous than the ADA, have also done better than ADA claims.[141] Other successful claims often involve overt, intentional discrimination directed at an employee with a long history of career success who has been recently stricken and asked for accommodations. Contrary to what might be expected, "pure" discrimination claims, in which an employee did not ask for any accommodations but rather claimed that

---

[134]Martyne v. Parkside Medical Services, 2000 U.S. Dist. LEXIS 8019 (N.D. Ill. June 8, 2000) (the plaintiff had suffered from her psychiatric problems since she was a child); Krocka v. Bransfield 969 F. Supp. 1073 (N.D. Ill. 1997), *aff'd and remanded* by Krocka v. City of Chicago, 203 F.3d 507 (7th Cir. 2000).

[135]Weigel v. Target Stores, 122 F.3d 461 (7th Cir. 1997).

[136]Martyne v. Parkside Medical Services, 2000 U.S. Dist. LEXIS 8019 (N.D. Ill. June 8, 2000); Davidson v. Midelfort Clinic, 133 F.3d 499 (7th Cir. 1998), *but see* EEOC v. Amego, Inc., 110 F.3d 135 (1st Cir. 1997).

[137]Colwell v. Suffolk County Police Dept., 158 F.3d 635 (2d Cir. 1998). This is true in all disability cases, not just mental disability cases; *see* Ruth Colker, "Winning and Losing Under the Americans With Disabilities Act," *Ohio State Law J.* 62 (2001): 239.

[138]Witter v. Delta Airlines, 138 F.3d 1366 (11th Cir. 1998).

[139]F. F. v. City of Laredo, 912 F. Supp. 248 (S.D. Tex. 1995).

[140]Lewis v. Quaker Chemical Corp., 2000 U.S. App. LEXIS 22321 (6th Cir. Aug. 24, 2000).

[141]Olson v. G. E. Astrospace, 101 F.3d 947 (3d Cir. 1996) (N.J. Law Against Discrimination [known as LAD]).

he or she could do the job and had been discriminated against on the basis of disability or perceived disability, have not done well.[142] In many cases, courts perceived the absence of any request for accommodations as an indication that the person was not truly disabled. Often, terminated employees who are successful in promptly obtaining new employment are deemed by courts to be neither disabled nor perceived as disabled by their former employers.

Successful cases reflect high-quality lawyering or at least competent lawyering. Discrimination cases have lost on appeal because the plaintiff's lawyer neglected to order the transcript of the previous trial, so the appellate court had no way to determine if the trial court's evidentiary rulings were erroneous.[143] Courts are becoming increasingly testy and impatient with incompetent attorneys, and this has surfaced in a number of ADA cases. Typical comments include

> we would like to note that all three parties have done an abysmal job of creating a factual record for this court. Both sides have failed to tell a clear, cohesive and comprehensible story of the facts supporting their respective position. And we are particularly disturbed by the number of times the defendants have cited to portions of depositions that do not support the facts that they cite the depositions to support.[144]

A 7th Circuit Court panel was more detailed in enumerating the failures of the plantiff's counsel, including failure to catalogue or tab exhibits in opposition to the defendant's motion for summary judgment or to properly authenticate or verify them.

> Needless to say, between the unauthenticated documentation and the failure to put it in any coherent form, confirming and identifying the facts that Golliday argues in her brief has taken far more time than in cases far more complex. To make matters worse, Golliday periodically refers to an entire exhibit or all the exhibits in support of her arguments, failing to be more specific. . . . We admonish [the] plaintiff's counsel to pay closer attention to the burden of adequately identifying evidence in any future cases before us and the district courts.[145]

Discrepancies Between Deposition Testimony and Affidavits

Increasingly, courts are disregarding substantial portions of the plaintiff's affidavits, or even the entire affidavit, submitted in opposition to the summary judgment motions when those affidavits appear to contradict the deposition testimony.[146] In one case, the court pointedly noted the difference between the clear, crisp statements of the affidavit and the frequent refusal to respond in the deposition to questions relevant to the matters sworn to in the affidavit.[147] In other cases, courts have noted that the plaintiffs in depositions tend to emphasize the positive—the extent to which they

---

[142] Again, this is also true in physical disability cases, *see Colker, supra* n. 137, at 239.

[143] Marks v. Lanzilotti, 2000 U.S. App. LEXIS 22144 (9th Cir. Aug. 4, 2000); Robert E. Lee v. City of Aurora, 1996 U.S. App. LEXIS 1601 (10th Cir. Feb. 6, 1996).

[144] Di Benedetto v. City of Reading, 1998 U.S. Dist. LEXIS 11804 (E.D. Pa. July 16, 1998).

[145] Hunt-Golliday v. Metropolitan Water Reclamation District, 104 F.3d 1004, 1010 (7th Cir. 1997).

[146] Mork v. Manpower, 1998 U.S. Dist. LEXIS 11312 (N.D. Ill. July 23, 1998); Patterson v. Chicago Association for Retarded Citizens, 150 F.3d 719, 724 (7th Cir. 1998).

[147] Patterson v. Chicago Association for Retarded Citizens, *id.*

are capable of doing a job—while their affidavits accentuate the negative—the extent of their disability.

Courts frequently point out the deficiencies of expert testimony in ADA cases generally and in psychiatric disability cases particularly. Expert testimony is necessary to establish the nature of a plaintiff's disability; more importantly, the expert must establish a nexus between requested accommodations and the disability.[148] If a plaintiff provides expert testimony addressed specifically to these issues, a defendant must counter with its own expert testimony related to the feasibility of accommodations requested by the plaintiff.[149]

It should be remembered that "winning" cases represent a small subset of "apparently meritorious" cases and that because of aspects of the ADA discussed in previous chapters, meritorious cases under the ADA represent a small sample of the experiences of discrimination that people with mental disabilities undergo in employment.

Conclusion

It should be apparent that there are many different ways of discriminating against people with mental disabilities in employment and that many of these forms of discrimination continue despite the enactment of the ADA. In some cases, this is due to inept lawyering, in others to Congress's failure to anticipate certain specific situations (e.g., psychotropic drugs are also revealed in tests for illegal drugs). However, it is fair to say that for the most part, the failure of the ADA to protect people with mental disabilities from discrimination is due to parsimonious interpretations of the statute by the courts, in some cases flying directly in the face of congressional intent.

Despite conservative jurisprudential axioms that legislatures rather than courts make laws, the American civil rights tradition has been that courts find civil rights protections in the U.S. Constitution, which are then codified by federal and state legislatures. The ADA and Section 504 of the Rehabilitation Act, along with the Age Discrimination in Employment Act, represent congressional initiative in the area of antidiscrimination law; in turn, the courts have been noticeably more restrictive in their interpretations of these laws. Although the ADA's individualized approach does leave more room for interpretation, the courts have repeatedly rejected evidence of congressional intent in fashioning restrictive interpretations of the ADA. This is particularly true in cases involving mental disabilities.

The most novel aspect of Section 504 of the Rehabilitation Act and the ADA is the requirement that employees offer reasonable accommodations to people with disabilities. Many employers have asked for guidance in how this requirement applies to people with mental disabilities. The next chapter discusses the requirement of reasonable accommodations for people with mental disabilities.

---

[148]Stern v. University of Osteopathic and Health Sciences, 220 F.3d 906, 909 (8th Cir. 2000) (dyslexia).

[149]Mustafa v. Clark County School District, 157 F.3d 1169, 1177 (9th Cir. 1998) (panic attacks and depression); Haschmann v. Time-Warner Entertainment Co., 151 F.3d 591, 596 (7th Cir. 1998).

Chapter 8
REASONABLE ACCOMMODATIONS FOR EMPLOYEES WITH PSYCHIATRIC DISABILITIES

Because of the enormous stigma attached to psychiatric disabilities, most employees with psychiatric diagnoses choose not to inform their employers of their conditions,[1] thereby forfeiting most of the legal protection provided by the Americans With Disabilities Act (ADA)[2] and any reasonable accommodations they might otherwise be entitled to under the ADA.[3] Labor and social sciences research, as well as

---

[1] Mellissa Roberts, Jacqueline Rotteveel, and Ed Manos, "Mental Health Consumers as Professionals: Disclosure in the Workplace," *American Rehabilitation* 21 (Mar. 22, 1995): 20; Laura Mancuso, "Reasonable Accommodations for Workers With Psychiatric Disabilities," *Psychosocial Rehabilitation J.* 14 (Oct. 1990): 3, 6; Jean Campbell and Caroline L. Kaufmann, "Equality and Difference in the ADA: Unintended Consequences for Employment of People With Mental Health Disabilities," in Richard Bonnie and John Monahan, eds., *Mental Disorder, Work Disability and the Law* (Chicago: University of Chicago Press, 1997) at 221, 229–233; Barbara Granger and Richard C. Baron, *A National Study on Job Accommodations for People With Psychiatric Disabilities: Final Report* (Philadelphia: Matrix Research Institute, Dec. 1996) at 6, 7 (people without job coaches are very reluctant to disclose psychiatric disabilities to their employers); *see also* Sherwin Rosen, "Disability Accommodation and the Labor Market," in Carolyn L. Weaver, ed., *Disability and Work* (Washington, DC: American Enterprise Institute Press, 1991) at 18, 22 ("It seems unlikely that the ADA will affect the propensity of workers to declare many types of covered disabilities"). The responses to the survey confirmed the conclusions of researchers on this topic. Respondents uniformly recognized the problem: "tough for people to 'out' themselves prior to hiring," N. D. B.; "same ole, same ole, people are afraid to tell employers because of non-help or it getting around the office," Survey No. 91. One respondent, in answering the question, "What do you want other people to know about . . . discrimination?" wrote, "Do not let your company know, if you can avoid it, of your psychiatric disability until after you are hired," Survey No. 43 (on file with author).

[2] Even if a person does not disclose a current disability, the ADA prohibits an employer from discriminating against an employee on the basis of a record of disability or because of a perceived disability, 42 U.S.C. § 12102(2) (defining *disability* to include a record of impairment that substantially limited one or more major life activities or being regarded as having such an impairment) and 42 U.S.C. § 12112(a) (prohibiting employers from discriminating against people with a disability). In addition, the ADA protects employees from discrimination on the basis of association with someone who has a disability, 42 U.S.C. § 12112(b)(4), from retaliation for asserting a protected right under the ADA or helping someone else assert their rights, and against coercing or intimidating or threatening anyone in exercising their rights or encouraging other people to exercise their rights under the ADA, 42 U.S.C. § 12203. None of these parts of the ADA require an employee to reveal his or her disability to the employer.

[3] It is crystal clear that an employer must be informed of a disability to trigger its obligations under the ADA, Hedberg v. Indiana Bell, 47 F.3d 928, 932 (7th Cir. 1995). Precisely what constitutes "informing an employer" about a disability is subject to differing interpretations. Some courts have tended to be quite harsh and legalistic about this, *see, e.g.,* Miller v. National Casualty Co., 61 F.3d 627 (8th Cir. 1995) (when the plaintiff's sister both telephoned and visited the employer to say the plaintiff was "mentally falling apart and the family was trying to get her into a hospital," the employer was not sufficiently notified that the plaintiff had suffered from a mental disability); Taylor v. Principal Financial Group, 93 F.3d 155 (5th Cir. 1996) (the plaintiff who informed his employer that he had bipolar disorder did not sufficiently notify his employer of a disability when he did not inform the employer of the specific limitations that result from the disability); Morisky v. Broward County, 80 F.3d 445, 447–448 (11th Cir. 1996) (the prospective employer's knowledge that the applicant had taken special education

the writings of people with psychiatric disabilities, shows that one of the most significant issues for people with psychiatric disabilities in the employment setting is
concern that disclosing a psychiatric disability will result in more harm than any
benefit to be gained from the protection granted by disability discrimination law.[4]
Unfortunately, given the current state of the case law under Title I of the ADA, the
choice to not disclose is probably prudent because the law appears to offer little
protection against anything but the most overt and blatant discrimination, and courts
rarely grant employees with psychiatric disabilities the accommodations they seek
through litigation. This chapter presents the range of accommodations that may be
made for these employees.

In any event, accommodations are often achieved without denominating them
as such. Employers may work out accommodations without realizing either that an
employee is psychiatrically disabled or that they are providing what would technically be called an "accommodation."[5] However, if an employer refuses to provide
the accommodation, court decisions to date provide little hope to the employee to
enforce his or her rights in a legal setting.

This is not because the accommodations requested by people with psychiatric
disabilities are enormously expensive. One of the key mistakes that critics of the
ADA have made is to equate the reasonable accommodation requirement with some
form of economic subsidy provided by employers to employees.[6] Some commentators have concluded that the federal government should reimburse employers for the
cost of reasonable accommodations.[7] However, as study after study has shown, the
cost of most accommodations is low, and the people with disabilities who suffer the
most discrimination are not the people whose accommodations cost the most. In
other words, discrimination against people with disabilities is not economically ra-
tional in the sense that it is chiefly directed against applicants or employees whose
accommodations would be the most expensive.

The economically oriented critique misapprehends the fundamental, irrational

---

courses in school and could not read or write was insufficient to put the employer on notice that the
plaintiff was disabled); Gruber v. Entergy Corp., 1997 U.S. Dist. LEXIS 3591 (E.D. La. Mar. 24, 1997).
In contrast, in the context of a case involving psychiatric disability, the 7th Circuit Court recognized
that the disability itself may have an impact on an employee's ability to articulate a request for a
reasonable accommodation, and "if it appears that the employee may need an accommodation but doesn't
know how to ask for it, the employer should do what it can to help," Bultemeyer v. Fort Wayne
Community Schools, 100 F.3d 1281 (7th Cir. 1996).

[4]*See, e.g.,* Jean Campbell and Caroline L. Kaufman, *supra* at n. 1; Laura Mancuso, *supra* at n. 1;
Barbara Granger and Richard Baron, *supra* at n. 1. As one researcher noted, "those who do achieve
employment forego the protection of the law in order to avoid disclosure of their psychiatric disability
and the stigmatization which inevitably follows"; Laura Mancuso, "Reasonable Accommodations for
Workers With Psychiatric Disabilities," *Psychosocial Rehabilitation J.* 14 (Oct. 1990): 3, 6.

[5]Mancuso, *supra* n. 1; Granger, *supra* n. 1.

[6]Sherwin Rosen, "Disability Accommodation and the Labor Market" in Carolyn Weaver, ed., *Dis-
ability and Work: Incentives, Rights, and Opportunities* (Washington, DC: American Enterprise Institute
Press, 1991) at 18, 29; Walter Y. Oi, "Disability and a Workfare–Welfare Dilemma," in Carolyn Weaver,
ed., *Disability and Work: Incentives, Rights, and Opportunities* (Washington, DC: American Enterprise
Institute Press, 1991) at 40; Richard A. Epstein, *Forbidden Grounds: The Case Against Employment
Discrimination Laws* (Cambridge, MA: Harvard University Press, 1992) at 480–494.

[7]Epstein, *supra* n. 6.

nature of employers' discrimination,[8] the huge costs (generally borne by the government and private individuals rather than employers) of *not* providing accommodations for disabled people, and the kind of reasonable accommodations people with psychiatric disabilities need. Case after case, anecdote after anecdote, shows employers acting contrary to their own economic interests in order to discriminate against someone with a disability.[9]

In addition, the kinds of accommodations people with psychiatric disabilities need are generally relatively inexpensive or free. The crucial issue is not cost, but workplace culture. The kinds of accommodations needed by people with psychiatric disabilities (when they need accommodations at all) can be divided into three categories, none of which raise major cost issues.

First, people with relatively severe disabilities sometimes ask for accommodations such as giving instructions in writing,[10] allowing the presence of or telephone calls to a job coach,[11] access to water at the employee's work space,[12] and room dividers.[13] These kinds of accommodations are often requested on behalf of the worker through a social service agency or a job coach.

Second, accommodations such as flexibility in working hours, the ability to work at home, time off during the work day for doctor's or therapist's appointments, and leaves of absence are often simply workplace issues common to employees with and without disabilities. These types of accommodations are usually worked out informally without reference to disability discrimination law. They also are requested more often by higher-income professionals with psychiatric disabilities, are rarely labeled *accommodations,* and are rarely the subject of litigation.[14] For example, a

---

[8]Even Evan Kemp chided economists for their "failure to recognize the tremendous prejudice against disabled people that exists in our society. Incentive-based policies, which do away with disincentives and create effective incentives, would work well only if there were no prejudice"; Evan Kemp, Jr., "Disability in Our Society," in Carolyn Weaver, ed., *Disability and Work: Incentives, Rights and Opportunities* (Washington, DC: American Enterprise Institute, 1991) at 57.

[9]Martinelli v. Montana Power Co., 886 P.2d 421, 428 (Mont. 1994) (a request of a productive employee whose medication for endometriosis caused various side effects, including depression, to work the day shift was refused by the employer, even when the employee produced day-shift employees ready to trade with her; the employer argued she was not disabled because "her condition was at all times curable by means of a hysterectomy and . . . she had the remedy of abating her symptoms temporarily by becoming pregnant as an alternative to a hysterectomy or drug therapy"). The business outcry attendant on the EEOC publication of guidelines related to employees with psychiatric disabilities was enormous, and none of it related to the expense of accommodating workers with psychiatric disabilities.

[10]Laura Mancuso, "Reasonable Accommodations for Workers With Psychiatric Disabilities," *Psychosocial Rehabilitation J.* 14(3) (Oct. 1990): 15 (using as an example of an accommodation based on an actual work situation, "arranging for all work requests to be put in writing for a library assistant who becomes anxious and confused when given verbal instructions").

[11]Sherman v. New York Life, 1997 WL 452024 (S.D. N.Y. Aug. 7, 1997); EEOC v. Hertz, 1998 WL 5694 (E.D. Mich. Jan. 6, 1998). For regulations regarding job coaches, 29 C.F.R. pt. 1630, App. § 1630.9

[12]This modification, which many take for granted, is described as a "reasonable accommodation" provided by employers in Barbara Granger and Richard Baron, *A National Study on Job Accommodations for People With Psychiatric Disabilities: Final Report* (Philadelphia: Matrix Research Institute, Dec. 1996).

[13]Mancuso, *supra* n. 10, at 15, "purchasing room dividers for a data entry operator who has difficulty maintaining [her] concentration (and thus accuracy) in an open work area."

[14]Research studies on employer provision of accommodations to people with psychiatric disabilities uniformly find that many employers provide these accommodations with little knowledge of the ADA

survey of professionals and managers with psychiatric conditions found that "common accommodations used were flexibility to modify daily duties (49%) and flexible schedules (33%). However, in general, accommodations were not formally negotiated, and for many, they were received irrespective of their psychiatric condition."[15]

Third, some very productive workers cannot function without accommodations that involve changes in the workplace environment and attitudes rather than the expenditure of funds. Chief among these often requested, but seldom granted, accommodations are receiving "more positive feedback," changing a supervisor, transferring the employee, being "gentler," fostering a "non-hostile working environment,"[16] reducing work hours (usually from 80–90 hours a week to about 50–70 hours a week), and trying to make the job less stressful. These accommodations are resisted with a ferocity that makes clear that, regardless of the theories of the law and economics school of thought, employers value retaining certain cultural aspects of the workplace far more than a financial calculus can justify. In litigation regarding these accommodations for workers with psychiatric disabilities, the plaintiff loses almost every one of the cases. For people with all kinds of disabilities, changing the workplace to permit people with disabilities to have access to employment opportunities involves something far deeper than simply paying for changes in the workplace, and people with psychiatric disabilities are the best example of this truth.

Courts are proving to be unwilling to mandate the kinds of workplace changes that would be of greatest assistance to people with mental disabilities. Indeed, for the most part, they are unwilling to make any changes that might assist people with psychiatric disabilities. It is particularly striking that courts that are willing to mandate fairly expensive accommodations to benefit people with physical disabilities[17] are almost completely unwilling to mandate changes needed by people with mental disabilities at no cost that would redound to the benefit of all employees. A few courts are even beginning to hold (contrary to the language of the ADA and its regulations) that mental disabilities caused by workplace stressors are somehow not covered under the ADA.[18]

The problem is that "reasonable accommodations" have been constructed as environmental accommodations, such as ramps, parking spaces, and even readers and interpreters. What people with psychiatric disabilities often require as accommodations is what the ADA seeks to ultimately accomplish: the transformation of

---

and no familiarity with the term *reasonable accommodation*; Granger and Baron, *supra* n. 12, at 31; Mancuso, *supra* n. 13, at 169.

[15]Marsha Langer Ellison and Zlatka Russinova, "A National Survey of Professionals and Managers With Psychiatric Conditions," Center for Rehabilitation, Boston University, Boston, MA, *available at* http://www.bu.edu.SARPSYCH/research/rtc/1999/si_3.html.

[16]Hunt-Golliday v. Metropolitan Water Reclamation District, 104 F.3d 1004, 1012 (7th Cir. 1997).

[17]Readers for blind employees were mandated by Nelson v. Thornburgh, 567 F. Supp. 369 (E.D. Pa. 1983); Fink v. New York City Department of Personnel, 855 F. Supp. 68 (S.D. N.Y. 1994); and Carter v. Bennett, 840 F.2d 63 (D.C. Cir. 1988).

[18]Webb v. Baxter Healthcare Corp., 57 F.3d 1067, (4th Cir. June 13, 1995) (holding no ADA claims when emotional problems were a result, not a cause, of hostile work environment). Defendants also tried to make this argument in Krocka v. Bransfield, 969 F. Supp. 1078, 1084 (N.D. Ill. 1998) (the court did not reject the premise of the argument but found that "the depression may have both caused difficulties and been exacerbated by them"). *But see* Wilson v. Daimler Chrysler Corp., 236 F.3d 827, 829 (7th Cir. 2001) (apparently permitting claims that disability was caused by sexual harassment in ADA case but finding plaintiff did not meet her burden of proof).

attitudes about disabilities and changes in how people deal with each other. A work environment in which workers are treated with respect and dignity would have obviated a substantial amount of the employment discrimination litigation discussed in this volume.

What Makes a Qualified Employee?

To be "qualified" for employment, an employee must be able to perform the essential functions of the job with or without reasonable accommodation. An "essential" function of the job is not a marginal function. The determination of whether a function is essential involves several factors such as the "number of employees among whom the performance of that job function may be distributed" and the "consequences of not requiring the employee to perform the function."[19] If the function that the employee cannot perform is not essential to the job, the employer may not base adverse job actions on the employee's inability to perform the function.[20]

One of the most striking aspects of employment discrimination cases involving employees with psychiatric disabilities is that, unlike physical disability cases, the ability to actually perform the substantive requirements of the job is rarely at issue.[21] Most ADA plaintiffs with psychiatric disabilities have the skills to perform the job.

However, as related in chapter 6, difficulties with employees with psychiatric disabilities arise in two areas. First, the employee may have difficulty complying with the employer's shift, overtime, or extra work requirements, which do not involve job-related skills but reflect the employer's desire to maximize profits with the minimum number of workers. Second, the employee often has difficulty interacting with a specific person in the workplace, usually his or her supervisor.

Attendance as an Essential Element of the Job

Many courts have decided a variety of very different ADA claims with the simple assertion that regular, predictable attendance at work is an essential element of the job as a matter of law, and an employee who cannot fulfill that requirement is not otherwise qualified for employment. These decisions have been made without the benefit of further factual inquiry or a trial.[22] To make findings about either regular

---

[19] 29 C.F.R. § 1630.2 (n)(2)(ii) and (iv) (2000).

[20] Rebecca Hanner-White, "Modern Discrimination Theory and the NLRA," *William and Mary Law Rev.* 39 (Oct. 1997): 99, 126.

[21] Bombard v. Fort Wayne Newspapers, 92 F.3d 560 (7th Cir. 1996); Grenier v. Cyanamid Plastics, 70 F.3d 667 (1st Cir. 1995); Doe v. Region 13 Mental Health Mental Retardation, 704 F.2d 1402 (5th Cir. 1983) (Rehabilitation Act); Allen v. GTE Mobile Communications, 1997 U.S. Dist. LEXIS 3539 (N.D. Ga. Feb. 25, 1997).

[22] Rogers v. International Marine Terminals, 87 F.3d 755, 759 (5th Cir. 1996); Carr v. Reno, 23 F.3d 525, 530 (D.C. Cir. 1994); Tyndall v. National Educational Centers, 31 F.3d 209, 213 (4th Cir. 1994); Vande Zande v. Wisconsin Department of Administration, 44 F.3d 538 (7th Cir. 1995); Jackson v. Veteran's Administration, 22 F.3d 277 (11th Cir. 1994); Bernard v. Rockwell, 869 F.2d 928 (6th Cir. 1989); Barfield v. Bell South, 886 F. Supp. 1321, 1326 (E.D. Miss. 1995); Hendry v. GTE, 896 F. Supp. 816 (N.D. Ind. 1995). The plaintiffs were denied the opportunity to present to a jury the questions of whether the accommodation they were requesting was reasonable within the constraints of that particular job, and the employers could avoid the burden of having to show that granting the plaintiffs' request would constitute an undue burden.

or predictable attendance at work as a matter of law flies in the face of the ADA focus on individualized assessments of both the needs of the employee and the capacity of the employer to accommodate him or her.

The cases in which courts find that attendance is an essential function of the job include short-term leave,[23] lengthier leaves of absence,[24] and work at home.[25] In some cases, the employee asks to use vacation leave as sick leave;[26] in others, the employee wants only to use sick leave, to which he or she is already entitled, for unpredictable flare-ups of the disabling condition.[27] Sometimes these absences are excessive, but predictable,[28] and sometimes they are both excessive and unpredictable.[29] The courts invoke the "attendance is an essential element of the job" mantra when the employee does not ask to miss any work but to work a different shift or to come to work at a later time and leave at a later time.

In the case of employees with psychiatric disabilities, courts are particularly dismissive of "unscheduled absences"[30]; this is less evident in cases involving physical disabilities. In cases involving persons with physical disabilities, some courts have held that employers must show that regular attendance is an essential function of the specific position involved and that reasonable attempts were made to accommodate the employee to enable him or her to satisfy attendance requirements.[31]

This simplistic approach threatens to completely eviscerate the protections of the ADA. Although this issue is important to many people with disabilities, because disabilities tend to require more medical care and supervision, and some have unpredictable exacerbations, it has particular impact on people with psychiatric disabilities, for whom leaves of absence or flexible scheduling may be especially crucial.

Courts have stated that "attendance is generally an essential function of any job"[32] to support findings that leave is not a reasonable accommodation, even though the statutory language of the ADA and the Equal Employment Opportunity Commission (EEOC) regulations interpreting that language have specifically found otherwise. The use of medical leave or unpaid leave to seek treatment was identified by Congress within the statutory language of the ADA as a reasonable accommodation. In addition, many workers whose requests for leave as a reasonable accommodation are rejected have been found entitled to receive it under the Family and Medical Leave Act (FMLA). In fact, a court found in one case that an individual was not otherwise qualified to perform her job because she took too much leave for her migraines, while holding that she might be entitled to leave under the FMLA.[33] Finally, some of the employers making these arguments have leave policies for all

---

[23] Hypes v. First Commerce Corp., 134 F.3d 721 (5th Cir. 1998); Daris v. Lockheed Martin Operators Support, 84 F. Supp. 2d 707 (D. Md. 2000); Vanderford v. Parker Hannifin Corp., 971 F. Supp. 1079 (N.D. Miss. 1997).

[24] Rogers v. International Marine Terminals, 87 F.3d 755 (5th Cir. 1996).

[25] Vande Zande v. Wisconsin Department of Administration, 44 F.3d 538 (7th Cir. 1995).

[26] Hendry v. GTE North, 896 F. Supp. 816 (N.D. Ind. 1995).

[27] Jackson v. Veteran's Administration, 22 F.3d 277 (11th Cir. 1994).

[28] Tyndall v. National Educational Centers, 31 F.3d 209 (4th Cir. 1994).

[29] Carr v. Reno, 23 F.3d 525 (D.C. Cir. 1994).

[30] Morgan v. Hilti, 108 F.3d 1319 (10th Cir. 1997).

[31] Fritz v. Mascotech Automotive Systems Group, 914 F. Supp. 1481 (E.D. Mich. 1996).

[32] Cisneros v. Wilson, 226 F.3d 1113, 1129 (10th Cir. 2000).

[33] Hendry v. GTE North, 896 F. Supp. 816 (N.D. Ind. 1995).

employees that are more generous than the leave requested by the employee as a reasonable accommodation and refused by the employer.[34]

Not all courts have been so harsh. Several circuit courts have explicitly held that regular and predictable job attendance is not an essential function of any and every job as a matter of law and have emphasized the individualized nature of each case.[35] Some have pointed to the FMLA as evidence that uninterrupted job attendance is not necessarily an essential element of employment and that leave may well be a reasonable accommodation. Appellate courts have also reversed district courts for finding that leave was not a reasonable accommodation when the employer's regular leave policy would have permitted the employee to take leave had he or she requested it under that policy.

Clearly, an individual may not be qualified for a job if that job requires predictable, regular presence when the individual is excessively, unpredictably absent and no reasonable accommodation exists. But this is a heavily fact-specific inquiry, not a circumstance for summary disposal as a matter of law.

To assess whether an absence can be reasonably accommodated, the job as well as its requirements must be analyzed. Some jobs may be done from home[36]; others may require face-to-face contact at work. Some employees have jobs and skills that are relatively fungible with those of other employees, so that it might be reasonable to expect a large employer to grant a leave of absence of a year or more.[37] Indeed, many employers have generous maternity leave policies that permit leaves of absence for three months, six months, or a year.[38] In determining the level of attendance necessary for a particular job, courts find it helpful to look at the employer's leave policies and how other employees are treated. In terms of requested leave, courts have found that if an employee with a disability requests leave that is within the employer's existing leave policy or would be required by the FMLA, granting the leave is a reasonable accommodation.[39]

The level of attendance that is essential to a job must also be examined. "Regular attendance is no doubt an essential part of a job, but the question is one of degree."[40] One court warned against conflating allegations of poor performance by an employee with a conclusion that a certain level of attendance was an essential element of the job: "To show that [attendance] is an essential element, defendants must demonstrate the job could not be performed, by anyone, without a particular level of attendance."[41]

---

[34]Rascon v. U.S. West Communications, 144 F.3d 1324 (10th Cir. 1998).

[35]Humphrey v. Memorial Hospital Association, 239 F.3d 1128, 1135 (9th Cir. 2001) (a medical transcriptionist with obsessive–compulsive disorder was permitted to attempt to show that working at home is a reasonable accommodation); Cehrs v. Northeast Ohio Alzheimer's Research Center, 155 F.3d 775 (6th Cir. 1998).

[36]Langon v. HHS, 959 F.2d 1053 (D.C. Cir. 1992) (computer programmer with multiple sclerosis).

[37]Norris v. Allied-Sysco Systems, 948 F. Supp. 1418, 1440 (N.D. Cal. 1996).

[38]Dutton v. Johnson County School Board, 859 F. Supp. 498, 507 (D. Kan. 1995); Walton v. Mental Health Association of Southeast Pennsylvania, 1997 U.S. Dist. LEXIS 18224 (E.D. Pa. Nov. 17, 1997) (cannot hold as a matter of law that attendance or, more precisely, a particular level of attendance is an essential element of a job without further factual inquiry).

[39]Cehrs v. Northeast Ohio Alzheimer's Research Center, 155 F.3d 375 (6th Cir. 1998); Criado v. IBM, 145 F.3d 437 (1st Cir. 1998).

[40]Dutton v. Johnson County Board of Commissioners, 859 F. Supp. 498, 508 (D. Kan. 1994).

[41]Walton v. Mental Health Association of Southeast Pennsylvania, 1997 U.S. Dist. LEXIS 18224 at *13 (E.D. Pa. Nov. 17, 1997).

In terms of unpredictable absences, some courts have held that even a small number of unpredictable absences means an employee cannot fulfill an essential element of the job, whereas others have pointed out that the very nature of sick leave is to accommodate employees' unpredictable illnesses. Again, the employer's policies are a significant benchmark. One court found that attendance could not be an essential function of the job because the company had no policy on unscheduled absences.[42]

When a qualified employee with a disability asks for an accommodation, whether it is to take leave, to return to work part-time, to work a more flexible schedule, or to work at home, the employer must show that granting the accommodation would be an undue hardship. Many courts never reach the point of analyzing whether granting the accommodation would be an undue hardship, which is also an individualized inquiry. It should be noted that even if attendance is not viewed as an essential function of the job, in some cases, courts frame the issue as presenting a nondiscriminatory reason for the adverse action, that is, the employee was not fired because of disability but because she violated the employer's attendance policy.[43]

Many ADA cases involve employees leaving the workplace without permission for reasons related to an emotional or physical condition. Courts react very differently depending on the nature of the condition. In cases involving physical conditions, courts find that "a single instance of leaving the work site without permission, the result of his disability, did not render him unqualified for the assignment given his otherwise perfect employment record."[44] However, similar cases involving employees who left the work site because of emotional difficulties are treated far less sympathetically, regardless of the employees' excellent work histories.[45]

Long Hours and Double Shifts: Are They Essential?

As employers strive to be competitive and maximize their profits, "downsizing" or its even more euphemistic cousin "rightsizing" have become household words. As a result, the average American works longer and longer hours.[46] Although labor law imposes certain requirements about paying overtime for nonprofessional workers, and many collective bargaining agreements impose notice requirements on employers before requiring overtime, no ceiling has been created by any U.S. labor statute on the number of hours an employer can expect its employees to work or on the degree to which an employer can require employees to work double, triple, or night shifts. Despite a great deal of research about the health dangers associated with long working hours, which prompted detailed worker safety rules in Europe, in the United States little reform has resulted from social science research and the popular press exposés of the effect of increasing time demands on workers' health.

---

[42]Carlson v. Inacom Corp., 885 F. Supp. 1314, 1321 (D. Neb. 1995).

[43]Price v. S.-B. Power Tool, 75 F.3d 362, (8th Cir. 1996).

[44]Sunkett v. Olsten Temporary Services, No. C-94-20027 (N.D. Cal. 1995) (an employer discriminates against an epileptic employee by firing him for throwing things and leaving the worksite without permission during a seizure), aff'd, 116 F.3d 486 (9th Cir. 1997).

[45]Simpkins v. Specialty Envelope, 94 F.3d 645 (table), 1996 WL 452858 (6th Cir. Aug. 9, 1996); Van Stan v. Fancy Colours and Co., 125 F.3d 563 (7th Cir. 1997).

[46]Larry Wilham and Mary Otto, "America: A Divided Journey," Miami Herald (Sept. 6, 1999): PA17.

Cases brought under the ADA constitute indirect testimony concerning the effect of employer downsizing on workers. Employers' requirements that employees work more than 10 hours a day or more than 5 days a week on a regular basis are leading to medical problems, collapse, and disability.[47] It is a sad commentary on the state of the American workplace that employees are requesting to work 40-hour weeks, or even 50-hours a week, plus one Saturday a month as "reasonable accommodations."[48] For the most part, these people are losing. Courts have used several techniques to defeat claims by plaintiffs for reasonable accommodations related to escalating work demands.

Ironically, courts find that the inability to meet extreme demands placed on employees by employers does not render the employees disabled,[49] even though plaintiffs have expert testimony directly connecting their disability with the inability to meet employers' requirements. For example, in some cases, employees have asked as a "reasonable accommodation" to work only a traditional 40-hour work week[50] and have been terminated or left the job after this request was denied. In these cases, courts find that anyone who can work a 40-hour work week cannot be disabled, and they dismiss the case.[51] Often, the fact that the plaintiff obtained another job elsewhere is used to support the finding that he or she cannot be disabled.

In other cases, courts actually find that working long hours is an "essential function" of the job.[52] This conclusion seems to fly in the face of the meaning of the term "essential function" of a particular job. Essential functions relate to the skills, training, and experience required to perform the position in question. Requirements that are related to minimizing labor costs and maximizing employer profits (often at the expense of employee health) should not be considered essential functions. Otherwise, any employer could determine that working 50, 60, 70, or more hours a week is an essential function of each position. Although the EEOC says in its *Technical Assistance Manual* at 2.3(a) that the ADA does not restrict an em-

---

[47]Kellogg v. Union Pacific, 233 F.3d 1083 (8th Cir. 2000) (plaintiff's job required him to work 60–80 hours per week and be on call 24 hours a day); Washington v. HCA Health Care Services of Texas, 152 F.3d 464 (5th Cir. 1998) (the plaintiff collapsed after being required to work 60–80 hours a week; his doctor recommended that his work be limited "to ten hour days or 50 hour weeks"); Settle v. S. W. Rogers Co., 998 F. Supp. 657 (E.D. Va. 1998) ("in general, [the] plaintiff was required to work [as a diesel mechanic] 11-hour days Monday through Friday and occasionally Saturday as well"); Soto-Ocasio v. Federal Express, 150 F.3d 14 (1st Cir. July 16, 1998) (the plaintiff arrived at work at 6 a.m. and "some days [was] required to work until 4 or 5 p.m. with only [a] one hour break").

[48]Voytek v. University of California, 1994 U.S. Dist. LEXIS 12453 (N.D. Cal. Aug. 25, 1994) (this very complex case involved other factors, but the request to work only 50 hours a week plus one Saturday a month was clearly made by Voytek and rejected by the court as not being congruent with the job Voytek was hired to do); Simmerman v. Hardee's Food System, 1996 U.S. Dist. LEXIS 3437 (E.D. Pa. Mar. 22, 1996) (40-hour week); Kralik v. Durbin, 130 F.3d 76 (3d Cir. 1997) (requesting an 8-hour day as a reasonable accommodation).

[49]Roth v. Lutheran General Hospital, 57 F.3d 1446, 1454–55 (7th Cir.) ("we cannot say that inability to fulfill long shifts or 36 hour call duties . . . necessarily proves the plaintiff is disabled"); Shpargel v. Stage and Co., 914 F. Supp. 1468 (E.D. Mich. 1996).

[50]Hemsing v. Philips Semiconductors, 1999 U.S. App. LEXIS 15152 (10th Cir. July 9, 1999); Simmerman v. Hardee's Food Systems, 1996 U.S. Dist. LEXIS 3437 (E.D. Penn. Mar. 22, 1996), *see* chap. 6, n. 30.

[51]Kolpas v. G. D. Searle, 959 F. Supp. 525 (N.D. Ill. 1997); Duff v. Lobdell-Emery Manufacturing Co., 926 F. Supp. 799 (N.D. Ind. 1996).

[52]Simmerman v. Hardee's Food Systems, 1996 U.S. Dist. LEXIS 3437 (E.D. Penn. Mar. 22, 1996).

ployer's ability to establish the content, nature, or functions of a job, this statement should apply to the actual job functions, not the length of time an employee works.

In one case involving a manager at a fast food restaurant, the court found that working 50 hours a week was an essential function of the job. The reasons provided were singularly unconvincing: The night managers might not be good enough; therefore, they need extra supervision. Stores and fast food restaurants that are open 24 hours a day have learned to cope with the reality that their managers cannot be expected to be on duty for the entire time, and it does not seem to be much of a strain to suggest that inadequate night managers should be replaced, instead of requiring all fast food restaurant managers to work 50 hours a week.

Courts are thwarting the intentions of Congress and of the EEOC to require employers to at least consider some accommodations such as flexible scheduling, job restructuring, reducing overtime work, and changing shift requirements.[53] Not all courts have agreed that lengthy hours are an essential function of the job. One interesting case under state disability discrimination law in California involved an attorney with depression who asked for one half day off every time he worked more than 45 hours for 2 weeks in a row. His employers turned him down flat, and when he sued, they argued that an essential element of being a lawyer was working 50- and even 60-hour weeks. The attorney was awarded $300,000 in compensatory damages (and $800,000 in attorney's fees). In addition, the occasional case involving a request for 40-hour work weeks has at least survived motions for summary judgment.[54]

Ability to Work Certain Shifts as Essential Elements of the Job

One of the central features of many disabilities is a lessening of stamina, or an inability to work irregular shifts, either because of the disability itself or because of side effects caused by medication used to treat the disability. As employers lay off workers and consolidate positions, employees who were productive day workers before downsizing are being fired because their medical condition prevents them from working night shifts, which the employer now requires.[55]

Once again, courts are eviscerating the ADA by finding that employer cost-saving measures are "essential functions" of the job rather than looking to the individual skills or training required to accomplish the functions of the job. Thus, courts have found that the ability to work rotating shifts, or "flexibility in scheduling," is an essential function of a job,[56] which, by definition, cannot be accommodated by greater employer flexibility in scheduling employees. Similar to the argument about whether working excessive hours can be an essential requirement, it is not clear that it is an essential function of any job that it be done by the same person for 12 hours or for two shifts in a row (astronaut may be an exception, but even

[53]See 29 C.F.R. § 1630.2 (o)(2)(ii).

[54]EEOC v. Union Carbide Chemical & Plastics Co., 4 1995 U.S. Dist. LEXIS 12444 (E.D. La. Aug. 18, 1995).

[55]Newman v. Silver Cross Hospital, 1998 U.S. Dist. LEXIS 11094 (N.D. Ill. July 14, 1998) (narcolepsy).

[56]Jasany v. U.S. Postal Service, 755 F.2d 1244, 1251 (6th Cir. 1985) (decided under the Rehabilitation Act); Mackie v. Runyon, 804 F. Supp. 1508, 1511 (M.D. Fla. 1992).

astronauts get plenty of rest) or that an individual be available to work different shifts at different times. By the same token, not being able to work a night shift because of one's condition has rarely been found to be enough of a limitation to constitute a disability, even though that is the only reason that the employee has been terminated.[57]

Social Skills as Essential Functions of the Job

Courts have enumerated a growing list of social skills as essential to employment, without any analysis and regardless of the technical skills required by a job. Courts have found that essential functions of a job include the avoidance of violent behavior that threatens the safety of other employees[58]; the ability of an employee to accept and follow instructions[59]; the ability of an employee to refrain from contentious arguments and insubordinate conduct with supervisors, coemployees, or customers[60]; the ability to serve as a role model for other staff[61]; and the ability to promote "harmony and cooperation."[62]

These findings are often framed in terms that make them difficult to dispute, although not necessarily reflecting the facts of the case. This is a particularly interesting development in light of the EEOC being specifically asked to enumerate certain kinds of social skills, such as getting along with others, as examples of essential elements of employment and refusing to do so.[63]

In fact, in cases in which the court deems social skills to be an essential function of the job, it has almost never been shown that the employee lacks social skills. These cases almost always involve a specific personality conflict, usually between an employee and a new supervisor, and often involve a request by the employee for

---

[57]Newman v. Silver Cross Hospital, 1998 U.S. Dist. LEXIS 11094 (N.D. Ill. July 14, 1998).

[58]Mazzarella v. U.S. Postal Service, 849 F. Supp. 89, 94 (D. Mass. 1994); Boldini v. Postmaster General, U.S. Postal Service, 928 F. Supp. 125, 131 (D. N.H. 1995).

[59]Boldini v. Postmaster General, *id.*; Schmidt v. Bell, 1983 U.S. Dist. LEXIS 13961 (E.D. Penn. Sept. 9, 1983) (failed to follow procedures and could not accept authority).

[60]Boldini v. Postmaster General, *id.*

[61]EEOC v. Amego, 110 F.3d 135, 138 (1st Cir. 1997).

[62]Husowitz v. Runyon, 942 F. Supp. 822, 831 (E.D. N.Y. 1996) (an employee with bipolar disorder was an individual with a disability but was terminated for legitimate reasons).

[63]U.S. Civil Rights Commission, *Helping Employers Comply With the ADA: An Assessment of How the United States Equal Opportunity Commission Is Enforcing Title I of the Americans With Disabilities Act* (Washington, DC: EEOC, Sept. 1998) at 69, 70. The commission noted that one of the comments to the EEOC's proposed ADA regulations "wrote that sections 1630.2(m) and (n) in the proposed regulations describe the essential functions of a job in terms of job 'duties' but they explicitly focus on the active or mechanical operations of a given position. The attorney argued that these proposed rules neglected to address the 'less tangible job requirements' such as the need to work compatibly in a team environment. The attorney mentioned that individuals with protected disabilities, such as mental or psychological disorders, can have involuntary emotional outbursts which may not directly disrupt the active performance of the disabled employee, but would nevertheless severely hinder team members in the same work environment. The attorney stressed that the final Title I regulations should make explicit that 'essential functions' can include more abstract job requirements, such as the ability to (a) work effectively and constructively on a team or (b) avoid disruptive behaviors that directly and significantly affect the performance of co-workers. The final Title I regulations did not include these proposed changes. The definition of 'essential function' does not refer to 'abstract job requirements' or 'less tangible job requirements.'"

a transfer as a reasonable accommodation. Although employers grant and courts endorse transfers for people with physical disabilities, courts almost universally refuse transfers for those with mental disabilities, because the need for them arises from the employee's inability to get along with a particular supervisor. Yet if a plaintiff attempts to show through a history of being fired from work that he or she is substantially limited in the major life activity of interacting with others, the defendant can argue that "his [or her] poor work history amounted to nothing more than an 'inability to follow work rules' that an employer is not required to tolerate."[64]

Getting along with coworkers and supervisors has been universally held to be an essential function of jobs. Courts do not even require a showing that transfer would be difficult. Responsibility for the inability to get along with a supervisor has generally been seen as resting with the employee. In spite of clear legislative history and regulatory language to the contrary, employers have not been held to the slightest burden of training employees or supervisors on working with people with mental disabilities. Like many accommodations,[65] such training would probably redound to the benefit of employees without disabilities as well.

"Otherwise Qualified": The Disability Benefits Dilemma

A recurring issue in claims of disability discrimination in employment is whether an application for disability benefits precludes a claim for discrimination. Because of the "otherwise qualified" requirement, employers have argued that an employee cannot logically be both "otherwise qualified" and totally unable to work, which is required to qualify for disability benefits. This issue arises frequently in both mental and physical disability cases. Often, the court castigates the plaintiff in these cases as a liar or a fraud. Courts frequently chastise the plaintiff for even bringing claims for employment discrimination under these circumstances, for example, "plaintiff cannot have it both ways"[66] and "federal courts facing similar arguments have refused to permit a plaintiff to 'speak out of both sides' of his or her mouth."[67]

However, the U.S. Supreme Court has established that applying for disability benefits does not preclude an individual from filing an ADA claim. In *Cleveland v. Policy Management Systems Corp.*,[68] the court held that "pursuit, and receipt of SSDI [Social Security disability income] benefits does not automatically estop the recipient from pursuing an ADA claim."[69] A close look at these cases finds plaintiffs in excruciating dilemmas. Almost always, the filing for benefits takes place after termi-

---

[64] Krocka v. Bransfield, 969 F. Supp. 1073, 1083 (N.D. Ill. 1997).

[65] Weare v. City of Malland, 887 F. Supp. 1249 (N.D. Iowa 1995) (curb cuts); Kenney v. Jerusalem, 9 F.3d 1067 (3d Cir. 1993); Zande v. State Department of Administration, 44 F.3d 538 (7th Cir. 1995) (ramps).

[66] Miller v. U.S. Bancorp., 926 F. Supp. 994 (D. Ore. 1996).

[67] *Id.* at 999, quoting Reigel v. Kaiser Foundation Health Plan of North Carolina, 859 F. Supp. 963, 967–970 (E.D. N.C. 1994).

[68] 526 U.S. 795 (1999).

[69] *Id.*

nation of employment.[70] Often the plaintiff is older and his or her job prospects are not hopeful, in part because of the disability itself. Often the lengthy period of time between the last day on the job and the filing for benefits makes it clear that the individual filed for benefits only because he or she needed some source of income.

The law providing disability benefits assumes that some people receiving disability benefits can work. People receiving disability benefits can engage in a "trial work period" for up to nine months without losing their benefits,[71] and after that they may work without receiving benefits for up to three years,[72] during which time they can resume receiving benefits at any time without any new determination that they are entitled to disability benefits.

This assumption certainly fits Deborah Stone's theory that disability benefits in part serve as a way for employers to get rid of marginally employable workers in times when there are plenty of workers in the labor market.[73] Disability benefit claims are higher among groups that are historically discriminated against in employment: older workers, minority workers, and female workers.[74]

Reasonable Accommodations

Self-Accommodation: The Invisible Accommodation

Many people with disabilities self-accommodate, that is, they figure out techniques for accommodating themselves to the work environment so that coworkers and supervisors are never aware of the efforts they make. People with psychiatric disabilities in general are often self-accommodators.[75] One survey respondent wrote, "I work every day but in terror of some unknown/unseen monster who is always ready to overwhelm me. I am so exhausted trying to keep up at work I cannot cope with more or friends. I hibernate all weekend."[76]

The concept of self-accommodation is not just a fancy term for an individual's adaptation skills; it represents a significant breakthrough of social understanding of the nature of disability in general. Every time we congratulate ourselves for feeling completely comfortable with or "not noticing" someone's disability, we are simply unaware of how much that person has accommodated himself or herself to us, to our environment, and our expectations.[77]

---

[70]Cline v. Western Horsemen Inc., 922 F. Supp. 442 (D. Colo. 1996); Baker v. Asarco, 1995 U.S. Dist. LEXIS 16852 (D. Ariz. Nov. 7, 1995); Pegues v. Emerson Electric, 913 F. Supp. 976 (N.D. Miss. 1996).

[71]20 C.F.R. § 404.1592(a) (current through Sept. 8, 2000).

[72]*Id.*

[73]Deborah Stone, *The Disabled State* (Philadelphia: Temple University Press, 1984) at 181, 182.

[74]*Id.*

[75]*See* Jean Campbell and Caroline L. Kaufman, "Equality and Difference in the ADA: Unintended Consequences for Employment of People With Mental Health Disabilities," in Richard Bonnie and John D. Monahan, eds., *Mental Disorder, Work Disability and the Law* (Chicago: University of Chicago Press, 1997) at 230.

[76]Survey No. 148.

[77]*Id.* (quoting a blind man as follows: "People frequently say, 'I don't consider you disabled.' That's because I make accommodations to my disability. . . . I'm accommodating all the time, but they don't know it or realize it.")

The degree to which this self-accommodation is invisible has a tremendously negative social impact because when disabled people *do* ask for reasonable accommodations, society often reacts as though it is being asked to do all the work of accommodation, rather than understanding that the requested accommodation is probably just the tip of the iceberg.

Employer Obligations: The Requirement of an Interactive Process

Unlike other laws prohibiting discrimination, the ADA was drafted in an era more sensitive to the potential of mediation, negotiation, and other means of avoiding litigation. Thus, not only does the ADA have a provision requiring courts to consider alternative dispute resolution and mediation,[78] but the process by which reasonable accommodations are determined, the so-called "interactive process," has acquired a legal significance of its own.[79]

The 7th Circuit has led the way in holding that an employer has "at least some responsibility in determining the necessary accommodation."[80] Significantly, the cases in which the 7th Circuit has articulated this duty most strongly involve plaintiffs with psychiatric disabilities.[81] These cases, which have been followed with some modifications in some circuits, and flatly rejected in others, hold that an employer's responsibilities in the area of reasonable accommodation may be affected by both the nature and the severity of the employee's disability.

In some cases, failure to engage in the interactive process has been seen as shifting the burden to the defendant because the employer did not even consider a request for accommodation by the worker with a disability.[82] In other cases, the employer need not consider the accommodation request if it can be proven later that no reasonable accommodation existed that would have assisted the employee in performing the essential functions of the job.[83]

---

[78] 42 U.S.C. § 12212 (West 2000).

[79] Although the ADA does not explicitly require "an interactive process," the EEOC interpreted the ADA's requirement that the employer offer an employee with a disability reasonable accommodations to mean that in determining the appropriate reasonable accommodation, "it may be necessary for the covered entity to initiate an informal, interactive process with the qualified individual with a disability. . . . This should identify the precise limitations resulting from the disability and the potential reasonable accommodations that could overcome those limitations"; 29 C.F.R. § 1630.2(o)(3).

[80] Beck v. University of Wisconsin, 75 F.3d 1130, 1135 (7th Cir. 1996); Feliberty v. Kemper Corp., 98 F.3d 274, 280 (7th Cir. 1996).

[81] Beck v. University of Wisconsin, *id.*; Bultemeyer v. Fort Wayne Community Schools, 100 F.3d 1281 (7th Cir. 1996).

[82] Humphrey v. Memorial Hospital Association (MHA), 239 F.3d 1128, 1139 (9th Cir. 2001) ("given MHA's failure to engage in the interactive process, liability is appropriate if a reasonable accommodation without undue hardship to the employer would otherwise have been possible"); Jacques v. Clean-Up Group, 96 F.3d 506, 515 (1st Cir. 1996) ("there may well be situations in which the employer's failure to engage in an informal interactive process would constitute a failure to provide reasonable accommodation that amounts to a violation of the ADA"); Fjellestad v. Pizza Hut of America, 188 F.3d 944, 952 (8th Cir. 1999) ("for purposes of [a] summary judgment, the failure of an employer to engage in an interactive process to determine whether reasonable accommodations are possible is prima facie evidence that the employer may be acting in bad faith").

[83] Hansen v. Henderson, 233 F.3d 521, 523 (7th Cir. 2000); Willis v. Conopco, 108 F.3d 282, 285 (11th Cir. 1997); White v. York International Corp., 45 F.3d 357 (10th Cir. 1995).

The regulations to the ADA promulgated by the EEOC contemplate that once an employee has asked for a reasonable accommodation,

> it may be necessary for the covered entity to initiate an informal, interactive process with the qualified individual. . . . This process should identify the precise limitations resulting from the disability and potential reasonable accommodations that could overcome those limitations.[84]

The interpretive guidance to the regulations reiterates that "the appropriate reasonable accommodation is best determined through a flexible, interactive process that involves both the employer and the qualified individual with a disability."[85]

The interactive process takes on particular significance in the light of psychiatric disabilities, because these disabilities often manifest most critically in "interactive" kinds of ways. Thus, some circuits have placed particular requirements on employers in the interactive process if an employee has a severe psychiatric disability.[86] Other circuits appear to consider all disabilities equally in terms of the employee's obligation to identify a needed accommodation and request it.

Specific Accommodations

In rare cases, a plaintiff alleging a psychiatric disability successfully runs the gauntlet of convincing a court that factual questions exist[87] regarding the existence of a disability and further persuades the court of his or her ability to perform the essential functions of a job with a reasonable accommodation. At this point, the plaintiff must still persuade the court that the accommodation requested is reasonable and will enable him or her to perform the essential functions of the job.

Courts often fail to understand the connection between the accommodation being requested and the plaintiff's disability. Sometimes, the minimal nature of the request for accommodation convinces the court that the plaintiff is not truly disabled.[88] In other cases, courts apparently see no connection between stress and a hostile work environment:

> Golliday has provided nothing to show that even if she were a qualified individual with a disability Metro Water failed to make reasonable accommodations for her. . . . In regard to her second request for accommodation, the record shows that at the civil service hearing she *merely* asked for a non-hostile working environment. *Even if this could be considered a genuine request for accommodation for her mental condition*

---

[84] 29 C.F.R. § 1630.2(o)(3).

[85] 29 C.F.R. pt. 1630, App. § 1630.9.

[86] Bultemeyer v. Fort Wayne Community Schools, 100 F.3d 1281, 1284 (7th Cir. 1996); Taylor v. Phoenixville School District, 174 F.3d 142 (3d Cir. 1999); *see also* Loulseged v. Akzo Nohel, 178 F.3d 731, 736 (5th Cir. 1999) (suggesting that an employer is subject to heightened requirements for the interactive process when the employee has a mental rather than physical disability).

[87] Almost all of these cases are disposed of on motions for a summary judgment; virtually all resulted in findings favorable to the employer.

[88] Soileau v. Guilford of Maine, 105 F.3d 12 (1st Cir. 1997) (because the plaintiff asked only to be relieved of having to facilitate meetings, a relatively minor part of his duties, the court concluded he was not substantially impaired in the activity of working).

involving panic attacks and stress, it occurred about 1/2 years after her suspension and long after she filed this complaint—and that was way too late.[89]

Courts' hostility to requests for reasonable accommodations by plaintiffs with psychiatric disabilities is not confined to relatively unusual requests, such as for a "nonhostile working environment." Even when the plaintiff requests an accommodation that was specifically identified as such by Congress in the language of the ADA, courts often find that the accommodation is not reasonable. Sometimes the same court has granted similar accommodations to individuals with physical disabilities.

Other than interpersonal accommodations, the kinds of accommodations that people with mental disabilities need are explicitly listed in the ADA and its implementing regulations as reasonable accommodations. Specifically, these include job restructuring,[90] part-time or modified work schedules,[91] and reassignment to a vacant position.[92] Plaintiffs also request accommodations specifically identified in the EEOC regulations as examples of reasonable accommodations, including modifications or adjustments to the work environment,[93] the use of accrued paid leave or providing additional unpaid leave for necessary treatment,[94] reallocating or redistributing marginal, nonessential functions,[95] and altering when and how an essential function is performed, for example, rescheduling an essential function from morning to afternoon.[96]

Leaves of Absence

The most frequently requested accommodations, regardless of the kind of disability, relate to job attendance. An employee may need time off to see a doctor, a few days off because of a flare-up of a condition, short-term leave for intensive treatment, or long-term leave to facilitate recovery. It is not surprising that these kinds of accommodations are among the most frequently requested: Disabilities in general require the care of physicians, who are rarely open at night or on weekends. Although doctors' appointments can be arranged ahead of time, the exacerbation of symptoms of a disability cannot be scheduled. The EEOC specifically discusses these examples in its regulations and lists leave as a type of reasonable accommodation.

Case law reflects that employers often grant these requests initially or even suggest leave (although sometimes, depending on the length of the leave requested,

---

[89]Hunt-Golliday v. Metropolitan Water Reclamation District of Greater Chicago, 104 F.3d 1004 (7th Cir. 1997) (emphasis added).

[90]42 U.S.C. § 12111(9); 29 C.F.R. § 1630.2(o)(2)(ii) (West 2000).

[91]*Id.*

[92]*Id.*

[93]29 C.F.R. § 1630.2(o)(1)(ii) (West 2000).

[94]This is an example of another specific reasonable accommodation that may be appropriate for particular situations listed in the EEOC's *Interpretive Guidance,* which notes that the examples of reasonable accommodations listed in the regulations are only "the most common types of accommodations that an employer or other covered entity may be required to provide"; 29 C.F.R. pt. 1630 App. § 1630.2(o) (Reasonable Accommodation).

[95]29 C.F.R. pt. 1630 App.

[96]*Id.*

they refuse the first request for leave). Nevertheless, the issue of leave as a reasonable accommodation is one that crops up frequently in case law.

One frequent question is how much leave is an employee entitled to as a reasonable accommodation? Some courts have used reasoning reminiscent of Joseph Heller's *Catch 22*. For example, the court in *Johnson v. Foulds*[97] held that if the employee asked for a temporary leave of absence, she was temporarily disabled at most; therefore, she was not covered by the ADA, whereas a request for a longer or unlimited leave of absence showed that she could not work and, therefore, she was not otherwise qualified for the job.

Obviously, one key indication about what constitutes a reasonable leave of absence is the employer's own leave policies as well as applicable state and federal laws and regulations. Congress has concluded that it is not unreasonable to require employers with more than 50 employees to permit employees to take up to 12 weeks of unpaid leave; therefore, that may serve as a "floor." Many big companies, such as Walmart,[98] Hardee's,[99] U.S. West,[100] and IBM,[101] have leave policies of up to a year. If a leave of absence would be allowed under a company's normal policies, it is difficult to imagine that it is an unreasonable accommodation. Many companies have generous maternity leave policies, which indicate that they have concluded that they can hold a given employee's position for up to a year.

In determining whether a leave of absence for a particular period of time is a reasonable accommodation, courts recently have begun examining how long an employer takes to fill a job vacancy, reasoning that if the employer could do without filling the job, it could also have granted the employee leave for that period of time.[102] Courts have also looked to whether policies on other types of leave such as sick leave were actually followed by the employer in its dealings with other employees.[103]

Requests for Specific Shifts

People with psychiatric disabilities,[104] as well as people with many other kinds of disabilities,[105] have requested work on day shifts as a reasonable accommodation. In

---

[97] 1996 U.S. Dist. LEXIS 9596 (July 8, 1996).

[98] Nunes v. Walmart, 164 F.3d 1243 (9th Cir. 1999) at *1.

[99] Simmerman v. Hardee's Food Systems, 1996 U.S. Dist. LEXIS 3437 (E.D. Pa. Mar. 22, 1996).

[100] Rascon v. U.S. West, 143 F.3d 1324 (10th Cir. 1998).

[101] Criado v. IBM Corp., 145 F.3d 437 (1st Cir. 1998).

[102] Haschmann v. Time Warner, 151 F.3d 591 (7th Cir. 1998).

[103] Walton v. Mental Health Association, 168 F.3d 661 (3d Cir. 1998).

[104] Guice-Mills v. Derwinski, 967 F.2d 794 (2d Cir. 1992) (a nurse with depression sought accommodation because her medication made it difficult for her to work night-shift hours); Doe v. Town of Seymour, 1998 WL 26410 (D. Conn. Jan. 16, 1998) (depression, dysthymia, and alcoholism); Gile v. United Airlines, 95 F.3d 492 (7th Cir. 1996) (depression); Simmerman, 1996 U.S. Dist. LEXIS 3437 (depression); Shea v. Tisch, 870 F.2d 786 (1st Cir. 1989) (anxiety disorder) (Rehabilitation Act case); Krocka v. Bransfield, 96 F. Supp. 1073 (N.D. Ill. 1997); Callison v. Charleston Area Medical Center, 909 F. Supp. 391 (S.D. W.Va. 1995) (bipolar disorder); McCall v. Myrtle Beach Hospital, 1997 U.S. App. LEXIS 23745 (4th Cir. Sept. 10, 1997); Webb v. Mercy Hospital, 103 F.3d 958 (8th Cir. 1996).

[105] Newman v. Silver Cross Hospital, 1998 U.S. Dist. LEXIS 11094 (N.D. Ill. July 14, 1998) (a narcolepsy case); Rhone v. U.S. Department of the Army, 665 F. Supp. 734 (E.D. Mo. 1987) (sarcordosis) (Section 501 of the Rehabilitation Act); Jones v. Lorain County Council on Alcoholism and Drug Abuse, 1996 WL 170344, (Ohio App. Apr. 10, 1996) (retinitis pigmentosa); Ventura v. City of Independence,

some cases, people are willing to work night shifts as long as they work them regularly; in other words, for these people, the reasonable accommodation requested is relief from rotating shifts (working day and night shifts alternately).[106]

Congress explicitly envisioned these requests as reasonable accommodations. One House of Representatives report states that "allowing constant shifts or modified work schedules provide ways of accommodating an individual with a disability to allow him or her to do the same job as a non-disabled individual."[107] The Senate report even more explicitly notes that

> some people with disabilities are denied employment opportunities because they cannot work a standard schedule. For example, persons who need medical treatment may benefit from flexible or adjusted work schedules. A person with epilepsy may require constant shifts rather than rotation from day to night shifts. . . . Allowing constant shifts or modified work schedules are examples of means to accommodate the individual with a disability to allow him or her to do the same job as a non-disabled person.[108]

Courts considering these cases have come up with inconsistent results. Sometimes, a court finds that a plaintiff whose condition does not prevent him or her from performing a job, only from working the night shift, is not disabled, thus precluding any consideration of reasonable accommodation.[109] In addition to providing expert evidence regarding the disability, an attorney should also be careful to link aspects of the disability or its treatment to the plaintiff's inability to work the night shift or rotating shifts. Neither the average juror nor the average judge is aware of the crucial importance of time of day or light to various kinds of disabilities. Specialists in this particular area can be called on to educate the judge and jury.

A plaintiff must also show that he or she can meet the essential functions of the job, with or without reasonable accommodations. This is a highly fact-specific inquiry. Is the shift part of the job description inherent in the job (such as night shift for a night watchman)? Has everyone who ever held the particular job at issue had to work rotating shifts? Have there ever been any exceptions to this rule in the past, such as changing the requirement to meet the needs of pregnant women, new mothers, people with sick relatives, or people whose religious beliefs prevent them from working certain days or shifts? How are shifts scheduled? Are there sufficient other employees that this function could be distributed among them? The EEOC specifically says in its interpretive guidance that "the second factor in determining whether a function is essential is the number of other employees available to perform that

---

108 F.3d 1378, 1997 WL 94688 (6th Cir. 1997) (table case) (asthma); McCall v. Myrtle Beach Hospital, 122 F.3d 1062, 1997 WL 560015 (4th Cir. 1997) (table case) (brittle diabetes); Hudson v. Lorotex Corp., 1997 U.S. Dist. LEXIS 4320 (N.D. N.Y. Apr. 2, 1997) (epilepsy).

[106]EEOC v. Union Carbide, 1995 U.S. Dist. LEXIS 12444 (E.D. La. Aug. 18, 1995) (an employee with bipolar disorder requests regular shifts—either day or night—and limitation to 8-hour shifts).

[107]House Committee on Labor and Education, H.R. Rep. No. 101-485, pt. 2, at 63 (1990).

[108]S. Rep. No. 101-116, at 31 (1989).

[109]Ventura v. City of Independence, 1997 U.S. App. LEXIS 4102 (6th Cir. Mar. 4, 1997) (not being able to work the night shift is not a substantial limitation on work; other limitations caused by asthma are insufficient to meet statutory standards).

job function or among whom the performance of that job function can be distributed."[110]

If the shift requirement is not an essential function of the job, the case should be over. If it is an essential function of the job, the first question is whether a person with a disability can be accommodated. Is there a way of trading assignments with fellow employees? Are there any accommodations that would permit an employee to stay in his or her position? If not (and this step is reached only if no accommodation permits the employee to stay in his or her position), is there a job available to which the employee could be transferred? (See "Transfer" on p. 190.)

These cases have achieved mixed results. There is some indication that courts are more sympathetic to the need of people with physical disabilities to work day shifts[111] than to assertions by people with psychiatric disabilities of the same need, although many people with physical disabilities have also lost cases relating to the need to work day shifts.

The fact that an enterprise is self-evidently a 24-hour-a-day operation, such as a hospital, means that requests to be relieved from the night shift are far more likely to be unavailing.[112] The conclusion is intuitively appealing, although not particularly logical. Even if having night shifts is an essential requirement of the enterprise in general, the EEOC requires courts to take into consideration whether this function can be distributed among available employees before determining that it is an essential function of a particular employee's job.[113] For example, in some of these cases, senior employees do not have to work the night shift[114]; in others, the employer rejected offers by other employees to trade shifts with the plaintiff or did not bother to thoroughly investigate the possibility.[115] This is clearly illegal under the ADA. The employer would have to show that shifting the employee to the day shift would be an undue hardship, but if the employee arranged for shift trades, even that defense would vanish: "The employer cannot avoid making the accommodation if the individual with a disability . . . can otherwise arrange to provide the accommodation. Under such circumstances, the necessary accommodation would no longer pose an undue hardship."[116]

This is particularly surprising in light of the substantial number of reasonable accommodation cases involving religion in which courts have required far more of employers in terms of investigating the possibility of trading shifts.[117] Congress un-

---

[110]EEOC *Interpretive Guidance to Title I Regulations,* 29 C.F.R. § 1630.2(n).

[111]Hudson v. Lorotex Corp., 1997 U.S. Dist. LEXIS 4320 (N.D. N.Y. Apr. 2, 1997) (epilepsy).

[112]Guice-Mills v. Derwinski, 967 F.2d 794 (2d Cir. 1992); Laurin v. Providence Hospital, 150 F.3d 52 (1st Cir. 1998); Callison v. Charleston Area Medical Center, 909 F. Supp. 391 (S.D. W. Va. 1995). In the few hospital cases where the plaintiff won, there was usually an indication of underlying discriminatory animus, McCall v. Myrtle Beach Hospital, 1997 U.S. App. LEXIS 23745 (4th Cir. Sept. 10, 1997).

[113]*See* 29 C.F.R. § 1630.2(n)(2)(ii).

[114]Laurin v. Providence Hospital, 150 F.3d 52 (1st Cir. 1998).

[115]Martinelli v. Montana Power Co., 886 P.2d 421, 428 (Mont. 1994); Neveau v. Boise Cascade, 902 F. Supp. 207 (D. Ore. 1995).

[116]*See* EEOC *Interpretive Guidance* to 1630.15(d).

[117]Opuku-Boateng v. California, 95 F.3d 1461 (9th Cir. 1996) (the circuit court said that the employer must prepare and post a tentative schedule asking other employees if they are willing to trade shifts); McGuire v. GMC, 956 F.2d 607 (6th Cir. 1992). *See* 29 C.F.R. § 1605.2(d)(1)(ii) and (iii) (EEOC regulations provide that employers letting employees choose when they work or permitting transfer or shift change constitutes reasonable accommodation of religion).

derscored that reasonable accommodations in ADA cases required far more of employers than reasonable accommodations in religion cases[118]; however, even a su-
perficial comparison of disability cases and religion cases shows that courts are more
favorably disposed toward people's scheduling requests in the latter cases. No court
has dismissed a religion accommodation case by noting that employee scheduling
flexibility is an essential function of the job that the employer need not accommodate,
as has happened in many disability discrimination cases.[119]

Lurking beneath the surface of these disability discrimination decisions is an
attitude of skepticism on the part of courts. In one case in which a nurse with a
seizure disorder who had small children and who was attending school requested
day shift work, the court explicitly sympathized with the hospital's concern that it
would be deluged with requests for the day shift from nurses with small children.
The court thus implicitly discounted the significance of the seizure disorder in the
nurse's desire for the day shift.

There is in fact an enormous body of medical research on the specific health
hazards of working the night shift, as well as a growing array of innovative business
solutions, that meets both the worker's and the employer's needs. Working the night
shift does exacerbate depression and anxiety,[120] in part because people with depression are already more likely to be suffering from sleep disorders[121] and in part because medication for depression makes it more difficult to work the night shift.[122]
Other research relevant to ADA claims by people with other disabilities confirms
that asthma attacks are more likely to occur at night and that working the night shift
increases the chances of ulcers and heart disease.

---

[118] "The Committee wishes to make it clear that the principles enunciated by the [U.S.] Supreme
Court in TWA v. Hardison, 432 U.S. 63 (1977) are not applicable to this legislation." In *Hardison*, the
Supreme Court concluded that under Title VII of the Civil Rights Act of 1964, an employer need not
accommodate people with religious beliefs if the accommodation would require more than a de minimis
cost for the employer. By contrast, under the ADA, reasonable accommodations must be provided unless
they arise to the level of "requiring significant difficulty or expense on the part of the employer, in light
of the factors noted in the statute, i.e., a significantly higher standard than that articulated in *Hardison*.
This higher standard is necessary in light of the crucial role that reasonable accommodation plays in
ensuring meaningful employment opportunities for people with disabilities"; Committee on Education
and Labor, H.R. Rep. No. 101-485, pt. 2, at 68 (1990). *See also* EEOC and *Interpretive Guidance* to
1630.15(d) ("the concept of undue hardship that has evolved under Section 504 of the Rehabilitation
Act and is embodied in this part is unlike the 'undue hardship' defense associated with the provision of
religious accommodation under Title VII of the Civil Rights Act of 1964. To demonstrate undue hardship
pursuant to the ADA and this part, an employer must show substantially more difficulty or expense than
would be needed to satisfy the 'de minimis' Title VII standard of undue hardship.").

[119] Jasany v. U.S. Postal Service, 755 F.2d 1244 (6th Cir. 1985); Mackie v. Runyon, 804 F. Supp.
1508 (M.D. Fla. 1992).

[120] R. J. Cole, R. T. Loving, and D. F. Kripke, "Psychiatric Aspects of Shift Work," *Occupational
Medicine: State of the Art Reviews* 5 (1990): 301–314; J. M. Waterhouse, S. Folkard, and D. S. Minors,
Shiftwork Health and Safety: An Overview of the Scientific Literature 1978–1990 (London: Her Majesty's
Stationery Office, 1992); Ethel Gofen, "Sleep: More Than Meets the Shuteye," *Current Health* 17 (Jan.
1991): 4.

[121] National Heart, Lung, and Blood Institute, "Breathing Disorders During Sleep" (Aug. 1994); N.
Brunello, R. Armitage, I. Feinberg, "Depression and Sleep Disorders: Clinical Relevance, Economic
Burden and Pharmacological Treatment," 42 *Neuropsychobiology* 3 (2000): 107–119.

[122] *See* Guice-Mills v. Derwinski, 967 F.2d 794 (2d Cir. 1992); Dees v. Austin Travis County MH-
MR, 860 F. Supp. 1186 (W.D. Tex. 1994).

It is hard to tell from only reading the cases, but the body of adjudication about day shifts as a reasonable accommodation leaves the impression that lawyers have not made a real effort to assemble all the medical literature and bring in the expert witnesses necessary to educate the court about the links between night shift work and health conditions. For that matter, employers are constantly bemoaning the rise in health care costs, yet few seem to focus on the contributions of the conditions and requirements of work in the downsized world to these costs.

Some employers, however, are coming up with solutions where everyone wins. One hospital in Rhode Island encourages people who are admitted for acute care to identify a "care partner," a spouse, sibling, parent, or friend. This person is admitted along with the patient. A hotel-style bed is provided for the care partner, who learns all about the patient's condition, including how to administer medication, how to chart, and how to care for the patient on discharge. One benefit of this system for the hospital is that fewer nurses are required on the night shift.[123]

Many employers resist requests for accommodation relating to shift changes by pointing out that such accommodations would be in violation of seniority, collective bargaining agreements, or both. The U.S. Supreme Court agreed to decide whether an employer is required to bypass a seniority system that is *not* the result of collective bargaining in granting an accommodation to a disabled employee.[124]

Requests for Shorter Hours

Case after case under the ADA reflects, sometimes in passing, that the 40-hour work week is going the way of the nuclear family: a cherished norm that bears no resemblance to reality in our lives.[125] Accommodation requests for shorter working hours usually involve an employee's request for a normal work week or work day, that is, a 40- or even 50-hour week or an 8-hour day. In these cases, the fact that the request for accommodations is so reasonable is often used to support a court's conclusion that the individual is not really disabled (after all, the plaintiff can work an ordinary work day); therefore, the individual does not qualify for protection under the ADA, even when the employer fired the employee because he or she could not work overtime due to a physical or mental condition.[126]

In Europe, research on the adverse health effects of long working hours led to legislation giving almost all workers[127] the right to refuse to work more than 48 hours a week (including overtime) without losing their jobs, the right to not have to work more than 13 hours in any work day, to have 1 rest day a week; to not be required to work more than 8 hours at night, and to 4 weeks of leave a year.[128] All

---

[123] "Cooperative Care Acutely Less Costly," *Modern Health Care* (Sept. 19, 1994): 32–34.

[124] U.S. Airways v. Barnett, 149 L.Ed.2d 467 (Apr. 16, 2001) (granting cert. on the following question: "Did the 9th Circuit err in holding that the ADA requires an employer to assign a disabled employee to a different position as a 'reasonable accommodation' even though another employee is entitled to hold the position under the employer's bona fide and established seniority system?").

[125] Fritz v. Mascotech, 914 F. Supp. 1481 (E.D. Mich. 1996) (after being hired, the employee agreed to a 50- to 56-hour work week).

[126] *See, e.g.*, Shpargel v. Stage and Co., 914 F. Supp. 1468 (E.D. Mich. 1996).

[127] There are a few limited exceptions, including, notably, medical students and doctors in training. E. C. Council Directive 93/104, *Official Journal of Law,* 12/13/1993, pp. 0018–0024 (1993 OJL 307).

[128] *Id.*

members of the European Union were required to adopt these standards according to the Treaty of Rome.[129] Great Britain fought these standards fiercely but was ultimately forced to adopt them by the European Court of Justice.[130]

Ironically, some of the research that caused the Europeans alarm was conducted in the United States, such as an old study showing that California workers who worked more than 56 hours a week were at much more serious risk of death from heart disease.[131] In Japan, there is a specific term for "death from overwork"—*karoshi*—and the country is concerned and investigating. In the United States, the concept of death from overwork is not even part of the national vocabulary. That does not mean it does not happen, nor does it mean that the only casualties of 60- and 70-hour work weeks are fatalities. Many of them are showing up as people who are making claims for disability benefits or claims of failure to reasonably accommodate under the ADA.

Working at Home

Up to one third of Americans do at least some of their work at home.[132] A growing number of these workers are "telecommuters" who use new technology to do their work from home. Although the number of telecommuters is difficult to measure, all studies agree that they are in the millions and increasing by as much as 15% a year.

Working at home may be particularly suitable for people with disabilities for a variety of reasons.[133] A person with Crohn's disease that involved serious bowel control problems might work at home[134]; a person who is depressed or suffers from anxiety or panic disorder might prefer it.

---

[129]Ralph H. Folsom, "Part One: Foundational Treaties," in *European Union Business Law: Sourcebook* (St. Paul, MN: West Publishing Co., 1995). Article 118a of the Treaty of Rome provides the following:

1. Member States shall pay particular attention to encouraging improvements, especially in the working environments, as regards the health and safety of workers, and shall set as their objective the harmonization of conditions in this area, while maintaining the improvements made.

2. In order to help achieve the objective laid down in the first paragraph, the Council, acting in accordance with the procedure referred to in Article 189c and after consulting the Economic and Social Committee, shall adopt by means of directives minimum requirements for gradual implementation, having regard to the conditions and technical rules obtaining in each of the Member States. [Fnaa8] . . .

3. The provisions adopted pursuant to this Article shall not prevent any Member State from maintaining or introducing more stringent measures for the protection of working conditions compatible with this Treaty.

[130]European Report 2174, United Kingdom of Great Britain and Northern Ireland v. Council of the European Union, Case C-84/94 (694 J0084) (Court of Justice of the European Communities Nov. 12, 1996), 1996 ECJ CELEX LEXIS 5915.

[131]P. Buell and L. Breslow, "Mortality From Coronary Heart Disease in California Men Who Work Long Hours," 11 *J. of Chronic Disease* 11 (1960): 615–626.

[132]Patricia Braus, "Homework for Grownups," *American Demographics* (Aug. 1993): 38.

[133]*See* Jacqueline Shaller, "Disabled Finding Wider Job Opportunities," *N.Y. Times* (July 9, 1989): Section 12 (NJ) 1; Caryn Eve Murray, "Charting a New Course: Disabled Overcome Obstacles to Become Entrepreneurs," *Newsday* (Aug. 18, 1997): C6.

[134]*See* Harris v. Chater, 998 F. Supp. 223 (E.D. N.Y. 1998).

In this context, some people with disabilities have asked their employers to be able to work at home as a reasonable accommodation.[135] In some cases, the request is to be permitted to work at home temporarily[136] and in some cases, permanently. In some cases, the requested accommodation is to be allowed to perform some, but not all, of the functions of the job from home.

The legislative history of the ADA makes it clear that "essential functions of the job" refers to the tasks to be performed and not the place in which they are performed.[137] Much harm has been generated by courts' confusion of cases involving unauthorized leaves of absence with cases involving employees' requests to work at home on a scheduled, regular basis.

Ironically, this area that bursts with potential for increasing the employment of people with disabilities has been virtually shut off by courts, which have been finding that working at home is not a reasonable accommodation as a matter of law. One of the key early cases involving the request to work at home was *Vande Zande v. State of Wisconsin Department of Administration.*[138] The facts in *Vande Zande* are important in understanding the infirmity of the court's reasoning.

Lori Vande Zande was a woman with paraplegia who intermittently developed pressure ulcers requiring her to stay home. She requested as an accommodation that she be allowed to work at home for 8 weeks and be provided with a desktop computer to do so. Her employer refused, stating there was at most only 15–20 hours of work for her to do at home and said she would have to make up the rest through sick leave or vacation. "In the event, she was able to work all but 16.5 [at home] hours in the eight week period."[139] Less than a page later, the court concludes, in a broad generalization of law applicable to all jobs and apparently without realizing that the facts in this case contradict its finding, that "most jobs in organizations public or private involve team work under supervision rather than solitary unsupervised work, and team work under supervision generally cannot be performed at home without a substantial reduction in the quality of the employee's performance."[140]

If there is any evidence in the record as to the quality of Vande Zande's work at home, the reader is not made privy to it. If there is information in the record as to the Department of Administration's ability to fax, conduct conference calls, and use other technological capabilities, it is not shared. Judge Posner concluded,

> An employer is not required to allow disabled workers to work at home, where their productivity *inevitably* would be greatly reduced. No doubt to this as to any generalization about so complex and varied an activity as employment, there are exceptions, but it would take a very extraordinary case for the employee to be able to create a triable issue of the employer's failure to allow the employee to work at home.[141]

If there is one concept that is fundamental to the ADA, it is that each case must

---

[135]Paleologos v. Rehab Consultants, 990 F. Supp. 1460 (N.D. Ga. 1998) (the court found that the plaintiff was not disabled but in any event would not have found working at home to be a reasonable accommodation).

[136]Vande Zande v. Wisconsin Department of Administration, 44 F.3d 538 (7th Cir. 1995) (employee with pressure ulcers asked to work full time at home for 8 weeks).

[137]H.R. Rep. No. 101-485, pt. 3, at 33 (1990), *reprinted in* 1990 U.S.C.C.A.N. 445, 453.

[138]44 F.3d 538 (7th Cir. 1995).

[139]*Id.* at 544.

[140]*Id.*

[141]*Id.* at 545 (emphasis added).

be considered individually. The 7th Circuit is in fact the champion of the notion of the interactive, individualized process by which employer and employee work out individualized accommodations that are suitable to both. To find that a given accommodation is unreasonable as a matter of law, without benefit of evidence in the record as to its tenability in general, and with every indication that it worked in the case before the court, seems perplexing at best.

No person with a psychiatric disability has ever won a reported court case requesting working at home as a reasonable accommodation. Although people with physical disabilities such as a back injury[142] or multiple sclerosis[143] have fared better in requests to work at home, the majority of courts follow the lead of the 7th Circuit and exclude working at home as a reasonable accommodation as a matter of law. But these courts have confused cases involving attendance requirements and unexpected, excessive absences with cases involving the request to work at home. The former cases implicate an employer's need for predictability, whereas the latter cases raise the question of whether one of the essential elements of the position is presence at the work site. Several commentators have critiqued this confusion and suggested that working at home may well be a reasonable accommodation.[144] At the least, it ought to be examined on a case-by-case basis under the ADA.

Transfer

Transfer may be a reasonable accommodation if no accommodation can be made to keep an employee in his or her present position. Congress indicated that the first goal of reasonable accommodations should be to maintain an individual in the job he or she was hired to fill:

> Reasonable accommodation may also include reassignment to a vacant position. If an employee, because of a disability, can no longer perform the essential functions of a job that she or he has held, a transfer to another vacant job for which the person is qualified may prevent the employee from being out of work and the employer from losing a valuable worker. Efforts should be made, however, to accommodate an employee in the position that he or she was hired to fill before reassignment is considered.[145]

Both the ADA and traditional employment practices support transfer as a reasonable accommodation, and in fact courts have been open to transfer in cases involving people with physical disabilities.[146] In some psychiatric disability cases, if

---

[142] Anzalone v. Allstate Insurance Co., 1995 WL 35613 (E.D. La. Jan. 30, 1995).

[143] Langon v. U.S. Department of Health and Human Services, 959 F.2d 1053 (D.C. Cir. 1992) (a Rehabilitation Act case).

[144] Kristen M. Ludgate, "Telecommuting and the Americans With Disabilities Act: Is Working at Home a Reasonable Accommodation?" *Minnesota Law Rev.* 81 (May 1997): 1309, 1331; A. E. Smith, "The 'Presence Is an Essential Function' Myth: The ADA's Trapdoor for the Chronically Ill," *Seattle University Law Rev.* 19 (Fall 1995): 163.

[145] H.R. Rep. No. 101-485, at 63 (1990), *reprinted in* 1990 U.S.C.C.A.N. 345.

[146] Aka v. Washington Hospital Center, 156 F.3d 1284 (D.C. Cir. 1998) (*en banc*) (diabetes and heart condition); Hurley-Bardige v. Brown, 900 F. Supp. 567, 570 (D. Mass. 1995).

the request for transfer is due to reasons other than failure to get along with a supervisor, transfer is sometimes seen as a potentially appropriate accommodation.[147]

One of the most common features of an employment discrimination action involving mental disability or perceived mental disability is clashes with the employee's supervisor.[148] One of the most commonly requested accommodations—sometimes the only requested accommodation—is not having to work with a particular supervisor. Courts have reacted with uniform hostility to the suggestion that such separations be considered reasonable accommodations.

Everything in the ADA and in traditional labor law points to transfer as a logical reasonable accommodation. However, courts have adamantly refused to consider transfer in situations involving mental disabilities. Thus, although in cases involving mental disabilities the courts have characterized transfer as simply not a reasonable accommodation, what the courts actually appear to be saying is that transfer is not a reasonable accommodation for people with mental disabilities.[149] Occasionally, cases involving requests for transfer because of job stress, which do not implicate interpersonal difficulties with supervisors, make it past motions to dismiss and for summary judgment.[150]

Personalized Accommodations

Often the best accommodations for people with psychiatric disabilities are those that are individually responsive to their needs, cost-free,[151] and generally demonstrate that the employer cares about the employee's well-being. These are more likely to be effective and, on a more cynical level, very likely to win court approbation. For example, in one case, the employer allowed the plaintiff to select coworkers to sit with her and read the Bible during her panic attacks.[152] As a practical matter, this employer was fairly certain to win a case that accused it of not making sufficient reasonable accommodations to the employee, and it did.

---

[147]Stradley v. La Fourche Communications, 869 F. Supp. 442 (E.D. La 1994) (a transfer to a different, less stressful, nonsupervisory job may be a reasonable accommodation); Sharp v. Abate, 887 F. Supp. 695 (S.D. N.Y. 1995); Przybylak v. New York State Thruway Authority, 1996 U.S. Dist. LEXIS 2786 (W.D. N.Y. Feb. 16, 1996) (an employee with depression, panic disorder, and agoraphobia requested a transfer to a smaller, less congested toll plaza. The union claimed that transfers between toll plazas are governed by seniority. Because the court did not have the collective bargaining agreement in front of it, it refused to grant the union's motion to dismiss). *See also* Poindexter v. Atchison Topeka and Santa Fe Railroad, 168 F.3d 1228 (10th Cir. 1999).

[148]Weiler v. Household Finance Corp., 1995 U.S. Dist. LEXIS 10566 (N.D. Ill. July 25, 1995); Boldini v. Postmaster General, U.S. Postal Service, 928 F. Supp. 125 (D. N.H. 1995).

[149]Siemon v. AT&T Corp., 117 F.3d 1173 (10th Cir. 1997).

[150]Stradley v. La Fourche Communications, 869 F. Supp. 442 (E.D. La 1994) (a transfer to a different, less stressful, nonsupervisory job may be a reasonable accommodation); Sharp v. Abate, 887 F. Supp. 695 (S.D. N.Y. 1995); Przybylak v. New York State Thruway Authority, 1996 U.S. Dist. LEXIS 2786 (W.D. N.Y. Feb. 16, 1996). *See also* n. 146.

[151]Of course, nothing is cost free that involves time, but most of these accommodations involve relatively little time from other employees or the worker.

[152]Larkins v. CIBA Vision, 858 F. Supp. 1572 (N.D. Ga. 1994).

Measures That Provide More Workplace Structure

Among accommodations discussed in the literature and in case law are various means of making work more structured. Many of these practices described as accommodations are free, make good business sense in any event, and might be reframed as traditional business practices. For example, in one case, an employer accommodated an employee with a psychiatric disability by providing her with a "written description of objectives and tasks" related to her job.[153] If this was a daily or weekly written directive, it would indeed be an accommodation, because employers do not routinely provide such instructions. However, it might have been only a job description, a relatively routine business practice, which, nevertheless, is requested by many plaintiffs in ADA actions. The defendant in this case also "made technical persons available [to the plaintiff] to answer all questions" and "required a supervisor to meet with her weekly to discuss her progress and assist her."[154]

A consultant on accommodations for people with psychiatric disabilities has suggested that project management software might be "especially helpful for someone with a mental disorder by keeping track of to-do lists and reminding them of deadlines."[155] This software could be useful for all employees.

Increasing Light and Reducing Noise

Almost every guide to accommodating people with psychiatric disabilities mentions as possible accommodations the decrease of extraneous noise, the increase of light or sunlight, or both.[156] These issues do not come up in the litigated cases: Whether because people with psychiatric disabilities are not asking for them or because they are easily accommodated is not clear.

Accommodations That Are Not Required

Both courts and the regulations have made clear that an employer need not reinstate an employee,[157] even if the employee resigned during an episode of depression,[158] nor may an employer be required to fund a job coach as a reasonable accommodation.[159] The question of whether sensitivity training for other staff members can be a required accommodation remains an open one.

---

[153] Allen v. GTE Mobile Communications Service Corp., 1997 U.S. Dist. LEXIS 3539 (N.D. Ga. Feb. 25, 1997).

[154] Id.

[155] "Reserved Parking Could be Accommodation for Worker's Mental Condition," *Disability Compliance Bull.* 10(8) (Oct. 9, 1997): 7.

[156] See EEOC *Enforcement Guidance on Psychiatric Disabilities*; Office of Technology Assessment, *The Biology of Mental Disorders* (Washington, DC: Government Printing Office, 1992); "Reserved Parking Could be Accommodation for Worker's Mental Condition," at n. 154.

[157] Siefken v. Village of Arlington Heights, 65 F.3d 664, 666 (7th Cir. 1995) (an employer was not required to give an employee a "second chance" as a reasonable accommodation).

[158] Wootten v. Acme Steel, 986 F. Supp. 524 (N.D. Ill. 1997).

[159] EEOC v. Hertz, 1998 WL 5694 (E.D. Mich. Jan. 6, 1998).

Can Individuals Be Required to Take Medication or Accept Treatment as a Reasonable Accommodation?

A few cases have raised the question of whether an employer or a court can make continued employment contingent on the taking of psychotropic medication. This has been characterized as the employer offering the employee a reasonable accommodation. EEOC regulations provide that this is *not* a reasonable accommodation and that the decision to take medications remains the individual's choice. ADA regulations say

> a qualified individual with a disability is not required to accept an accommodation, aid, service, opportunity or benefit which such qualified individual chooses not to accept.[160] However if such individual rejects a reasonable accommodation, aid, service, opportunity or benefit that is necessary to enable the individual to perform the essential functions of the job held or desired and cannot, as a result of that rejection, perform the essential functions of that position, the individual will not be considered a qualified individual with a disability.[161]

Generally, cases have held that an employee may not be forced to enter treatment as a reasonable accommodation.[162]

Conclusion

It is important to remember that the ADA prohibits both intentional discrimination (i.e., disparate treatment) and unintentional discrimination. An action can constitute disparate treatment even if undertaken for apparently benign motivation or out of ignorance. A situation may exist that is discriminatory without malice or animus on the part of an employer. However, once this situation is brought to the employer's attention in the form of a request for reasonable accommodations, the employer has a duty to take the request seriously.

The employer may certainly ask for documentation of the disability and its impact on the employee's ability to work and may ask for explanations or reassurances of how the proposed accommodation will work to permit the employee to perform his or her job. If the employer is satisfied that the individual is disabled but does not want to provide the accommodation, the employer has a duty to engage in an interactive process with the employee to determine what accommodation could be provided, unless it is absolutely clear that no accommodation is available.

It should be said that employers reach this conclusion unilaterally at their peril. There is little cost to sitting down with an employee and trying to come to an agreement about an accommodation, and it benefits the employer as good business practice and in any subsequent litigation to have made efforts to understand and meet

---

[160]This sentence appears almost verbatim in the statute, 42 U.S.C. § 12201(d) (2000).

[161]29 C.F.R. § 1630.9(d).

[162]Miners v. Cargill Communications, 113 F.3d 820 (8th Cir. 1997); Roberts v. County of Fairfax, Virginia, 1996 U.S. Dist. LEXIS 11812 (E.D. Va. Aug. 13, 1996) (it is not discrimination to fail to require an employee to enter treatment); Jones v. Corrections Corp. of America, 993 F. Supp. 1384 (D. Kan. 1998).

the employee's needs. Although not all employers who are successful in litigation made offers of accommodation, many employers who lose ADA cases are seen as either having made no efforts whatsoever or having actively undermined and sabotaged the employee after learning of his or her disability.

Employees, however, should be prepared to clearly inform the employer of the nature of the disability, the way in which it affects work performance, the accommodation desired, and the way in which the accommodation would meet the employee's needs. Employees are caught between a rock and a hard place because it is better to never have to tell an employer about psychiatric disabilities; many employees inform their employers only after trouble has been brewing for some time, and the timing of employer notification makes courts extremely suspicious.

Chapter 9
CONCLUSION

The Americans With Disabilities Act (ADA) was passed and signed amid high expectations that it would be a potent weapon to combat discrimination against people with disabilities. Congress focused particularly on employment discrimination because one of the principal aims of the ADA was to reduce disability benefit rolls by enabling people who could work to enter the employment market.

The ADA has failed to provide people with mental disabilities with the kind of protection from discrimination that Congress envisioned. It has proven to be a hollow promise, and people with mental disabilities remain better off concealing their condition from employers and colleagues at work.

The reasons that Title I of the ADA has been a failure in protecting Americans with mental disabilities are complex and varied. At the most general level, the structure of antidiscrimination law makes it difficult because of its strict separation of discrimination into discrete categories—race discrimination, gender discrimination, age discrimination, disability discrimination—which belie the lived experience of individuals who often report discrimination at the intersections of these categories. If an employer is afraid that a black man with a diagnosis of mental illness will be violent, or an older person with a disability will not have the stamina to complete the job, how are these stereotypes to be parsed? The categories of the law demand an accounting which is not true to life.

In addition, the ADA itself is difficult to analogize to pre-existing antidiscrimination law. Its specific protections were established by Congress in the first instance, rather than being codified by Congress from pre-existing court rulings as was the case with race and gender discrimination law, and judges are therefore unfamiliar with concepts such as "reasonable accommodation."[1] Unlike race and gender, disability is seen as a category open to ambiguity and subjectivity, and psychiatric disabilities are seen as representing the extreme end of this ambiguity and subjectivity. Judges—and the public—conceptualize disability as static, visible, and immune to environmental influences.

When judges do recognize the existence of mental illness, their notion of what constitutes mental illness operates to virtually guarantee defeat in an employment discrimination case. The most pernicious stereotype is the "all or nothing" belief that a mental illness takes over a person's life and identity to the extent that it necessarily precludes him or her from all but the most menial employment. The visible "second world" of people with mental disabilities are often in such jobs; the invisible "first world" of people with psychiatric diagnoses can only continue to be doctors, judges, pilots, and administrators because their diagnoses are hidden from their colleagues. When people from this latter group bring lawsuits, it is difficult for courts to accept that a person who performs competently in a job, or who successfully

---

[1]Although a much narrower version of "reasonable accommodation" is required in laws prohibiting discrimination on the basis of religion, judges see few cases alleging discrimination based on religion.

obtains another job after being fired, has a psychiatric disability at all. Therefore, the question of whether the person was fired because of stereotypes about mental illness, or whether the workplace could have been changed to permit them to continue to work, never even gets asked.

On the other hand, someone whose psychiatric disability is manifest is considered unqualified for employment, and therefore he or she is not covered under the ADA. In few of these cases do courts bother to examine whether a reasonable accommodation would permit the person to accomplish the job. Courts often sweep away requests for reasonable accommodations such as flexible hours or work at home, applying the broad generalizations that the ADA was meant to extinguish.

In both of these situations—a person whose manifest competence precludes a court from perceiving his or her disability, and a person whose disability precludes a court from recognizing his or her competence—courts assume that the person's condition will continue indefinitely. The truth about psychiatric disabilities rattles our settled frameworks about both the continuity and the complexity of people's emotional states. People who are in the grips of the most real and terrifying psychoses can go back to being teachers, parents, scientists, doctors, lawyers, and professors. This concept is difficult enough for the public and the judiciary to grasp. What is impossible to grasp is that people can be teachers, journalists, scientists, doctors, lawyers, and professors *while* experiencing the most severe suffering and emotional turmoil, including being suicidal, cutting, and having hallucinations. It does not mean that the schizophrenia is not real, that the hallucinations and delusions are diluted or made up or not terrifying. Nor does it mean that the person with these disabilities is not really being a competent lawyer, doctor, or journalist. Harvard students have received literary and journalism awards while they were suicidally, chaotically depressed and behaving in ways that would get people in other places involuntarily committed.[2] Even when courts understand that psychiatric disability is episodic or cyclical, they are prone to write it off as a "temporary" disability not covered by the ADA.[3]

Another stereotype is that to be a "real" disability, a disability must not vary according to context or environment. Psychiatric disabilities flare up in certain environments and in response to certain stresses, as do many physical disabilities. In particular, interpersonal relationships have a great impact on psychiatric disabilities. Courts have responded by creating a per se rule that disabilities brought on by stressful contact with a supervisor cannot be covered under the ADA. But the increased vulnerability to abuse and tension at work is the hallmark of psychiatric disability, and this is the only area where courts have eliminated a disability-based cause of action by looking at the origin of the disability.

Courts also fail to understand the dynamic between discrimination and psychiatric disability. Although race discrimination does not cause someone to become African American, and gender discrimination does not make someone a woman, when a person with a psychiatric diagnosis who is otherwise functioning well is

---

[2] Elizabeth Wurtzel, *Prozac Nation: Young and Depressed in America* (Boston: Houghton Mifflin, 1994).

[3] Brown v. Northern Trust Bank, 1997 U.S. Dist. LEXIS 13184 (N.D. Ill. Sept. 2, 1997); Sanders v. Arneson Products, 91 F.3d 1351 (9th Cir. 1996); Williams v. Health Reach Network, 2000 U.S. Dist. LEXIS 9695 (D. Me. Feb. 22, 2000).

subjected to discrimination on the basis of that diagnosis (e.g., the teacher trainee who is not allowed to student teach or the employee who is transferred or demoted when his diagnosis becomes known), he or she may have a breakdown. Courts then bar the individual's discrimination claim because he or she is not qualified to hold the position. This means that the more painful the consequences of discriminatory action, the less likely the individual is to prevail in challenging that discrimination.

In part, these stereotypes can be addressed by new regulations or new regulatory interpretations by the EEOC. In part, they can be addressed by helping judges and the public reach a better understanding of the nature of psychiatric disability. The rest of the problems are inherent to the ADA as drafted or to the structure of litigation and are less easily resolved.

By far the most substantial problem facing people with psychiatric disabilities —and people with all disabilities—is that the EEOC and the courts have interpreted the requirement that a physical or mental disability "substantially limit one or more major life activities" in a way that insulates blatant discrimination by employers based on stereotypes about impairments. The most direct way to resolve this problem would be to amend the ADA to require only the showing of an impairment and adverse employment action based on the impairment if the employee was not asking for a reasonable accommodation. Another solution would be for Congress to amend the ADA to simply list covered disabilities.

These approaches are unlikely to be successful. A more likely solution would be for the EEOC to clarify that an employee whose condition was the basis for adverse employment action was "regarded as disabled" by the employer. This has a substantial foundation in ADA and Section 504 legislative history.

The ADA, even in the wake of the Supreme Court trilogy of *Sutton/Murphy/Kirkingburg*, is of some use to Americans with psychiatric disabilities. Principally, the ADA is extremely helpful because it prohibits employers from asking questions about mental health treatment or hospitalization in employment applications and job interviews. This provision assists employees with psychiatric conditions in doing what is unfortunately the single most useful thing they can do in today's environment: conceal their condition from their employer.

The ADA may have some effect simply by its existence. It can be seen as an organizational tool to educate employers and the public about psychiatric disabilities, and to promote research, discussion, and dialogue. However, this is a far cry from being an effective employment discrimination law. Ten years after the passage of the ADA, social sciences research and media reports suggest that employers and the public retain many of the harmful and damaging stereotypes about mental illness that preceded its enactment.

The need for public education about psychiatric disability is recognized by all; but the most potent kind of education occurs when a friend or family member reveals that he or she has a psychiatric diagnosis. Like disclosure of sexual orientation, the courage that this takes is a measure of the depth and virulence of social bias against people who have psychiatric diagnoses. Unlike the gay community, for whom life and death in the form of the AIDS epidemic made social consequences seem less significant, most people with psychiatric disabilities have yet to organize publicly and in large numbers. People with physical disabilities—many of whom do not have the choice of whether to disclose their disabilities—are beginning to be represented in Congress, on the EEOC, and in other high positions in the Executive Branch.

Since the passing of Lawton Chiles, the Governor of Florida, the only person in high
political office to have acknowledged a psychiatric history is Congresswoman Nydia
Valazquez (D.N.Y.), who did not do so voluntarily. In fact, she sued successfully
over the revelation of her psychiatric history after a hospital employee revealed her
records to the *New York Post*. Even the National Council on Disability did not
appoint its first representative of the community of people with psychiatric disabilities until the 1990s.

The lesson of this is that the law to a large extent follows political trends rather
than shaping them; enforces consensus rather than creating it; and—even in the face
of a federal mandate to do so—will not hand out rights to a community insufficiently
organized to insist that the federal mandate be honored. This is not to say that efforts
to enforce the ADA are useless, but they must be accompanied by political action.
In other words, the relationship between anitdiscrimination law and the people it
purports to protect has never been a one-way-street. People who look to the law to
protect their rights must look to themselves and each other to protect the law, and
to give it meaning and substance. If they do not, the law will remain a hollow
promise.

APPENDIX A
Survey

Susan Stefan is writing a book about discrimination against people with diagnoses or labels of psychiatric disability. She would like to learn more about the perspectives and experiences of people who have these diagnoses and labels. Please take a few minutes to fill out this form. As you can see, it is anonymous, and it will help her a great deal. **Please return the survey to Susan Stefan, University of Miami School of Law, P.O. Box 248087, Coral Gables, FL 33124-8087.** Thank you very much.

1. Do you believe you have a disability?
   _____ Yes   _____ No

1a. How would you define or describe "having a disability?"

   _____

   _____

2. Do you believe that other people regard you as having a disability?
   _____ Yes   _____ No

3. Do you believe that you have a physical or mental impairment?
   _____ Yes   _____ No

3a. If yes, does the impairment substantially limit you in one or more major life activities?
   _____ Yes   _____ No

3b. If you answered yes to 3a, please describe:

   _____

   _____

4. Are you vulnerable to abuse because you have or are perceived as having a disability?
   _____ Yes   _____ No
   If yes, explain and/or give examples.

   _____

5. Have you ever been discriminated against?
   _____ Yes   _____ No

5a. If yes, please check all the categories that apply:

_____ housing	_____ access to stores, movies, etc.
_____ access to medical care	_____ how people treated you
_____ employment	_____ courtroom situations
_____ insurance	_____ institutional settings
_____ education	_____ other (specify below)

_____

_____

_____

5b. Did you feel as though you were discriminated against because of

_____ race	_____ religion
_____ sex	_____ sexual preference
_____ age	_____ psychiatric disability or perceived disability
_____ physical disability	_____ a combination of one or more of the above

6. In what areas of your life have you experienced the worst discrimination?

_____

_____

_____

7. Please give examples of the worst discrimination you have encountered.

_____

_____

_____

8. Please explain how you felt afterward, for how long this effect lasted, and what impact it had on the way you lived your life after that.

_____

_____

_____

9. What do you think is the best thing that can be done to make sure these kinds of things don't keep happening?

_____

_____

_____

10. Do you think the Americans With Disabilities Act can prevent these things from happening to people?

_____ Yes   _____ No   _____ Yes, if: _____

_____

11. Do you know anyone who sued or was sued under the Americans With Disabilities Act?

_____ Yes   _____ No

If yes, what was the case about? What happened? _____

_____

_____

12. Do you feel part of the community where you live? Why or why not? _____

_____

13. I am writing a book about discrimination, law, and psychiatric disability, including perceptions of psychiatric disability. What do you want to know about that I should include?

_____

_____

_____

14. What do you want other people to know about psychiatric disability, perceptions of psychiatric disability, discrimination, or law that I should include?

_____

_____

_____

May I quote from your responses to this survey in my book? The quote would be anonymous. Unless you want me to use initials, I will simply number all the survey responses, and cite to the response by its number.

_____ Yes you may quote from this.

_____ I would like you to use my initials, which are _____.

_____ I prefer that you cite the survey by its number.

APPENDIX B
A Sample of Disability Discrimination Cases Involving Mental Disabilities

The Americans With Disabilities Act, Title I

Acrophobia
> Forrisi v. Bowen, 794 F.2d 931 (4th Cir. 1986) (Rehabilitation Act)
> Lindenau v. Wortz Co., 2000 U.S. App. LEXIS 21415 (10th Cir. Aug. 23, 2000)

Adjustment Disorder With Mixed Emotional Features
> Stauffer v. Bayer Corp., 1997 WL 588890 (N.D. Ind. July 21, 1997)
> Stradley v. LaFourche Communications, 869 F. Supp. 442 (E.D. La. 1994) (although the plaintiff concedes that this disorder does not qualify under the ADA, he argues that the defendant regarded him as having depression; court finds a material dispute of fact on this question)
> *Wallis v. Runyon, No. 01950510 (EEOC, Nov. 13, 1995) (EEOC awards postal employee damages for discrimination on the basis of emotional disability and retaliation for filing EEO claim. EEOC rejects argument by Postal Service that Wallis did not prove damages because his pre-existing emotional condition caused the distress he claimed as damages from the discrimination)
> Witter v. Delta Airlines, 138 F.3d 1366 (11th Cir. 1998)

Adjustment Disorder With Depressive Features
> *Barton v. Tampa Electric Co., 1997 WL 128158 (M.D. Fla., Mar. 11, 1997) (later diagnoses include depression, bipolar disorder, and "possible schizoaffective disorder") (denying defendant's motion for summary judgment on discrimination claim even though plaintiff was on long-term disability and finding that defendant's actions may have contributed to or exacerbated plaintiff's mental disability)
> Wood v. County of Alameda, 1995 U.S. Dist. LEXIS 17514 (N.D. Cal. Nov. 17, 1995)

Adjustment Disorder
> *Presta v. SEPTA, 1998 U.S. Dist. LEXIS 8630 (E.D. Pa. June 11, 1998) (also anxiety disorder and posttraumatic stress disorder)
> *McKenzie v. Dovala, 2001 U.S. App. LEXIS 3844 (10th Cir. Mar. 13, 2001)

Cases marked with an asterisk indicate that the plaintiff prevailed in the particular motion before the court—usually defendant's motion to dismiss or motion for summary judgment. This does not mean that the plaintiff ultimately prevailed in the case, only that in the particular issue before the court, the plaintiff prevailed. The reader will note how rarely plaintiffs in Title I cases experience even this kind of limited victory.

Agoraphobia

    Mears v. Gulfstream Aerospace Corp., 905 F. Supp. 1075 (S.D. Ga. 1995), *aff'd*, 87 F.3d 1331 (11th Cir. 1996) (also "dythmia") [sic]

    *Ofat v. Ohio Civil Rights Commission, 1995 WL 310051 (Ohio App. May 17, 1995) (with panic disorder) (state law case)

    *Przybylak v. New York State Thruway Authority, No. 95-CV-0707E(F), 1997 WL 662346 (W.D. N.Y. Oct. 16, 1997) (also depression and panic disorder) (question whether collective bargaining agreement supersedes request for transfer; court refuses to dismiss because collective bargaining agreement is not in the record before it), *aff'd in part, vacated in part*, 198 F.3d 234 (2d Cir. 1999) (affirming dismissal of the case after stipulation between plaintiffs and defendants, but vacating trial court order setting out the terms of the stipulation as an inappropriate ruling on the lawfulness of the accommodations involved)

    Rio v. Runyon, 972 F. Supp. 1446 (S.D. Fla. 1997) (also clinical depression and anorexia nervosa) (hostile work environment)

Anorexia

    Morgan v. Hilti, Inc., 108 F.3d 1319 (10th Cir. 1997) (also depression) (employee terminated for excessive absenteeism, not discrimination because of her condition)

Anxiety Disorder

    Alba v. Upjohn Company, No. 95-12788-JLT, 1997 WL 136334 (D. Mass. Feb. 21, 1997) (also depression)

    Ali v. Brown, 998 F. Supp. 917 (N.D. Ill. 1998) (also depressed)

    Andrews v. United Way of Southwest Alabama, Inc., 2000 U.S. Dist. LEXIS 1969 (S.D. Ala., Jan. 26, 2000) (summary judgment granted, dismissed 2000 U.S. Dist. 8439) (S.D. Ala., June 5, 2000) (also depression)

    Bey v. City of New York, 1998 U.S. Dist. LEXIS 15522 (S.D. N.Y. Oct. 1, 1998) (also depressive disorder) dismissed 1999 U.S. Dist. LEXIS 113791 (S.D. N.Y. July 23, 1999)

    Bultemeyer v. Fort Wayne Community Schools, 100 F.3d 1281 (7th Cir. 1996) (also severe depression and schizophrenia)

    Childs v. National Jewish Center For Immunology and Respiratory Medicine, 129 F.3d 130 (10th Cir. 1997) (severe anxiety disorder)

    Cisneros v. Wilson, 226 F.3d 1113 (10th Cir. 2000) (also depression) (plaintiff failed to show she was a "qualified individual with a disability" under the ADA)

    Cody v. Cigna Health Care of St. Louis, 139 F.3d 595 (8th Cir. 1998) (fact that employer "offered" nurse with anxiety and depression medical leave and a psychiatric examination, did not prove that employer regarded her as disabled)

    *Criado v. IBM Corporation, 145 F.3d 437 (1st Cir. 1998) (also attention deficit disorder and depression) (plaintiff awarded $200,000 in compensatory damages and $250,000 in punitive damages; lowered to statutory cap of $300,000)

    Dee v. Odili Techs, 1999 Conn. Super. LEXIS 3120 (Conn. Super. Ct. Nov. 18, 1999) (also depression)

    *EEOC v. Staten Island Savings Bank, 207 F.3d 144 (2d Cir. 2000) (also depression) (insurance coverage for mental health conditions)

Emberger v. Deluxe Check Printers, WL 677149 (E.D. Pa. Oct. 30, 1997) (manic depression and anxiety) (hostile work environment claim loses; employee disobeys order to leave female employee alone)

Gaul v. Lucent Technologies, Inc., 134 F.3d 576 (3d Cir. 1998) (request to be transferred away from workers who caused him prolonged and inordinate stress was unreasonable as a matter of law: "ADA not intended to interfere with personnel decisions") (anxiety and depression)

Gonzagowski v. Widnall, 115 F.3d 744 (10th Cir. 1997)

Hess v. Allstate Ins. Company, 2000 U.S. Dist. LEXIS 12258 (D. Me. Aug. 2, 2000) (insurance coverage of mental health conditions)

Ketcher v. Wal-Mart Stores, Inc., 122 F. Supp. 2d 747 (S.D. Tex. 2000)

Kushner v. NationsBank of Texas, 1998 U.S. Dist. LEXIS 12708 (N.D. Tex. Aug. 12, 1998)

*Lally v. Commonwealth Edison, 1996 U.S. Dist. LEXIS 19386 (N.D. Ill. Dec. 19, 1996)

*Lewis v. Kmart Corp., 180 F.3d 166 (4th Cir. 1999) (also depression) (insurance coverage of mental health condition)

Linser v. Ohio Dep't of Mental Health, 2000 U.S. App. LEXIS 25644 (6th Cir. Oct. 6, 2000) (employee with anxiety disorder and depression failed to establish she was disabled under the ADA)

Menes v. CUNY University, 92 F. Supp. 2d 294 (S.D. N.Y. 2000) (also depression)

Moore v. Board of Education of Johnson City Schools, 134 F.3d 781 (6th Cir. 1998).

*Nash v. Chicago Transit Auth., 1998 U.S. Dist. LEXIS 12668 (N.D. Ill. Aug. 7, 1998) (defendant's motion to dismiss is denied) (also hypertension)

Querry v. Messar, 14 F. Supp. 2d 437 (S.D. N.Y. 1998) summary judgment granted in part, denied in part by, 66 F. Supp. 2d 5631 (S.D. N.Y. 1999)

*Presta v. Southeastern Pennsylvania Transportation Authority, 1998 U.S. Dist. LEXIS 8630 (E.D. Pa. June 11, 1998) (also adjustment disorder and posttraumatic stress disorder)

Rivera-Flores v. Bristol-Myers Squibb Caribbean, 112 F.3d 9 (1st Cir. 1997) (also posttraumatic stress disorder) (release of ADA claims approved by court)

Savoie v. Terrebone Parish Sch. Board, 2000 U.S. Dist. LEXIS 1223 (E.D. La., Feb. 4, 2000) (also depression, anxiety, and stress)

Shea v. Tisch, 870 F.2d 786 (1st Cir. 1989) (Rehabilitation Act case involving employee with anxiety disorder; no duty to assign to less stressful location, in part because of collective bargaining agreement)

Stola v. Joint Industry Board, 889 F. Supp. 133 (S.D. N.Y. 1995).

Thurston v. Henderson, 2000 U.S. Dist. LEXIS 2410 (D. Me. Jan. 5, 2000), aff'd, 230 F.3d 1347 (1st Cir. 2000) (also posttraumatic stress disorder)

*United States v. City and County of Denver, 49 F. Supp. 2d 1233 (D. Colo. 1999), aff'd in part, Davoll v. Webb 194 F.3d 1116 (10th Cir. 1999) (also depression)

*Wood v. County of Alameda, 1995 U.S. Dist. LEXIS 17514 (N.D. Cal. Nov. 20, 1995) (employee with anxiety and clinical depression wins a motion for preliminary injunction requiring the employer to reassign her to a vacant position, even though court finds that factual issue exists as to whether she has a disability under the ADA)

Aphasia

Cleveland v. Policy Management Sys. Corp., 526 U.S. 795 (1999) (application for disability benefits does not create a presumption that an individual is not otherwise qualified for employment under the ADA)

DeMarv v. Car-Freshner Corp., 49 F. Supp. 2d 84 (N.D. N.Y. 1999)

Paul v. Wisconsin Department of Industry, Labor & Human Relations, 1999 U.S. App. LEXIS 20362 (7th Cir. Aug. 24, 1999)

Schneider v. City and County of San Francisco, 1999 U.S. Dist. LEXIS 3001 (N.D. Cal. Mar. 9, 1999)

Williams v. Health Reach Network, 2000 U.S. Dist. LEXIS 9695 (D. Me. Feb. 22, 2000)

Apraxia

*Arneson v. Sullivan, 946 F.2d 90 (8th Cir. 1991) (moving employee to a location that is less distracting is a reasonable accommodation)

Attention Deficit Disorder

*Criado v. International Business Machines Corp., 145 F.3d 437 (1st Cir. 1998), 1998 U.S. App. LEXIS 11743 (1st Cir. June 18, 1998) (also attention deficit disorder and depression) (plaintiff awarded $200,000 in compensatory damages and $250,000 in punitive damages; lowered to statutory cap of $300,000)

*Davidson v. Midelfort Clinic Ltd., 133 F.3d 499 (7th Cir. 1998) (sufficient factual questions on whether plaintiff had a record of disability to avoid summary judgment)

Lancaster v. City of Mobile Alabama, 1996 WL 741371 (S.D. Ala. Aug 14, 1996), aff'd, 110 F.3d 798 (11th Cir. 1997)

*Menkowitz v. Pottstown Memorial Medical Center, 154 F.3d 113 (3d Cir. 1998)

Attention Deficit Hyperactivity Disorder

Bercovitch v. Baldwin School, Inc., 133 F.3d 141 (1st Cir. 1997)

Autism

EEOC v. CEC Entertainment, Inc., 2000 U.S. Dist. LEXIS 13934 (W.D. Wisc. Mar. 14, 2000) (defendant's motion for judgment was denied; the evidence was sufficient to support the jury's determination that plaintiff's employee was a qualified individual and was discriminated against because of his disability)

Taylor v. Food World, Inc., 133 F.3d 1419 (11th Cir. 1998)

Bipolar Disorder (or "Manic–Depression")

Alexander v. Margolis, 921 F. Supp. 482 (W.D. Mich. 1995), aff'd, 98 F.3d 1341 (6th Cir. 1996)

Bagwell v. Wake County, 1999 U.S. App. LEXIS 4820 (4th Cir. March 22, 1999)

Bennett v. State Farm Mutual Automobile Insurance Company, 1994 WL 728282 (N.D. Ohio 1994)

Birchem v. Knights of Columbus, 116 F.3d 310 (8th Cir. 1997)

Brundage v. Hann, 57 Cal. App. 4th 228, 66 Cal. Rptr. 2d 830 (Cal. App. 1997) (woman did not show employer knew of her condition when she was fired; reinstatement not a reasonable accommodation)

Callison v. Charleston Area Medical Center, Inc., 909 F. Supp. 391 (S.D. W.Va. 1995) (ERISA preempts claims that discriminatory discharge deprived employee of disability benefits)

Carrozza v. Howard County, Md., 45 F.3d 425 (4th Cir. 1995)

Christopher v. Adam's Mark Hotels, 137 F.3d 1069 (8th Cir. 1998), *cert. denied*, 119 S. Ct. 62 (1998)

Crandall v. Paralyzed Veterans of America, 146 F.3d 894 (D.C. Cir. 1998)

*Duda v. Board of Education of Franklin Park Public School District No. 84, 133 F.3d 1054 (7th Cir. 1998)

Dudley v. Augusta School Department, 23 F. Supp. 2d 85 (D. Me. 1998) (also stress)

Equal Employment Opportunity Commission v. CNA Insurance Companies, 96 F.3d 1039 (7th Cir. 1996) (insurance coverage of mental health conditions) (also depression)

EEOC v. Bath Iron Works, Corp., 1999 U.S. Dist. LEXIS 10600 (D. Me. Feb. 8, 1999), adopted summary judgment granted 1999 U.S. Dist. LEXIS 10596 (D. Me. Mar. 19, 1999) (insurance coverage of mental health conditions)

*EEOC v. Union Carbide Chemicals Plastics Company, Inc., 1995 WL 495910 (E.D. La. Aug. 18, 1995) (court rejected employer's argument that because employee controlled his condition with lithium he was not disabled)

Emberger v. Deluxe Check Printers, 1997 WL 677149 (E.D. Pa. Oct. 30, 1997) (manic depression and anxiety) (hostile work environment claim loses; employee disobeys order to leave female employee alone)

Esfahani v. Medical College of Pennsylvania, 919 F. Supp. 832 (E.D. Pa. 1996)

F.F. v. City of Laredo, 912 F. Supp. 248 (S.D. Tex. 1995) (bus driver could not perform essential functions of position)

Fitts v. Federal National Mortgage Assn., 2001 U.S. App. LEXIS 448 (D.C. Cir. Jan. 12, 2001) (also depression)

Glowacki v. Buffalo General Hospital, 2 F. Supp. 2d 346 (W.D. N.Y. 1997) (not a disability when it did not limit major life activities)

Green v. Geo. L. Smith II Ga. World Congress Ctr. Authority, 987 F. Supp. 1481 (N.D. Ga. 1997) (also schizophrenia) (if conduct occasioning discharge occurs before employer has knowledge of disability, no ADA liability)

Hess v. Allstate Ins. Company, 2000 U.S. Dist. LEXIS 12258 (D. Me. Aug. 2, 2000) (also depression and panic disorder)

Hill v. North Carolina Department of Corrections, 1999 U.S. Dist. LEXIS 5639 (E.D. N.C. Feb. 24, 1999), *aff'd*, 201 F.3d 436 (4th Cir. 1999) (table case) (also chronic fatigue syndrome)

Hoeller v. Eaton, 149 F.3d 621 (7th Cir. 1998) (plaintiff not substantially limited in one or more major life activities)

Hogarth v. Thornburgh, 833 F. Supp. 1077 (S.D. N.Y. 1993)

Husowitz v. Runyon, 942 F. Supp. 822 (E.D. N.Y. 1996) (plaintiff's termination was because of his disability; court rejects conduct/disability dichotomy but finds plaintiff was not otherwise qualified for his position)

Keoughan v. Delta Airlines, 113 F.3d 1246 (10th Cir. 1997) (because plaintiff failed to take her lithium, district court found her not qualified; appeals court affirms on basis that employee was not qualified because she missed too much work)

Landefeld v. Marion General Hospital, 994 F.2d 1178 (6th Cir. 1993) (Rehabilitation Act)

Lewis v. Zilog, 908 F. Supp. 931 (N.D. Ga. 1995), *aff'd*, 87 F.3d 1331 (11th Cir. 1996)

Maes v. Henderson, 33 F. Supp. 2d 1281 (D. Nev. 1991) (also depression)

Matzo v. Postmaster General, 685 F. Supp. 260 (D. D.C. 1987), *aff'd*, 861 F.2d 1290 (D.C. Cir. 1988) (Nov. 14, 1988) (Rehabilitation Act)

Mawson v. U.S. West Bus. Resources, 23 F. Supp. 2d 1204 (D. Colo. 1998)

McConnell v. Pioneer Hi-Bred International, 2000 U.S. Dist. LEXIS 3335 (D. S.D. Jan. 24, 2000) (also depression)

Miller v. Runyon, 77 F.3d 189 (7th Cir. 1996), *cert. denied*, 519 U.S. 937 (1996) (manic depressive disorder insufficient to toll statute of limitations on employment discrimination charge)

Mork v. Manpower, 1998 U.S. Dist. LEXIS 11312 (N.D. Ill. July 23, 1998) (also attention deficit disorder) (employee did not show he was harassed on the job and was not disabled when his affidavit contradicted his deposition testimony about his ability to perform various kinds of work)

Office of the Senate Sergeant at Arms v. Office of Senate Fair Employment Practices, 95 F.3d 1102 (Fed. Cir. 1996)

Passamonti v. Itochu International, 1998 WL 107165 (S.D. N.Y. Mar. 11, 1998), (ADA liability under Title I for individual defendants; cannot bring administrative proceeding and judicial proceeding at the same time)

Przbylak v. New York State Thruway, 1996 WL 107125 (W.D. N.Y. Feb. 21, 1996) (also agoraphobia and panic disorder) (question whether collective bargaining agreement supersedes request for transfer; court refuses to dismiss because collective bargaining agreement is not in the record before it), *vacated in part and remanded*, 198 F.3d 234 (2d Cir. 1999)

Scott v. American Airlines, Inc., 1997 WL 278129 (N.D. Tex. May 15, 1997) (earlier diagnosed as depression and obsessive compulsive disorder) (arrival at work on time essential function of job; McDonnell-Douglas Title VII analysis appropriate in ADA cases; employer not liable for failure to accommodate employee if employee does not specify accommodation she needs)

Seaman v. C.S.P.H., Inc., 1997 WL 538751 (N.D. Tex. August 25, 1997), *aff'd*, 79 F.3d 297 (5th Cir. 1999)

*Stewart v. Bally Total Fitness, 2000 U.S. Dist. LEXIS 10047 (E.D. Pa. July 20, 2000) (also depression, stress)

Taylor v. The Principal Financial Group, Inc., 93 F.3d 155 (5th Cir. 1996) (must advise employer not only of diagnosis but of limitations caused by disability in order to be entitled to accommodation)

*Taylor v. Phoenixville School District, 998 F. Supp. 561 (E.D. Pa. 1998), 12 N.D.L.R. 142 (E.D. Pa. 1998) *rev'd and remanded*, Taylor v. Phoenixville School District, 184 F.3d 296 (3d Cir. Pa. 1999) on remand, Taylor v. Phoenixville School District, 113 F. Supp. 2d 770 (E.D. Pa. 2000)

Threatt v. County of Mecklenburg, 1998 U.S. Dist. LEXIS 8081 (W.D. N.C. Apr. 7, 1998)

Van Stan v. Fancy Colours and Co., 125 F.3d 563 (7th Cir. Sept. 15, 1997)

Wallin v. Minnesota Dept. of Corrections, 153 F.3d 681 (8th Cir. 1998) (depression and alcoholism)

Walton v. Mental Health Association of Southeastern Pennsylvania, 168 F.3d 661 (3d Cir. 1998) (depression) (employee loses because her absences were causing decline in program and no reasonable accommodation was possible) (also agoraphobia and depression)

Webb v. Mercy Hospital, 102 F.3d 958 (8th Cir. 1996)

Wilking v. County of Ramsey, 983 F. Supp. 848 (D. Minn. 1997), *aff'd*, 153 F.3d 869 (8th Cir. 1998)

Witter v. Delta Air Lines, Inc., 138 F.3d 1366 (11th Cir. 1998) (plaintiff who was permanently grounded as a pilot not substantially limited because "piloting airplanes" too narrow a range of jobs to constitute a "class of jobs")

Wooten v. Acme Steel, 986 F. Supp. 524 (N.D. Ill. 1997) (reinstatement not a reasonable accommodation as a matter of law under the ADA)

*Yount v. S & A Restaurant Corp., 1997 WL 573463 (N.D. Tex. Sept. 8, 1997)

Zihala v. Illinois Department of Public Health, 1999 U.S. Dist LEXIS 2445 (N.D. Ill. Feb. 26, 1999)

Borderline Personality Disorder

Hatfield v. Quantum Chemical, 920 F. Supp. 108 (S.D. Tex. 1996)

Houck v. City of Prairie Village, 978 F. Supp. 1397 (D. Kan. 1997) (also post-traumatic stress disorder, depression, psychosis from mania, and others), *aff'd*, 166 F.3d 347 (10th Cir. 1998)

Marshall v. Metal Container Corporation, 1998 U.S. App. LEXIS 27863 (7th Cir. Oct. 20 1998) (also dissociative identity disorder and major depression) (employer had sufficient grounds for termination; therefore, court did not reach the issue of whether she was disabled under the ADA)

Weigert v. Georgetown University, 120 F. Supp. 2d 1 (D. D.C. 2000)

Bulimia

Equal Employment Opportunity Commission v. Amego, 110 F.3d 135 (1st Cir. 1997)

Claustrophobia

Commission on Human Rights v. General Dynamics, 1991 Conn. Super. LEXIS 2704 (Nov. 22, 1991)

Neveau v. Boise Cascade Corp., 902 F. Supp. 207 (D. Ore. 1995) (state disability discrimination law)

Chronic Fatigue Syndrome

Dufresne v. Venneman, 114 F.3d 9525 (9th Cir. 1997)

Durley v. APAC, Inc., 236 F.3d 651 (11th Cir. 2000)

Kennedy v. Applause, Inc., 90 F.3d 1477 (9th Cir. 1996)

Martinez v. PacifiCorp, 2000 U.S. App. LEXIS 8542 (10th Cir. April 28, 2000)

Depression (or Depressive Disorder)

Adams v. Rochester General Hospital, 977 F. Supp. 226 (W.D. N.Y. 1997)

Allen v. GTE Mobile Communications Service Corp., 1997 WL 148670 (N.D. Ga. Feb. 26, 1997), 6 AD Cases 1063

Bacon v. Great Plains Manufacturing, Inc., 958 F. Supp. 523 (D. Kan. 1997) (no liability when employer did not know about plaintiff's depression–problem with supervisor)

Barfield v. Bell South Telecom, Inc., 886 F. Supp. 1321 (S.D. Miss. 1995)

Bazile v. AT&T Bell Laboratories, Inc., 1997 WL 600702 (N.D. Tex. Sept. 19, 1997) (disability benefits receipt disqualified plaintiff from claiming that he was otherwise qualified), *aff'd*, 142 F.3d 1279 (5th Cir. 1998)

Boldini v. Postmaster General U.S. Postal Service, 928 F. Supp. 125 (D. N.H. 1995) (Rehabilitation Act)

Bombard v. Fort Wayne Newspapers, Inc., 92 F.3d 560 (7th Cir. 1996)

*Boob v. Northwestern Mutual Life Insurance Company, 77 F. Supp. 2d 211 (D. N.H. 1999)

Breiland v. Advance Circuits, Inc., 976 F. Supp. 858 (D. Minn. 1997) (also schizoid personality disorder) (plaintiff found not to be "substantially impaired in a major life activity"; court explicitly rejects EEOC Compliance Manual's listing of "interacting with others" as a major life activity; in addition, court finds that placing disciplinary notes in plaintiff's employment file is not sufficient adverse employment action to support any claim for retaliation)

Brown v. Northern Trust Bank, 1997 WL 543098 (N.D. Ill. Sept. 2, 1997)

Brumley v. Pena, 62 F.3d 277 (8th Cir. 1995), *reh'g en banc denied*, Sept. 10, 1995 (severe depression)

Bultemeyer v. Fort Wayne Community Schools, 100 F.3d 1281 (7th Cir. 1996) (also anxiety attacks and schizophrenia)

Bunevith v. CVS Pharmacy, 925 F. Supp. 89 (D. Mass. 1996) (employer did not know about depression, and in any event, plaintiff did not have a disability that substantially impaired life activity)

Burch v. Coca-Cola Co., 119 F.3d 305 (5th Cir. 1997) (also alcoholism)

*Carlin v. Trustees of Boston University, 907 F. Supp. 509 (D. Mass. 1995) (B.U. refused to readmit graduate student in pastoral psychology after leave of absence for depression; court denied defendant's motion for summary judgment, finding that student had provided sufficient evidence of pretext to raise material dispute of fact)

Childs v. National Jewish Center For Immunology and Respiratory Medicine, 129 F.3d 130 (10th Cir. 1997)

Cody v. Cigna Health Care of St. Louis, Inc., 139 F.3d 595 (8th Cir. 1998) (nurse with anxiety and depression was "offered" medical leave and a psychiatric examination; this action did not prove that employer regarded her as disabled)

*Cornwell & Taylor, LLP v. Moore, 2000 Minn. App. LEXIS 1317 (Ct. of Appeals of Minn. Dec. 22, 2000) (defendant had duty to reasonably accommodate plaintiff's husband's handicap) (also schizoaffective disorder)

*Criado v. IBM, 145 F.3d 437 (1st Cir. 1998) (also attention deficit disorder and depression) (plaintiff awarded $200,000 in compensatory damages and $250,000 in punitive damages; lowered to statutory cap of $300,000)

Debose v. Nebraska, 207 F.3d 1020 (8th Cir. 1999)

*Dertz v. City of Chicago, 1997 WL 85169 (N.D. Ill. Feb. 24, 1997) (issues of material fact as to whether the city perceived officer treated for depression as disabled and whether he was otherwise qualified for active duty as a policeman; also issues of retaliation for bringing this litigation)

Dikcis v. Indopco, 1998 WL 13323 (N.D. Ill. Jan. 7, 1998)

Dikcis v. Nalco Chemical Company, F. Supp. 669 (N.D. Ill. 1997)

*Doe v. Town of Seymour, 1998 WL 26410 (D. Conn. Jan. 16, 1998) (also dysthymic disorder and alcoholism) (refusing to grant summary judgment on the question of whether reasonable accommodations were available for plaintiff's shift requirements)

EEOC v. Aramark Corp., 208 F.3d 266 (D.C. Cir. 2000)

EEOC v. CEC Entertainment, Inc., 2000 U.S. Dist. LEXIS 13934 (W.D. Wis. Mar. 14, 2000)

EEOC v. CNA Insurance Companies, 96 F.3d 1039 (7th Cir. 1996) (and bipolar disorder) (employee not a qualified individual with a disability under the ADA)

Equal Employment Opportunity Commission v. Amego, 110 F.3d 135 (1st Cir. 1997) (plaintiff loses)

Fitzgerald v. Allegheny Corp., 904 F. Supp. 223 (S.D. N.Y. 1995) (New York Human Rights Law)

Formosa v. Miami Dade Community College, 990 F. Supp. 1433 (S.D. Fla. 1997) (college secretary who attempted suicide not disabled because her onset of depression was limited to interaction with a particular supervisor)

*Fromm-Vane v. Lawnwood Medical Center, Inc., 995 F. Supp. 1471 (S.D. Fla. 1997) (if employee requests accommodation after decision to terminate but before effective date of termination, employer still may have duty to respond to request for accommodation)

Gaul v. Lucent, 134 F.3d 576 (3d Cir. 1998) (anxiety and depression)

*Gile v. United Airlines, Inc., 95 F.3d 492 (7th Cir. 1996) (reassignment to a completely different position can be a reasonable accommodation)

Gillette v. City of Farmers Branch, 2001 Tex. App. LEXIS 391 (Tex. Ct. App. 5th Cir. Jan. 19, 2001)

Gruber v. Entergy Corp., 1997 WL 149966 (E.D. La. March 24, 1997) (employer knew of depression, but not of limitations resulting from it; therefore, plaintiff loses)

Guice-Mills v. Derwinski, 967 F.2d 794 (2d Cir. 1992) (head nurse not otherwise qualified for position; accommodations offered by VA were reasonable) (Rehabilitation Act)

Hatfield v. Quantum Chemical Corporation, 920 F. Supp. 108 (S.D. Tex. 1996) (plaintiff loses)

*Haysman v. Food Lion, Inc., 893 F. Supp. 1092 (S.D. Ga. 1995) (also posttraumatic stress disorder and somatization) (plaintiff loses all claims on summary judgment except harassment but is permitted to proceed with that claim in light of evidence that plaintiff was subjected to "negative stereotyping, threats, verbal abuse and other conduct which created an intimidating and hostile environment")

Henry v. Guest Services, Inc., 902 F. Supp. 245 (D. D.C. 1995), aff'd, 98 F.3d 646 (D.C. Cir. 1996)

Hetreed v. Allstate Insurance Company, 1999 U.S. Dist. LEXIS 7219 (N.D. Ill. May 11, 1999) (also posttraumatic stress disorder)

Hollestelle v. Metropolitan Washington Airports Authority, 145 F.3d 1324 (4th Cir. 1998) (depressed employee's chronic tardiness made him unable to perform essential functions of job; employer's attempts to accommodate were "extraordinary")

Horton v. Delta Air Lines, Inc., 1993 WL 356894 (N.D. Ca. Sept. 3, 1993)

Hunt-Golliday v. Metropolitan Water Reclamation District of Greater Chicago, 104 F.3d 1004 (7th Cir. 1997)

Jerina v. Richardson Automotive, Inc., 960 F. Supp. 106 (N.D. Tex. 1997) (also chronic fatigue syndrome and panic disorder) (employee not disabled although he died during pendency of litigation)

Johnson v. Boardman Petroleum, 923 F. Supp. 1563 (S.D. Ga. 1996)

Johnson v. Foulds, 1996 U.S. Dist. LEXIS 9596 (N.D. Ill. July 9, 1996)

Johnston v. Morrison, Inc., 849 F. Supp. 777 (N.D. Ala. 1994) (waitress who experienced "meltdown" when restaurant became crowded could not perform essential functions of job)

Johnson v. New York Medical College, 1997 U.S. Dist. LEXIS 14150 (S.D. N.Y. Sept. 18, 1997) (fact that plaintiff was hospitalized for two weeks for depression and was taking medication for depression insufficient to support finding of "substantial impairment of major life activities")

Katz v. Metropolitan Life Insurance, 1998 WL 132945 (S.D. N.Y. Mar. 20, 1998) (employer offered reasonable accommodation of job sharing; employee terminated because of poor performance, not for discriminatory reasons)

Kolivas v. Credit Agricole, 125 F.3d 844 (2d Cir. 1997) (employer did not know of depression until after employee was fired for "poor attitude")

Kotlowski v. Eastman Kodak Company, 922 F. Supp. 790 (W.D. N.Y. 1996)

Krocka v. James Bransfield and the City of Chicago, 969 F. Supp. 1073 (N.D. Ill. 1997)

Larkin v. CIBA Vision Corporation, 858 F. Supp. 1572 (N.D. Ga. 1994) (also posttraumatic stress disorder and panic disorder) (answering phones essential function of job; employer sufficiently offered accommodations)

Lawson v. CSX Trans. Inc., 101 F. Supp. 2d 1089 (S.D. Ind. 1999)

Lee v. Publix Supermarkets, 1998 U.S. Dist. LEXIS 8921 (N.D. Fla. March 16, 1998) (later diagnosed with bipolar disorder)

Liff v. Secretary of Transportation, 1994 WL 579912 (D. D.C. Sept. 22, 1994)

*Martini v. Boeing Company, 945 P.2d 248 (Wash. Ct. App. 1997) (state antidiscrimination law) (employee wins jury trial; upheld on appeal except that employer was entitled to subrogation of future workmen's compensation payments)

McClain v. Southwest Steel, 940 F. Supp. 295 (N.D. Okla. June 25, 1996) (plaintiff with depression and high blood pressure survives motion for summary judgment on discriminatory discharge and FMLA claims, loses on hostile environment claim when the fact that co-workers called him "crazy" or "a lunatic" and talk about people on Prozac or going to a mental health institution and that his supervisor asked him "what the f***'s wrong with you?" did not create a hostile environment as a matter of law)

Mendez v. Gearan, 947 F. Supp. 1364 (N.D. Cal. 1996) (Rehabilitation Act, rather than Administrative Procedures Act, applies to Peace Corps applicant's challenge to Peace Corps' refusal to hire her because she was taking antidepressant drugs) *summary judgment granted in part denied in part*, 956 F. Supp. 1520 (N.D. Cal. 1997)

Miles v. General Services Administration, 1995 WL 766013 (E.D. Pa. Dec. 27, 1995) (also diabetes and carpal tunnel syndrome) (employee fired for misconduct making him not otherwise qualified for the position)

Moore v. The Board of Education of Johnson City Schools, 134 F.3d 781 (6th Cir. 1998)

Morgan v. Hilti, Inc., 108 F.3d 1319 (10th Cir. 1997) (also depression) (employee terminated for excessive absenteeism, not discrimination because of her condition)

Morrill v. Lorillard Tobacco Company, 2000 U.S. Dist. LEXIS 18810 (D. N.H. Dec. 7, 2000) (also posttraumatic disorder and dissociative disorder)

Morton v. GTE North, Inc., 922 F. Supp. 1169 (N.D. Tex. 1996), *aff'd*, 114 F.3d 1182 (5th Cir. 1997), *cert. denied*, 522 U.S. 880 (1997) (N.D. Tex. Jan. 23, 1996)

Nave v. Wooldridge Construction of Pennsylvania, 1997 U.S. Dist. LEXIS 9203 (E.D. Pa. June 30, 1997) (plaintiff with stage II-A Hodgkin's disease, for which he received radiation therapy and spent two weeks in the hospital undergoing various surgical procedures, was diagnosed with major depression secondary to the radiation; plaintiff found not to be disabled) (depression and Hodgkin's disease)

Office of the Senate Sergeant at Arms v. Office of Senate Fair Employment Practices, 95 F.3d 1102 (Fed. Cir. 1996) (depression and alcoholism—employee not entitled to accommodation when he did not disclose his disability before disciplinary action being instituted against him)

Olson v. General Electric Astrospace, 101 F.3d 947 (3d Cir. 1996) (also multiple personality disorder and posttraumatic stress disorder)

Overton v. Reilly, 977 F.2d 1190 (7th Cir. 1992) (Rehabilitation Act)

Pack v. K-Mart, 166 F.3d 1300 (10th Cir. 1999) (sleeping is a major life activity but concentration is not; plaintiff did not present sufficient evidence that her depression substantially limited her in sleeping), *cert. denied*, 528 U.S. 811 (1999)

Pelletier v. Fleet Fin. Group, Inc., 2000 U.S. Dist. LEXIS 16456 (D. N.H. Sept. 19, 2000) (also panic disorder)

*Poindexter v. Atchison, Topeka and Santa Fe Railroad Company, 914 F. Supp. 454 (D. Kan. 1996) (also panic disorder and separation anxiety) 168 F.3d 1228 (10th Cir. 1999)

*Pritchard v. Southern Company Services, 92 F.3d 1130 (11th Cir. 1996) (court revives ADA claims)

Przybylak v. New York State Thruway Authority, No. 95-CV-0707E(F), 8 N.D.L.R. 3 (W.D. N.Y. 1996), 1996 WL 107125 (W.D. N.Y. Feb. 21, 1996) (also agoraphobia and panic disorder) (question whether collective bargaining agreement supersedes request for transfer; court refuses to dismiss because collective bargaining agreement is not in the record before it) vacated 198 F.3d 234 (2d Cir. 1999)

Ramsey v. United Airlines, Inc., 2000 U.S. Dist. LEXIS 13775 (N.D. Ill. Sept. 14, 2000).

Rivera-Flores v. Bristol Myers Squibb, 112 F.3d 9 (1st Cir. 1997) (upholds waiver of any legal claim as including ADA claim even though employee was "'very depressed'" at the time he signed the waiver)

Rizzo v. Children's World Learning Centers, Inc., 173 F.3d 254 (5th Cir. 1999), *cert. denied*, 121 S. Ct. 382 (2000)

Sarko v. Penn-Del Directory Company, 968 F. Supp. 1026 (E.D. Pa. 1997)

Sarver v. BellSouth Telecommunications, 1996 WL 478871 (E.D. La. Aug. 22, 1996) (employee's waiver of all termination-related claims against employer barred ADA claim, noting that employee did not return lump sum payment employer sent him)

*Sawhill v. Medical College of Pennsylvania, 1996 WL 509844 (E.D. Pa. Aug. 30 1996) (statute of limitations extended because clinically depressed psychologist did not know discharge was disability related until deadline had passed)

Schneider v. City and County of San Francisco, 1999 U.S. Dist. LEXIS 3001 (N.D. Cal. Mar. 10, 1999) (also attention deficit disorder/hyperactivity)

Schwertfager v. City of Boynton Beach, 42 F. Supp. 2d 1347 (S.D. Fla. 1999)

Scott v. American Airlines, 1997 WL 278129 (N.D. Tex. May 15, 1997) (early diagnosis, along with obsessive compulsive disorder; later diagnosed as "manic depression") (arrival at work on time essential function of job; McDonnell-Douglas Title VII analysis appropriate in ADA cases; employer not liable for failure to accommodate employee if employee does not specify accommodation she needs)

*Scott v. Leavenworth Unified Sch. Dist., 1999 U.S. Dist. LEXIS 20053 (D. Kan. Dec. 23, 1999)

*Senate Sergeant at Arms v. Senate Fair Employment Practices, 95 F.3d 1102 (Fed. Cir. 1996)

*Shannon v. City of Philadelphia, 1999 U.S. Dist. LEXIS 2428 (E.D. Pa. Mar. 5, 1999) summary judgment granted, 1999 U.S. Dist. LEXIS 18089 (E.D. Pa. Nov. 23, 1999).

Siemon v. AT&T Corp., 117 F.3d 1173 (10th Cir. 1997)

Simmerman v. Hardee's Food Systems, Inc., 1996 WL 131948 (E.D. Pa. March 22, 1996), *aff'd*, 118 F.3d 1578 (3d Cir. 1997) (E.D. Pa. 1996) (ability to work 50-hour week and multiple shifts is essential function of job)

Smith v. Blue Cross Blue Shield of Kansas, Inc., 894 F. Supp. 1463 (D. Kan. 1995), *aff'd*, 102 F.3d 1075 (10th Cir. 1996), *cert. denied*, 522 U.S. 811 (1997), 7 N.D.L.R. 152 (D. Kan. 1995) (individual who was depressed and under stress and said she was completely unable to work was not a qualified individual)

Snead v. Metropolitan Prop. & Cas. Ins. Company, 2001 U.S. App. LEXIS 853 (9th Cir. Jan. 23, 2001) (also posttraumatic stress disorder)

Staffier v. Sandoz, 78 F.3d 577 (1st Cir. 1996), No. 95-2154 (1st Cir. Feb. 16, 1996) (employer can request medical clearance after worker absent from work for nine years due to depression and emotional stress)

Stewart v. County of Brown et al., 86 F.3d 107 (7th Cir. 1996)

Stradley v. LaFourche Comm. Inc., 869 F. Supp. 442 (E.D. La. 1994)

Sturm v. UAL Corp., 2000 U.S. Dist. LEXIS 13331 (D. N.J. Sept. 5, 2000)

Thompson v. Warner Lambert Company, 1995 WL 864544 (E.D. Mich. Dec. 15, 1995)

Thompson v. City of Arlington, Texas, 838 F. Supp. 1137 (N.D. Tex. 1993)

Tumbler v. American Trading and Production Corp., 1997 WL 230819 (E.D. Pa. May 1, 1997)

Walton v. Mental Health Association of Southeastern Pennsylvania, 1997 WL 717053 (E.D. Pa. Nov. 17, 1997) (depression) (employee loses because her absences were causing decline in program and no reasonable accommodation was possible), *aff'd*, 168 F.3d 661 (3d Cir. 1999)

Webb v. Baxter Health Care Corp., 57 F.3d 1067 (4th Cir. June 13, 1995) (plaintiff loses on ADA claims; court revives sex discrimination claims)

Webb v. Mercy Hospital, F.3d 958 LEXIS 32671 (8th Cir. 1996)

Weyer v. Twentieth-Century Fox Film Corp., 198 F.3d 1104 (9th Cir. 2000)

Williams v. Health Reach Network, 2000 U.S. Dist. LEXIS 9695 (D. Me. Feb. 22, 2000) (also stress)

*Williamson v. International Paper Company, 85 F. Supp. 2d 1184 (S.D. Ala. 1999), motion granted 85 F. Supp. 2d 1999 (S.D. Ala. 1999); judgment entered, 2000 U.S. Dist. LEXIS 2473 (S.D. Ala. Jan. 27, 2000)

Wilson v. Globe Specialty Prods., 117 F. Supp. 2d 92 (D. Mass. 2000)

Wisniewski v. Ameritech, 1996 WL 501737 (N.D. Ill. 1996), 1996 U.S. Dist. LEXIS 12822 (N.D. Ill. Sept. 3, 1996) (no indication that depression substantially impaired major life activities)

*Wood v. County of Alameda, 875 F. Supp. 659 (N.D. Cal. 1995), 1995 U.S. Dist. LEXIS 17514 (N.D. Cal. Nov. 20, 1995) (employee with anxiety and clinical depression wins a motion for preliminary injunctive relief requiring the employer to reassign her to a vacant position, even though court finds that factual issue exists as to whether she has a disability under the ADA)

Wallin v. Minnesota Dept. of Corrections, 153 F.3d 681 (8th Cir. 1998) (depression and alcoholism)

Wilking v. County of Ramsey, 983 F. Supp. 848 (D. Minn. 1997), *aff'd*, 153 F.3d 869 (8th Cir. 1998)

Wooten v. Acme Steel, 986 F. Supp. 524 (N.D. Ill. 1997) (reinstatement not a reasonable accommodation as a matter of law under the ADA)

Depressive Neurosis

Kemer v. Johnson, 900 F. Supp. 677 (S.D. N.Y. 1995), *aff'd*, 101 F.3d 683 (2d Cir. 1996), *cert. denied*, 519 U.S. 985 (1996) (and schizotypal disorder)

Dysthmia

Krocka v. James Bransfield and the City of Chicago, 969 F. Supp. 1073 (N.D. Ill. 1997)

Mears v. Gulfstream Aerospace Corp., 905 F. Supp. 1075 (S.D. Ga. 1995), *aff'd*, 87 F.3d 1331 (11th Cir. 1996) ("dythmia," also agoraphobia)

Soileau v. Guilford of Maine, 928 F. Supp. 37 (D. Maine 1996), *aff'd*, 105 F.3d 12 (1st Cir. 1997)

Wellman v. Wheeling and Lake Erie Railway, 11 N.D.L.R. 254, 134 F.3d 373 (6th Cir. 1998), No. 97-3084, 1998 WL 25005 (6th Cir. Jan. 12, 1998) (employee loses because he fails to show he was replaced and because his poor decision making and insufficient work habits were sufficient reason for his termination)

Explosive Personality Disorder

Mazzarella v. United States Postal Service, 5 N.D.L.R. 48 (1994), 849 F. Supp. 89 (D. Mass. 1994) *aff'd*, 185 F.3d 885 (Fed. Cir. 1999), *cert. denied*, 528 U.S. 905 (1999)

Learning Disability

Anderson v. General Motors Corporation, No. 96-2090-GTV, 1992 WL 279818 (E.D. Mich. Aug. 10, 1992), *aff'd*, 991 F.2d 794 (6th Cir. 1993)

Bermer v. Moskowitz, 117 F. Supp. 2d 126 (D. Conn. 1999)

Gonzales v. National Bd. of Med. Examiners, 225 F.3d 620 (6th Cir. 2000)

*Haswell v. Marshall Field & Company, 16 F. Supp. 2d (N.D. Ill. 1998)

Killculler v. New York State DOL, 205 F.3d 77 (2d Cir. 2000)

Lancaster v. City of Mobile, Alabama (S.D. Ala. Aug 15, 1996), 1996 WL 741371 (S.D. Ala. Aug. 15, 1996), 5 A.D. Cases 1845, *aff'd*, 110 F.3d 798 (11th Cir. 1997)

Lane v. Wal-Mart Stores, Inc., 2000 U.S. Dist. LEXIS 13935 (D. Md. Aug. 28, 2000)

Lewis v. Aetna Life Ins. Company, 7 F. Supp. 2d 743 (E.D. Va. 1998) (plaintiff entitled to continued payment of monthly disability benefits as long as plaintiff remains disabled within the meaning of the plan, until the age of 65)

Matthew v. Kennecott Copper Corp., 2000 U.S. App. LEXIS 3078 (10th Cir. Feb. 28, 2000)

Schneider v. City and County of San Francisco, 1999 U.S. Dist. LEXIS 3001 (N.D. Cal. Mar. 9, 1999)

*Walstead v. Woodbury County, 113 F. Supp. 2d 1318 (N.D. Iowa 2000) (plaintiff had a genuine issue regarding her impairment substantially limiting the major life activity of learning, reading, thinking, and concentrating)

Multiple Personality Disorder

Doe v. County of Milwaukee, 871 F. Supp. 1072 (E.D. Wisc. 1995)

Olson v. General Electric Astrospace, 101 F.3d 947 (3d Cir. 1996) (also depression and posttraumatic stress disorder)

"Nervous Breakdown"

Glidden v. County of Monroe, 950 F. Supp. 73 (W.D. N.Y.)

Leland v. U.S. Bank N.A., 1999 U.S. Dist. LEXIS 15344 (D. Ore. Sept. 22, 1999)

"Nervous Disorder"

Horton v. Board of Trustees of Community College Dist. No. 508, 1996 U.S. Dist. LEXIS 6879 (N.D. Ill. May 16, 1996), *aff'd*, 107 F.3d 873, 1997 WL 66514 (7th Cir. Ill. Feb. 7, 1997)

Obsessive–Compulsive Disorder

Childs v. National Jewish Center For Immunology and Respiratory Medicine, 129 F.3d 130 (10th Cir. 1997)

Newberry v. East Texas State University, 161 F.3d 276 (5th Cir. 1998)

Scott v. American Airlines, 1997 WL 278129 (N.D. Tex. May 15, 1997) (early diagnosis, along with depression; later diagnosed as "manic depression") (arrival at work on time essential function of job; McDonnell-Douglas Title VII analysis appropriate in ADA cases; employer not liable for failure to accommodate employee if employee does not specify accommodation she needs)

Smith v. Ciba-Geigy Corp., 1996 WL 437458 (S.D. Tex. May 23, 1996), *aff'd*, 114 F.3d 1181 (5th Cir. 1997), *cert. denied*, 118 S. Ct. 301 (1997)

Organic Mental Syndrome, Not Otherwise Specified

Holihan v. Lucky Stores, Inc., 87 F.3d 362 (9th Cir. 1996) (also diagnosed with "stress related problems precipitated by work" and "depression and anxiety" by other doctors)

Panic Attacks or Panic Disorder

EEOC v. Staten Island Sav. Bank, 207 F.3d 144 (2d Cir. 2000) (panic disorder with obsessive–compulsive symptoms)

*Ferrier v. Raytheon, 1998 WL 249204 (E.D. La. May 13, 1998) (jury verdict of $500,000 in compensatory damages reduced to $300,000 in compliance with cap and jury's award of punitive damages eliminated)

Francis v. Chemical Banking Corp., 62 F. Supp. 2d 948 (E.D. N.Y. 1999) (plaintiff is not disabled, employer's reason for firing him is not pretextual, and racial epithets are too "isolated" to constitute hostile work environment on the basis of race), *aff'd*, 2000 U.S. App. LEXIS 11896 (2d Cir. N.Y. May 24, 2000)

*Holland v. Chubb American Service Corp., 944 F. Supp. 103 (D. N.H. 1996) (employee's termination two days after employer ceased accommodating him with flexible schedule raised sufficient inference of discrimination to withstand employer's motion for summary judgment)

Hunt-Golliday v. Metropolitan Water Reclamation District of Greater Chicago, 104 F.3d 1004 (7th Cir. 1997)

Jerina v. Richardson Automotive, Inc., 960 F. Supp. 106 (N.D. Tex. 1997) (also chronic fatigue syndrome and panic disorder) (employee not disabled)

Johnson v. Morrison's, Inc., 849 F. Supp. 777 (N.D. Ala. 1994)

Keys v. Joseph Beth Booksellers, 1999 U.S. App. LEXIS 1581 (6th Cir. Feb. 1, 1999) (summary judgment affirmed against plaintiff failed to show he was otherwise qualified)

Moore v. The Board of Education of Johnson City Schools, 134 F.3d 781 (6th Cir. 1998)

Mustafa v. Clark County Sch. Dist., 157 F.3d 1169 (9th Cir. 1998) (finding that plaintiff could be substantially limited in his ability to work because he suffered from depression, posttraumatic stress disorder, and panic attacks)

*Ofat v. Ohio Civil Rights Commission, 1995 WL 310051 (Ohio Dist. Ct. App. May 17, 1995) (with agoraphobia) (state law case), *dismissed, appeal not allowed*, 74 Ohio St. 3d 1417, 655 N.E. 2d 737 (Ohio, 1995)

*Poindexter v. Atchison, Topeka and Santa Fe Railroad, 914 F. Supp. 454 (D. Kan. 1996) (also major depression and separation anxiety), *rev'd*, 168 F.3d 1228 (10th Cir. 1999)

Przybylak v. New York State Thruway Authority, 1997 WL 662346 (W.D. N.Y. Oct. 16, 1997) 1996 WL 107125 (W.D. N.Y. Feb. 21, 1996) (also agoraphobia and depression) (question whether collective bargaining agreement supersedes request for transfer; court refuses to dismiss because collective bargaining agreement is not in the record before it), *vacated in part and affirmed in part*, 1999 U.S. App. LEXIS 35270 198 F.3d 2341 (table case) (2d Cir. 1999)

Querry v. Messar, 14 F. Supp. 2d 437 (S.D. N.Y. 1998), 1998 U.S. Dist. LEXIS 11677 (S.D. N.Y. July 27, 1998)

Reeves v. Johnson Controls World Services, Inc., 140 F.3d 144 (2d Cir. 1998) (plaintiff's panic disorder not a disability under the ADA because "everyday mobility" not a major life activity but plaintiff stated a claim under New York state antidiscrimination law)

*Wixsted v. DHL Airways, 1998 U.S. Dist. LEXIS 4601 (N.D. Ill. April 7, 1998) (Wixsted's co-plaintiff D'Avila diagnosed with depression, posttraumatic stress disorder, and panic disorder)

Zirpel v. Toshiba America Information Systems Inc., No. 96-2293SD, 9 N.D.L.R. 298, 111 F.3d 80 (8th Cir. 1997) (panic disorder, sexual harassment) (plaintiff was not disabled, in part because she promptly found another job)

Paranoid Thought Disorder

Palmer v. Circuit Court of Cook County, Ill., 117 F.3d 351 (7th Cir. 1997)

Schwartz v. Comex, 1997 WL 187353 (S.D. N.Y. Apr. 16, 1997)

Posttraumatic Stress Disorder

*Berry v. City of Savannah, 1999 U.S. App. LEXIS 6278 (6th Cir. April 1, 1999)

Blackwell v. Runyon, 116 F.3d 1489 (10th Cir. 1997) (claims were time barred; posttraumatic stress disorder did not toll statute of limitations)

Coaker v. Home Nursing Services, 1996 WL 316739 (S.D. Ala., 1996), *aff'd*, 98 F.3d 1354 (11th Cir. 1996)

Dockery v. City of Chattanooga 134 F.3d 370 (6th Cir. 1997)

Freeman v. City of Inglewood, 1997 U.S. App. LEXIS 11789 (9th Cir. May 16, 1997) 113 F.3d 1241 (9th Cir. 1997) (table case)

Graehling v. Village of Lombard, 58 F.3d 295 (7th Cir. 1995)

Hamilton v. Southwestern Bell Telephone Company, 136 F.3d 1047 (5th Cir. 1998) (posttraumatic stress disorder not a disability when it did not prevent employed from performing a job or a broad range of jobs; employee terminated for misconduct, not because of discriminatory reasons)

*Haysman v. Food Lion, Inc., 893 F. Supp. 1092 (S.D. Ga. 1995)

Hoffman v. Brown, 1997 U.S. Dist. LEXIS 18800 (W.D. N.C. Oct. 24, 1997), *aff'd*, 145 F.3d 1324 (4th Cir. 1998) (Section 501 of Rehabilitation Act)

Houck v. City of Prairie Village, 978 F. Supp. 1397 (D. Kan. 1997) (also borderline personality disorder, depression, psychosis from mania, and others)

*Kvintus v. R.L. Polk, 3 F. Supp. 2d 788 (E.D. Mich. 1998), *aff'd*, 194 F.3d 1313 (6th Cir. 1999)

Maciejewicz v. Oak Park Public Library, 1998 WL 559785 (N.D. Ill. Aug. 24, 1998) (unable to perform essential functions of job)

Marschand v. Norfolk and Western Railroad, 876 F. Supp. 1528 (N.D. Ind. 1995), *aff'd*, 81 F.3d 714 (7th Cir. 1996) (employee with posttraumatic stress disorder not disabled because inability to work in operation of public transportation vehicles or protection of public safety was not significantly limiting on ability to work)

Miller v. Honeywell, Inc., 1996 WL 481525 (Minn. App. Aug. 27, 1996)

Newman v. Chevron U.S.A., 979 F. Supp. 1085 (S.D. Tex. 1997) (posttraumatic stress disorder) (fact that employee's misconduct may have been caused by disability was immaterial; also, driver of gasoline truck who "blanked out" was not otherwise qualified for the job)

*Olson v. General Electric Astrospace, 101 F.3d 947 (3d Cir. 1996) (also multiple personality disorder and posttraumatic stress disorder)

Pavone v. Brown, 1997 WL 441312 (N.D. Ill. July 29, 1997), *aff'd*, 165 F.3d 32 (7th Cir. 1998)

Porter v. Mesquite Independent School District, 1998 U.S. Dist. LEXIS 9036 (N.D. Tex. June 11, 1998)

*Presta v. Southeastern Pennsylvania Transportation Authority, et al., 1998 U.S. Dist. LEXIS 8630 (E.D. Pa. June 11, 1998) (also adjustment disorder and posttraumatic stress disorder)

*Rascon v. U.S. West, 922 F.2d 584 (10th Cir. 1998), 1998 U.S. App. LEXIS 8992 (10th Cir. May 6, 1998) (upholding determination that in failing to grant employee leave to attend inpatient posttraumatic stress disorder clinic and firing him instead, employer discriminated)

Schmidt v. Bell, 1983 WL 631 (E.D. Pa. Sept. 9, 1983) (individual who resented authority and whose "violent, explosive personality is exacerbated under stress" cannot be otherwise qualified for employment) (Rehabilitation Act)

*Sherback v. Wright Automotive Group, 987 F. Supp. 433 (W.D. Pa. 1997) (issue of fact existed as to whether plaintiff's posttraumatic stress disorder was a disability under the ADA even though it was mitigated by medication; also, plaintiff regarded as having a disability)

Separation Anxiety

Poindexter v. Atchison, Topeka and Santa Fe Railroad, 914 F. Supp. 454 (D. Kan. 1996) (also major depression and panic disorder), *rev'd*, 168 F.3d 1228 (10th Cir. 1999)

Schizoaffective Disorder

Morgan v. City and County of San Francisco, 1998 WL 30013 (N.D. Cal. Jan 13, 1998) (employer wins; although it took a year to enter into an accommodation agreement, it did provide accommodations such as careful selection of supervisors; ultimately, plaintiff missed too much work), *aff'd*, 202 F.3d 278 (9th Cir. 1999)

Schizoid Personality Disorder

Breiland v. Advance Circuits, Inc., 976 F. Supp. 858 (D. Minn. Sept. 16, 1997) (also major depression) (plaintiff found not to be "substantially impaired in a major life activity;" court explicitly rejects EEOC Compliance Manual's listing of "interacting with others" as a major life activity. In addition, court finds that placing disciplinary notes in plaintiff's employment file is not sufficient adverse employment action to support any claim for retaliation)

*DiBenedetto v. City of Reading, 1998 U.S. Dist. LEXIS 11804 (E.D. Pa. July 16, 1998)

Schizophreniform Disorder

Blankenship v. Martin Marietta Energy Systems, 83 F.3d 153 (6th Cir. 1996) (Ohio state law claims)

Miller v. Champaign Community Unit School District, 983 F. Supp. 1201 (C.D. Ill. 1997)

Schizophrenia

Arroyo v. New York State Insurance Dept., 1995 WL 611326 (S.D. N.Y. Oct. 18, 1995), *aff'd*, 104 F.3d 346, 1996 U.S. App. LEXIS 23914 104 F.3d 349 (2d Cir. 1996) (table case) (employer granted summary judgment on Section 504 claim because it did not receive federal funds)

Bultemeyer v. Fort Wayne Community Schools, 100 F.3d 1281 (7th Cir. 1996) (also severe depression and anxiety attacks)

Castorena v. Runyon, 1994 WL 146343 (D. Kan. April 4, 1994)

Franklin v. United States Postal Service, 687 F. Supp. 1214 (S.D. Ohio 1988) (plaintiff not otherwise qualified when ability to work the window at a small post office was an essential function of the job)

Fuentes v. United States Postal Service, 989 F. Supp. 67 (D. P.R. 1997) (Rehabilitation Act) (plaintiff was not otherwise qualified—and perhaps not even disabled—because her disability arose from her refusal to take her medication) (Rehabilitation Act)

Green v. George L. Smith II Georgia World Congress Center Authority, 987 F. Supp. 1481 (N.D. Ga. 1997)

Lane v. Hillsborough County Hospital Authority, 1997 U.S. Dist. LEXIS 9891 (M.D. Fla. July 10, 1997) (complaint did not plead sufficient facts to support allegation that plaintiff was qualified for employment)

Miller v. Runyon, 77 F.3d 189 (7th Cir. 1996), *cert. denied*, 519 U.S. 937 (1996) (refusing to toll statute of limitation)

Tyler v. Runyon, 70 F.3d 458 (7th Cir. 1995) (Rehabilitation Act)

Wilson v. Chrysler, 172 F.3d 500 (7th Cir. 1999)

Young v. Ford Motor Company, 1997 U.S. Dist. LEXIS 9213 (E.D. Mich. May 7, 1997) (defendant's motion for summary judgment granted in failure to rehire case when plaintiff did not respond to it)

Schizotypal Personality Disorder

Kemer v. Johnson, 900 F. Supp. 677 (S.D. N.Y. 1995), *aff'd*, 101 F.3d 683 (2d Cir. 1996), 1996 WL 219402 (2d Cir. Apr. 30, 1996), *cert. denied*, 519 U.S. 985 (1996) (and depressive neurosis)

Seasonal Affective Disorder

Robinson v. Banker's Life and Casualty Company, 899 F. Supp. 848 (D. N.H. 1995)

Sleep Disorder

Olson v. General Electric Astrospace, 101 F.3d 947 (3d Cir. 1996)

Somatization

Haysman v. Food Lion, Inc., 893 F. Supp. 1092 (S.D. Ga. 1995) (also posttraumatic stress disorder and depression)

Stress

Bey v. City of New York, 1999 U.S. Dist. LEXIS 11379 (S.D. N.Y. July 27, 1999)

Davoll v. Webb, 194 F.3d 1116 (10th Cir. 1999) (jury verdict affirmed)

*Fritsch v. City of Chula Vista, 1999 U.S. Dist. LEXIS 11013 (S.D. Cal. Jul. 14, 1999) (plaintiff's mental health records subject to discovery because plaintiff put her mental health in issue by asking for damages for emotional distress) summary judgment granted, dismissed 2000 U.S. Dist. LEXIS 14820 (S.D. Cal. Feb. 17, 2000) (also depression)

Holmes v. Pizza Hut of America, Inc., 1998 WL 564433 (E.D. Pa. Aug. 31, 1998)

Jordan v. Storage Techn. Corp., 2000 U.S. Dist. LEXIS 12941 (E.D. Pa. Sept. 6, 2000)

Langford v. County of Cook, 965 F. Supp. 1091 (N.D. Ill. 1997) (employees' inability to work under specific supervisor not disabilities within meaning of the ADA)

McKibber v. Hamilton County, 2000 U.S. App. LEXIS 12123 (6th Cir. May 30, 2000)

McVarish v. New Horizons Community Councilling and Mental Health Services, 1999 U.S. App. LEXIS 8508 (10th Cir. May 4, 1999)

Mundo v. Sanus Health Plan of Greater New York, 966 F. Supp. 171 (E.D. N.Y. 1997) (finding job-related stress not a disability for ADA purposes)

O'Neal v. Atlanta Gas and Light Company, 968 F. Supp. 721 (S.D. Ga. 1997), *aff'd*, 122 F.3d 1079 (11th Cir. 1997) (employee not disabled when his condition only precluded him from working certain shifts)

Paleologos v. Rehab Consultants Inc., No. Civ. 1:96-CV-2193-JEC (N.D. Ga. Jan. 16, 1998), 990 F. Supp. 1460 (N.D. Ga. 1998) (not reasonable accommodation to work at home)

Palmer v. Dalton 1995 WL 705132 (N.D. Ca. Nov. 7, 1995)

*Roberts v. Progressive Independence, Inc., 183 F.3d 1215 (10th Cir. 1999)

Transexualism

*Conway v. City of Hartford, 1997 WL 78585 (Conn. Super. Ct. Feb. 4, 1997) (transexualism or gender dysphoria a mental disorder for purposes of state antidiscrimination statute even though not covered under the ADA)

Vertigo

Armstrong v. Turner Indus., 141 F.3d 554 (5th Cir. 1998)

Cefalo v. New York Medical College, 577 N.Y.S.2d 405 (N.Y. App. Div. 1991) (plaintiff who went on permanent disability status could not show discrimination in failure to rehire without a showing that he had recovered from his disability)

Miscellaneous

Atypical Trigeminal Neuralgia

Misek-Falkoff v. International Business Machines Corp., 854 F. Supp. 215 (S.D. N.Y. 1994), *aff'd*, 60 F.3d 811 (2d Cir. 1995), *cert. denied*, 517 U.S. 1230 (1996)

Von Recklinghausen's Disease[1]
> Thompson v. Vacco, 1997 U.S. Dist. LEXIS 13042 (S.D. N.Y. Aug. 29, 1997)
> (abstention in suit charging state statute relating to child custody violates ADA
> in light of pending child custody suit)

Mental Disability Unspecified
> *Solomon v. New York City Board of Education, 1996 WL 118541 (E.D. N.Y.
> March 6, 1996)
> *Ward v. State of Connecticut Commission on Human Rights and Opportunities,
> 1996 WL 383357 (Conn. Super. Ct. June 13, 1996)

Psychological Reaction to Cancer
> Sanders v. Arneson Products, Inc., 91 F.3d 1351 (9th Cir. 1996) (psychological
> reaction to cancer too temporary to fall under the definition of disability)

Title I Cases Involving Claims That the Plaintiff Was Regarded as Having a Mental Disability

Alvarado v. Chicago Board of Education, 1996 WL 166947 (N.D. Ill. March 14,
1996)

Balliet v. Heydt, 1997 U.S. Dist. LEXIS 14913 (E.D. Pa. Sept. 25, 1997)

Barnes v. Cochran, 944 F. Supp. 897 (S.D. Fla. 1996), aff'd, 130 F.3d 443 (11th Cir.
1997)

Burke v. Nalco Chemical Company, 96 U.S. Dist. LEXIS 10190 (N.D. Ill. July 18,
1996)

Cody v. Cigna Health Care of St. Louis, Inc., 139 F.3d 595 (8th Cir. 1998)

Does v. District of Columbia, 962 F. Supp. 202 (D. D.C. 1997)

Fenton v. Pritchard Corp., 926 F. Supp. 1437 (D. Kan. 1996)

Fronczak v. New York State Department of Correctional Services, 2001 U.S. App.
LEXIS 2167 (2d Cir. Feb. 8, 2001)

Glidden v. County of Monroe, 950 F. Supp. 73 (W.D. N.Y. 1997)

Greenberg v. New York State, 919 F. Supp. 637 (E.D. N.Y. 1996)

Hawkins v. Microfibres, 1995 U.S. Dist. LEXIS 21611 (N.D. Miss. May 10, 1995),
aff'd in part, 78 F.3d 582 (5th Cir. 1996)

McConnell v. Pioneer Hi-Bred International, 2000 U.S. Dist. LEXIS 3335 (D. S.D.
Jan. 25, 2000)

Pouncy v. Vulcan Materials Company, 920 F. Supp. 1566 (N.D. Al. 1996)

Ruhlman v. Ulster County Department of Social Services, 194 F.R.D. 445 (N.D. N.Y.
2000) (holding that defendants were not entitled to five years of plaintiff's mental
health records because plaintiff's claim is that he was perceived as disabled)

Schwartz v. Comex, 1997 WL 187353 (S.D. N.Y.)

Siciliano v. Chicago Local 458-3M, 1997 U.S. Dist. LEXIS 20519 (N.D. Ill. Dec.
18, 1997) 1997 WL 792977 (N.D. Ill.)

---

[1] Also called neurofibromatosis, this is a disease which manifests itself in psychotic or schizophrenic-like episodes, see, e.g., Lomax v. Brown, 1994 WL 8745 (Vet. App. Jan. 6, 1994).

Stewart v. County of Brown, 86 F.3d 107 (7th Cir. 1996)

Varnagis v. City of Chicago, 1997 U.S. Dist. LEXIS 9031 (N.D. Ill. June 20, 1997)

Vinson v. Cummins, 36 F. Supp. 2d 1085 (S.D. Ind. 1999)

Walton v. City of Manassas, 1998 U.S. App. LEXIS 19169 (4th Cir. Aug. 18, 1998)

Webb v. Mercy Hospital, 102 F.3d 958, 960 (8th Cir. 1996)

Wilking v. County of Ramsey, 153 F.3d 869 (8th Cir. 1998)

APPENDIX C
Contacting the EEOC

Information provided here was accurate at the time this book went to press, September 2001.

HEADQUARTERS
U.S. Equal Employment Opportunity
  Commission
1801 L Street, N.W.
Washington, D.C. 20507

Phone: 202-663-4900
TTY: 202-663-4494

FIELD OFFICES
To be automatically connected with the
  nearest EEOC field office, call:

Phone: 1-800-669-4000
TTY: 1-800-669-6820

Albuquerque District Office
505 Marquette Street, N.W.
Suite 900
Albuquerque, NM 87102

Phone: 505-248-5201
TTY: 505-248-5240

Atlanta District Office
100 Alabama Street
Suite 4R30
Atlanta, GA 30303

Phone: 404-562-6800
TTY: 404-562-6801

Baltimore District Office
City Crescent Building
10 South Howard Street
3rd Floor
Baltimore, MD 21201

Phone: 410-962-3932
TTY: 410-962-6065

Birmingham District Office
Ridge Park Place
1130 22nd Street
Suite 2000
Birmingham, AL 32205

Phone: 205-731-0082/3
TTY: 205-731-0095

Boston Area Office
1 Congress Street
10th Floor, Room 1001
Boston, MA 02114

Phone: 617-565-3200
TTY: 617-565-3204

Buffalo Local Office
6 Fountain Plaza
Suite 350
Buffalo, NY 14202

Phone: 716-551-4441
TTY: 716-551-5923

Charlotte District Office
129 West Trade Street
Suite 400
Charlotte, NC 28202

Phone: 704-344-6682
TTY: 704-344-6684

Chicago District Office
500 West Madison Street
Suite 2800
Chicago, IL 60661

Phone: 312-353-2713
TTY: 312-353-2421

Cincinnati Area Office
550 Main Street
Suite 10019
Cincinnati, OH 45202

Phone: 513-684-2851
TTY: 513-684-2074

Cleveland District Office
1660 West Second Street
Suite 850
Cleveland, OH 44113-1454

Phone: 216-522-2001
TTY: 216-522-8441

Dallas District Office
207 S. Houston Street
3rd Floor
Dallas, TX 75202-4726

Phone: 214-655-3355
TTY: 214-655-3363

Denver District Office
303 E. 17th Avenue
Suite 510
Denver, CO 80203

Phone: 303-866-1300
TTY: 303-866-1950

Detroit District Office
477 Michigan Avenue
Room 865
Detroit, MI 48226-9704

Phone: 313-226-7636
TTY: 313-226-7599

El Paso Area Office
The Commons, Building C, Suite 100
4171 N. Mesa Street
El Paso, TX 79902

Phone: 915-832-6550
TTY: 915-832-6545

Fresno Local Office
1265 West Shaw Avenue, Suite 103
Fresno, CA 93711

Phone: 559-487-5793
TTY: 559-487-5837

Greensboro Local Office
801 Summit Avenue
Greensboro, NC 27405-7813

Phone: 336-333-5174
TTY: 336-333-5542

Greenville Local Office
Wachovia Building, Suite 530
15 South Main Street
Greenville, SC 29601

Phone: 864-241-4400
TTY: 864-241-4403

Honolulu Local Office
300 Ala Moana Boulevard, Room 7123-A
P.O. Box 50082
Honolulu, HI 96850-0051

Phone: 808-541-3120
TTY: 808-541-3131

Houston District Office
1919 Smith Street, 7th Floor
Houston, TX 77002

Phone: 713-209-3320
TTY: 713-209-3367

Indianapolis District Office
101 W. Ohio Street
Suite 1900
Indianapolis, IN 46204-4203

Phone: 317-226-7212
TTY: 317-226-5162

Jackson Area Office
Dr. A.H. McCoy Federal Building
100 West Capitol Street, Suite 207
Jackson, MS 39269

Phone: 601-965-4537
TTY: 601-965-4915

Kansas City Area Office
400 State Avenue
Suite 905
Kansas City, KS 66101

Phone: 913-551-5655
TTY: 913-551-5657

Little Rock Area Office
425 West Capitol Avenue
Suite 625
Little Rock, AR 72201

Phone: 501-324-5060
TTY: 501-324-5481

Los Angeles District Office
255 E. Temple
4th Floor
Los Angeles, CA 90012

Phone: 213-894-1000
TTY: 213-894-1121

Louisville Area Office
600 Dr. Martin Luther King Jr. Place
Suite 268
Louisville, KY 40202

Phone: 502-582-6082
TTY: 502-582-6285

Memphis District Office
1407 Union Avenue
Suite 521
Memphis, TN 38104

Phone: 901-544-0115
TTY: 901-544-0112

Miami District Office
One Biscayne Tower
2 South Biscayne Boulevard
Suite 2700
Miami, FL 33131

Phone: 305-536-4491
TTY: 305-536-5721

Milwaukee District Office
310 West Wisconsin Avenue
Suite 800
Milwaukee, WI 53203-2292

Phone: 414-297-1111
TTY: 414-297-1115

Minneapolis Area Office
330 South Second Avenue
Suite 430
Minneapolis, MN 55401-2224

Phone: 612-335-4040
TTY: 612-335-4045

Nashville Area Office
50 Vantage Way
Suite 202
Nashville, TN 37228

Phone: 615-736-5820
TTY: 615-736-5870

Newark Area Office
1 Newark Center, 21st Floor
Newark, NJ 07102-5233

Phone: 973-645-6383
TTY: 973-645-3004

New Orleans District Office
701 Loyola Avenue
Suite 600
New Orleans, LA 70113-9936

Phone: 504-589-2329
TTY: 504-589-2958

New York District Office
7 World Trade Center
18th Floor
New York, NY 10048-0948

Phone: 212-748-8500
TTY: 212-748-8399

Norfold Area Office
Federal Building, Suite 739
200 Granby Street
Norfolk, VA 23510

Phone: 757-441-3470
TTY: 757-441-3578

Oakland Local Office
1301 Clay Street
Suite 1170-N
Oakland, CA 94612-5217

Phone: 510-637-3230
TTY: 510-637-3234

Oklahoma Area Office
210 Park Avenue
Oklahoma City, OK 73102

Phone: 405-231-4911
TTY: 405-231-5745

Philadelphia District Office
21 South 5th Street
4th Floor
Philadelphia, PA 19106

Phone: 215-440-2600
TTY: 215-440-2610

Phoenix District Office
3300 N. Central Avenue
Suite 690
Phoenix, AZ 85012-1848

Phone: 602-640-5000
TTY: 602-640-5072

Pittsburgh Area Office
1001 Liberty Avenue
Suite 300
Pittsburgh, PA 15222-4187

Phone: 412-644-3444
TTY: 412-644-2720

Raleigh Area Office
1309 Annapolis Drive
Raleigh, NC 27608-2129

Phone: 919-856-4064
TTY: 919-856-4296

Richmond Area Office
3600 West Broad Street
Room 229
Richmond, VA 23230

Phone: 804-278-4651
TTY: 804-278-4654

San Antonio District Office
5410 Fredericksburg Road
Suite 200
San Antonio, TX 78229-3555

Phone: 210-281-7600
TTY: 210-281-7610

San Diego Area Office
401 B Street
Suite 1550
San Diego, CA 92101

Phone: 619-557-7235
TTY: 619-557-7232

San Francisco District Office
901 Market Street
Suite 500
San Francisco, CA 94103

Phone: 415-356-5100
TTY: 415-356-5098

San Jose Local Office
96 North 3rd Street
Suite 200
San Jose, CA 95112

Phone: 408-291-7352
TTY: 408-291-7374

Savannah Local Office
410 Mall Boulevard
Suite G
Savannah, GA 31406-4821

Phone: 912-652-4234
TTY: 912-652-4439

Seattle District Office
Federal Office Building
909 First Avenue, Suite 400
Seattle, WA 98104-1061

Phone: 206-220-6883
TTY: 206-220-6882

St. Louis District Office
Robert A. Young Building
1222 Spruce Street
Room 8.100
St. Louis, MO 63103

Phone: 314-539-7800
TTY: 314-539-7803

Tampa Area Office
501 East Polk Street, 10th Floor
Tampa, FL 33602

Phone: 813-228-2310
TTY: 813-228-2003

Washington Field Office
1400 L Street, N.W., Suite 200
Washington, D.C. 20005

Phone: 202-275-7377
TTY: 202-275-7518

TABLE OF AUTHORITIES

Laws

Cases

INDEX

ABOUT THE AUTHOR

Susan Stefan, JD, is an attorney at the Center for Public Representation in Newton, Massachusetts. Until 2001, she was a professor of law at the University of Miami School of Law, where she taught disability law and mental health law. She graduated magna cum laude from Princeton University in 1980, received a master's in philosophy from Cambridge University in 1981, and received her law degree from Stanford University Law School in 1984. Ms. Stefan writes about disability and mental health law. She also continues to litigate cases involving the Americans With Disabilities Act and its application to people with psychiatric disabilities.